MANAGING BY DESIGN

Using QFD to Transform Management Performance

Michael Clargo

TESSERACTS

MANAGING BY DESIGN
Using QFD to Transform
Management Performance

Copyright © Michael Clargo 2002

All Rights Reserved

ISBN 0 9543021 0 9

First Published 2002 by Tesseracts
www.tesseracts.com

MANAGING BY DESIGN

PREFACE

A new battleground...

They say that the world is getting smaller; that the Internet and world-wide communication are turning us into the global village. But for me, and probably for you, the opposite is true. I live in a village in England, I regularly exchange information with a colleague in mainland Europe, I buy my books from an American bookshop (yes that one!), and I access information from all around the world. And every time I want to buy something, I am faced with literally thousands of options from hundreds of different sources.

In a very practical sense, our world is not getting smaller; it is getting much bigger. Businesses now have competitors they have never even heard of, in places they'll probably never see. Some of these businesses are old and established, and have just had the barriers of distance and communication lowered enough to compete. Some of them are brand new or in fields up to now not considered as competition, but the barriers of habit and history have fallen away.

What is more, the overwhelming vista of options that are now available to potential customers has spawned a new web-based industry; of agencies that gain power and influence by guiding people through the many choices that they face. They collate the options, and provide objective comparisons to make the choice quicker and simpler. Increasingly, potential purchasers can see comprehensive information on a business's offering, performance and track record, and compare it instantly with its competitors'.

...with different rules...

Together, these two factors – increasing competition and ready comparison – are demanding a huge shift in the mindset of business. Historically, constraints on choice and information have provided a degree of stability in most markets. Competitiveness has been sustained by incremental improvements such as reducing waste and overhead costs, and steadily improving product and service quality. But now markets are more immediately susceptible to new solutions, to creative alliances, and to innovative ways of working; and failure to keep pace is being rapidly exposed, and exploited.

It is no longer enough for businesses simply to consider how to do the same thing a bit better or a bit quicker. The competition has become bigger and more aggressive. The future is not linear with the past. Businesses will only survive if they can grasp fully the emerging risks and opportunities of their new situations, and configure the best of their organisation and resources to meet them in new and creative ways.

Fortunately the problem is, at least in part, also the solution. The same forces that are pressing organisations to step-up their competitive game are also providing a far greater wealth of options and opportunities for doing so.

Unfortunately, traditional methods of business planning provide little facility for handling the resulting complexity; and managing complexity – configuring a wealth of creative options to deliver ground breaking performance – is what business in the new century is all about.

Sadly, the lack of good approaches for deploying ambitious goals, and the consequences of getting things wrong, have driven managers to maintain a conservative approach to business planning; the very antithesis of what is now needed. As a result, they have set mediocre goals; perpetuated inferior practices; failed to inspire the imagination of their people; and have seen survival as success. Most companies have consistently failed to harness the full creativity and enterprise of their organisation to achieve anything like their full potential, because of the weakness of traditional methods for business planning. In the future, this will prove fatal.

...needs new weapons!

It is therefore clear that, if organisations are to be empowered to thrive in the new business world, they will need far more effective business-planning tools than most that are currently in use. There is however, one approach which is more than capable of meeting this need; a tried and tested process that has already had dramatic results for companies like Smith & Nephew, Emerson, Siemens and Microsoft. It is called Quality Function Deployment (QFD), and it provides a structured and participative approach for effectively harnessing the new levels of challenge and complexity inherent in business planning today.

QFD is probably the best kept management secret going (albeit not intentionally). Originating in Japan, it is an extremely effective tool for working out what you are trying to do and how you are going to do it, and for exploring the opportunities in both. It is powerful enough to transform a global business, simple enough to be developed on a flipchart, and flexible enough to design anything from a complete organisation to an isolated activity or product.

And it is the combination of these qualities that make it so effective in business planning. One tool, linking top to bottom, strategy to decision, purpose to action, intent to desire and mission to culture. It links them simply, visibly and inexorably, across all levels of the organisation; guiding and harnessing every effort. Yet, at every level, it provides opportunities for new ideas and creativity, inspiration and commitment.

QFD enables any organisation, large or small, to map out its objectives; to explore how each of its functions, activities or business processes can leverage its attainment of them; and to translate this into clear strategies. It is an extremely powerful tool for this kind of work, and has enabled a major research organisation to achieve 40% performance improvement in one year, across all of its objectives, and a European-wide assembly facility to make a three-fold improvement in its delivery performance. It is the only tool that can reliably and objectively drive the focus and creativity that businesses will need to excel in the future.

The dramatic performance improvements quoted above, impressive though they may be, are only part of the story. The clear and methodical objectivity of the approach both enables companies to target and deliver huge step-changes in performance, and provides a sustainable basis for them to build on these for the future. QFD does this because it drives improvement through the management team, in a way that develops their identity, using a process that they can replicate. It equips them to:

- identify and prioritise goals that strategically focus the organisation on its opportunities
- align all their potential – people, resources and facilities – behind achieving those goals
- minimise inefficiency and distraction by objectively challenging activities that no longer fit their strategy
- provide a framework to harness the creative energies of their people in driving performance improvement
- effectively monitor and manage their progress, at all levels, to ensure success.

Quality Function Deployment

Surprisingly, QFD is not a new tool; it was developed at the end of the 1960s in Japan. So the question needs to be asked: If it is so successful, why aren't more people using it? The answer lies in the cultural divide between technical and business issues. For a large proportion of the intervening years, the tool has predominantly been the domain of highly technical product design teams. It has transformed their performance, but in doing so it has developed along ever more detailed and complex lines, away from the simple pragmatic style that appeals to management teams.

Clearly, if more managers are to benefit from this approach, the literature needs to be made more accessible to them. They need a more robust and less onerous version of the approach, they need to be inspired with examples they can relate to, and they need to be supported with tools they can readily apply. In short, they need a pragmatic guide to implementing QFD in their business.

That is the purpose of this book.

INTRODUCTION

What do we mean by 'Managing by Design'?

On one hand, it implies a sense of intention and predetermination, and on the other it reflects a spirit of creativity, free-thinking and innovation. Both perspectives should be true of effective management, and you will find both heavily represented in the pages of this book. But more than this, 'Managing by Design' reflects the conscious application of a design perspective within the responsibilities of management.

Why?

Because it is extremely effective!

It is also liberating, empowering and inspiring.

However, for many people it is an unorthodox concept and, despite the logic of the concept and the overwhelming benefits that arise from its adoption, people can struggle to assimilate the idea and its implications into their day-to-day thinking.

It is, therefore, a real challenge to attempt to equip the reader with all that they need to practically exploit 'design thinking' through the medium of a book (albeit supported by a website). We rise to this challenge by adopting a number of principles.

- We promote the reading of this book as discovery. 'Unlearning' poor practice is as important to effective management as learning good practice. 'Discovery' provides us with a device in which the reader can challenge conventional wisdom, and adopt new ideas in the context of a deeper understanding of what they are trying to do. For this reason, the main subject of this book is not fully explained until Chapter 6, after the early chapters of the book have taken a quite confrontational look at traditional management.

- We equip the reader with everything needed to successfully adopt a design approach to management. We do not restrict ourselves to the basic mechanics of implementing design thinking. Instead, we explain the personal and organisational implications of a success-ful implementation and so establish a firm and sustainable founda-tion for the approach.

- We use a wide, interesting (and perhaps unexpected) variety of means to engage and support the reader in their exploration of design thinking. Effective learning requires a balance of approaches, and we each have different preferences within that. We use story, expla-nation, exercises, illustrations, diagrams, questions, and unashamedly copious quantities of other people's wisdom (quotes) to make and reinforce the key learning points.

■ We create a 'journey' for the reader: a clear flow in the information presented. By employing a novel as the backbone of the book, we suggest a logical, chronological sequence that will make sense to most managers. Readers who are already expert users of the tools we present, may be dismayed at how different aspects of the tools have been split up into different sections of the book. It is important to realise, however, that the order in which we present the ideas is driven by a management agenda, not a purist/technical one.

■ We have created a path that can be followed practically. Our goal has been to promote and extend a design perspective on manage-ment, irrespective of the specific tools used. To make this perspec-tive useful and practical we focus on one specific design tool: quality function deployment (QFD). The reason for this is that it is the best design tool currently available for exploring and defining complex systems simply. QFD has already proven its practicality and bene-fits in management.

■ We have tried to minimise the barriers to applying the learning from the book efficiently. The ideas presented can be applied as a com-plete system or as isolated practices – this journey really can begin with a single step. Also, we provide a range of supporting materials that can be downloaded without charge from the Internet and adapted to your own particular needs.

The book has been consciously designed to provide you with everything you need to effectively implement and employ 'Managing by Design' within your own organisation. It contains clear guidance, techniques and insight, ensuring that the ideas of design are effectively and practically harnessed; these will deliver the business performance transformation that you will need to compete effectively in the new e-global economy.

By the end of the book, you will know how to:

■ establish the need for transformation in your organisation, and commit to QFD as the means of bringing that about

■ build a team around you, that is determined to use QFD to deliver clear worthwhile goals and to create a more effective organisation

■ co-ordinate and lead the effective implementation of QFD, and ensure that your resources are efficiently focused on delivering the results

■ work through the personal challenges and opportunities that QFD pro-vides and to develop a greater personal effectiveness

■ adapt and adjust your management forums and routines to support and make full use of the effective application of QFD

■ ensure that QFD remains in tune with the changing needs of your busi-ness environment, and continues to provide an effective basis for harnessing the creativity and industry of your people in transforming your performance.

These 'learning points' correspond to the six main sections of the book, sections A to F.

In order to maximise its effectiveness in preparing you to implement QFD, this book is written in a number of complementary styles.

(a) On the left-hand pages, the book is written as a text, providing guidance, insight, challenge and practical tips for putting QFD into practice in your organisation.

(b) On the right-hand pages, the book is a novel, providing a continuous illustration of what it may feel like to implement QFD, and how you might address the issues that it raises.

(c) In the appendices, numerous cameos of real QFD applications provide examples that you can adapt to your own situation

(d) Through the Internet, a complementary web-site provides a portal to professionally developed practical tools, materials and handouts, which you can apply to get a flying start in implementing QFD.

How you use the book is entirely up to you and your personal learning style. But feedback to date indicates that the most effective way of approaching the book is as follows.

- Read the novel through first (right-hand pages) to develop an overall picture of the ideas being promoted and their implications (this takes between 2 and 4 hours).

- Scan the pictures, quotes, and titles of the text (left-hand pages) as you are reading the novel, to develop richer depth of understanding, and a grasp of how the text relates to the novel.

- Think through some clear applications for the book in your organisation, and how you would like it to impact on current management practices - develop these thoughts into clear objectives for taking this forward.

- Read the text pages, and then explore in more depth the text sections that are relevant to your stated objectives, and undertake any exercises in them; pay particular attention to the section on 'Personal Effectiveness'.

- Use the Appendices and the associated web-site to equip yourself with any relevant tools and ideas for implementation.

- Set yourself a target for re-reading the book and resetting your objectives at some later date.

The structure of the book is outlined diagrammatically on the next page.

Book Structure

		Text
	Introduction	Preface
		Introduction

Novel

1 Introduction

2 Confront confused direction

3 Confront inferior organisation

4 Confront impoverished management practice

5 Confront deficient awareness

6 Confront undisciplined planning

7 Establish clear and explicit common goals

8 Define the structure of the organisation

9 Exploring ways of working together to deliver

10 Encouraging commitment

11 Leading the change

12 Proposal reconciliation

13 Managing upwards

14 Driving a consistent approach

15 Balancing work and home

16 Personal values

17 Clarifying your purpose

18 Reconsidering and re-evaluating your role

19 Designing your role

20 Making hard decisions

21 Systematic management meetings

22 Tackling issues (Pursuing the goals)

23 The Roof

24 Process management reporting

25 Pulling it all together

Epilogue

Conclusion

Appendices

Sidebar labels:

- **A** Confront the need for transformation
- **B** Build a team that is determined to drive transformation
- **C** Lead and coordinate the implementation of QFD
- **D** Develop a greater personal effectiveness
- **E** Adapt management practice to fully exploit QFD
- **F** Coordinating QFD in large organisations

This book owes a vast amount to the experience and generosity of my past clients (and current friends). Together we have made most of the mistakes that it is possible to make, and this book borrows heavily on the experiences that we have worked through together. As a result the novel has been inspired with plenty of real life illustrations – in fact it almost wrote itself.

Managing by Design has been written so that others can obtain the benefits that we have gained out of applying a design perspective to management[1], without having to repeat all of the painful experiences (although we fully anticipate you may create a few new ones of your own).

Design perspectives in general, and QFD in particular, are immensely powerful tools that will transform the quality and impact of your goal-setting and thereby transform your business. As such it has implications for your whole management approach. This book provides the thinking, the guidance and the tools to enable you to implement them in their fullness and use them effectively.

Good luck, and may God bless you.

Michael Clargo

What the symbols mean

Relevant quotations and comments[2]

Exercise / opportunity to explore the ideas

Example / more detail on the topic

Guidance and reference meaterials

Tools and techniques to support application

---

1   In order to differentiate the concepts and ideas proposed by this book, we have referred to them as 'Managing by Design', but to us they are just 'management'. The danger of putting a label on any new management idea is that by doing so you immediately position it in people's minds as a programme, with a shelf-life, and not as 'the way of working'.

2   Many of the quotes in this book have been drawn from one excellent source: The Manager's Book of Quotations, edited by Eigen & Segal and published by Amacom.

Overview of the book

The novel covers a five-month period in the life of a fictional company, Cylek UK, as it grapples with the issues illustrated below. The numbered shields represent the chapters of the novel. The textbook runs parallel to this and works through the topics reflected in the blue bars. In any particular chapter, both novel and textbook relate complementary themes, and many of the examples and diagrams in the text can be related to the corresponding part of the novel.

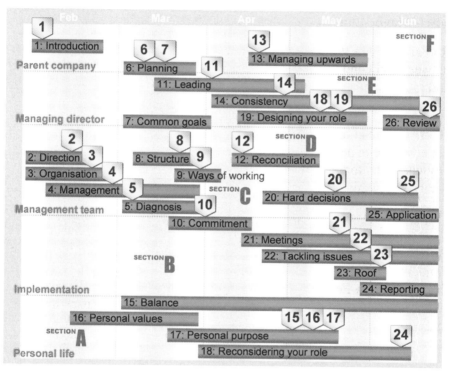

A more detailed plan for the book can be found in Appendix 1, and a more sophisticated cross reference between novel and textbook can be obtained by means of the glossary and index at the end of the book.

Cylek UK is the British subsidiary of a much larger American corporation; it manufactures modems (electronic equipment for linking computers over telephone lines) and other electronic networking products. A more detailed explanation can be found in Appendix 2.

Neither Cylek UK, nor any of the characters associated with it, are intended to represent any organisation or persons, either living or dead. However, Cylek does provide an opportunity for reflecting real situations that we have encountered in our work, and for making them available to the reader without embarrassing any of our past clients.

Chapter 1

Only one window showed any sign of life on the dark, rain drenched trading estate. Behind it a man looked balefully at the phone ringing on his sparsely furnished desk. He let it ring, waiting for it go to voice mail. He knew who it was and he did not want to speak to them, not yet, not now! Maybe tomorrow? Maybe next week? Maybe!

Richard Frewer was at that point of prolonged indecision, somewhere between fight and flight, somewhere between taking the long walk home and launching himself at the chasm that separated him from achieving his goals. Goals he once thought he could achieve easily.

He was alone in the deserted office block, and he felt that way. His mind flitted between determination, resentment, blame, and escape, but never anywhere for long. The arguments raging in his tired brain seemed to want to draw him into the grey middle ground, away from any sense of solidity, away from any sense of concrete action. He was alone, and he was lonely, with only his thoughts for company. Some company!

But it could be worse: he could answer the phone. It would not matter to the mid-western drawl at the other end that it was 9pm on a wet, black Friday night in February. He imagined Frank Delaney in the sunshine of his air-conditioned splendour, a spread of deli sandwiches on his desk and eager, enthusiastic people rushing around outside the glass walls of his office. Lunch time in Houston; it all seemed so different over there.

But that was the problem. Their sunshine-inspired picture never seemed to take account of the gritty reality of the canvas. The vision they sold him did not give any indication of the dilapidated state of the road he had to travel to get there. He resented that, he resented them, and he resented the whole damn situation. He could pick up the telephone, but what would he say? There was nothing to say.

The ringing stopped, the tense feeling in his stomach eased, and he returned to the solitude of his dark, rainy Friday evening.

He could speak to the Americans, but what would he say? What stance would he take? Bullish optimism? Humble compliance? Righteous indignation? Each had its virtues. But each had even more risks.

No, he could not talk to the Americans. They sold him this sack of shit in the first place. What would they understand about the hard realities? What did they really care about him?

No, he was right to not answer the telephone.

He sat back in his chair and his gaze took in the office around him. He focused on the coat on the back of the door. The one Laura bought him for their anniversary. He fastened on it as a metaphor for home and family, as the icon for the choice to go home and seek comfort there, but he knew that would not work. The coat's lifeless drape reminded him of what had gone out of their marriage.

He had tried to sell her the same story that the Americans had sold to him. But she had never bought it. Yes, she had gone along, but only because she had run out of arguments. And every day of the last six months had born out her fears. And every day of the last six months he had denied it and explained it as another step to the vision. And every day of the last six months the gap between them had widened.

He could not discuss it with her; he was not ready to admit defeat. He was in the office at 9pm, precisely because he could not go home like this. She would see him, and recognise the confusion, and the façade that protected him from the discussions he wanted to avoid would be breached. He was too weak to engage in that, and he knew he would lose, not because he was wrong, but because he was not strong enough to win. After all, that was the way that Laura had lost the argument six months ago!

Friends? No there were no friends he could discuss it with. Who has time for anything other than acquaintances when you have a high-flying career and a family?

His mind drifted to those old 50's private-eye movies where the guy pulls out a bottle of bourbon from the desk drawer. He had never done that, and there was nowhere he could get one, but he could identify with the character, and the image made him smile at himself. And, following the theme, he began to review the whole sorry story in his mind. "It was a black November evening in Gloucester, and the rain beat against the window …"

Richard had been headhunted for the job at Cylek. A past colleague had given his name to the recruitment agency, and he had been flattered by the attention - he had never been headhunted before. He had been running the New Products facility at Ektracom for three years, and had really pushed things forward. He had put in a lot of change, some of it a bit flaky perhaps, but it looked good, and performance had improved, and the cracks did not show too badly.

But the Board was a clique, and the Managing Director, Simon, felt Richard was a bit of a maverick, and not really good enough to be one of the elite few that really ran the business. Richard also felt his last appraisal had been politically engineered to keep him sweet, but out of their way. For his part, Richard felt that Simon was arrogant, aloof, and frankly not particularly good, and it irked him that lesser people who thought themselves superior were holding him back.

The job at Cylek was a big jump. A really big jump. It was in fact a bigger job than Simon's. What better way to show them the true standing of his talent. In one bound he would be ahead of them, and still 20 years younger. Yes!!!

The salary was virtually double what he was getting, and the car, better than any in the director's slots at Ektracom. And Richard went for it for all he was worth. If they thought he could do it, then he could. No challenge had ever beaten him, it was just a matter of thinking it through logically, and lets face it he was probably the best person he knew at doing just that! And Cylek looked at him, and reviewed his resume of success, and agreed with him wholeheartedly.

Explaining his resignation to Simon, had almost been as sweet as having his new Jaguar delivered to the Ektracom car park on his last day. Rubbing their noses in it had been every bit as good a feeling as he had hoped it would be.

The new job would be a challenge, but that was what being the Managing Director was all about wasn't it?

The challenge was in the form of an 800-person organisation, under-performing the industry, and needing to make a 50% improvement in margins. Richard had been to the site and seen the waste, he had spoken to the people and seen their blind spots, and he had looked at the methods and seen the inefficiency. He felt he knew the answer almost before he started. It was like going into the exam having already seen the paper beforehand.

Laura did have a few problems with the move. She had grown up in the Northeast, and she hated the idea of Gloucester, but even she could not deny him this break. Richard had to admit that she spent most of the time pointing out the risks and pitfalls, but that was typical of someone facing such a change, and Richard knew she would grow to like it. A bigger house and more luxurious holidays would, he thought, soon put the rest in perspective.

Yes, it was a really big change. It was what they call the 'big break'. Richard was good, he was very good, and now he was about to demonstrate it to the world and to his family. This was the step to real success and Richard could almost taste it.

But he had not counted on having his hands tied behind his back. From day one it seemed his time was not his own. The telephone never stopped ringing. He was expected to attend every meeting with every customer, and to get personally involved in every problem. An early attempt to drop out of a sales meeting brought a lecture from the States about the importance of customer relationships and the need to remain in touch with the pulse of the market and its players. And an unsolved problem in delivery bought him an unscheduled and unwelcome visit from the VP for logistics and a personal telephone call from the President himself.

His days were not his own, and he soon found himself working later and later in order to get some time to plan and develop his ideas to transform the business. But the States soon took up that time to involve him in conference calls. It seemed that every department wanted the "European Perspective", and he was it!

He had raised the matter with his immediate boss, Frank Delaney, but Frank made it very clear that he had enough problems of his own without having to worry about Richard's as well.

He started to come in early, and at weekends. It was the only chance he had to make a difference that was truly him.

Laura was not happy, but it would not be for long. Just long enough to buy him some time. But when he did get his thoughts straight, and develop a plan, and sold it to his people, he found it swept away by one central initiative after another: The Central Licensing Initiative, The Global Purchasing Initiative, The Relationship Marketing Initiative, The Cost of Quality Initiative, The Inventory Reduction Initiative, The New Appraisal System, The … .

He had added them up. During the past six months, he had been expected to make a contribution to, or report progress on, no less than 15 different, seemingly unconnected, initiatives. His people had lists of tasks that were up to a hundred items long, of things they needed to do to support these initiatives, and they consistently failed to make serious progress on any of them. And they consistently failed to make any progress for him either.

As the nights drew in and the days got shorter, he drove in the darkness to be at the office for 6.30 am. He regularly had a feeling of queasiness, almost of dread, on that short journey in. He sensed a futility in it all, and sometimes wanted to cry, but then the mask went back on, the optimism switch was flicked, and he was ready to take on the new day. At least the States would not be telephoning him until after lunch.

He struggled hard, and though the progress was slow, he was almost on top of things.

But now the last month's performance figures were out, and the small increase in the last three months of that year, that appeared to dip in January, were now showing that this dip was not just some small blip - some spurious anomaly. The trend was clearly down. Conclusion: He had done nothing materially to improve things; he had failed to deliver what had been expected of him. How could it have been otherwise? It had not been him who had been working there. It had been some marionette pulled by the strings of routine and desperation. As he reflected on his own failure a small sense of fear gnawed his stomach and he looked at the telephone again, wondering if Frank had given up trying to contact him for the evening, or whether he was currently speaking to Laura at home. A sense of depression seemed to descend upon him, enveloping him like a heavy black cloak.

Cylek could be a good company; it could be a great company, if only he had had the chance to do what was needed rather than what was wanted. Oh how Simon would laugh at him now! And what about Laura? He had taken her trust, and he had gambled it, and he had lost, and now he had to face up to admitting it. He had never felt so alone.

He felt more and more depressed as he thought about it. But he was not going down without one last attempt. He couldn't admit defeat yet. He had nothing to lose. He did not know what to do about Laura, but he knew he was not going to waste the trust she had put in him and the disruption she had endured for him.

And he wasn't yet sure what he'd do about the States, but playing possum wasn't going to do anybody any good, and nor was continuing to play by their rules.

By 9 o'clock on the following Monday morning, everybody became aware that something had changed over the weekend. Secretaries were heavily in negotiation, reshuffling meetings, trying to find space in overburdened diaries. Hushed conversations abounded. There was a buzz about the place.

Amongst the hustle and bustle of the office, a portly grey-haired man sauntered in to the office of Peter Kale. He leaned ostentatiously on the filing cabinet, a self-satisfied smile on his face, as he stared at the frantic form of Cylek UK's financial wizard. Peter looked up. "What are you looking so smug about Daniel? You can't have escaped this? The whole thing is impossible! I've got the auditors in next week, appraisals to complete, the task force on Corporate Tax is meeting on Wednesday, and there's the first quarter's forecast to sort out. And he expects us to drop everything and come running."

Peter's outburst only served to increase Daniel's smile. He replied, "It's okay, it's only a temporary glitch. Mark my words we will be free of this crap in a few weeks."

Peter paused, and looked intently at Daniel, as though trying to read new information in his eyes. Confident he had Peter's undivided attention, Daniel continued.

"Wonder-Boy's finished!" He let the drama of the words hang in the air, forcing Peter to push him further. He was enjoying the moment.

Peter continued to look at Daniel, seeming to weigh up whether to play Daniel's game. Was Daniel just playing 'Company Gossip', or did he really have some inside information?

Daniel Matthews, Cylek's Sales and Marketing Director was legendary for his contacts in the States. Heavily political, he had used his network to secure power and to survive many of his past colleagues and superiors. But his contacts had not been enough to secure him the top job six months ago. He deeply resented the fact that they had chosen an unknown, almost twenty years his junior, over him, and he had never concealed it.

Many had thought that this would be the last straw, that Daniel would walk. But in his early fifties, and separated from his political contacts and power, Daniel knew his limitations on the open jobs market only too well. However, he believed that Cylek had made a huge mistake in appointing Richard Frewer, and he was eager and determined to ensure that they realised the fact as quickly as possible.

Peter decided to play along with Daniel's game "Yes? What makes you so sure?"

Daniel played out a bit more line. "Well you've seen last month's figures, you can't say that this is anything more than panic! Wonder-Boy hasn't a clue! He is out of his depth!"

"And...?" said Peter. He knew his part in the charade.

"And he spent four hours on the telephone to Frank over the weekend. Three separate telephone calls!"

Peter allowed his expression to change to critical scepticism. "It's a bit thin Daniel!" But Daniel's smug smile did not waver, and Peter knew there really was something more. He had known Daniel for ten years - Daniel had something pretty conclusive.

"Okay, I'll buy it! What else do you know?"

Daniel's smile deepened yet further as he anticipated the impact of the news on Peter. "The Old Man's sending over a trouble-shooter. Three month assignment!" He watched Peter's expression change, and having achieved the result he wanted, he continued. "And I'll lay odds that Wonder-Boy is out on his ear in half that time." He turned on his heel and walked straight out. Then with an additional touch of drama he paused at the door and finished with "By the way, this is all confidential, even Wonder-Boy doesn't know yet!" He paused just long enough to relish Peter's shocked expression and left abruptly.

Section A

Confront the need for transformation

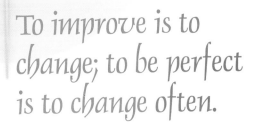

To improve is to change; to be perfect is to change often.

Winston Churchill

CONFRONT THE NEED FOR TRANSFORMATION

Managing by Design ...

...as a textbook

...as a novel

The fact that you are reading this book may well mean that you are already aware of a need to improve your management approach - to establish more effective goals and ensure your people pursue them harmoniously, diligently and cre-atively. But unless your people are also able to see the same compelling need that you do, then they are likely to lose their enthusiasm for change as soon as serious effort is required. So the first question we need to address is: 'How do you create that compelling need in them?'

In part, selling the logic and benefits of the QFD approach creates that need, but the attraction will unfortunately weaken as the going gets tough. The other part of the equation is to establish a burning platform of the problems in the existing approach. How this is achieved is the subject of this first section; chapters two to six.

It isn't what people think that is important, but the reason they think what they think.

Eugene Ionescu
French playwright

- Confront confused direction - identify areas where goals and priorities create conflict and confusion.

- Confront inferior organisation - chal-lenge the lack of objectivity and analy-sis that has allowed poor practices and structures to continue unchallenged.

- Confront impoverished management practice - expose the mindset that binds management into detail.

- Confront deficient awareness - ques-tion the evidence that says things are okay, and take a clear critical look at how you fare in practice.

- Confront undisciplined planning - expose the inferior planning practices that fail to identify or address these issues effectively.

Text continues on left-hand pages...

A small steel peg clicked out, snapping the square aluminium channel into position, and the flip-chart stand clattered back onto its other two legs. Colin Park stood back to survey his handiwork, and absentmindedly continued his conversation with Amanda Carr who was laying out the tea and biscuits.

"If y'ask me Mand, the writin's bin on the wall for the last six months or more. I seen it all before. We've 'ad months of moanin' and carpin' and nuthin' much 'appenin'. Now we're in ta the bit where they all flap around like 'eadless chickens, an' the next thing, phut! Takeover, shut down, sack! I seen it all before. Still we're neither of us far off our retirement are we Mand?"

"You speak for yourself you cheeky beggar! I've got a good few years to go yet, thank you very much."

Colin grinned to himself at Amanda's outburst.

After a few moments of silence Amanda spoke again. "Col, do you really think we're for the chop then?"

"Best thing for it, if y'ask me. They spend 'alf their time arguin' and the other 'alf wonderin' what to argue 'bout next. There's not one of 'em really knows what they're doin'. But they talk a good game all right, well at least enough to convince 'emselves. Rest of us stopped listenin' long ago. Anyways, we'll be all right, there's plenty of jobs goin' beggin'. Any chance of a cuppa tea?"

Amanda simply gave him one of 'her looks'.

"Ah well, I'll be off then and make me own. Can't be spendin' all day chattin' to you. See ya!" And with that, he was gone, leaving only his signature trademark, a pungent smell of Brut aftershave.

Novel continues on right-hand pages...

Confront confused direction

Over recent years the quality of objectives in business has improved markedly. The introduction of concepts like SMART[1] has had a positive impact on the quality and clarity of thinking in many organisations. And yet, despite the quality of the wording of objectives, many organisations continue to suffer from:

- conflict and disagreement between people pursuing different objectives

- the delivery of an 'event' or activity being seen as an end in itself

- a detachment and ambivalence to the objectives at junior levels of the organisation.

In other words, while the quality with which objectives are expressed and defined has improved, the quality with which they are determined, reconciled and deployed remains largely unchanged.

In part, this is because managers tend not to check on the practical effectiveness of their goal-setting process. They may recognise confusion between themselves and their colleagues as a result of a weak goal-setting process from above, but they are prone to assume that their own goal-setting processes are immune to similar problems. However, the practical reality of most goal-setting processes today, is that they need to improve how effectively they:

- align objectives with the hopes and aspirations of the individuals pursuing them

- define objectives at appropriate levels of detail

- ensure objectives effectively mesh and engage with each other.

---

1 SMART is an acronym for Specific, Measurable, Agreed, Realistic, and Time-bound - five characteristics that can be used to assess whether an objective is clear to those expected to pursue it.

Confusion of goals, and perfection of means seems to me to typify our age.

Albert Einstein
Nobel Laureate in Physics

Does your team have clear direction?

How consistent would your people's answers be to the following questions?

1. If you suddenly found yourself with a significant amount of spare time and resources, where would you invest it and why?

2. If you suddenly found you were overloaded with work, what service would you suspend and why?

3. What for you are the most important goals you are pursuing and why?

4. What are the most important goals your colleagues are pursuing and why?

Chapter 2

Richard looked at the clock and decided to give the three missing managers until ten past two, and if they were not there by then, he would start without them. The other four managers appeared more than usually subdued, as though they expected something momentous and were wrapped in their individual thoughts. Normally they would be lobbying him for this or that, or deep in conversation with each other about some event or issue. The atmosphere today reminded him more of a dentist's waiting room. Richard used the time to think through how they were likely to react to what he was about to propose.

The slim pale man on his left, Andrew Richardson, the HR Manager, would almost certainly be supportive. He valued anything that helped people to get their issues out and to think them through clearly. He was also very open to trying anything new, as was Deborah Lewis who sat next to him.

Deborah had been the Technical Director for the last 18 months. Ambitious and idealistic, she was less pragmatic than Richard would have liked, and while her grand schemes had stolen a march on the competition, they were also a major factor in the current drop in performance.

Across from her, the polished ebony form of Abs Halshaw, the Operations Director, could go either way. He would support it for as long as it appeared to be delivering clearly useful actions and decisions. But if the debate became in any way prolonged and esoteric he would switch off or become disruptive. This often put him in conflict with Deborah; more so recently as he worked to eradicate the production issues created by what he saw as her 'design excesses'.

The fourth member present was Peter Kale, the Finance Director. He would be an unknown in all of this. At 56, he was the oldest and longest serving member of the management team. He never seemed to get passionate about anything, either for or against, but he had a quick and lively mind that often served to express his cynicism in devastating wit, and too often carried the argument.

Peter was nobody's puppet, but Richard felt that too often he played to Daniel Matthew's agenda. Daniel was one of the three missing managers,

In the rest of this chapter, we explore the common issues in each of these three areas, and then consider an approach (Why-How charting) which can address them effectively.

Aligning objectives and individuals

People only pursue objectives that are important to them. If you are to success-fully deploy your objectives, the key thing to understand is: 'What makes these objectives important to my people?' The answer to this question is often found in a mixture of three possible factors:

- achieving the objective could provide them with some direct benefit, either material or spiritual (e.g. self esteem)

- achieving the objective could provide them with some indirect benefit (e.g. a linked bonus or salary increase)

- achieving the objective would provide them with increased influence and potential to achieve further objectives.

It is not uncommon to find situations where none of the above factors apply, and yet the organisation still expects the objective to be delivered. This is a paradox - com-panies often employ people for their abil-ities and interests in looking after the needs of the business, and yet they expect those same people to suppress those very aptitudes when it comes to their person-al needs.

The truth is that people behave in line with what they believe will benefit them per-sonally. Sometimes those benefits may be complex, deferred, and altruistic, but they are still the driving factors, not some loosely expressed aspirations of a distant management committee.

Companies often seem to forget this. A classic example of such inattention is where organisations develop vision state-

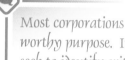

Most corporations do serve a worthy purpose. Individuals seek to identify with it. The competitive leader will make the connection between our souls and our work, and will benefit from the energies released.

Lawrence M. Miller
Business consultant
American Spirit (William Morrow, 1984)

Questions to engage people in vision:

What would make you really proud to work for an organisation?

How can working for an organisation help you to achieve your life goals and ambitions?

What can you contribute to making our organisa-tion what we want it to be?

What opportunities would our pursuit of the organi-sation's vision provide for you personally?

and had been on the management team almost as long as Peter. Richard often felt that Daniel carefully crafted the ammunition that he knew Peter would fire. It was almost as though Daniel knew that once Peter had expressed something he was committed to it, and Peter could not resist providing the punch line to Daniel's story craft. Daniel knew how to play Peter, and therefore how to influence much of the meeting.

John Trowell, the IT Manager, crashed into the meeting just before the deadline Richard had set himself. He was followed, more sedately, by Susan Dobbs, the Site Services Manager. John muttered an apology "Sorry, the system controlling the security pass access into the building was down".

"So John," replied Peter, "were you and Susan fixing it, or merely trapped in the broom cupboard by it?" There was general laughter, which broke some of the tension that had built up. Susan and John's romantic association had been a source of humour for some time now, but everyone knew that they never let it interfere with their work.

Susan put a mock glare on Peter, and retorted: "Well we have to use them for something and heaven knows we'll never get Finance to approve any new brooms".

Richard took advantage of the momentary upswing in energy to start his meeting. He stood up to capture their attention. "We'll start, and Daniel will just have to catch up when he gets here." He flicked on the OHP and a graph of the last five months' performance illuminated the end wall, its camel hump shape familiar to everyone in the room.

"You've all seen this," he said. "What does it represent?"

There was a prolonged pause, broken by Abs' tentative submission of the obvious. "Performance to date for the current financial year?" he said and then looked round to see what he had missed. The rest stayed silent. Richard was not known for being overly rhetorical, and they wanted a clue as to which direction to go. They were going to have to wait a while longer though.

"Performance of what?" Richard asked Abs.

"Of the business," replied Abs, continuing in his vein of submitting the obvious.

ments, and a series of value statements, and then simply publish them on the wall, or communicate them in a series of road-shows.

A consistent vision and values is, however, extremely important to the effectiveness of the business in moving forward, but it takes far more effort than simply working out and publishing a statement. An effective vision requires that:

- the future needs of the business are fully explored and described, and the implications for its people are understood

- these objectives for the business are reconciled with the 'natural' objectives and affinities of its people, and their current motivations [1]

- where direct reconciliation is not viable, indirect links, e.g. rewards and pay-offs, are established.

The objectives of the business are actually what is written on the hearts and minds of its people, and if that is not reconciled to the words on the wall, then the latter are not the vision of the business - despite what it states in the headline.

'Vision statements' are a tool to influence the vision of the business, but they are not that vision in themselves. They are a means, not an end, and as with all means, their effectiveness needs to be evaluated rather than simply assumed.

Defining objectives at appropriate levels of detail

Objectives should be sufficiently specific to provide guidance and direction, but not so specific that they constrain the organisation from perfectly valid and appropri-

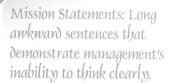

Mission Statements: Long awkward sentences that demonstrate management's inability to think clearly.

Scott Adams, in 'The Dilbert Principle'

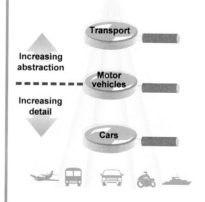

---

1 By explaining, involving and investing in the thinking and attitudes of its people, an organisation can develop a deeper and more effective commitment than by simply linking objectives to bonuses.

Managing by Design

"Of us! Of the management," chipped in Andrew, seeing that it might be an opportunity to explore the issues within the management team, and eager to progress it.

"Against what?" challenged Richard.

"Our objectives," submitted Andrew, keen to keep the door open on the management team issues. The others paused while they tried to discern the direction this was taking them.

"Is it?" asked Richard, looking around at each face in the room.

While most struggled to think how it could not be, Peter was getting increasingly frustrated by this kindergarten cat-and-mouse game, and interjected: "Clearly it is. The objective of any business unit is to maximise financial return, which is what that graph shows".

Deborah caught a whiff of short-termism in the reply, and appended: "Financial return, sustained over time - the graph doesn't show that!"

"Quite!" rejoined Peter, "anybody can see that our performance against objectives is declining!"

There was a tone of dismissiveness in his response that annoyed Deborah, but she continued calmly: "No! I mean that our objective of investing in longer-term performance is not reflected in that graph".

"Clearly not!" replied Peter quickly, beginning to see Deborah's point but choosing not to. He was just about to say: "Otherwise we wouldn't have that dip!" when Richard interjected.

"What are our objectives?" he asked. This brought him another quizzical look and the response that they were written in job descriptions. "Yes, okay, but what are our collective objectives?" He stepped quickly to the flip chart and wrote up 'Maximise Financial Return' in order to forestall Peter steam rolling the meeting to a unitary viewpoint, but he remained there, poised to capture other ideas.

They were not long in coming. 'Develop our People' from Andrew, 'Maximise our Future Potential' from Deborah, 'Conform to Legal Requirements' from Susan, 'Sustain the Environment' again from Deborah, and so the list continued.

At that point, Daniel strolled in. Without apology, he moved to a vacant place, remained standing with his files under his arm, and peered impe-

ate routes. In practice, companies err toward making objectives too detailed, and thereby restrictive and potentially ineffective. For instance, it is common to find objectives expressed in terms of *'Implement X by the end of March'* without any stipulation being made about the expected impact of 'X' on performance. As a result the team *'implementing X'* will have no criteria by which to judge the quality of their work, and thereby no understanding of when 'X' may be improved by further adapting it to 'Y'.

An objective is a tool just like any other; it needs to be designed to produce the optimum effect. Careful and appropriate wording of the objectives must do more than simply summarise an intended position. It must inspire people to pursue that position vigorously and creatively. while ensuring that the resulting effort and enthusiasm is focused, coherent and complementary. No small feat. And yet while well-designed objectives can have a dramatic impact on the effectiveness of a strategy, it is often the case that only a very small proportion of the total effort invested in them is allocated to defining them.

Poor design of objectives often arises in situations when they are considered in isolation. Objectives normally represent one element of a complete strategy. Each objective can be broken down into finer, more detailed objectives, and each can be built up with other parallel objectives into a higher-level broader objective. In this way objectives form part of a hierarchy. Ensuring this hierarchy is well balanced and that each objective plays its part is key to developing effective objectives.

Ensuring objectives mesh and engage efficiently with each other

Are all objectives equally important? What happens if it is not possible to support all the objectives at once? Which

Checking your objectives

Is there any valid activity or achievement that may be disqualified by each of these objectives?

Is there any invalid activity or achievement that may be encouraged by each of these objectives?

Are these objectives clearly required to support the strategy/higher objective?

Are these objectives fully achieved/guaranteed by delivering their defined sub objectives?

Are each of the objectives expressed in terms of a sustainable performance improvement?

An object of utility needs to be as simple as possible, but no simpler.

Albert Einstein
Nobel Laureate in Physics

riously at the flip chart. His stance seemed to exude the expectation that it was up to Richard to address him. Richard did so.

"Daniel, we are looking at what our objectives as a business are."

Daniel responded quickly and abruptly. "Well that's obvious! It's to serve customers. All of that list is subservient to serving customers!"

Peter bridled visibly at Daniel's comments, but held his peace.

Richard saw some real light in this, and took the opportunity to put his major opponents in conflict. "Surely it's to make money Daniel" he replied. "We serve customers to make money!"

His tone, the use of Daniel's name, and the patronising phrasing did their work. Daniel entrenched himself further and explicitly away from Peter's original stand. "A business is its customers," he proclaimed pompously. "We make money, in order to, and purely as a result of, serving them. And that is a direct quote from Cyrus Lerejecks last month. Case closed!" he said, and sat down. Cyrus Lerejecks was 'the Old Man', Cylek's esteemed founder and President.

"And, of course, Cyrus is happy for his vast financial wealth to dwindle in that cause is he?" Peter asked sarcastically.

Richard quickly forestalled Daniel's response with a question. "Where exactly does the Corporate Environmental Policy fit into this?" he asked.

"It's about our social responsibility," submitted Deborah.

"In part," responded Daniel, "but it's mostly about our image with our customers".

"Actually it's about the avoidance of costly litigation," challenged Peter.

"And Investors in People?" Richard queried. But before Andrew could get in with a response, Richard continued: "Actually, we have never sat down and clarified what our collective objectives are. We have all assumed them, but we have just demonstrated that, as a group, we have no clear consistent, coherent set of goals. Each of us may feel that we have a clear understanding of what we should be doing, as a business, but unless we can agree how everything fits together, then in practice we're likely to find ourselves working against each other. That is what we have experienced over the last two months. In practice!"

objectives take priority? And how do your team decide that?

If your objectives are not thought through, in terms of how they relate to each other and to higher objectives, it is extremely difficult to answer these questions. And this is often a cause of contention between people with responsibilities for delivering different objectives. For instance when there is conflict between cost reduction and key investments.

Having a hierarchy of objectives helps a team relate their objectives to the overall structure of objectives, and to make intelligent decisions in compromising one objective to optimise a more critical one.

For this reason, it is important to get the whole team involved in exploring the hierarchy of their objectives. This both ensures a deeper understanding of the strategy, and a greater commitment to the conclusions.

Why-How charting

A Why-How chart is such a hierarchy, and it provides an opportunity to address all of the three foregoing areas.

- To engage people in clarifying the objectives, and getting them to think through how they relate to them.

- To develop a complete hierarchical picture of the strategy, from the abstract to the detailed.

- To ensure that the relationship between different objectives is clearly understood.

It also provides a mechanism to expose where thinking is currently weak in these areas, and to strengthen it.

A Why-How chart is essentially a map of the logic of the organisation. It is a map of what the organisation is planning to achieve, and how it intends to deliver it.

Are all objectives of equal importance?

Managing by Design

Richard had their attention. He could see that it was a fragile grip in some areas, Daniel and Peter were itching to re-assert their views, but it would hold for the moment.

"If I am wrong, then this will be a very, very short meeting. Someone will state a simple set of clear objectives. We'll all agree with them, and that will be that. If I am right, then we will be spending quite a bit of effort in discussion and reconciliation, because my objective for this meeting is to leave here with a common explicit set of clear objectives for Cylek UK."

He waited for further challenges but gradually they all settled into their seats. They knew he was right. A number of them believed they could state the objective, but looking round the table, they could not identify anyone they could be sure would agree it in full.

Richard pulled out a number of pads of yellow sticky notes, and distributed them round the room. Daniel put on his best "Oh surely not this!" face, but Richard intentionally avoided catching his eye, and proceeded smoothly.

"What I'd like everyone to do," he said, "is to write what you believe our objectives, as Cylek UK, should be. One objective per sticky note. Large clear writing so that it can be seen at a distance. And when you've finished come and stick them on the wall over there so that everyone can read them."

Everybody thought, and wrote, and stuck their sticky notes up on the wall. Some in clumps, some randomly spread out, some in neat columns. Richard encouraged everyone to read the notes and ensure they understood what was meant. Then duplicates were taken away by agreement, and very similar notes were amalgamated.

"Now the difficult bit," said Richard. "We are going to identify the relationships between these objectives. To work through and agree which supports what and why. But first a few ground rules: One, this is not a democracy. I have the final say because it was me that was appointed to do so, and because it will be me who will be called upon to justify the conclusions. Two, in reaching my conclusions I will be strongly influenced by the view of the team. We will all listen carefully to all of the considerations expressed, and where there is still a difference of opinion, having heard all of the arguments, we will assume the majority is most likely to be right."

On a Why-How chart, boxes each containing a stated objective, are linked by upward pointing arrows. The arrowheads point to the reason why an objective exists, and the tails point to how an objective is to be fulfilled. The steps to develop a Why-How chart are listed on the right.

Organisations developing a Why-How chart for the first time may find that it takes them all day to complete. This time is typically taken up in reconciling disparate views amongst the management team. However, as a result of this, the first working through of the Why-How chart can provide tremendous insight and shared understanding on how the organisation works, providing the debates are efficiently managed.

This insight and understanding opens up new lines of thought, and the team finds that it can identify previously unseen opportunities and ideas for leveraging the assets of the organisation in pursuit of its goals.

In an ideal world, your Why-How chart may look like the neatly ordered diagram seen on the right, and progressive refinement of your thinking may eventually be rewarded by such a cleanly logical model.

In practice, however, it is far more likely that your finished result will look more ragged,[1] with arrows going everywhere, and sometimes even back on themselves.

This is not a problem. The key value in the Why-How chart is the discussion that takes place to develop it. Why-How charting is not a precise science, and its effectiveness is best judged by the level of engagement, and quality of discussion[2], from those involved in developing it.

Steps to produce a Why-How chart.

1. List the objectives we know we should have - write each on a separate sticky-note.

2. Place the first sticky-note on the board.

3. For each sticky-note placed ask "Why are we doing this?".

4. Find and place objectives that answer this question and continue the process.

5. For each sticky-note placed ask "How are we doing this?".

6. Find and place objectives that answer this question and continue the process.

7. Create new objectives as necessary to complete the logic of the model.

8. Resolve any disagreements through understanding each other's perspectives and explanations.

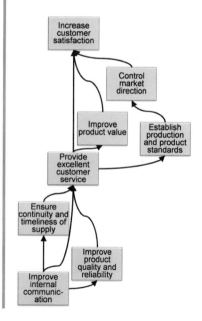

---

1   An example of a real Why-How chart for a retail IT facility can be found on the associated web-site. See Appendix 7.

2   Effective facilitation clearly helps in this.

Daniel was not keen on this, and he challenged it. "But supposing the minority just happens to be the one person who is the expert on the subject?" There were a few nods around the room.

Richard took it calmly in his stride. "Then it is very much up to that expert to articulate the arguments clearly so that the whole team can understand, and to maintain their credibility so that their colleagues are swayed by their opinion."

That seemed fair to most people, but one or two still appeared hesitant.

"Look," said Richard, "at the end of the day, confusion over our goals within this team and this company is costing us big time. We've lost two months on the launch of the MR4; we've lost two major accounts; we've lost four of our key people in the last month; we've wasted hours of our time in meetings; and we waste each other's energy through arguments and confusion. I am not willing for this situation to continue, and I would rather be 100% agreed on all our goals, and 100% wrong on some of them, than 0% agreed on our goals, and thereby 50% wrong on all of them. Frankly, we may make some mistakes in forcing the issue, but they won't in practice be big ones, and they will be overwhelmed by the progress that clarity and agreement will afford us."

Peter thought about this, carefully. He narrowed his eyes, looked up to the right and then he nodded. Daniel just looked sullen, but he did not challenge any further. So, be it!

Richard continued: "We are going to get a lot out of sharing our views on these objectives, and I don't want to lose that, so I'm going to ask Helen to come in and take notes of our discussions. These will be available to everyone to supplement the final conclusions we reach."

Richard started with the sticky note on serving customers, and with a series of 'Why?' and 'How?' questions he began, one by one, to link it to the other objectives. Every time another sticky note contained the answer to 'Why?' he placed it above the original note and joined it by an upward pointing arrow. Whenever another sticky note contained the answer to 'How?' he placed it below the original note and joined it by an upward pointing arrow.

New notes were written when no existing sticky note had the answer to 'Why?' or 'How?'

Turning the Why-How chart into effective objectives

The completed Why-How chart provides excellent insight into the interdependence of your organisation's objectives, and will do much to ensure a balanced perspective within your team. But for practical purposes, this logic now needs to be drawn back into a simple set of words: a limited number of complementary objectives that together reflect all that is important to your organisation.

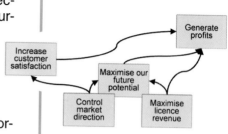

This can be achieved by taking a layer horizontally through the chart. Any line drawn from left to right through the chart will have to pass through all the strands that are required to make your organisation work. The challenge is to draw this line through a series of statements which effectively balance detail with direction. In doing this it is important to ensure that:

- everybody has included what is important to them in the diagram, and can see how it fits into the statements being selected

- the statements provide guidance, without undue constraint, and in particular that they reflect performance and impact rather than events and activity

- the objectives can be seen as a complete and complementary set, all of which are necessary to achieve the overall goal.

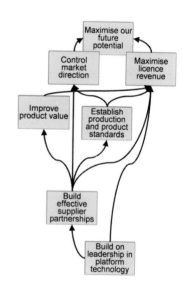

If the layer of statements to be developed into objectives is selected by discussion, with these points in mind, then you will have done much to ensure that your objectives will be fully effective, reconciled, and deployed within your organisation.

Gradually a diagram took shape. A map of the logic that held the objectives of Cylek UK together. Some discussions had been entrenched, but Richard had managed them well: taking the heat out of arguments; focusing on new information; ensuring people did not simply re-state the same points; checking that everybody felt they had heard all the arguments and were willing to abide by the majority decision.

He lost Daniel for at least ten minutes when 'Customer Satisfaction' had been made subservient to 'Generate Profits'. Privately Richard thought Daniel had a point. Money as a goal for its own sake was unhealthy. But he did not feel the rest of the team were ready for that discussion yet. In fact, he felt Daniel did not really believe it, it just met his needs to emphasise the importance of his own role.

By the end of the meeting, something had clearly been achieved. The objectives and sub-objectives of Cylek UK had been made a lot clearer, and new insights had been gained by everybody, including Richard. He now realised how much he had not understood about what Cylek was about. The biggest surprises for him concerned the role of suppliers in establishing production standards, and how big a factor production lead times were on their current inventory levels. It was frightening that he had run the organisation for six months with such blind spots.

In the event, Richard had not used his right to overrule once. He had not needed to. He kept the discussion open long enough to fully understand it himself, and found that every time he had come to a very firm conclusion, a majority of the team had reached the same point. And some very worthwhile points had been reached.

The diagram had opened up a whole new area of thinking for the team, in terms of how it could license the platform technology back into the market via certain suppliers. The links in the Why-How chart showed how this could secure not just additional revenue, but also have a dramatic influence over the future direction of the market. Richard's team were clearly excited about this insight, and there was a steady buzz of conversation around it.

At the end of the meeting even Daniel had to admit it had gone well, and it was sheer vindictiveness that made him ask: "Is there any truth in this rumour that Cylek are sending over a trouble shooter, Richard?"

In addition, the discussion will have high-lighted areas where you need to reconsider the alignment of any individual's personal objectives and reward system.[1]

Completed Why-How chart

The dotted line indicates a set of objectives which could be used to summarise the chart

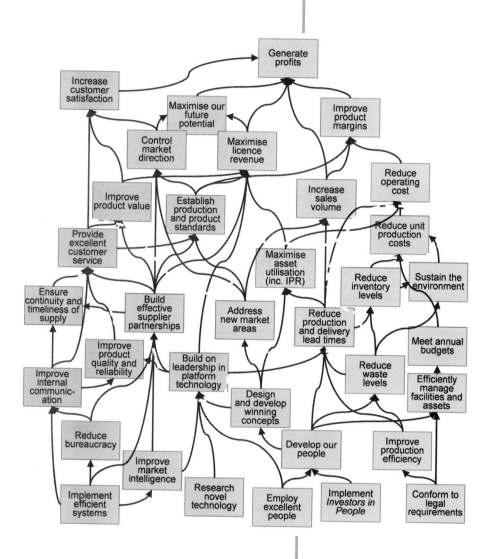

Richard responded immediately: "Good grief, no!" and then he realised who was asking and he felt a bit less comfortable. "What rumour Daniel?"

Daniel shrugged. "Just something of nothing," he said as he left the room. He felt good. Richard had been rattled, and he still did not know about it.

Confront inferior organisation

Competitive product design is difficult and complex: achieving the optimum balance between functionality and cost; seeking innovation while fully exploiting existing synergies; ensuring reliability from the new and radical; harnessing the potential of the organisation to the opportunities of the customer. Little wonder that a range of tools and disciplines have evolved to help the designer in getting those balances right.

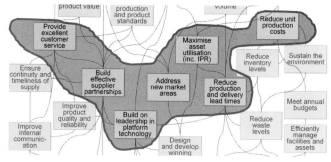

It seems strange then, to consider that business design[1], which is often more complex and critical than product design, should be undertaken largely without the benefit of similar disciplines and tools. More often than not, the design of a business remains static well past the point at which it would have been competitively advantageous to change; and only eventually changes following decisions that are largely bereft of the rigour applied to product design. Perhaps it is unsurprising that so many organisation changes fail or fall short of their potential.

The idea of applying the same rigour to business design as to product design is not a new one. As long ago as the end of the 19th century, Frederick Taylor applied some of the concepts then in use in product design, to radically improve the production performance of a steel plant. The result was so dramatic that the technique spread rapidly. However, because

Design: for products (or businesses)

Need and opportunity

Functionality		Cost
(Niche)	**C**	(Commodity)
Innovation	**O**	Standardisation
(Freedom)	**N**	(Synergy)
	F	
Sexiness	**I**	Reliability
(Image)	**G**	(Integrity)
	U	
Fashion	**R**	Consistency
(Responsiveness)	**A**	(Sustainability)
	T	
	I	
	O	
	N	

Potential and resources

---

1 Business design is the conscious configuration of resources, facilities, alliances, systems, people and methods to efficiently fulfil current and future business opportunities.

Chapter 3

That evening, Richard poured over the outputs from his meeting. In the pattern of the diagram he could see a number of stickies around which the whole diagram seemed to hang; pivotal objectives from which it appeared possible to derive the whole of the rest of the chart. Richard looked at them more clearly. There were seven of them, and together they captured all of the lines that went from the bottom to the top of the chart. Each of them appeared to make the sticky notes above them inevitable, and the sticky notes below them essential. He could see that together they represented the real objectives of his organisation.

The more he looked at the Why-How chart, the more he felt excited by the words on the page and how they linked together. He could see success written in the pattern. It all hung together in a form of symmetry that engineers find beautiful, and it would make Cylek UK work.

He used to get the same feeling when he poured over the concepts and proposals for a new design. It was almost an instinct that told him what would work and what would not.

The parallel struck a chord in him. What actually was the difference in designing a business from designing a new product? Thinking about it, it struck him as odd that designing a business was essentially more complex and important, but that designing new products was undertaken with more objectivity, analysis and care. On reflection, he felt that this was wrong, and he began to wonder whether he could not apply some of the design tools with which he was so familiar to his current situation. Clearly, the design tools would have to be modified to engage the whole of his management team, but that should be possible. He settled down to work out how.

By late on Thursday evening he had developed a clear plan for his team to work on the design and development of Cylek UK. It would start with defining a clear specification; working up each of the objectives into measurable targets of success. Then he would get his team involved in using design tools that he had found successful in his own design career, in particular one called QFD, to establish exactly what Cylek UK was

of the value set at the time, the impact on the people doing the work did not feature significantly in the design objectives. As our values evolved, the conclusions arising from Taylor's work were seen as dehumanising, but instead of re-running the design process with revised objectives, the whole design process fell into disrepute. Essentially, the baby was thrown out with the bathwater.

What happened was akin to abandoning musical notation, because of 'The Birdie Song'!

Since then, the mindset appears to have developed that if we want to retain 'soft' objectives we have to avoid 'hard' methodologies.

This is patently not so. Rigorous design approaches have delivered us increasingly people-centred products. From the Avent baby bottle to the Stannah stair-lift, the 'softness' you deliver at the end depends upon the objectives you put in at the start. The 'hardness' only comes in taking full responsibility for the conclusion. The issue is really one of our own preferences and prejudices. For as long as we can convince ourselves that innovative, humanistic, inspirational, radical solutions can only be produced by liberated, free-wheeling, unconstrained activity, we can justify avoiding the disciplines and duties that we would prefer to do without.

Subconsciously, we often equate discipline with constraint, and we confuse our conclusions with our identity. But discipline can force the exploration of new avenues, and the most constrained of people are often inspired to the most radical of solutions. Necessity *is* the mother of invention, and invention *is* 1% inspiration and 99% perspiration. Good

The great enemy of the truth is very often not the lie – deliberate, contrived, and dishonest – but the myth – persistent, persuasive and unrealistic.

John F. Kennedy
Thirty-Fifth President of the United States

... by chance you will say, but chance only favours the mind which is prepared.

Louis Pasteur
French chemist

going to do to deliver those targets. He had his whole plan worked out, including detailed agendas for each of the sessions with the management team. He felt confident and alive. This was going to work. He had the same feeling he had about his winning designs.

Happily, he packed up his case to leave for home. With luck, he would be home in time to put Nicholas to bed.

Just before he left, he checked his e-mails. One caught his attention in particular. It was direct from Cyrus Lerejecks, copied to Frank Delaney. It read:

Review of Cylek UK operations.

Following the recent downturn in the performance of our UK operations, the Board have agreed to undertake a full review of our Gloucester facility. To this end, we have appointed Ms Lucy Derring to join you from 5th March, for an undefined period. Her brief is to identify and oversee the implementation of improvements at Gloucester. In this capacity, she will report directly to me. Lucy has done some excellent work in a number of our other facilities over the last ten months, and I am sure you will extend to her every courtesy and assistance.   Cyrus

Richard went cold. He read, and re-read, the e-mail over and again. Surely, there was a mistake. He could not see how such an arrangement could be tenable. Who exactly would be accountable for what in practice?

He wondered why Frank Delaney hadn't warned him of this – Frank was his boss after all. Was this really coming direct from the Old Man, or was it simply Frank covering his ass?

He telephoned Frank, but he was in Wichita. He would not be contactable until tomorrow. He toyed with the idea of telephoning Cyrus, but that would be rash. He needed to be much better prepared for that call.

He put the telephone back down, leaving his hand on the receiver, undecided as to what to do next. So, Daniel had had the inside track again! Damn!

The news of the imposed trouble-shooter threw Richard's mind into turmoil. It was a cruel twist of fate that at precisely the time he was becoming confident that he really could change things, minds on the other

disciplines[1] ensure that the necessity and the perspiration are held in balance to generate the real quality of conclusion.

Whether your subject is a product or an organisation, the disciplines of an effective design process will ensure that the conclusions you reach are the best available, in all aspects, hard *and* soft.

The concept of business design

So, what actually do we mean by design?

Whether for organisations, or for products, design is essentially the basis for deploying objectives. In product design, a top-level specification is broken down into the performance requirements of individual components, and ideas are combined until there is confidence that those performance requirements can be fulfilled or exceeded. In business design, top-level goals are broken down into the performance requirements of the various areas of the organisation, and options developed until there is confidence that the performance can be delivered.

The effectiveness of the design is determined by the quality with which the objectives are broken down, to guide the selection and combination of winning solutions. This is true whether we are considering a new washing machine, the mix of business to achieve global presence, or the development of a new appraisal process.

Middle managers make nothing but the organisation

...

Earl Shorris
from The Oppressed Middle
(Anchor/Doubleday, 1981)

If, as the quote above might suggest, your sole role has been 'making the organisation', what tangible evidence can you claim as to the quality and productivity of your efforts over the past year?

....
....
....
....
....
....
....
....
....

---

1   The disciplines themselves need to be designed if they are to be fully effective in this. Design tools are a proven example of such design.

side of the Atlantic had clearly concluded that he could not. Or had they? The whole picture was so unclear.

Richard struggled over the following week to retain his enthusiasm for his plans, but as he explained them to his team his words sounded hollow, his commitment eroded by the uncertainty of the new arrangements.

"Where does Lucy Derring fit into all of this?" asked Peter, when Richard had finished outlining the plans for moving forward. "Supposing her agenda is totally different? Shouldn't we wait to see what she has to say?"

The whole group watched Richard in rapt attention. This was the question in all their minds. All of them wanted to understand what Lucy Derring's appointment would mean, and none of them wanted to waste time on activities that were going nowhere.

Richard looked steadily back at them. He was not sure that he had an answer to that question. All he knew was that he did not want to dance to someone else's tune when he had a good tune of his own. He did not know if, or how long, he would retain control of his company, but he felt sure that the easiest way to lose control was to have no clear ideas himself. And then a thought struck him. "Ms. Derring will not just be reviewing the situation here, she will also be reviewing us. Make no mistake about this. It is one thing to have a company with problems. It is something altogether worse to have a management team that is not doing something serious about them."

In the silence that followed, Richard looked intently at each one of them. Andrew and Susan nodded back at him, but others bowed their heads and looked away. Richard was not sure why. In hindsight his argument seemed pretty compelling.

And then Daniel, looking back defiantly, put the concealed reservations into brutal words. "Richard, she will be far more likely to be reviewing you. It's too late to mock up some sort of master plan now, and frankly if she's going to be reviewing my work I've other areas I'd prefer to invest in than saving *your* ass!"

There was an audible intake of breath as people looked at Daniel, shocked. But Richard noticed that no-one was leaping to disagree with Daniel. He looked back at them, and defeat seemed to creep into his bones.

Peter took a more conciliatory approach. "Richard, we really won't be able to do anything worthwhile in the few days that we have. Let us keep

Design, as a discipline for deploying objectives, works well because of the rigour it demands.

- The needs of the design are fully analysed to provide clear objectives, which are then tested with the 'customers'.

- An overall system is developed to deliver the objectives, and is broken down into logical subsystems to aid analysis and planning.

- The potential for each part of the system to deliver the objectives is explored, and performance targets set for each.

- New ideas and creative options are sought, evaluated against the performance targets, and combined into solutions, which are refined and proven through analysis and experimentation.

- A balanced solution is formulated to make optimum use of existing resources and to fully leverage new ones.

- The conclusions are fully tested against the original objectives.

Each element of the above list is simply a means to establish a contract for fulfilling the objectives. As such it is every bit as appropriate for business design as it is for product design.

The illustration on the next left-hand page explores how this works in practice.

On a scale of 0-5 (5 being best), how well did your most recent organisational change fulfil the bullet points on the left?

What would have been the result of moving to the right on each scale?

....
....
....
....
....
....

the plan you have proposed, but delay starting on it until we know what is going on. This woman will be here on Monday, and then we can see what she has in mind. There is nothing to stop us picking things up again as soon as we know."

Most people nodded at this, and Richard sensed he was not going to get any further. Clenching his teeth he nodded assent, and then watched as his team filed out of the room, the meeting clearly at an end.

Susan hovered toward the back and as she passed Richard, she paused, looked at him and said quietly, "We still have the plan, and that is almost as good as being three days into it. Added to which it gives us three days to paper over some of the other cracks." Then she moved on without waiting for an answer.

'Papering over the cracks'; Richard considered the statement with derision. But Susan was right, and he had some cracks of his own to paper over, and he would be damned if he would let this Derring woman in close enough to see the join.

The morning of Lucy Derring's arrival came quickly. Richard leafed through the pile of papers in front of him, but his eyes just went through the motions. His mind was somewhere else. He had got nowhere with either Frank or Cyrus in reversing the decision to send Lucy Derring, and now the infernal woman was camped outside his office door. He knew he was being childish, making Lucy wait, but he really resented her arrival and his options to express the fact seemed very limited.

Ten minutes after their meeting had been due to start, Richard finally gave up his charade, and buzzed Helen to show Lucy in.

Lucy was almost exactly as Richard had visualised her to be: young, slim, attractive, blonde, self-possessed, cool and dressed immaculately in a business suit. The image only served to reinforce his prejudices. He felt anger rise up again inside him, and he vented it by directing his attention back at the papers on his desk, continuing his game and thus forcing her to make the first move.

She walked up to the edge of his desk without hesitation, thrust out her right hand and said "Good morning, Richard!"

Stage 0: We start our design process with an organisation that is largely headed in the same direction, but where there are differences in the detailed interpretation of what that means. This creates conflict and confusion, which leads to loss of enthusiasm and wastage of effort.

Stage 1: The overall direction is clearly and unambiguously defined in terms of a quantified vision, which is tested against the market and the shareholders' aspirations.

Stage 2: The organisation is divided into logical 'components', each of which needs to play a distinct role in ensuring the vision is fulfilled.

Stage 3: Each 'component' reconsiders its activities and performance against its new role, and realigns itself to what is now expected of it.

Stage 4: Where a 'component' is complex, they may need to repeat Stages 1 to 3 locally in order to ensure all their targets are aligned.

Stage 5: Each 'component' harnesses all of their resources in pursuing the targets they have agreed with the rest of the organisation, and employs new and creative solutions where there are shortfalls.

Stage 6: Overall progress is regularly measured, and used to refresh and reinforce commitment to the overall strategy, and to identify where the logical model needs to be improved.

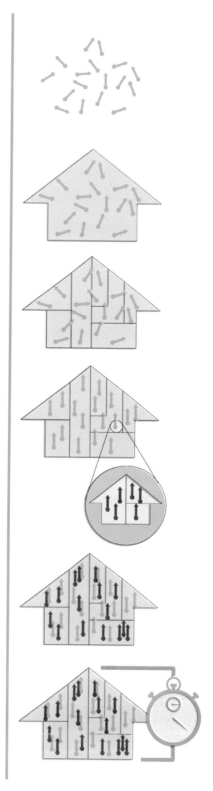

Richard delayed his response just long enough to be rude. He flicked through another page, before standing up, peremptorily shaking her hand, and responding in an aloof tone "Muzz Derring, please take a seat." It sounded more like an instruction than an invitation.

It seemed clear to Richard that this was to be a power struggle, and currently he had the power, and he wasn't going to roll over and play dead for anyone. The chairs were all neatly arranged around Richard's meeting table, but Richard sat back down behind his desk and resumed his charade of flicking through papers. Lucy appeared to take this in her stride. Her face showed no sign of irritation, or of it being 3am by her internal clock. She simply picked up a chair and brought it over to face Richard's desk.

As soon as Lucy had sat down in front of his desk, Richard picked up his pile of papers and moved over to the meeting table. Lucy hesitated, still sitting in front of Richard's desk. And Richard began to feel that he had gone too far. A sense of shame began to intrude on his annoyance. This was not like him. It was not worthy of him. What was he doing?

But Lucy simply picked up her chair again, moved it back to the meeting table and said: "I'm sorry, it's the jet lag! I get a bit confused," and then sat attentively, waiting for Richard.

The meeting was short and predictable. Richard remained cold almost to the point of rudeness. He made it clear that the review was unnecessary, and that on no account was it to intrude on the smooth running of the business, or on the progress of plans already in place to address performance issues.

Lucy remained calm, conciliatory and pleasant, noting Richard's objections and concerns in her file. Lucy had clearly been here before! She worked hard to understand the detail of Richard's concerns, drawing him out, and making copious notes. Richard recognised the technique, but Lucy appeared totally sincere in what she was doing, and gradually Richard became calmer and even a little more open.

When Richard had run out of steam, Lucy introduced her agenda. She slid a sheet of quarto paper across to Richard. It was a memo from Cyrus Lerejecks to Lucy, and it was headed 'Objectives for Review of Gloucester Facility', and on it were the following bullet points.

- Understand major factors in current performance issues

The quality of business design depends on the quality of each step. Design methods have developed to ensure that each step can be undertaken methodically and confidently, to maximise the effectiveness and efficiency of the final conclusion. Many organisations will claim that they undertake these steps, but the quality of the methods they use are suspect, and this is borne out by the levels of conflict and inefficiency (often unseen, or worse still, accepted as inevitable[1]) that remain in their business.

Planning to design the business

Business design, as we have shown, is an important, perhaps vital, task that should be undertaken with discipline and rigour[2] if it is to fully achieve its potential.

But not all business design takes place at the same time, or at the same level of the organisation. For business design to be effective, it needs to be undertaken where the best information exists to support it effectively. It also needs to be undertaken at the best time to make full use of that information.

To ensure that these things happen effectively requires careful planning. Time needs to be scheduled into existing work patterns and commitments, and attuned to existing planning and budgeting cycles.

Effective business design therefore involves management throughout the organisation. Every manager needs to be involved in the configuration of their specific areas of responsibility and knowledge.

"I think we may need a little more clarity around step 2"

Every moment spent planning saves three or four in execution.

Crawford Greenwalt
President, Du Pont

---

1   Waste and conflict are only inevitable to the extent that poor design makes them so.

2   Discipline and rigour are commonplace concepts in practically all professions, and yet they sometimes jar when we consider them in terms of management. Could this be because traditional approaches to management are amateurish?

- Work with management team to ensure strategy and effective management approaches to meet end of year performance targets
- Establish effective program of continuous improvement in line with Cylek standards
- Recommend further changes as required.

The final sentence on the memo clearly stated that Lucy was expected to report progress and findings, weekly, direct to Cyrus Lerejecks, according to the Plan of 18 February.

"What plan?" asked Richard abruptly. Lucy slid another quarto sheet in front of him. On it, a series of blue rectangles described how tasks would be completed in various timescales, and black diamonds set deadlines for various reports and deliverables.

Richard poured over the plan. The timescales were very tight, but even if they had been incredibly loose, Richard would have said what he said next. It was his means of negotiation. "There is no way we can do this!" he exploded.

Lucy remained calm. "What exactly?"

"Well, any of it!" responded Richard. "It will totally disrupt our schedules!"

"We can change the timescales," said Lucy, "but whatever we agree will have to be approved by the President."

Richard had to admire her strategy. She was presenting herself as a calm helpful ally. Her bottom line was anchored in the authority of the Old Man himself, and if Richard wanted to change that, he would be negotiating with Lerejecks. Very clever. He turned his attention back to the detail of the plan. He explored each task, and drew out the details. Each time, he would listen to her response and then, like a dodgy plumber, he would suck air through his teeth and shake his head, and move onto the next point.

Finally he sat back in his chair and said: "Clearly there are some practical details to be sorted out. Be back in my office at 8.30am tomorrow morning with a detailed breakdown and we will review how we might take it forward then."

He got up to walk back to his desk, the interview clearly at an end and Lucy's composure almost broke. She had been told that Richard Frewer was a good man who just needed a bit of help. She had bent over back-

This has both advantages and risks. On the one hand, effective involvement of the whole management team can ensure a well informed solution that has the commitment of all those needed to make it happen. On the other hand, the involvement of the whole management team can prove an unwieldy distraction that disrupts existing work and creates confusion. The difference lies in the quality of planning for management involvement, and the determination of:

- when a manager's input is most appropriate

- how the background/context is sold to them

- the way in which they are encouraged to contribute, and how conclusions are reached

- how their conclusions are accommodated in the overall model, and how they are involved in implementing the conclusions.

The diagram below illustrates an outline plan for achieving this.

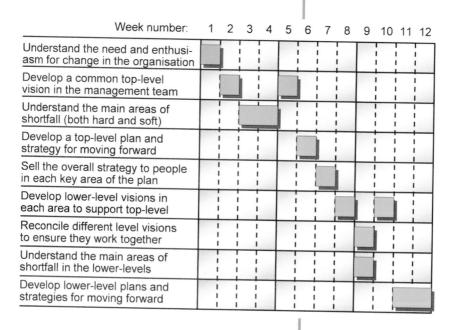

wards to enable him to show that side of his character. And he had just thrown it back in her face. There was no way she was going to play this game of submission and dismissal. She had seen it before: no involvement, a request for more detail, rejecting the conclusions, and being sent away to redo it. She could stay in that cycle forever.

What was her next approach? She had not prepared for this. Did it mean that her meeting with Richard's management team was now off for this afternoon? Was she to be held outside on a string?

Then a thought struck her, and she replied: "Good, I have an agenda for this afternoon's meeting that will deliver just that!" And she stood up quickly and walked out before Richard could gather his thoughts to reply.

As she closed the door and stood in the corridor she leant back against the doorframe for a moment and looked skywards for strength. She was infuriated! The sheer gall of the man!

She looked across to Helen, who was busily typing a document into the computer, and used this scene of normality to reset her frame of reference, and to regain the neutrality she needed to do her job. When she had fully recomposed herself, she approached Helen to find out what office arrangements Richard had put in place for her. On current showing, she half anticipated a broom cupboard in a separate portakabin.

Confront impoverished management practice

Once explained, the concept of 'business design' makes sense to nearly everybody who hears it. But most managers have great difficulty in reconciling the ideas of the foregoing chapters with what they do in practice day-by-day.

Faced with the hardness and reality of current issues, the less tangible concept of 'design' as a role simply evaporates away. This issue may be one you are beginning to struggle with at this very moment, and there are no easy ways to overcome it.

What we are attempting to deal with is a change in the basic assumptions about the role of management, and the first step is to fix very clearly in our minds what the new role we are proposing is. Two examples of how this might be achieved are:

- The competition question; which helps to establish the outcomes we are trying to achieve.

- The 'team of scientists' question; which begins to define how we are going to deliver the outcomes.

These are explained below.

The competition question

The competition question is designed to explore the concept of excellence in an organisation. Try it for yourself using the form on the right. In the blank labelled A, write the type of business you are in. In the spaces labelled B, write the names of three good organisations in the same business. And then in the area labelled C, write down the objective criteria that you would use to differentiate the winner.

Then when you have done this, ask what objective evidence you have of managing

Chapter 4

By the time the 2 o'clock meeting came around, the jet lag was really cutting in. Lucy had been without sleep for 26 hours and was really starting to feel it. She had used the intervening time to develop her agenda for the meeting, which was now a lot less about developing a common understanding of each other and a lot more about planning out the next four weeks. She knew if she could gain enough commitment from Richard's team, she could undermine his plans to keep her at arm's length.

The team were all in attendance, despite Richard almost encouraging them to find more important things to do. An imposed trouble-shooter carried all the drama of a soap opera script, and they were not going to miss out on the initial episode. Lucy met them one by one as they came into the room, introducing herself and memorising their faces against the organisation chart she already had in her mind.

Only Daniel was late, but barely so. Richard suspected it was to demonstrate his own importance, but there again he had always suspected that.

Lucy started:

"Good afternoon. Thank you for this opportunity to explain a bit about myself and what I am doing here. My name is Lucy Derring and I am here because companies fascinate me, and I get my kicks by asking many questions about them. No seriously, I do! While most kids I knew were having Barbie tea parties, my Barbie was having board meetings." This drew a laugh, but Lucy continued, "Seriously! I am not joking! I mean, who can get interested by 'Two Sugars?' when you can be planning a major construction project? Although I must admit most of my construction projects were stables and swimming pools - but I was only a kid." This drew another laugh. They were warming to her. Well, except for Richard of course.

"Yes! Questions about business! It really is what turns my wheels. Let me give you an example. This example will help you to see my role more clearly and it will also help me to see what is important to you." She paused and took a sip of water. "I want you to imagine that you have been appointed, as a group, to judge a competition, a competition of modem manufacturers, sponsored by Computer Monthly.

the improvement of those criteria in your own business. For that is the race you have chosen, and you have to run it better than your competitors, and to improve faster than them too.

The nature of the competition question illustrates the difference between conventional management and 'design' mentalities. By reflecting on other organisations, the question tends to encourage an objective 'design' perspective. However, when a group of managers are asked directly which criteria they want their business to be judged by, most tend to become subjective, and (at least subconsciously) filter out all criteria that they feel would reflect 'unfairly' on their current performance.

The scientific approach

This theme of objective distance is further developed in the 'team of scientists' question, illustrated on the right. By precluding any direct intervention, the question forces people to take a design perspective. You might like to try it yourself before you turn the page.

Ironically, despite being well versed in the disciplines and techniques of their craft, scientists and engineers are often the least prone to continue to use these principles in management. And yet, the performance of many of their facilities could be greatly improved by the rigorous application of their work place disciplines to the management of their organisations and processes.

The competition question

What might Cylek's answers have been?

Customer satisfaction survey score
Level of repeat business
Business growth (turnover)
Profitability (as % of turnover)
% Innovations introduced ahead of competition
% Sales from new products
% Competence growth
Employee satisfaction score
Business partner satisfaction score
% Vacancies recruited internally
% Levels of waste and rework
% Performance improvement
Product comparison ranking

'Team of scientists' question

Imagine you are a team of scientists and engineers appointed by the benevolent owner of 'Deep Thought' Ltd. (an organisation in the same business as your own) to improve its performance.

You have no management skills, but are expert in the creative thinking and objective analysis that your discipline requires. It is for this, and your naivety in traditional management, that you have been selected.

You are empowered to change anything, as long as you apply your professional discipline in doing so, but must not get embroiled in the day to day operation yourself.

How do you begin to delight your new boss?

"A number of companies have applied for the prize, 3 Com, US Robotics, Modular Technology, Psion, Hayes, Multitech Systems, and D-Link, but not Cylek, because they are supplying the judges. The competitors have agreed that you can see whatever you want, and talk to whoever you need to, in order to reach your decision as to which is the 'Best Modem Manufacturer'. What I want to know is on what criteria do you base your decision?

"Remember they are all going to be good, so you are going to be differentiating them more on the extent to which they have something, rather than whether they have it. I'll split you into two groups. You have twenty minutes, and I need a list of no more than ten criteria on which you will differentiate the winner from the also rans. Go!"

There was a real enthusiasm to tackle the problem she had posed. The question intrigued them and they seemed keen to get on and debate it. By the end of it, one group had identified 12 criteria, which they had selected down to 10, and the other had identified six by grouping ideas together. All of the suggested criteria were good ones.

Lucy looked at the lists. "So let me just check. What you are saying is that any modem manufacturer which scores highly on these criteria is necessarily a good company. Is that right?" The group thought about it for a while, and following a minimal amount of speculative challenges and responses, they nodded in agreement.

"Good!" she said. "Okay, now to be good criteria, these aspects of the business must be important, because otherwise you would have picked something else". She looked around for agreement, and then continued: "And they must be observable, or they would be of no use to you as the team of judges. You can't judge what you can't observe." The group nodded again, but a bit more tentatively, not fully sure of where she was going.

"And if, as we have agreed, they are each important and variable, and observable," here she began to emphasise the words carefully. "Then they must be key measures of the health of the business, and they must require management!"

She looked around the group again, but there were no nods this time, people seemed to be thinking about this, and possibly about its implications for them, the management team. But she knew they would not disagree. They could not. The logic was clear-cut.

This 'scientific' approach to management has, however, been increasing steadily in popularity (in spirit, if not in name) and a lot of what is now seen as 'best practice' management has clear parallels in the world of science and technology (see panels on the right).

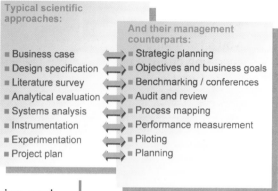

Typical scientific approaches:

- Business case
- Design specification
- Literature survey
- Analytical evaluation
- Systems analysis
- Instrumentation
- Experimentation
- Project plan

And their management counterparts:

- Strategic planning
- Objectives and business goals
- Benchmarking / conferences
- Audit and review
- Process mapping
- Performance measurement
- Piloting
- Planning

The key to the success of the scientific approach is that it is objective, analytical, comprehensive, and systemic. It considers all the things needed to make high-quality business decisions.

The top-box model

In fact, in most disciplines which relate to making something achieve of its best, the professionals in that discipline are the ones who apply an objective and analytical approach, whether they are doctors, or engineers, or biochemists, or architects.

The diagram on the right illustrates this by comparing a professional approach to medicine and a professional approach to engineering. In both cases, the practitioner is clear on the results that must be achieved and has quantified them. In both cases, the practitioner understands the key variables that they need to combine in order to deliver the results, and they understand the systems that impact on those variables. And in both cases, professionalism is reflected in the objectivity and analytical discipline that is used in deciding how to modify those variables and systems in order to deliver the results.

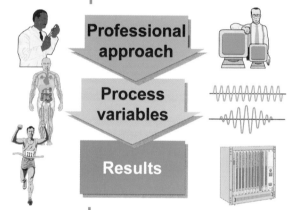

Professional approach

Process variables

Results

Could the same model be used to define professionalism in management?

She continued: "Furthermore, while performance on these criteria, which you have defined, is a measure of the quality of the company," she paused just long enough to ensure that she had everyone's attention. "Growth in that performance is a measure of the quality of the management of that company."

Several of the team anticipated with dread what they were sure was the next question: 'So, how does Cylek UK fare on these?' Or, 'How many of these do you measure/manage?' But Lucy never asked it. She let it hang and then instead of administering the coup de grace she continued in the abstract. She wanted friends, not enemies.

"So, imagine that company ABZ came bottom in your survey, and its Chairperson headhunted you as a group to manage ABZ to win the competition next year. And with presence of forethought he set the following rules: that you could change anything you wanted, but that you were not personally to become involved in the detail of the operations on a day-to-day basis."

She paused for a moment, and then asked: "How many here have scientific, engineering or technical backgrounds?" Over half the group raised their hands.

"Okay, so imagine the chairperson of ABZ has employed you for your analytical skills, your objectivity, and not for any managerial experience. How, using just those skills, and without getting involved in the detail, do you begin to make the ABZ chairperson a very happy man or woman? Same groups as before. Fifteen minutes to answer the question. Go!"

At the end of this second exercise, the groups fed back a good list of approaches, including 'Measure against the Criteria', 'Benchmark against the Winners', 'Analyse root causes of Deficiency', 'Establish clear Performance Targets'…

Lucy was pleased. She carried on her theme.

"Okay! Now imagine that you can invest all of your time in doing that." She paused, and looked intently at them as if to emphasise the question. "How likely is it that you could get ABZ to win the following year?"

Deborah had warmed to her now. She liked questions like this, and readily threw in a proposal. "Better than evens." Andrew had warmed to her too. "Yes, at least that!" he said. Nobody seemed inclined to disagree.

Certainly management is about 'making something achieve of its best'. And it too has results that can be defined or quantified: revenue; delivery performance; quality. And it too has variables and systems that affect the attainment of those results: competence; work patterns; reward systems; facilities. But, in management, how objective and analytical do the decisions on how to modify those variables and systems in order to deliver the results, tend to be?

Does the manager really understand the process variables that deliver results, and systematically develop them to do so? Can we see the evidence of data analysis, experimentation and logical conclusion in their records and their work?

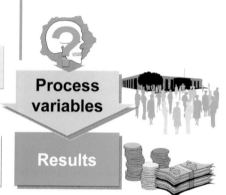

Not always!

Part of the reason for this is that traditionally most management work appears to have a far more operational focus. In this more 'operational' role the manager is heavily involved in sorting out problems, ensuring people are aware of issues, dealing with the business interfaces and acting as a specialist resource on issues that require his or her experience. Using a gearbox analogy, this role could be likened to a spectacularly advanced lubricant: easing friction, cooling the hot spots, providing a contact with other equipment, putting out fires and even compensating for missing cogs and sprockets.

From this intensely busy perspective it is very difficult to consider the other role: that of the designer who monitors the gearbox performance, models the key functions, experiments with different variables, and implements better ways of operating. That is the role that we have been advocating for management over the

Lucy continued, with only a small smile to acknowledge the contributions. "And, at a guess, if they were fairly typical of companies in the modem industry, maybe even using 'here' as an example, how much do you feel you could improve their performance in that year?"

The group thought for a while. Deborah was again first to break the silence. "Perhaps 50%."

"No, not that much!" interjected Abs.

"How much would you think then?" Lucy asked of Abs.

Abs thought a bit more then asked "If they were typical, and we could work full time on it?" he posed. Lucy nodded encouragingly and Abs continued: "Probably about 25%".

"I'd go for 40%," said John.

"Okay," said Lucy, "between 25 and 50%. And if ABZ was an 800 person organisation with a turnover of £130m?" She had drawn the link back to Cylek. "How much would that be worth?" She did not wait for an answer. The question had been rhetorical.

And then she continued with a passion that they had not seen before: "I am constantly frustrated and vexed that organisations like Cylek Inc. can take a group of enthusiastic capable people, and put them in a position where they can add £50m of value to the business year on year, and then tie them up in so much bureaucracy and activity that they don't have time to even think about it!"

Richard fought hard to keep the admiration out of his face. She had drawn them right onto the hook, and then not only let them go, but had swum away with them.

Lucy concluded: "That's why I get such a buzz out of my job. I have been given the privilege of helping management groups like yourself to get the time to take control of their business in a new way. In the way that you have described here this afternoon. But I am not the expert. I am just the catalyst. And my first step is to get to meet all of you individually so that I can tailor what I do to what you need.

"At the end of the day, if what we have just described is going to happen, it is going to be you that makes it happen. I will make an appointment to see each and everyone of you before the end of the week, and then we can have a follow up meeting early next week."

last ten pages. A role reflected in the top box of the diagram on the right.

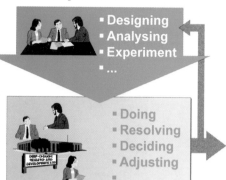

This 'top-box' role is what will ultimately determine the success of your organisation. It is what management is all about. But the transition from more traditional perspectives on management is far from easy.

In practice, managers find it difficult to spend the required time in the 'top box' for a number of reasons.

- All the urgent things are in the bottom box; the problems tend to be immediate, and things need to be sorted today if deadlines are to be met.

- We are more sure of our work in the bottom box; it is commonly being good at our work here that got us promoted in the first place.

- We don't feel comfortable with what we do in the top box; the tools and analytical techniques are often alien to us, particularly when applied to people and organisations.

- Work in the top box isn't valued; certainly not as much as fire-fighting - avoiding problems is a lot less visible than 'saving the day' when it all goes horribly wrong!

- We totally forget to think about going into the top-box; it is not uncommon to find that 5pm comes round, and your entire day has been driven by crises.

But the truth of the matter is that somebody must spend time redesigning your organisation to maintain its competitiveness as your business world expands.

If not you, who?

If not now, when?

Managers are the basic and scarcest resource of any business enterprise.

Peter F. Drucker
Management consultant and writer
in The Practice of Management
(Harper & Row, 1954)

Everyone nodded agreement. She had done it. Even Richard did not look too put out. One guy looked a bit sullen though - the one who had introduced himself as Daniel.

She would have to watch him!

Confront deficient awareness

Developing a clear hierarchy of well-defined and complementary goals that resolve conflict and confusion should do much to focus your organisation as a team on delivering greatly improved performance. This will be further enhanced by introducing the concept of business design as the means to ensure that those objectives harness your resources in the most effective and efficient manner, and by establishing management's role in that design.

The end result of this is likely to be a sense of shared intent and aspiration to improve

... always providing that it doesn't get too tough.

But change is tough!

Facing up to the need to change ourselves, and wresting with our behaviours, is not something we do easily, and some nebulous sense of theory is rarely enough to get us through the hard times (see the diagram on the right).

To bring about change, the issues, opportunities and implications have to be made real, practical, and specific to us. And that means that the theory of the last 65 pages has to be explicitly related to the situation in our own organisations. People need to be made aware of the real opportunities that face them personally, and of the real costs and consequences of not taking those opportunities, and they have to believe what they hear.

If your people are to be convinced that changes to their current practice are essential, then you will need compelling evidence to press your case. You must be able to objectively demonstrate a sufficient shortfall in current practice and performance to warrant change.

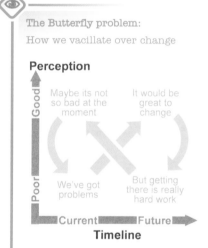

The Butterfly problem:
How we vacillate over change

An examination of cultural issues at the organizational level is absolutely essential to a basic understanding of what goes on in organizations, how to run them, and how to improve them.

Edgar H. Schein
Massachusetts Institute of Technology
in Organizational Culture and Leadership
(Jossey-Bass, 1985)

Chapter 5

A week later and Lucy was back in front of the group. Richard had accepted her plan for moving forward the previous Wednesday. It was not what he had tried to inflict on her, but he felt he could not very well do otherwise. His team had already virtually committed to what she had laid out on her planning sheet.

She had now completed all the initial interviews and the meeting was arranged for her to give her initial feedback and outline her proposed next steps. She had asked for a pre-meeting with Richard to explain the main points to him privately in advance of this feedback to the whole management group, but Richard had avoided it by claiming prior engagements. The truth was he did not want to commit himself before he had had a chance to see how the wind blew with his management team. He wanted to keep his powder dry.

Once again, the whole management team was present and almost on time. This fascinated Richard. He had rarely managed to achieve this with meetings planned months in advance. Clearly, his team was interested in the topic.

Lucy waited for everyone to arrive, and then started immediately by thanking everyone for their input and openness, and by expressing the hope that she had done justice to their time and ideas.

"As I agreed with you at the time of the interviews, the findings that I will be reporting today are non attributable. However, I believe that everything that was said to me was said in good faith, and I believe you will get a lot out of the conclusions. But before we start, perhaps it would be useful for you to understand the structure I used for the interviews and where it comes from."

Lucy waited for a general nod of assent, and then continued: "When I first started this work, I was involved in implementing Total Quality." There was a slight groan from some quarters of the group, and Lucy nodded. "Yes, that's not an uncommon reaction. But, in principle, Total Quality is simply a collection of excellent tools and attitudes. It is the implementation that so often lets it down. Don't get me wrong, my implementations were no better than anyone else's. I caused just as much

Fortunately, in most cases, this is not at all difficult.

Management survey

The best way to fully understand the need for change is to undertake surveys of current performance and practice. The first part of this, evaluating performance, may be done in a number of ways:

- comparing progress against past objectives

- looking at measures of customer satisfaction, waste, employee turnover, etc.

- looking at comparative indices with other organisations in similar industries.

The second part, evaluating the quality of current practice, should be done by comparing perceptions of what happens in your organisation with a model of good management practice.

A number of such models exist: The Baldrige Award; The European Quality Award; The Deming Prize. And there are also examples that can be gleaned from books written about exemplary companies.

In most cases their wisdom is reflected in six recurrent aspects of management (see the list on the right), which provide a useful framework for understanding and analysing current management practice.[1]

As reflected in models of good management practice, these six aspects of management: Purpose; Philosophy; People; Process; Predict; Perfect, are attributed to be crucial factors in the success of organisations. They are seen as important because there is a high correlation

Excellent management teams:

Purpose

Ensure a clear understanding of customer needs and issues, and inspire a desire to find new ways to serve them better

Philosophy

Establish clear targets for improvement of performance, at all levels, and develop a value culture which ensures they are actively pursued

People

Develop people's abilities and attitudes in a planned and productive manner, through a programme of challenges, experiences, team involvement, and training

Process

Develop and design the processes which effect performance, using methods which aid disciplined thinking and collective involvement

Predict

Measure process performance objectively, and use trends and analysis to drive a disciplined approach to solving current or potential performance issues

Perfect

Plan to continuously improve their approach to all of the above, through a strategy of actively learning from themselves and others

And deliver clear business benefits as a result of the above.

---

1 Material to support this is introduced later in the chapter.

bureaucracy and disinterest as the next person. And then I came across this quote."

Lucy flicked a switch on the data projector, and the screen behind her lit up with the words: *'Total Quality Management is more about the Quality of Management than it is about the Management of Quality.'*

Lucy continued: "TQ was based on some very sound principles, but all too often we spent our time getting people at the coal face to do things differently while their managers continued in the same old way. The result was not sustainable. Management behaviour determines organisation behaviour. If management don't change, ultimately their people won't either. But the quote got me to thinking. What actually is 'High-Quality Management'? Or in other words, since management is a profession, how would you describe quality in that profession? What would you say differentiated a professional manager from an amateur, apart from pay?"

She looked around. She had their attention. Clearly, the answer was not obvious to them.

"Then let me propose an answer to you, and see what you make of it." She clicked to the next slide in her presentation, and by drawing parallels between the professions of medicine and engineering, Lucy derived a model, which she then applied to management. From this she drew out six principles, which she put up on the screen:

Purpose: Ensure a clear understanding of how value is added to the customer

Philosophy: Ensure a consistent set of values which are commonly shared

People: Systematically develop and harness the potential of people

Process: Consciously and professionally design and develop all processes

Predict: Establish the data flows to invoke responsibility and enable accurate decisions

Perfect: Have a clear strategy to monitor and improve all of the above.

"Basically, it was this model which I explored with you in our interviews." She paused and looked round the room. "Yes, I can see most of you can

between their existence and success, and between their absence and failure.

However, these six aspects represent more than a serendipitous collection of features that are seen to be present in success. The six aspects are interrelated, and in most cases, sustainable success requires that all six are present. As such, the six aspects are not independent, but each represents one facet of a complete system, and the system requires all six aspects if it is to work effectively.

The system we refer to here is the model of systematic management, and it is directly analogous to the closed loop control model, which is the mainstay of effective systems design.

To explain the model in engineering terms: the *'process'* is established to deliver an *'output'*. The quality of the *'output'* is defined by the *'set point'*, and the *'measured value'* of the output is continuously evaluated against that. Any gap between the *'measured value'* and the *'set point'* is analysed by the *'controller'*, which calculates how to operate the *'actuator'* to make changes in the *'process'* and correct the *'output'*. The system is as effective as it is simple.

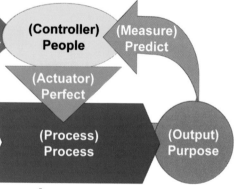

Looking at the same model again, but this time in management terms: *'purpose'* represents our understanding of the needs of our customer, which is delivered by the practices of our business *'process'*. The intended quality of our work is defined by our *'philosophy'* and we monitor and model our outputs to *'predict'* whether our outcomes will fulfil that expectation. Any gap needs to be accurately presented to our *'people'* so that they can analyse the underlying

Managing by Design

recognise it. Essentially it is an engineering model called a 'closed-loop feedback'."

At this, Richard started to pay very close attention. He hadn't heard Lucy's so-called theories of management before, and he wasn't really interested in them, but as soon as she started to talk about engineering, she was on what he considered to be his territory. He felt sure she would slip up. He shifted position to more intently listen to what Lucy was putting forward, and to be ready to exploit the first piece of flawed thinking.

Lucy continued: "Let me explain a bit more. In a closed-loop feedback system, the result or output is measured and compared against a target value, or set point. The difference between the set point and the measured value is evaluated by an algorithm, and the conclusion is used to make changes in the process, such as opening a valve or increasing a voltage, in order to influence the output toward the target value." As she talked through the theory her hand flicked over a diagram on the screen. "The model is critical to effective control of engineering processes from electronics to steel plant, from deep sea drilling to space exploration."

Seeing Richard's attention on her, she asked: "Do you have anything to add at this point Richard? I know this is your area of expertise!"

Caught off guard, he just said: "No. That seems right to me. Carry on."

She paused for a moment more, and then said: "It is also critical to effective control of an organisation," and one by one, she related the principles she had drawn out to the principles of the 'closed-loop feedback diagram'. Richard sat there stunned, all thoughts of destroying Lucy's arguments flushed from his mind. Why had he never seen it before? It was so beautifully simple.

Lucy continued: "Management's role is in the top half of this diagram. Management are the algorithms that hold the whole thing together, but all too often, they are forced down into the process: replacing missing parts, cooling things down and ensuring the product flows. If you ask most groups of managers how much time they get here, in the top box: setting goals, analysing outputs and designing and experimenting with the process - many will tell you it is less than 10%, which is far less time than they need to do the job properly."

There were nods of agreement round the table.

issues, and make changes to *'perfect'* the *'process'*. In some cases those changes may simply mean a correction, but in others they may warrant a complete redesign of part of the system.

Adopting the systematic management model

The model explained above is both logically and empirically valid, and for this reason most managers have little difficulty in accepting its veracity. However, such acceptance should not be taken for granted, and before the model is used as a basis for evaluating current practice it is important to reach explicit agreement with your management team on its adoption.

The six columns below represent one means of beginning that discussion. Each column represents five different levels of proficiency in each of the six aspects.

Effective deployment of objectives, particularly where they have a reasonable degree of ambition, requires a fairly high positioning on each column. This ensures that:

Knowledge and desire to ensure 'delight'	A clearly designed value set is evident	Development has been designed into work patterns	All processes deliberately designed to 'perform'	All activity consciously analysed and modelled	Systematic improvement of overall 'fitness'
Systematic focus on customer satisfaction	Comprehensive standards rigorously prosecuted	System of growth through challenge and coaching	Key/critical processes have been 'designed'	Rigorous prediction drives problem solving	'Fitness' is understood and steadily improved
Clear desire to satisfy customers	Standards exist and are actively pursued	Clear effort to involve, support and encourage	Processes have been mapped and developed	Measured deviations are clearly analysed	Clear strategy for improving performance
Customer awareness is evident	A direction is evident but goals are unclear	Effort largely a result of observed deficiencies	Some clear documenting and control of processes	Performance objectively monitored and recorded	Improvements take place on an ad-hoc basis
Largely task rather than role focus	Value set, if any, largely depends on individuals	No serious attempt to address development	Concept of processes is not evident	No objective performance monitors	There is no clear planned improvement

- the goals are based on an effective understanding of the organisation's role
- the goals are totally clear and unambiguous

"I can see that the feedback is unlikely to hold any real surprises for you then. But before I get into it properly, I'd just like to try a little exercise in observation. In a few seconds I will hold up a normal sheet of lined A4 paper, and I'd like you to take a really good look at it." At that point, she produced from inside her file, a ragged and marked sheet of paper, which she held up to the group for a moment, and then returned to her file.

Turning back to the group, she asked: "What can you remember about it?"

Various points were thrown in almost immediately. "It was torn halfway down the left-hand-side", "It had a smudge mark in the bottom right corner", and "The top left corner was crumpled".

She quickly stopped the group and pulled the paper back in front of them again. "Interesting that," she said. "Interesting that no-one mentioned how straight these lines are, or how flat and thin the sheet is or what a wonderful right-angle is formed here." She paused. "You see we tend to take our expectations of a sheet of A4 paper for granted, and talk about how the sheet differs from those expectations." She paused again. "The same thing happens when I speak to people about their companies. There is a lot that is good about Cylek UK, but you won't see it fairly represented on the following slides. That is not because it is unimportant, or it does not exist, it is just because you didn't tell me about it. Is that okay?"

People nodded, and Lucy was about to move on, when Daniel interjected: "Surely it is your job to produce a balanced picture. It is up to you to find out the facts and if our views are biased to compensate for them."

Richard was surprised at the interjection. An unexpected ally? He was not sure that Daniel was the sort of ally he wanted. But before he could work out what to do, Lucy had responded: "I agree! And eventually we will collectively pull together such a statement. But for the moment, all I am doing is presenting back to you what you see, and what is at the forefront of your minds. Nothing more!"

Lucy went to move on, but Daniel hadn't finished with her. "What use is that?" he retorted. Lucy caught herself just before she responded and paused, apparently in thought.

- people are fully developed and prepared to take responsibility for delivering them

- processes are clearly defined, in control, and are fully aligned to the goals

- issues in achieving the goals are rapidly identified and effectively addressed

- the potential to pursue goals is continuously improved.

By asking your team to agree what level on each column is required, to sustainably deliver performance improvement, you begin a debate that will both deliver insight, and validate the framework as an acceptable basis for reviewing current practice.[1]

Mechanics of evaluation

Once the model for evaluation has been agreed, there are a number of mechanisms that exist to help management teams evaluate the quality of management practice within their organisation. These include the following.

- Interviews[2] with groups and individuals to elicit current perceptions and anecdotal evidence, e.g. managers; staff; customers; suppliers and other business partners; local community; shareholders.

- Quantitative surveys[3] to ascertain the extent and depth of good or poor practice.

- Operational audit results against nationally or internationally recog-

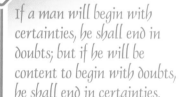

If a man will begin with certainties, he shall end in doubts; but if he will be content to begin with doubts, he shall end in certainties.

Francis Bacon
Lord Chancellor of England 1561-1626

---

1 A PowerPoint™ version of the diagram can be found on the associated web-site (see Appendix 7). A practical example of using this approach can be found on page 465.

2 An example interview form for customers and employees can be found on the associated web-site (see Appendix 7).

3 An example survey form for customers and employees can be found on the associated web-site.

The pause was long enough for Andrew to answer the question. "Well, it will help us to reach a common agreement on where we are. We've never really had that!"

Susan then supplemented that with: "We'll need a shared picture in order to agree our priorities for moving forward."

Others nodded, and Daniel sensed it was not worth pursuing, but he had to have the last word. "I'll reserve judgement," he said.

Sensing the group were largely with her, Lucy moved ahead to the feedback. She presented the findings sensitively enough, but it was clear that she had unearthed a whole range of issues in her discussions with Richard's team, and not one of them could they argue against. Lucy really had been very thorough. Finally, after twenty-seven minutes, of uninterrupted feedback, she concluded her presentation.

"Please don't take from what I have said that you are particularly poor. I have seen and heard a lot of good things over the last week. But, if you are intending to sustainably improve your performance, there are a number of issues that you will need to overcome, and they are these."

At this she put up a simple slide of six bullet points, said "Thank you for your time," and walked out of the room.

The six bullet points read:

- Few people outside of sales have any real understanding of customers, either external or internal. People are task focused rather than role focused.

- Targets and standards are ambiguous, confused and often non-existent. There is no consistent set of values promoted within the organisation.

- The appraisal system is effective, but is not well linked to development. People's skills are not effectively harnessed against business opportunities. Teamwork is weak.

- Outside of manufacturing, there appears to be no real understanding of process. Procedures do exist where ISO 9000 requires it, but are not developed or refined.

- Measures are largely purely financial. Decision making and problem-solving are largely ad-hoc and poorly informed.

- There is no clear program of continuous improvement, or of strategically harnessing corporate initiatives. There is no process for learning from own or other companies experience.

nised quality standards such as IiP, ISO 9000, EQA, QRS, Baldrige, etc.

- Process review of operational practice.

- Cost of quality analysis and problem tracking.

Some companies may already have elements of these data, and can use them to provide some of the answers. Very rarely do companies need to undertake all of the above review mechanisms to develop an accurate evaluation of their current management practice.

In the case of your own organisation, you might use the objectives you defined[1] at the end of the introduction to guide you as to how deep and comprehensive your survey needs to be.

Reviewing these objectives is likely to raise a number of questions in your mind about the extent and effectiveness of your current management practice. The level and type of review you undertake should be designed to provide accurate, objective answers to those questions.

It's only the companies that you're unfamiliar with that are well managed.

Fred Vanderschmidt
Director, Abt Associates Inc.

---

1   See page 11.

It was a very subdued management group that left the meeting room that evening.

Richard watched them go, but he himself sat quietly in his chair staring at the projection screen, his fingers steepled in front of his nose.

He sat there undisturbed for what seemed like an age, deep in thought over what he had seen: reconciling Lucy's model of management with his own thinking; reflecting on how closely Lucy's analysis paralleled his own concerns; and admiring how deftly she had managed the whole thing.

He still did not know where Lucy was coming from, but she would make an awesome ally.

As he pushed himself out of his chair, he made a decision to fully understand Lucy's agenda, and see if there was some scope in joining forces. All of a sudden, Lucy as an ally seemed a lot less risky than Lucy as an enemy.

Confront undisciplined planning

So, now you know the issues in your organisation, what has that to do with QFD? Well, whatever performance or practice shortfalls currently exist in your organisation, they are almost certainly a result of weaknesses in your planning process.

If that sounds a bit harsh, consider the following: those performance and practice deficits can only exist if one or more of the following is true.

- The planning process failed to identify the potential for improvement.

- The planning process didn't set objectives that would force the improvement to take place.

- The planning process didn't schedule and prioritise the resources to enable improvement.

- The planning process didn't establish the means to highlight lack of improvement.

- The planning process didn't address the issues that prevented improvement.

In short, the issues remain because the current planning system has failed to identify, demand or pursue the necessary improvement. This is directly analogous to deficiencies arising in a product due to weaknesses in the design process.

The intention of implementing QFD is to establish a planning and management system that ensures that the potential of the business is fully exploited in pursuing its current and future goals.

The purpose of this chapter is to provide a brief overview of the core tool in Quality Function Deployment: the QFD diagram; what it is; and how it works.

On a scale of 0-5 (5 being best), how well does your own planning process fare?

Ensuring all improvement opportunities are identified

Setting objectives that drive improvement to happen

Ensuring the right level of resources are available at the right time

Defining the means and mechanisms to objectively monitor progress

Addressing the barriers that have limited improvements in the past

How much would your organisation gain if it could score 5 in all of these areas?

Chapter 6

The following day found Lucy in Richard's office at 8.30 in the morning, for only the second time in the ten days she had been in the UK. Richard had dropped all of his previous charades of dismissal, and welcomed her in. This was much more like his normal approach, but he realised how incongruous the difference seemed to her when he glimpsed a wry smile of amusement as she sat down.

He thought about explaining this was his normal approach, by apologising for his behaviour to her last week, but he realised that this would make him seem even worse, like a Dickensian bank manager who had suddenly discovered his cleaner was a multi-millionaire. He did not even feel he could compliment her on her presentation for exactly the same reason. And there was no way he was going to validate her findings by remarking on their quality, especially since he was probably going to need to undermine them subsequently to his bosses in the States.

Instead, he busied himself with pouring them both a cup of coffee and getting straight in his own mind what he wanted out of this meeting. He had decided that he needed to better understand her agenda, and where she was coming from, and so without any preamble he asked: "So, what do you see as the next steps?"

Lucy caught the emphasis on 'you'. Richard was clearly not giving anything away here. He wanted to emphasise that Lucy's views were simply her own opinion, and carried no authority for him, his business, and what they might do in the future. Lucy parried. It actually was not her modus operandi to come in with a shopping list of actions and suggestions. She knew from experience that it did not work. People tended to be a lot more committed to plans and ideas that they developed themselves, and Richard was going to need a lot of commitment if he was going to fix the problems in Gloucester.

The best way was to identify what the client already had planned, understand where their enthusiasm and strengths lay, and then build on these. So, she asked: "What do you want to do next?"

Richard's face told her that he did not like that response, and he was just thinking how to phrase 'You tell me, you're the expert!' into something a bit less clichéd when she pitched in with: "What's QFD?"

QFD was first applied in Japan in 1972, at the Mitsubishi Kobe Shipyards, where engineers were struggling to make sense of how to break down exacting customer specifications into the complex of assemblies and systems that are a ship.

The problem was that all of the systems and assemblies were interrelated, and achieving the optimum performance in apparently conflicting requirements meant that some exacting compromises needed to be made. Conventional means of breaking down the specification into the various design areas limited the engineers' scope for finding the optimum solution, and was in danger of creating conflict and rework as the true needs of each component became clear. (Does any of this sound familiar to you in your management role?)

Shigeru Mizuno and Yoji Akao hit on the simple idea of creating a matrix of relationships between the main areas of the specification and the key systems and assemblies required to deliver them.

The matrix revolutionised the Mitsubishi engineers' thinking and helped them to see possibilities and potential that had previously been dormant in the design. Since then the tool has spread within the automotive and computer industries, where its potential for reconciling conflicting requirements and sophisticated mechanisms has been fully exploited.

As has been discussed earlier, the concept of a complex design clearly has parallels with the nature of business and companies. They too, often have challenging and apparently conflicting requirements placed upon them (e.g. increase market share and cut inventory), and can certainly be viewed as complex systems of processes and resources. It was there-

Richard was visibly taken aback by the quick change in topic, so she continued: "A number of people I spoke to said you had plans to focus Cylek UK on its objectives through a tool called QFD, but they weren't able to tell me what it was. I've never heard of it and it intrigued me. What does it stand for?"

This made Richard smile. He could not think of a worse way to introduce QFD to someone than to explain what the letters stood for. For him, personally, the acronym was the biggest turn-off about the tool. But Richard was quite torn. On the one hand he didn't want to expose his cards until he knew where Lucy was coming from. And on the other hand, here was a great opportunity to win Lucy over to his way of things. He was convinced that Lucy's apparent interest in engineering would make her vulnerable to the charms of a design tool like QFD, but he wasn't yet sure of her.

He looked at her for a moment, while he made up his mind how best to respond. Her appearance was one of innocent interest, and he felt so proud of his own thinking on this matter that he really didn't want her to hear it from anybody else.

Eventually his enthusiasm for his own ideas overrode his caution. "Let me show you," he said. He went to his desk and pulled out the list of seven objectives for Cylek UK that he had developed from the Why-How chart, and pinned them to his notice board by the side of the organisation chart that was already there.

"These are the objectives for Cylek UK. They haven't been approved by Frank yet, but if you look at them you will see that they are comprehensive and cover everything we need to deliver."

He invited Lucy up to take a closer look. She did so, and then she went back to her file and pulled out the business objectives for Cylek UK that had been sent from the States. She held them up against Richard's list and compared them.

After about a minute she said: "I can see that they might encompass your actual objectives, but they seem far more vague. I can't see Frank approving these!"

"No, he wouldn't," replied Richard. "But that's because they don't have measures and targets established for them yet. Interestingly, your little exercise last week helped a bit there, and I've used some of the ideas from it." He went back to his desk and picked up another sheet of A4

fore likely that QFD would also add value in this area of design.

This idea of applying the tool of QFD to the design of an organisation was explored by the American Supplier Institute and Ford, in the late 1980's, based on research undertaken in Japan.[1] It was successfully applied to the holistic design of an organisation in the UK in 1993 (Siemens Congleton), and it has since been used successfully in other parts of Siemens, and also in parts of Emerson, Sainsbury's, Microsoft, and Smith & Nephew, where it has generated previously inconceivable performance improvements.

How (organisational) QFD works

At its simplest, QFD is a matrix: a series of rows and columns. Each row reflects a clear business objective, and each column reflects a separate mechanism (see example right), e.g. function, unit, department or process of that business.

Each cell then represents the potential for that business mechanism to influence the attainment of the objective. Developing the framework for the matrix provides an opportunity for the management team to reconsider the organisation's mission, its logic, and its operating structure.

The business objectives (rows of the QFD matrix) may be drawn from the Why-How chart (right), choosing a series of statements that together represent exactly what the organisation is trying to achieve (see Chapter 2). Each objective should be further clarified to the extent of having clear measures associated with it, and a quantified target performance defined. These will be addressed in the following chapters.

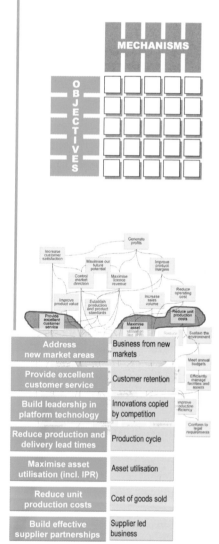

Objectives and measures

---

1   Reported in 'Policy management through QFD', Lawrence P Sullivan, Quality Progress, June 1988.

with a number of measures on it, some of which she recognised from her first session with the management team.

"Now, this is in no way complete. We still have to do some work on anchoring exactly what we mean by those objectives. But when we have finished, delivering these objectives would guarantee the delivery of what the States have requested, and more."

"So what is wrong with just using these?" asked Lucy, waving the objectives she had in her hand.

"They are incomplete," replied Richard, and when Lucy looked sceptical he continued: "They focus only on the financial aspects of the business such as turnover, capital employed and market share, and yet we know that the States is also interested in customer satisfaction and employee development."

"But they are interested in customer satisfaction and employee development because they lead to the financial targets," interjected Lucy.

Richard was just about to respond with: "Yes, tomorrow's! Not today's!" when a thought struck him. "Don't give me that! It was you who ran the exercise on measures last week. It was you who was emphasising the importance of a balanced management focus." Lucy smiled as she realised she had been hoist by her own petard. "Well that's what this will become," concluded Richard in a slightly less aggressive tone.

"Okay," said Lucy, "let's say that I buy that. How does all this relate to QFD?"

"Imagine our objectives are now fully defined. The next question is how do each of the departments contribute to delivering those objectives?"

"Management by Objectives," put in Lucy.

"No, not Management by Objectives," responded Richard. "MBO leads to a number of problems and missed opportunities."

"Such as?" prompted Lucy.

"MBO can be very divisive. Departments tend to focus on the more obvious objectives, and miss out on considering their potential to influence others, even adversely. And often when the objectives are cascaded down, they lead to sub-optimisation and sections working against each

The quality of insight that QFD can provide depends greatly on the care with which the 'mechanisms' are defined. The 'mechanisms' (columns of the QFD matrix) are the means by which the organisation fulfils its goals - they are logical subdivisions of your organisation. Some means of dividing up the business provide a richer depth of understanding within QFD than others, and in practice the most useful models tend to be ones based on business processes. For some companies, this has caused them to rethink how they organise themselves (see example process diagram on the right, and Appendix 2).

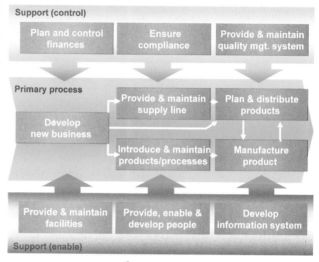

By discussing each cell of the resulting matrix, the managers develop a complete understanding of how the business must work as a whole if is to succeed. This provides new insights as to how the potential of each mechanism can be exploited in new and innovative ways, and, equally importantly, how they can have adverse effects that need to be controlled.

Through a simple mathematical relationship (see Appendix 5), QFD provides a mechanism for ranking the objectives, and prioritising improvement of the mechanisms. Teams responsible for managing each mechanism can then draw up additional QFDs, to think through how each mechanism can be creatively developed to best fulfil its potential.

By further developing the basic diagram, QFD also provides for the management team to think through their communication and reporting needs. A triangular, half-matrix on top of the main QFD

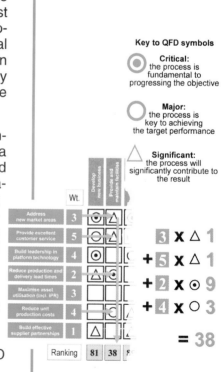

other. Objectives get achieved, but potential is lost and overall the business suffers."

"MBO does not have to be like that!" retorted Lucy.

"No, it doesn't, but in all of the practical applications of it that I have seen, it has either turned out that way in practice, or it has been toned down to a series of wish lists that carry no effective teeth. It might work for a year or two when it is first implemented and all the gross inefficiencies are ironed out, but how many implementations can you name where it has been sustained effectively without causing sub-optimisation or lost opportunities?"

Lucy nodded to accept the point.

Richard continued: "We used to design products in a similar way to MBO. The overall specification was broken down into specifications for systems and subsystems in a very linear way, and that too created sub-optimisation and conflict in the design. But then the Japanese came up with the idea of QFD. QFD was developed for product design, and that's where it has been used, but I want to apply it to the development of this business, so I'll explain it to you in those terms."

Lucy nodded. She could sense an enthusiasm and a passion building in Richard that she had not seen before, and she was as interested in that as she was about the explanation.

"Imagine if we created a grid between the objectives and the departments, where the departments are the columns and the objectives are the rows. And then imagine if, as a team, we explored the potential of each department to contribute to, or to detract from, each objective.

"The whole management team would be drawn into a complete understanding of how the business could work, and could be encouraged to think creatively about untapped potential. For instance," he jabbed with his finger at an imaginary cell, "they could explore the potential of the invoicing system to develop customer loyalty, or," he jabbed at another cell, "they could explore the role of our IT system in personal development."

Lucy conjured up possibilities in her mind as Richard spoke. She was intrigued by the idea of a management team using these types of discussions to design new functionality and focus into their business. She was developing a sense of how businesses could proactively shift com-

diagram (shown below) provides an opportunity to look at the interaction of each of the business 'mechanisms' (be they processes, departments, business groups or whatever) and to consider the extent to which they are likely to work in harmony or conflict. This helps those who will manage those 'mechanisms' to think through the level of communication they need to arrange between them.

Benefits of QFD

QFD thus provides each manager with a clear understanding of what his or her area should deliver, in the context of how the organisation needs to operate as a whole.

Within this, the rigour and structure that QFD provides gives freedom for the management team to consider goals and strategies that they might otherwise consider unthinkable or irresponsible, even to the extent of entirely redefining themselves, their role, and their operations.

The structure provides a means to examine every part of the organisation, and to succinctly document[1] the conclusions, but the real value of QFD is in the discussion. The valuable outcomes leave the room in people's minds and not on the piece of paper that is the QFD. The QFD diagram is not the goal of the exercise, it is simply a tool within it.

The discussions on the other hand will do much to:

■ build deeper understanding of the organisation's objectives, and

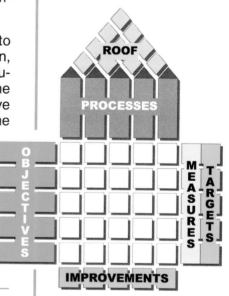

---

1 The QFD diagram can be further enhanced as a summary document by including measures and targets for the objectives, and by reflecting relationships between the various mechanisms in the 'roof' of the diagram (as explained earlier). See illustration on the right.

   Information on Measures and Targets can be found in Chapter 7. Information on developing the roof can be found in Chapter 23.

petitive goal posts by leveraging the potential of their 'Cinderella' process-es.

Richard continued: "And when the grid is complete, and the discussions documented, the departments can review their performance against their potential, and redesign themselves where there are advantages to be gained. And through some simple maths, priorities can be determined and resources allocated to where they have the best competitive lever-age, just like in product design.

"And just as in product design, each department can develop their own QFD, to better focus themselves on their enhanced goals."

Richard went silent, and he watched Lucy gaze at the blank space on his notice board, and he imagined the pictures that were floating in front of her eyes.

She turned and looked at Richard appraisingly, and said: "You really have a vision for this place don't you?" Richard looked back at her. Her face was a guileless picture of enthusiasm that in that moment seemed to mirror his own. In that moment, he just wanted her to know the true him, to appreciate his thoughts and dreams. He nodded, and she continued: "So, let me ask you again. What do you want to do next?"

Richard smiled, accepting this was where they started out, and then began to explain his plans for refining the measures and targets, and for the schedule of meetings he had prepared to develop and implement the QFD approach. His enthusiasm was infectious.

At the end of it Lucy said: "You know, there is tremendous potential in this to address a lot of the issues that were raised yesterday!"

"I know," said Richard, a trifle ruefully.

"For instance," continued Lucy, "it could dramatically improve target setting and performance measurement. It could give people a better understanding of role, and could therefore improve how they are used. It could provide better focus on the processes, and it would provide an excellent platform for continuous improvement."

Richard simply stared blankly back at her. He was quite amazed at how quickly she had grasped the concept. "But you still haven't told me what it stands for," challenged Lucy.

greater clarity of exactly what they mean and how they fit together

- ensure a holistic grasp of the organisation and how the various parts need to interact and function together

- inspire new insights into the potential for each part of the organisation to contribute to achieving the objectives, and build a greater appreciation of the contributions being made

- equip the management team members to inspire and encourage their own teams to commit themselves to achieving their potential.

All of these factors are key to developing a real sense of teamwork in transforming your organisation, and it is this teamwork that will make the difference in effectively harnessing the talents and energies of your people in transforming their performance.

In the next section we look in more depth at precisely how QFD will help you to do this, and we work through the practical mechanics of developing a QFD for your own organisation.

"Oh," said Richard, "I'm afraid that is probably the least endearing aspect of the whole tool. It stands for Quality Function Deployment." Lucy gave him a quizzical look. "Well you did ask!" he retorted, "but personally I only ever refer to it as QFD."

Lucy looked back at the wall where Richard had created the makeshift QFD, and after a few moments she said: "I have some consulting tools that might make bits of your planned meetings more effective, and if you want I would be happy to facilitate them for you."

Richard hesitated. He still was not sure about her. It was his job to lead the team. Was she trying to take over?

Lucy sensed Richard's uncertainty, and some intuition told her it was a concern about losing control of his plans, so she chipped in quickly: "Look, I think this QFD is a brilliant idea. I've never seen anything like it. A lot of my success has stemmed from the fact that I'm an outsider and that people think I have the ear of the board. Most of what I do, quite frankly, they already have the ability to do for themselves. But this is different. I've got a feeling that, with this approach, I can really add something new to my clients. I want to learn about it. I want to see it work. I want to introduce it to other companies. But this is your company, and your tool. You would lead the workshops of your people, and I'd just be the hired hand, facilitating selected sessions so that you could take a full part in leading the discussions. How about it?"

Richard had been touched by her honesty, and slightly reassured by what she was proposing, but he still was not fully sure about this.

"Look, what say we sit down and plan out the first of your sessions together. I'll chip in some approaches that you can take or leave, and at the end you can choose whether you get me involved, and how! What do you say?" And before he could respond, she said: "We can plan it tomorrow, over dinner at my hotel. Now that the conference call on the next range of products has been cancelled, I know you're free from 7pm onwards. I'll book the table!"

As she watched her departing back, he smiled. It was the first real evidence he had seen of the aggressiveness he often associated with American consultants. And actually, the thought of dinner with her was beginning to appeal to him.

Summary

Most practical approaches to organisation management fail to fully deploy clear business goals, or to efficiently harness all the available creativity and resource in pursuit of them. But, it is one thing to accept this logically, and another thing altogether to see it clearly within your own situation, and to get your people to see it too.

In this section we have reflected on a number of practical tools to think through the concepts of:

- clarifying and reconciling goals and objectives

- relating the disciplines of design to business

- taking a 'top-box' approach to management

- evaluating the quality and effectiveness of management practice in an organisation

- addressing the deficiencies through QFD.

How will you implement this thinking in your own situation?

....

....

....

....

....

....

....

....

....

Relevant materials available on the web-site to support discussion and application of the ideas in this section

Presentation materials in MS PowerPoint™ format:

    Why-How charting and how it works

    The concept of business design

    The 'top-box' role of management, and its responsibilities

    Surveying current management practice

    Introduction to QFD.

Survey materials in MS Word™ format (editable to suit):

    Customer interview and questionnaire forms

    Employee interview and questionnaire forms

    Basic interviewing guidelines.

Discussion exercises in MS PowerPoint™ format:

    Competition question

    Team of scientists question.

Copies of key diagrams in MS PowerPoint™ format.

Section B

Build a team that is determined to drive transformation

If you have built castles in the air, your work need not be lost; that is where they should be. Now put the foundations under them.

Henry David Thoreau

BUILD A TEAM THAT IS DETERMINED TO DRIVE TRANSFORMATION

Whatever goals you have set your organisation, you can be sure of one thing: If they are sufficiently worthwhile and ambitious, they will require good teamwork from your people to ensure that they are delivered successfully.

Essentials of effective teamwork

Clear and common goals	Shared processes and frameworks
Defined roles and responsibilities	Committed interpersonal relationships

But good teamwork doesn't just happen. Good teamwork depends on four key factors being in place: shared objectives; agreed roles; effective ways of working; and interpersonal commitment. Where teams work well it is possible to see that all these things are in place, and where they fail it will be due to a deficiency in one or more of these areas.

Developing the QFD diagram provides a means to address all four of these factors.

- Establishing clear and explicit common goals within the rows of the QFD.

- Defining the structure of the organisation in the columns of the QFD and thereby the roles and responsibilities of each team member.

- Constructively exploring, through the grid of the QFD, how every part of the organisation can work together to efficiently deliver the goals.

- Building commitment through deploying the QFD and encouraging people to submit their own dreams and ideas for making things happen.

Over the next four chapters, seven to ten, we will look at this in more detail.

"'Alf day then?" asked Colin, as he moved the cleaning trolley from in front of the door to let Richard pass. "Or 'ave you been sacked after all?"

Richard smiled at Colin's affront. He liked his blunt friendly manner, and felt some companionship from the number of times Colin had been his only company in the building.

"Is there a book on it then?" he replied. "What odds are you giving at the moment?"

"Pretty damn slim, I'd say, if you can't pull this shower int' a decent team."

Richard took the opportunity to straighten up the collar on his coat before stepping out into the rain spattered darkness.

"Better team than the Robins though eh?" challenged Richard taking a side swipe at Colin's beloved Swindon Town F.C. "What was it? Three one to Pompey?"

Colin retorted "Yeah well, at least we found the goal. 'Alf your lot would-n't know what a goal looks like, and I'm convinced other 'alf are all tryin' ta be the number eight."

"That's rugby!" countered Richard, before he noticed he'd be drawn neatly to where Colin wanted him.

"Precisely!" retorted Colin triumphantly. "Anyway 'ave a good evenin'. And watch out for that young Miss Derrin'. She'll 'ave you for break-fast!"

Richard smiled ruefully, and navigated his way round the trolley and into the cold night, ruminating that not much found its way past Colin.

Establish clear and explicit common goals (Rows of the QFD)

The single most important factor in effective teamwork is having a clear and shared objective. It is the crucial factor that differentiates teams from committees. In a committee, each participant has their own responsibilities or goals, which are more important to that person than the work of the committee. Progress is made by finding routes that don't unduly compromise each member's agenda. A team is formed when the members are able to wholeheartedly commit to a common goal that is more important than their personal agendas. Individual objectives become whatever will progress the common goal. Unfortunately a lot of management teams are really committees.

The rows of a QFD provide a means to ensure that the goals of the organisation are clear, agreed, unambiguous, and used to drive all activity within the organisation.

In Chapter 2 we looked at how Why-How charting[1] could be used to develop a clear understanding of an organisation's goals, and at how the chart could be translated into an effective set of objectives. In this chapter we look at how those objectives can be further refined to provide a clear focus for the team and its work on QFD.

There are three steps which help to ensure that whatever objectives have been set out of the Why-How chart are unambiguous. These are:

- make sure that the objectives are few in number, ideally less than ten

Objectives are not fate; they are direction. They are not commands; they are commitments. They do not determine the future; they are a means to mobilise the resources and energies of the business for the making of the future.

Peter F Drucker
Management Consultant & Writer
in People & Performance
(Harper & Row, 1977)

---

[1] The Why-How chart provides an excellent basis for identifying a balanced set of organisational objectives, but it is not the only means. Other methods include reconsidering existing objectives, or brainstorming a list of objectives onto yellow sticky-notes and then grouping them down into a limited number of top-level objectives for your organisation.

Chapter 7

Over coffee Richard asked, as casually as he could: "Have you submitted your initial report to Cyrus yet?"

"No, not yet, but he will be expecting it soon. I'll pull together something for early next week. Do you want to see it before it goes?"

Richard was taken aback. The offer seemed genuine and he could not detect any sarcasm. "What? See your report to Cyrus?"

Lucy laughed. "You really don't get it do you? I am on your side!" Richard looked sceptical.

"Look at it from my point of view," she said. "I love this job. I love waltzing into a company. I love making a difference. And I love waltzing back out again knowing that I have."

She paused for a second, "Okay, and yes, I love the paycheques too. But to be able to do that I have to work with the management team. If I damage or destroy them, I either don't get to waltz back out or I don't get to make the difference, at least not in the way I want to. The only exception to that is where the MD is a complete dunderhead, and fortunately for me, Cylek doesn't seem to appoint any of those." Then she scrutinised his head with mock seriousness, and said: "Unless …"

Richard laughed.

"It really is important to me, Richard, that we work as a team. We do have the same objective. We both want to see Gloucester's performance dramatically improve, yes?"

Richard looked at her carefully, and felt she was being sincere and open. He nodded.

"And, actually, we both have the same process for achieving that goal. We both believe that it is by improving the management practices, and we both agree that QFD seems to be the best opportunity for beginning to do that. So now that's two hurdles out of the way – we agree on the goal and the means."

Lucy paused and took a sip of her coffee.

- define clear measures of success to describe what progress means against each objective
- specify numeric targets for each measure, so that the magnitude of the objective is clear.

These points are expanded below.

Limiting the number of objectives

The greater the number of objectives, the more difficult it is to keep them all in mind, and yet that is what a team must do. If there are too many objectives, then members of the group will tend to focus on some and forget others, and this can have uncontrolled, and therefore unfortunate, consequences. If they are selected with care, it is possible to describe all that an organisation is trying to do in five to ten objectives, and seven is about the limit of most people's easy retention. If you have too many objectives, you should consider redefining and regrouping them until you have a practical number. Reference to a Why-How chart will help to ensure that there is no loss of quality in this process.

Establishing measures

Objectives can remain remarkably ambiguous and woolly until they are described in terms of the measurable impact that achieving them will have. Unfortunately, developing appropriate measures for business operations is one activity that organisations tend to find exceedingly painful.

There is something about the combination of the creativity that it requires, and the judgement it implies, that makes the task seem almost impossible. As the mind seeks to free itself to find new possibilities, our internal critic is thinking how the measure could be misused if applied to us personally. The result tends to be a prolonged silence.

That which can be measured is known, but if you cannot measure something, if you cannot express it in numbers, then your knowledge is of a meagre and unsatisfactory kind.

Lord Kelvin
British Physicist

Which is the tallest figure?

Without measurement to guide us, our frames of reference and past experience can influence us to judge things inaccurately.

"The only other things that could stop us being a team is if we get our roles confused, or if we just can't get on. As for the roles, well we're working on those, but from my perspective your role is sacrosanct, and I'm here simply to assist you in implementing change. And as for getting on together, well frankly I'd rather have someone give me paper cuts and rub lemon juice into them!"

Richard smiled lopsidedly, and wondered if Lucy was reflecting back to their initial meeting. "Yes, I'm sorry about last Monday morning!" he said sheepishly.

Lucy laughed back at him.

"I think we'll get along just fine, but I know that trust is a major part of that, and so everything I send to Cyrus you get to see. That is actually part of my agreement with him for doing this work. I love helping people and I hate politics. Cyrus knows that the day he asks me to do the dirty on one of his people is the day he finds another consultant." She paused, and then continued: "But to be fair, I think Cyrus thinks that way too!"

It was 11pm and the evening was coming to an end. They had come up with a very good programme for the first QFD meeting, and Lucy had greatly improved Richard's ideas on how to arrange things. He had built more trust in her, and he thought he had presented a more accurate impression of himself. The environment away from the office had been very relaxing, and let's face it, the company had been delightful.

As Richard lay in bed that night, he replayed the evening in his mind.

In his mind, the ambitious, political harlot had been replaced by a caring, enthusiastic woman. In his mind, the scheming enemy had been replaced by an intelligent ally. In his mind, the sterile target of his resentment had been transformed into an attractive soul mate.

It was true, they had so much in common it was uncanny. Here was a woman who not only understood and appreciated his dreams, she also had the ability to help him achieve them. And on top of that, she was distinctly sexy.

Richard couldn't remember enjoying an evening so much in years. In his imagination, the management consultant was transformed into the subject of his fantasies, and his hand stole down toward the waistband of his boxer shorts.

The key to developing good measures lies in separating the creative from the critical, and applying them at different times. The competition question[1] provides one mechanism for doing this.

Evaluating the extremes of performance of fictitious organisations can illuminate useful measures of performance.

It achieves this by invoking a fictitious third party, and thereby frees the individual to be more objective. Other similar mechanisms can be found in the Guide to Measurement,[2] one example of which is illustrated on the right.

What would a company look, feel and work like if its human resource function…	
…worked very well?	…worked very poorly?
Happy people	Discontent
Low turnover	Waves of people leaving
Leaving for more senior roles	Leaving for similar roles
Competence growth	Steady or declining competence
Lots of ideas	Few suggestions

In each case the result is usually both creative and objective, and the next step is simply to apply the critical. This can be achieved by asking in what way the conclusions apply to you in your particular situation. This question enables the group to refine such measures before they accept them as valid evaluators of their efforts, but in many cases the team will adopt most of their conclusions.

Where a group is less inhibited in considering objective self evaluation, the Why-How chart becomes a useful device for thinking through potential measures. By looking at why an objective exists we gain insight as to how we might measure whether it has been successful.

Setting targets

Establishing measures helps to clarify what is meant by the words of the objective. They describe the dimensions along which success will be judged. Setting targets on those dimensions is equally critical to a complete understanding of the objective. For instance, a target of 'increase output by 5%' requires a totally

1   See page 56.

2   See Appendix 7.

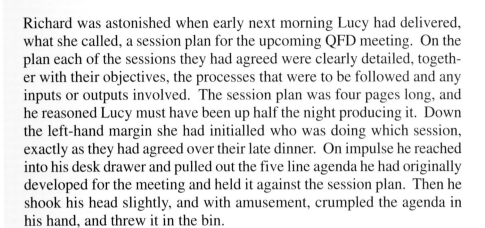

Richard was astonished when early next morning Lucy had delivered, what she called, a session plan for the upcoming QFD meeting. On the plan each of the sessions they had agreed were clearly detailed, together with their objectives, the processes that were to be followed and any inputs or outputs involved. The session plan was four pages long, and he reasoned Lucy must have been up half the night producing it. Down the left-hand margin she had initialled who was doing which session, exactly as they had agreed over their late dinner. On impulse he reached into his desk drawer and pulled out the five line agenda he had originally developed for the meeting and held it against the session plan. Then he shook his head slightly, and with amusement, crumpled the agenda in his hand, and threw it in the bin.

In the top right-hand corner of the session plan Lucy had scribbled an internal telephone number. He presumed it was hers. It was certainly a number in the accounts department where he had asked Helen to find Lucy a desk, well away from where she might eavesdrop on the real issues.

He thought back to the affinity he had felt with her the evening before. Was the scribbled telephone number an encouragement to call? He wanted to. He pictured her in his mind, and how the candlelight had sparkled in her eyes and reflected enticingly from her lip gloss. He felt a strange tightness of anticipation in his chest as he picked up the telephone and dialled her number. The pressure increased as he heard the ringing tone in the receiver.

"Lucy Derring!"

"Hi Lucy, it's Richard. Did you get ANY sleep last night?"

Lucy laughed. "Good morning Richard. I just claimed some credit back from my jet lag. How are you this morning?"

"I'm very well," Richard replied. "Just a little astonished. Do you do this for all your meetings?"

"Most of them," affirmed Lucy. "At the end of the day, effective meetings can make a huge difference to the end result, and they are practically impossible to rework when they are producing the wrong result. A carefully planned process might look like an expensive overhead but

different strategy to one of *'increase output by 500%'.*

The targets, in large part, define whether the approach taken needs to be incremental or radical; whether we are talking about evolution or revolution.

The key to setting effective targets is to identify in which places you want to focus your revolution, and in which places you are happy for evolution.

Revolution (major increases in performance) requires creativity and innovation to achieve it. Creativity and innovation are, by their very nature, risky and time consuming. Every item of creativity you require increases your chances of failure. Where one innovation relies on another for success, your risks are compounded. Rolls Royce discovered this principle on the RB211 engine to the cost of their entire business.[1] Innovation is necessary for transformational performance, but it should be used frugally, and focused on where it has the greatest leverage.

When you have identified which objectives should have stretch targets, and which should not, the next step is to have the team agree what the actual targets should be. The clothes-line method, as described on the right, is an excellent method of exploring all the arguments, and reaching consensus on the final targets, based on those arguments.

It is essentially a physical number line, along which people can stand to indicate where they would like a target to be set. One end of the number line may be current performance (say 50) and the other end may be global best practice, or a different value depending on the highest aspiration in the room (say 100).

---

1 The RB211 was a radical jet-engine development in the 1960s. Sadly the extent of innovation compounded the risks, and the cost and time implications bankrupted Rolls-Royce.

The concept of number is the obvious distinction between the beast and the man. Thanks to number, the cry becomes song, noise acquired rhythm, the spring is transformed into a dance, force becomes dynamic, and outlines [become] figures.

Joseph Marie d Maistre
French philosopher and statesman.

Target setting process (clothes-line method):

Everybody considers what target they would set and writes it clearly on a card provided

We identify the highest and the lowest and peg them on the clothes-line, others peg their cards at appropriate points in between

Everyone stands where they currently believe the target should be

We hear the arguments for and against the extremes, and people move up and down the line (to different target values) as they are swayed by the arguments they hear

After five minutes, or after all the arguments are heard, we take the point at which most people are standing.

it is actually a very valuable investment. See what you think after the meeting on Monday."

Richard could see her point, but he could not see himself buying into that sort of effort. Then on impulse he said: "Are you free for lunch today?"

"Sure," she said.

"I just wanted to run back through your plan, and check I fully understand it."

"Yeah, fine," she responded.

"Okay, see you at 12.30 in the canteen," he said, and put the telephone back on its rest.

Richard sat and stared into space for a moment. He didn't really need to run through the plan, it was all perfectly clear, but there was a strange desire in him, almost a compulsion, to see Lucy again. It was the same feeling he'd had when he started dating Laura. It was weird how he felt nervous. A bit like a schoolboy.

A slight sense of guilt developed, and he dismissed it with rationality. It is not like I am breaking any rules, and he focused on Laura, and then he focused on the rules.

And then he let his mind drift onto breaking the rules, and as it drifted back on to Lucy his pulse quickened. He caught himself, and blinked and cleared his head.

What an awful name, the thought, 'Loo Sea'. He accentuated the syllables for effect, then focused back on the report in front of him.

The canteen seemed unusually busy for a Friday. Tray in hand, Deborah scanned the ranks of pale green tables for a set of friendly faces to join for lunch. She spotted Richard and Lucy chatting happily in the corner. Intrigued she walked over to join them. The relaxed style of their conversation seemed quite at odds to the vibes she had picked up earlier in the week.

"So what are you two plotting?" she challenged jokingly.

"Lucy's trying to convince me I need a clothes-line!" responded Richard.

Somebody standing half way along such a line would then be reflecting a proposed target half way between the two (say 75), and that person may move up and down the line as influenced by hearing the arguments of those stood at different positions.

When well facilitated, the targets tend to be ambitious, practical and, most importantly, have the buy-in of the whole team.

Weighting the objectives

The steps outlined above will do much to clarify exactly what you mean by your objectives, however, in separating the objectives from the Why-How chart and placing them into the QFD there is a real danger that we begin to lose sight of their context, and therefore their relative importance to the overall goal.

The QFD, however, provides a means to reflect that relative importance and to use it to influence priorities within the grid. The weighting column is used to rank the importance of the objectives on a scale of five to one - five being the most important and one the least.

The importance, like most aspects of the QFD, is best determined by objective and open discussion. Weightings[1] can be defined by working through the objectives one by one, and ranking each on the scale of one to five through consensus, guided by the relationships in the Why-How chart. But we have found that it often works better in practice to identify the most and least important objectives first, and then to use this as a scale to rank the next.

In the finished QFD, the weighting will be used to help prioritise the efforts of your team in making things happen.

---

1 More sophisticated mechanisms of weighting can be found in Appendix 5

Deborah maintained her quizzical expression as she slid her tray out from under her plate.

Lucy clarified. "It's a means of getting a group to agree performance targets. In essence it is a human number line."

Deborah looked even more intrigued, so Lucy continued "Basically we run a length of string across a room and peg numbers to it to create a scale. People then go and stand under the number they want the target to be. Everybody then puts forward their reasons, and people move up and down the scale as they feel influenced by the arguments they hear. The idea is that once everybody has had their say, people will have taken on board the balance of the arguments, and will have tended to group themselves under the most appropriate target value. It might sound a little strange but it works surprisingly well."

"Sounds fun," said Deborah, who had a liking for anything new or different.

"Okay," said Richard, "we'll have the clothes-line! Will I be able to use it to agree the weighting of the objectives as well?"

"I don't see why not," replied Lucy.

Define the structure of the organisation (Columns of the QFD)

Establishing a clear set of common goals will ensure that your team are all headed in the right direction, but it won't ensure that they will work as a team to get there. Teamwork implies that the team members each play their part in achieving the goal, and that each part is complementary and combines with the other parts efficiently and effectively - like a football team for instance. If the parts that people are required to play are unclear, then the result is often a free-for-all, with some tasks being done twice and others completely forgotten. Clarifying and agreeing a defined role for each team member is vitally important if the team is to work efficiently and effectively in pursuit of the goal.

In this chapter, we look at how the columns of the QFD can be used to establish what those roles are by:

- clarifying the structure of the organisation, and

- clarifying responsibilities within that structure.

Because QFD is simply a matrix that relates 'what you want to do' to 'how you want to do it', it places no restrictions on the models you might use for 'how'. As such, how the management team choose to view the structure of their organisation through the QFD is entirely up to them. They could, for instance, view it as:

- divided into market areas, with each column representing a separate product line

- divided into geographic areas, with each column representing a separate region

- divided into disciplines or specialisms, with each column representing a different skill set

Chapter 8

Back at the hotel, Richard and Lucy celebrated the success of their first joint project. The meeting had been a tremendous success all round.

Richard had to admit his reservations about what Lucy called 'The clothes-line' had proved foundationless The idea of his management team standing along an imaginary number line, moving up and down it, and arguing their positions had seemed a bit bizarre. And yet in practice it had proved to be the most focused and efficient discussion they had ever had.

At the end of the meeting, everyone had bought into the outcomes, and felt they had developed a clear set of measures and targets that they could commit to delivering by the end of September – Cylek's financial year-end.

Correction – make that nearly everyone. Daniel was proving an increasing concern to Richard. On a number of occasions he had taken a different stance from the group and refused to consider other viewpoints. The process had highlighted his differences, and had ultimately isolated him in them. His attempts to steamroller the conclusions fell foul of Lucy's ground rules for the meeting, and he had grown increasingly sullen. Richard was worried about how he might bring him back on board.

Yet he did not regret the process in the slightest. It had illustrated to him how the price for Daniel's involvement had been acceptance of Daniel's agenda and politics. And it was a cost, that now Richard had been clearly shown the price tag, he knew he could not afford to keep paying. Working with the session plan had been a real eye-opener for Richard, and he was beginning to see meetings more clearly as a process. A process which, in the past, had been all too often wasteful and ineffective.

Lucy put down her fizzy water and said: "Richard, you know you were explaining developing the QFD between the objectives and the departments? Well I was wondering, have you considered linking it to business processes instead of departments?"

"Say some more," prompted Richard.

- divided into improvement areas, with each column representing a different project or initiative
- divided into traditional business functions, with each column representing a different department
- divided into areas of functionality, with each column representing a different business process.

In practice, however, most of these have limited value as an ongoing management tool. In the case of the first two options we tend to find that the columns on the QFD become very similar, because in practice geographic and market areas represent microcosms of the complete business and have to fulfil all of the objectives - so the debate becomes sterile and provides little new insight. In the case of the third option, we may develop a good understanding of the skills we need to develop and recruit, but little insight into how they should be integrated into the systems and facilities of a multidisciplinary organisation. The fourth option provides excellent guidance on how improvement should be focused - but in practice, because it separates improvement activity from day-to-day performance responsibilities, it tends to become a wish list.

The fifth option reflects the position many companies adopt when they first start to use QFD. It ensures that increased clarity is brought to bear on the existing lines of responsibility in the organisation, but it does not require any reorganisation of those responsibilities, or the attendant disruption and potential confusion that that may entail. By retaining current models of operating, organisations can evaluate most of the potential of QFD without committing themselves to its use.

The sixth option, however, combines real insight with the means to focus it on the day-to-day management of the business.

The benefits of process thinking:

Breaks down functional silos

Focuses on customers and delivery

Links operation with improvement

Highlights hand-over problems

Better flexibility and responsiveness

Increased efficiency / reduced cost

Reduced cycle times / more speed

Better teamwork and communication

More fulfilling involvement/activity

Improved quality assurance.

"Well, I was extending the concept of product design, and how it might work in business. If you think about the sub-assemblies, are they not more likely to represent various forms of systems? Yes?"

"Ye-e-es, go on."

"For instance, in telescope design, I imagine the QFD works better if you separate out optics, casing, and adjustment into columns than if you have columns of eyepiece, object lens assembly and main tube, each of which might contain elements of all three."

Richard thought about this for a while and related it back to his own experience of QFD. "Yes, much better!"

"Well, if we were to extend that thinking to Cylek UK. Would the QFD work better if we considered a process such as 'logistics' for the storage and movement of goods, rather than a series of activities grouped separately under Operations, Site Services and IT?"

Richard thought about it.

Lucy let him ponder briefly and then cut in with: "You see, process thinking is adding a lot to business improvement currently. Good tools have been developed to help design processes and manage their performance."

Richard nodded. He was aware of some of them. "But some of our departments are processes," he responded.

"Some, but not all, and not completely," challenged Lucy. "Wouldn't it make sense to refine the model of Cylek UK to better reflect processes before we launch into QFD properly?"

Richard thought some more. She had a point. But there were a number of down-sides. "Possibly," he allowed, "but, point one, it could take a long time to think that out and get it agreed, and, point two, it would confuse the accountabilities and that could be disastrous for us."

"Well perhaps, but taking those points in turn: firstly, I'm sure we could come up with an approach that would have business processes sufficiently defined and agreed by the next meeting, and secondly, accountabilities can often become a lot clearer when they are defined in terms of processes."

Richard sat back, and look upwards for a while. It certainly made sense, but it was more ambitious than what he had in mind.

In practice we have found this by far the best basis for the columns on the QFD. So the rest of this chapter is dedicated to ensuring a clear understanding of:

- the concept of business process
- business process modelling
- the steps to developing an effective business process model
- roles and responsibilities within the process model.

The concept of business processes

All businesses contain processes, whether we recognise them as such or not. A process is simply described as a sequence of activities that transform an input into an output, whether that output is a product, a service, or your expenses claim.

Processes can be defined as short sequences of activities, such as *'assembling a wheel nut'* or long sequences, such as *'building a complete car from new materials'*. Processes can be described specifically, such as *'fitting the driver's seat in a Ford Focus'*, or generically, such as *'making a phone call'*. Processes can be directly related to delivering output, such as *'producing product'*, or indirectly related to it, such as *'maintaining facilities'*, or even more indirectly related, such as *'planning improvement'*.

What then do we currently do that is not a process? The short answer to that question is 'nothing'. Even the activity of identifying processes, is in itself a process, or at least part of one. As a process, it can be defined, evaluated, improved and managed. And that is the benefit of seeing activities as processes, or parts of processes - the opportunity to improve, objectively and systematically, the per-

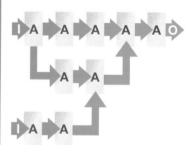

Examples of process concepts

Not only is there but one way of doing things rightly, but there is one way of seeing them, and that is, seeing the whole of them.

John Ruskin
English art critic and historian.

"Try this," she said. "You and I sit down and develop a logical model between us. Not too radically different, but with the processes defined a bit more clearly. Then we propose the model to the management team, and conclude any further refinements, and agree the model in principle. And then you appoint numbers of the management team to take responsibility for those processes and adjust any remaining confusions."

"Yes," he said hesitantly, "but will we really get extra advantage out of it?"

Lucy thought for a moment. She was a little puzzled that Richard seemed to be struggling with something that seemed so obvious to her.

"I'm sure we will," she replied, "but let's go over the logic step by step and see that I haven't missed anything. Firstly, processes give us a way of breaking down the business into clear sequences of activities which lead to identifiable performance." She looked at Richard to ensure he was with her on this point, and he half shrugged and then nodded in reply.

"Secondly," she continued, "assigning responsibility for these processes means that each manager has a clear picture of what he or she is intended to achieve, and has direct influence over the means to achieve it." She looked at Richard again, and again he nodded.

But then he stopped and challenged. "But how does that differ from what we have now?"

"Well in some cases it doesn't," she replied, "because in areas like production the clarity is already there. In fact they already are a process! But in other areas performance and responsibility are a lot more woolly."

Richard looked at her quizzically, so she continued, "Well, take the problems you are having with availability of components at point of use. Who has clarity over performance and responsibility over putting it right? Wouldn't it be more clear it if was seen as one process rather than three parts of separate departments?"

Richard nodded, but Lucy could see he was still slightly hesitant.

"We could take an initial stab at it right now, and if it doesn't get us anywhere we can abandon the idea from the outset. Shall I see if they've got a room we can work in? I imagine we are going to have to spread out a bit for this one."

formance of that activity in the context of what the organisation is trying to achieve.

Because all work that takes place in an organisation can be defined as part of a process, it is possible to develop a model of the business, which is comprised entirely of interlinking and complementary processes. The performance of the organisation can then be described in terms of the performance of its processes. Examples of such models for a number of different organisations may be seen on the right.

Because of the variety of work that takes place in an organisation, there are clearly different types of processes. The four most common types of processes are as follows.

- Direct processes, which are concerned with the routine activities of directly producing and delivering the main products and services of the organisation to its customer.

- Indirect processes, which are concerned with the routine of supporting the operation of direct processes through the provision of facilities, labour, finance, paperwork, etc.

- Control processes, which tend to be cyclical, and manage the operation of other processes, through measuring their performance and effecting adjustments where required.

- Design processes, which tend to either be on an annual cycle or more ad-hoc, and establish the parameters and means for improvement.

Business process modelling

There is, however, no preordained model of business processes. There is not one set and constant answer stating exactly what the business processes for a company should be (see the variety in the examples of the diagram on the right).

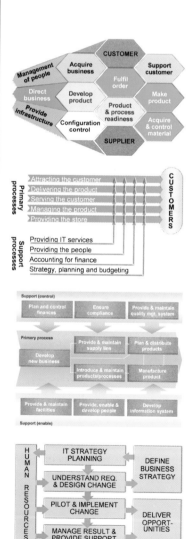

Richard nodded, and Lucy headed for the reception desk, glass in hand. He watched her shapely legs, which were accentuated by her high-heeled shoes, and how they blended into a very attractive bottom. As his thoughts wandered, he realised that it was becoming increasingly difficult for him to keep them focused on business, and that he would have to fight to keep his mind on the subject in hand.

He was still fighting when Lucy returned to wake him out of his reverie.

"No luck! They are fully booked, but we could always use my room. It is big enough!"

Richard's imagination temporarily took him hostage and demanded a ransom, he paid in full with images that caused him to flush. But he caught himself quickly, and looked back obviously embarrassed. "No, I couldn't do that," he said tightly.

Lucy saw the expressions on his face, and heard the tone of his voice, and caught on quick. "Excuse me. Let me get one thing straight. I don't screw my clients. I'm a country girl from the Bible Belt and I still have my faith and my values!"

Richard was taken aback by her bluntness, and blustered: "I never thought for one minute…" but he stumbled to a halt, realising that his face was telling quite a different story. He caught himself and started again. "My apologies. I was taken off guard. I merely meant that it would not seem right. That it could be misinterpreted by others."

Now it was Lucy's turn to look embarrassed. "I'm sorry! People tell me that I'm too open, that things I do and say get misinterpreted. And then I get paranoid that people have got the wrong end of the stick, and I change from Dr. Jekyll into Miss Hyde. I didn't mean anything by it. Of course you didn't think that!"

Richard was once again disarmed by her frankness, and felt guilty that he was going to let her think that it was she who had been in the wrong. He could not, or would not, do anything about that. But he could at least take a more conciliatory approach.

"We're business colleagues. We are responsible senior people in a large multi-national and we have work to do. If people around us want to mis-interpret that, that's their problem. Lead on McDuff!"

Each organisation is free to consider the main elements of how they do business in many, equally valid, different ways. The key is to develop a model which provides the greatest insight and potential for improvement and control of your business. And to accept that the chosen model is unlikely to be perfect, but should provide a practical basis for targeting improvement.

One other important note to make from the models shown on the previous page, is that none of them reflects metaprocesses: the processes which 'control' and 'design' the organisation.

These metaprocesses are the mechanisms which ensure your management team works effectively. While such mechanisms benefit from improvement in their own right, such considerations are best separated from the consideration of how to manage and improve the more functional aspects of the organisation. An analogy would be to consider the designing of a washing machine, and whether considering the designer's set square or drafting pen in the product QFD would be apt to clarify or confuse things. To include the control and design processes within the business QFD tends to create circular arguments and confusion, and it is best to restrict your QFD to routine 'direct' and 'indirect' processes.

The steps to developing an effective business process model

Developing process models can be a fun activity, and can in itself provide new insights into how your organisation can be developed. What follows here is a practical guide to developing an effective process model with your management team. It breaks process modelling down into five steps.

Examples of direct and indirect processes for a manufacturing business

Direct processes:

Sales Order Management

Product Manufacturing

Purchasing

Order Despatch

Product Distribution.

Indirect processes:

Quality Assurance

People Development

Facilities Management

Financial Management.

She looked at him with slightly narrowed eyes, as if to say 'Are you sure?' and he responded: "Sexual equality! If you were Daniel, would people assume I was gay?"

"And down on your luck," she said, and laughed.

Lucy's room turned out to be opulent and massive. "Wow, I'm glad this isn't out of my budget!" he said. And then with the faintest note of anxiety: "It isn't, is it?"

She smiled, and went over to her briefcase to pull out the ubiquitous sticky notes. "It's all part of the strategy," she replied. "If people think you cost a lot they seem to value the outcomes more." Richard gave her a disbelieving look. "It's true actually!" she replied, and then conceded: "And, of course, it is more fun to live in luxury."

This was a side to Cylek that he wanted to explore further. "And Cyrus doesn't have any problem with that?" he asked.

She looked at him quizzically. "I'm not actually employed by Cylek, I'm just retained by them. These," she indicated the surroundings, "are part of my normal terms. It is just as important that Cyrus values what I have to say. And anyway, I've made him many more times in benefits what I've cost him in fees."

She sat down at a large circular mahogany table, put down the sticky notes and a pen, and cleared the various hotel literature on to the bed behind her. Richard sat down opposite, and waited.

"Let's take the departments one by one, and list out the activities that each is responsible for. I'll write each activity on a separate sticky note and we'll stick them up on that wall over there. We'll put them up initially in their departments, then we'll try moving them round and see if we can develop a better, more process focused model. How does that sound?"

"Fine," said Richard, shrugging.

"Okay. Go!" she said.

They worked through the task as she had outlined it. When the sticky notes were up on the wall, Richard spotted a few activities he had missed.

- List the activities of the organisation.
- Develop a number of possible models.
- Review the models' strengths and weaknesses.
- Select a model and refine it.
- Define the scope and boundaries of each process within the model.

This approach is intended for the management group that will ultimately develop the QFD, and take responsibility for the processes. It is intended to enable them to contribute their ideas and experience, and to build their commitment to implement the conclusions.

List the activities of the organisation

The first step is to list the activities of the organisation. It is important that the activities listed are at a similar level of detail. This can be achieved by asking each member of the management group to break down the area he/she is responsible for into ten to fifteen activities that collectively represent all that their department/section etc. should be doing.[1] The next step is to get the group to call these out, and to list them not only on a flipchart but also separately on four sets of sticky-notes.[2] Calling out the activities helps people to identify areas they have forgotten, and to ensure that the final list is comprehensive.

When the list is finished the group should have four complete sets of sticky-notes, each one identifying an activity that takes place in the organisation.

Develop a number of possible models

The group is then split up into three syndicate teams, each with a set of all the

Example of listing activities under headings of existing departments

HR	Technical	Operations
Catering	Returns and repairs	Packing and despatch
Recruitment	Special products	Equipment maintenance
Pay awards	Product design	Manufacture
Safety management	Product quality inspection	Industrial engineering
Succession planning	Competitor analysis	Goods receiving
Training	Platform research	Machine setups
Library	Standards development and liaison	Stores
	Legal and IPR	
	Vendor selection	
	Complaints management	

---

1   Listing what 'should' be happening ensures that valuable activities which are not currently happening are considered in the model.

2   The reason for this will become clear in the next step.

Lucy wrote them up and added them to the wall, but Richard became concerned with the overall integrity of what they were trying to do.

"If we have still got activities missing then our conclusions will be flawed," he protested.

Lucy stopped and sat down on the edge of the bed looking at the yellow rectangles that now decorated her wall. "We could end up missing out some of the activities," she conceded, "but I think we'll remember the key ones. Looking at this, I think we have a good chance of developing a logical framework that is right in principle. We can always get the management team to refine it further and ensure everything is included. That can be part of their buying into this."

Richard still looked sceptical. Lucy continued: "Look, we've come this far. Why don't we just try moving things round a bit and see what emerges. If we're not happy with what we get, we can abandon it at that point, and stick with the departments as they are. But don't you think it's worth a try to explore our options before we lock in the existing solution?"

She had spoken to the designer in him, and he responded. Within a couple of minutes he was enthusiastically shuffling the sticky notes, conjuring up new arrangements and visualising the result. Every so often, Lucy would seen an alternative pattern and start to build it, but it was as much to stimulate Richard's thinking, as it was to propose a solution.

Within half an hour, Richard had developed a pattern that he was reluctant to change any further. Lucy thought it looked good in process terms, even though three of the existing departments remained virtually the same as they were originally. She had earlier moved activities out of them, only to see Richard return them minutes later, so she was happy that they were not left by default.

"Okay," she mused. "Now, if these really are processes, we ought to be able to give each of them a simple description consisting of a verb and a noun, so let's give it a try." She pointed to one of the departments that had not changed. "How about this one to start?"

"That's Human Resources," said Richard.

"Ang Arrgh!" Lucy imitated a quiz show buzzer for a wrong answer. "Verb and noun, at least!"

activities on sticky-notes. The team's role is to group the activities into a logical set of business processes for the organisation. The fourth set of sticky-notes is developed into the current organisational model.

When the syndicates have completed their models they should present them back to the group, and explain their reasoning.

Review the models' strengths and weaknesses

The group, as a whole, should then work round each of the four models, including the current model, and for each one, they should list out what they see as its strengths and weaknesses. These should be flip charted into two columns, on one sheet of paper for each model. Extended debate of the feedback should be avoided. At the end of this step, each model should be pinned up on the wall, together with its sheet of strengths and weaknesses.

Select a model and refine it

The fourth step is to pick one of the models as a basis for developing it into the model for the organisation. This does not necessarily mean picking the best model, because it may be easier to correct and refine one of the other models. The preferred model should be agreed through consensus reaching[1], so that the whole group can support the conclusion.

Having selected a model, the next step is to refine it. This is done by working through the 'weaknesses' feedback, and incorporating ideas from the other models to address the issues. Consensus reaching should also be used through this process.

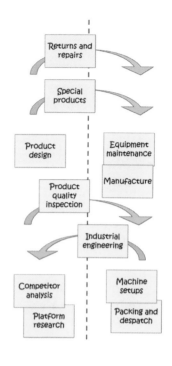

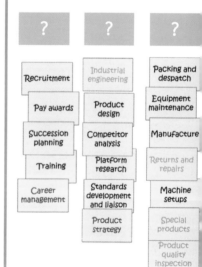

Examples of moving activities between department groups to create processes (above) and of identifying suitable process

---

1   See Appendix 9 for an explanation of Consensus reaching.

Richard thought about this for a while. "Okay," he said. "How about 'Providing and Growing Human Resources'?"

Lucy grimaced "'Human Resources'?" she said, as though she had tasted lemon juice. "Why don't people call them 'People'?"

"Who's process map is this?" challenged Richard in mock indignation. "But you're right! 'Providing and Growing People' it is!"

Lucy wrote the words up on a different colour sticky note and stuck it above the collection of activities. And so they worked though each of the groups. Sometimes, having defined a name, Richard would pull off one of the activities and find a better home for it, one that fitted it better. Sometimes he did it in reverse, pulling an additional sticky note into the new process, and twice he spotted activities that he had missed, and added them in.

By the time they'd finished he was very happy with the result. "Great! So what happens next?"

"You go home!" she said pointing to her watch. It was gone 11pm Where had the time gone?

"Uh, oh!" he said. "Major brownie point trade deficit!" Then he thought about it a bit more seriously. "Shit!" he expostulated, and shook his head. Things were bad enough with Laura at the moment. He did not need this. "Got to go," he said, "but thanks, you were right." And he left abruptly, all thoughts of next steps evaporated.

Laura closed the book in front of her and placed it on her bedside table with a sigh of resignation, and as she retracted her arm the duvet settled back over her recumbent form.

She had hoped that reading a few verses from its pages might stem the tide of resentment that was building inside her, but she hadn't really been able to see the words through the angry pictures in her mind, and as she looked at the hands of the clock wind their way past another hour a resurgent wave of bitterness engulfed her.

Shaking her head, she reached back out for the book, and placing her hand palm down on the large gold cross that was embossed in its cover she muttered a silent prayer.

Define process scope and boundaries

The fifth and final step is to remove ambiguity from the processes by clarifying their scope and boundaries. This is achieved by looking at each of the process groups in turn, and raising questions about exactly where their boundaries lie. The conclusions of these discussions normally result in some of the activities being rewritten or subdivided to ensure the scope and boundaries are clear.

At this point it would be beneficial to give the processes appropriate names that reflect what they are trying to achieve. Normal convention for naming processes is that the name should contain a verb and a noun, such as 'test product' or 'distribute report'. This is a valuable discipline that can help prevent subsequent problems.

Other methods of developing the process model

The method of developing the organisational model outlined above, while effective, can prove very disruptive in practice. This is not an issue if you are open to reconsidering your management and reporting structures, but can be problematic if there is a need to keep existing structures relatively stable, for instance if your management group is not confident with process management.

An alternative is to map up the current organisational model in sticky-notes, and then consider proposals to modify the model and bring it more in line with process thinking. In this way existing structures can be largely preserved. This method is the one used within the story on the right-hand pages.

There are also generic models of business processes, and models that have been developed by other organisations. It is

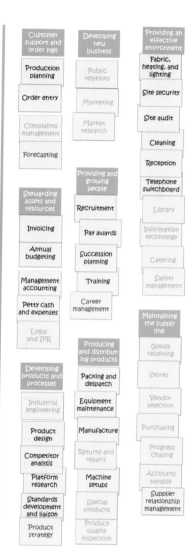

But the sound of the car pulling up outside the house gave renewed focus to her ire. She could see in her mind's eye her husband shutting the car door as though he hadn't a care in the world. Her mind dwelt on a picture of him out enjoying himself over some business dinner while she explained to her son that he couldn't stay up any longer to surprise his dad with his hard-won trophy. She imagined Richard's laughing face while Nicholas's look of broken disappointment, far more poignant than the expected tantrum, had torn a hole in her heart. Damn! She hated the man's insensitivity, his selfishness!

Richard shut the front door quietly, and carefully mounted the stairs, hoping that Laura had fallen to sleep. He looked into the bedroom. Laura was lying quietly, her back towards him. He switched off the light and stepped back into the hall to get undressed. Then he stealthily made his way up his side of the bed.

"This isn't fair!" Laura's voice was loud, abrupt, without any trace of sleep in it. Richard paused where he was, and then turned on the bedside light. Laura kept her back towards him as she spoke in measured tones, her resentment clear in the pauses between each sentence: "We came down here as a family. Nicholas and I left friends and a life we knew, because we're a family. And now we're not a family. You are Richard Frewer, business tycoon, and Nicholas and I might as well not exist!"

"That's not true!" retorted Richard.

"Oh no?" She sat up and twisted round to face him. "Then tell me exactly how many hours we've had as a family doing things together last month, and then tell me whether it's been getting better or worse!"

"Laura, it's not like that!" he pleaded.

She looked at him aghast. "Then tell me what it is like," she shouted. "Tell me what it is like, week in, week out, for Nicholas and I. Tell me from your expert position of the odd few minutes that you spend here. TELL ME!!!"

Her voice had risen to a crescendo, and the last two words were shouted at him. And then she burst into tears.

Simultaneously, he heard Nicholas cry out from his room. The unexpected noises had woken him. Richard got up to go to him, but, at the foot of the bed, Laura pushed past him barging him out of the way.

possible, with care, to adopt and adapt appropriate elements of these models for your own organisation.

Roles and responsibilities within the process model

There are two aspects to achieving improvement: design and operation. While the 'design' may make provision for improvement, that improvement is not actually delivered until the activity is operated effectively in line with the design requirements. In practice, we have found that improvement is best achieved when authority for these two aspects is held by one person, i.e. the manager responsible for delivering the performance is also responsible for designing how it is achieved. Whenever authority has not been coincident, we have found that the effectiveness of the improvement tends to be diminished by politics, communication issues, and wildly differing priorities.

The key factor in your success in delivering transformational performance depends on how well you identify and assign responsibility for process improvement.

If you appoint the right people as process owners, and establish them properly in that role, then your performance will take off.

If you appoint the wrong people as process owners, or fail to establish the authority and resources they need, then your performance will, at best, drift slowly to a plateau.

In many cases, however, you may have little choice over who your initial process owners are. They are most likely to be your current management team for two very good reasons.

- What will you do with them if they aren't managing the business?

"I can do it," he protested, but before he could continue she glared at him, her wet eyes full of anger and scorn. He backed away and let her go, and sat on the edge of the bed. The bedside light illuminated a single Polaroid photograph. It was of a kindergarten class. A small boy was holding up a trophy, and at the bottom Laura had written 'Nicholas awarded prize for best pupil', and today's date.

Under it was a piece of paper with a scribbled note that simply said, "Just in case you miss all of Nicholas's childhood!!" Richard looked back at the boy's face. He imagined his son waiting at home to tell Daddy the good news, and eventually going to bed sad and disillusioned. And as he thought about what might have transpired, he felt a lump rise up in his throat, and he slumped down onto the bed swearing forcefully: "Shit! Shit! Shit! Shit!" Then self-pity cut in, and he raged against the unfair demands placed upon him. He could not do everything!

In the subsequent management meeting, the management team was given a free hand to refine the processes that Richard and Lucy had defined. They changed surprisingly little, and, almost without exception, had eagerly taken on the roles of each taking a process forward, continuing to define it, and establishing its boundaries with the other processes.

Almost without exception! Daniel had refused to accept any perspective that had *'Customer Support and Order Management'* and *'Developing New Business'* as two separate processes. As the discussion progressed, and it became clear that he was in a minority in his view, his arguments became more and more entrenched and emotive, until he had isolated himself from the group entirely.

By the break, he had completely hijacked the meeting. He was ignoring any and all ground rules, and was fighting tooth and claw to return the protocol of the meeting to the style that he had triumphed in over the years. Richard was at his wits end, and spoke to Lucy urgently over coffee. "Do I concede, or do I fire him? Because it sure as hell looks like it's got to be one or the other?" Lucy cast her gaze down at the coffee counter and said quietly, "To be frank, I'm somewhat surprised that you haven't fired him already!"

Richard looked at her for a moment, and then adjusted his position to screen their conversation from the group behind him. Then he replied

- Who will you get to replace their knowledge and experience?

But you will have a lot of choice over exactly how you appoint and establish them in their roles. And it is here that you can turn things for good or ill. Appointing someone to the position of process owner is even more critical than it has been to appoint someone to your management team, and it needs to be done with even more forethought and care. Process ownership is a serious job, but if you appoint someone in a five-minute corridor conversation, or as part of another meeting, it is very unlikely to be seen that way.

In appointing process owners it is important to follow the same disciplines as you would for appointing someone to any other senior position.

- Let them know what jobs they are being considered for and give them time to prepare their questions and answers.

- Interview them properly for the job, outlining clearly the nature and expectations of the role, and drawing out their ideas for fulfilling it.

- Appoint people through the formal channels, and establish a clear job description, and objectives both for their role and for the process they are managing.

- Set up review and reporting expectations and clarify the criteria against which their performance in their role will be evaluated.

- Agree resources and authority levels for the role.

- Circulate relevant notices concerning the appointment, and consider a pay rise to reflect the increased responsibility.

The responsibilities of the process owner reflect a more intense and onerous role

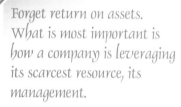

Forget return on assets. What is most important is how a company is leveraging its scarcest resource, its management.

Paul Strassmann
Former Vice President, Xerox

softly, "I guess I should have done in any normal circumstances, but it's really not that easy in this case."

Lucy tilted her head to one side and raised an eyebrow quizzically.

Richard continued, "Our business is very dependant on a limited number of good customer relationships, about twenty in all, and he tends to keep them very much to himself. He has kept the way things happen in his area very much a black-art, and as a result anybody who was any good has moved on."

Lucy grunted a quiet acknowledgement a gazed back down toward the coffee counter in thought.

"Added to which," continued Richard, "he has a lot of clout in head office. There are lots of people who think very highly of him, ironically precisely because of his 'black-art' approach and the results he gets through it. My credibility with them is not enough to withstand the resultant questioning of my judgement or the inevitable drop in sales while we tried to fill the void he has created around him."

Lucy continued to gaze at the counter for a few moments longer, and when she looked up again she had clearly come to a decision.

"We can afford to let this one go," she said. "After all you were originally going to go with departments anyway. The issue lies in how we let it go. How we let Daniel get his way without validating his behaviour. How about…" And she outlined how Richard might reach an agreement with Daniel.

"Daniel?" Richard approached Daniel holding court with Peter and Abs. Daniel looked up, clearly hostile, but he allowed himself to be drawn to one side. From her vantage point by the coffee counter, Lucy watched the body language intently for clues as to how things were going.

"We need to sort this out," Richard said and paused. "Perhaps I should apologise…"

Daniel was taken aback. This was not what he had been expecting. Richard had clearly spent too much time around that Derring woman, he was even beginning to speak like her.

than those of a traditional manager. It is vitally important that your team wake up early to this fact, and develop new habits quickly. An effective appointment process will help to initiate this.

To do anything less may leave your team with the feeling that this is just another add-on project to be handled in largely the same way as countless previous others.

Responsibilities of process ownership

When appointing process owners, it is vitally important that we don't confuse their responsibilities with those of the processes they own.

All too often we see managers' job descriptions written in terms of output, quality, customer satisfaction, etc. These are not the responsibilities of the manager, they are the responsibilities of the process and their team. The manager's responsibility is to ensure that their process and team are able to systematically fulfil *'output, quality and customer satisfaction'*.

To achieve this effectively they need to:

- understand clearly the needs and expectations of their process by the business, their customers, and their colleagues

- translate these needs and expectations (aspirations) into clear and specific performance improvement targets agreed by the business, their colleagues, and their customers

- convene a team of people who have a strong interest in the process, and to build a commitment in that team to improving its performance to meet the agreed targets

- develop and document (e.g. in a process map) an accurate under-

How do your people fare on these for their current areas of responsibility?

....
....

....
....

....
....

continued...

Richard continued: "I'm not sure I fully understood what you were saying in there."

Daniel grunted: "I think you did!"

"Okay, let me just make sure. Was the essence of what you were driving at, that Sales and Marketing, or rather, Customer Support, Order Management and Developing New Business, should be under the same person?"

Daniel stared back impassively. Richard pushed. "Was it?"

"You know it was!"

Richard had not actually known any such thing. Daniel had dragged them all round the houses and back again. Richard had just suspected that Daniel's motive was to avoid any reduction in his job.

"Okay," said Richard. "In order to move forward, let's say I accept that point, and that the person will be you. Let me then ask, although Sales and Marketing are closely linked, do they work in exactly the same way and produce exactly the same output?"

Daniel remained silent. The same argument had raged earlier and he had avoided it then too.

"Let me ask this another way. If sales and marketing reported to the same person, would there be anything to stop that person managing it as two or more, albeit closely linked, processes?"

Daniel sensed Richard was holding out an olive branch. If he did not take it, he could not see any practical way forward from here either. "No-o?" he said hesitantly.

Richard went for closure. "After the break I will appoint 'owners' for the various processes; people who will continue to work with the processes and refine them, and ultimately manage them. If the model I put forward for that fits in with what you think is required, will you support us in moving things forward?"

Daniel thought for a moment. Nodded, and then said pompously: "Yes, providing what you are proposing is practical, I will support you. But I do have to say that I am disappointed that we have wasted so much of this morning on things that have ultimately proven not to be in the best interests of the company. We could move forward a lot faster if we took

standing of how the process works in practice, and how its operation is controlled and influenced

- routinely measure process performance against target, graphically trend it, and undertake rigorous analysis of any adverse trends or performance deficiencies

- develop plans for addressing the root causes of any issues; ensuring commitment for their implementation; and forecasting the impact of this on future performance to meet target

- seek best practice related to their process, review it for applicability and implement it where appropriate.[1]

But above all of this, to adopt as their first responsibility, as part of the top team, the overall performance of the organisation as a whole.

It is these responsibilities that managers must be able to demonstrate that they are fulfilling effectively. And when they do, *'output, quality and customer satisfaction'* will be ensured.

continued...

---

1   These points are further developed in Chapter 14.

more account of the years of experience that we have available to us in the team!" And he turned and walked back into the room.

Richard looked at the ceiling for strength, and then looked at Lucy and nodded.

After that, the rest of the morning went without a hitch, and Lucy facilitated the meeting flawlessly.

Exploring ways of working together to deliver the goals (Grid of the QFD)

In the previous chapter, we considered how the design of the organisation could be understood and improved by breaking it down logically into business processes. We also looked at how team members should be appointed to be responsible for the operation and performance improvement of those processes.

Our next task is to understand exactly what we mean by *'performance improvement'* for each of the processes.

This is a complicated issue; the performance potential of our processes and the strategies for pursuing our objectives are highly interdependent.

Establishing the process role

How do we develop a winning strategy hand-in-hand with exploring the potential of each process for creatively contributing to it? And since the processes are interlinking, how do we define what we need of any one process while we are still defining what we need from all the others?

These are the questions that we need to answer if we are to get the very best out of our organisation, but the plethora of options, and complexity of interdependencies tend to create an impression of Pandora's box.

Fortunately, however, the grid of the QFD provides an excellent framework for exploring and addressing exactly these questions. Completing the grid of the QFD enables the management team to:

■ evaluate the potential of each process to contribute to the goals of the organisation

Chapter 9

Three days later, the team were gathered once again in the main meeting room.

As was now the custom, Richard introduced the meeting and sat down, and watched Lucy smoothly introduce the process for developing the grid of the QFD. Thinking back on it, he realised how much he owed his progress to Lucy. He had introduced the concept of QFD, but she was making it work. He considered how many pitfalls he would have fallen into without her ideas, her planning and her facilitation.

This meeting was the big one, the one in which they would develop the grid of the QFD. They had planned the whole day for this session. Fifty-six cells with ten minutes discussion for each. Nine hours plus breaks, introduction and wrap-up. Lucy was running the group through the agenda. Planned finish time was 8pm that evening, but they all had been forewarned of that, so there was no surprise.

A slide appeared on the screen, projected straight from the computer. It was the column and row headings for the first cell, along with fuller descriptions for each. At the bottom was an electronic bar graph that counted up the minutes. The bar started green, went orange at six minutes, and red at ten.

"Okay then, can I have an initial show of cards for the extent to which the process of *'Customer support and order management'* affects the objective of *'Address new market areas'*," Lucy asked. "Remember, the exact definition for what is meant by each symbol on your cards is explained on the flipchart over there." She pointed to the far right corner.

Some people had clearly anticipated the question, and had thrust the card with their chosen symbol on it up into the air almost immediately. Others wanted to think things through a bit, but eventually, hesitantly, the last card went up.

Lucy summarised the picture for the group: "So, nobody feels there is no relationship, a majority feel there is a major relationship, and we have one person who feels the relationship is critical, and two who have indicated they feel it is a minor relationship. Okay cards down. Daniel can you present the argument for it being a critical relationship?"

- develop clear strategies for achieving its goals based on fully exploiting that potential

- understand the interdependencies that are essential to meeting the goals (efficiently)

- establish a 'contract' with each process for what is expected of it.

In the process of developing the grid of the QFD, the whole management team works together, one objective at a time, developing a comprehensive under-standing of how each and every process influences its achievement or otherwise. In this way the interdependence of the business, and its untapped potential, is fully appreciated by the whole team.

Developing the grid of the QFD

However, maintaining this level of insight and attention to detail for each and every one of over 40[1] cells, for the whole man-agement team, is an awesome task. Particularly since it is important to achieve it working all together in one sitting.[2] However, it is possible, providing the process used ensures:

- a clear focus on the discussion in hand

- objective and balanced discourse

- clear and agreed conclusions

- regular breaks.

The following process is designed to achieve all of the above, and has been well proven on many occasions.

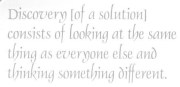

Discovery [of a solution] consists of looking at the same thing as everyone else and thinking something different.

Albert Szent-Gyorgyi
Nobel laureate in medicine and physiology

---

1   Assuming a grid at least six objectives by seven process-es. Very few top-level QFDs are smaller than 40 cells, but for reasons of focus and practicality you should endeav-our to keep your QFD to no more than 80 cells.

2   If the management team is split up to work through the grid, or if the work is split into two sessions with an interval of a day in-between, it becomes difficult to remain consistent in both the scoring and the arguments.

Daniel responded immediately and with a degree of derision. "Frankly, I'm surprised no-one else can see how crucial the way we treat our customers is to growing our business."

Deborah bridled at that, and responded coldly. "The question is about whether the way we treat existing customers stimulates purchases from new ones in different markets, and frankly," here Deborah mimicked Daniel's original tone, "I'm surprised you see things so simplistically."

Daniel sat bolt upright in his chair, and Lucy shot an urgent look at Richard who came in immediately. "Excuse me! I was under the impression that this was about sharing ideas and moving forward. If we bind the stances people take to their personal credibility then we will all have more at stake to lose than the argument.

"If someone explains simply that the sky is technically blue, then I can move from my original position of seeing it as grey. But if someone implies that anyone who thinks the sky is grey must be stupid, then I'm going to fight to the end to prove that person wrong. Because to accept that they are right means accepting that I'm stupid! Many of us will start with somewhat flawed or incomplete perceptions. When we have shared our knowledge we can develop, without stigma, slightly less flawed and somewhat more complete perceptions. Associating perceptions with characteristics about those who hold them, however indirectly or subconsciously, simply gets in the way of developing that common view. Let's keep things objective or we'll be here until midnight tomorrow."

Most people could see Richard's point, but Deborah and Daniel looked as though they had both been told off. "Ah well," thought Richard, "at least if they're quiet for a minute or two it will give the others a chance to get the discussion back on track."

The team finally concluded that it was a major relationship, largely on the strength of 'word of mouth', 'referrals', and the impact of satisfied customers on market image.

The second cell was more straightforward, but even so, it yielded new insights into how the current approaches for developing new business often failed to fully embrace new market areas, and tended to simply extend existing ones. As a result, the team could see exciting new possibilities in redesigning the process.

But each new insight was painful, and often hard won through determined and entrenched discussion. It was as if the old surface needed to be phys-

1. Ensure from the outset that everybody is willing to commit to the process; set ground rules for developing the grid and pin up written versions of these as a clear reminder to the group.

2. Work through the grid horizontally, taking one objective at a time, and considering, in turn, the contribution of each process to that objective.

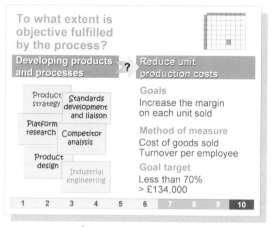

3. Plan a set time for each cell and unobtrusively keep the group informed of progress against it. The 'animation' facility in most presentation software provides an effective means for doing this. Ensure a short period for relaxation at the completion of each row of the grid.

4. Keep the specific process and objective that are under discussion at the forefront of the group's mind. Projecting slides with the process and objective clearly described helps to achieve this. Or alternatively, have two flipcharts, one with sheets of individual objectives and the other with sheets of individual processes, each turned to the right page. It is surprisingly easy without this facility for odd members of the group to begin discussing the wrong cell, and confuse their colleagues. All such confusion drains energy and enthusiasm very quickly.

5. Debate on each cell should be carefully managed to ensure time and energy is not wasted by repeated argument, discussion hogging, irrelevancies, or resentment. This can be helped by working through the following steps for each cell.

   Use simple cards to obtain an initial straw poll of how people view the relationship (see the examples shown on the right).

ically broken before the organisation would reveal new secrets and opportunities.

And yet, even though it was hard work, Richard could see in people's faces the new ideas taking root. The ploughing may have been taking its toll on his workers, but he knew there would be rich pickings when the process teams had time to go back over the furrows and see what had been churned up.

And so the process continued, with occasional breaks and hiccoughs, all the way to the forty-fifth cell.

Abs half closed his eyes and shook his head as Deborah concluded her opening argument, and almost before the last syllable had been uttered, he launched himself into a response.

"How can you say that? You've never really understood the damage your people do, have you?"

Lucy moved towards the middle of the room hoping that Abs would see she was ready to reinforce the ground rules that they had agreed at the outset. But Abs had his eyes fixed on Deborah, and his heart fixed on resolving all the frustration of a long festering issue. He continued determinedly. He pointed forcibly at the intersection between *'Developing products and processes'* and *'Reduce costs of poor quality'*.

"How can you say that your process has less of an impact on *'Costs of poor quality'* than mine, when 90 per cent of the wastage that I incur is down to problems that you've given me? It's stupid!" His eyes flashed angrily at the end of his sentence and his finger now pointed at Deborah. Lucy realised that she was not going to deal with this by presence alone.

"Points only please. Not personalities. We need to work through the grid logically and rationally. It's getting late and we're all tired, and we need to be even more careful that we are working to consensus." She looked from Abs to Deborah, and Deborah took this as her cue to respond. The damage had been done. Deborah took Abs' view that her point was 'stupid' as a personal affront to her. And she was all set to defend her point vigorously. After all, SHE was right!

"You incur wastage because you've never adjusted your processes properly to cope with the new products, and that is down to you. You never

Ask for the extremes of view to be explained simply, briefly and unemotionally.

Ask for other new points to be included objectively, one by one.

Avoid entrenched argument by carefully managing the sequence, asking only for new points, and keeping personalities out of it.

6. Reach a conclusion quickly and fairly.

Ensure that all of the important points have been made, and that people are content they have been listened to and understood. Correct any omissions.

Clarify that if everyone is now fully appraised of all the salient factors we can trust their conclusions to be an informed judgement, and therefore we should accept the balance of opinion of the team as a whole.

Ensure that people are willing to abide by a final vote.

Ask for a final vote, and accept the majority view.

	Wt.	Customer support and order management	Develop new business	Producing and distributing product	Maintaining the supply line	Developing products and processes	Providing an effective environment	Providing and growing people	Stewarding assets and resources
Address new market areas	3	◯	◉	△	◉	◯		△	
Provide excellent customer service	5	◉	△	◉	◉	◯	◯	◯	◉
Build leadership in platform technology	4		△	◉	◯	◉	△	◉	
Reduce production and delivery lead times	2	◉		◯	◉	◉	◉	◉	△
Maximise asset utilisation (incl. IPR)	3	◯	◯	△		◯	◉	△	◉
Reduce unit production costs	4	◯	△	◉	◯				
Build effective supplier partnerships	4								

It is vitally important to remember that it is not the final score on the QFD that is important, but the learning and insight that has arisen from the discussion. These discussions and conclusions are intensely valuable to the management team, and its subsequent work, and it is therefore important to ensure that they are preserved. If they are left to the memory of the participants, 80% of the value will be lost within a week. For this reason it is prudent to fully document the discussions and make them available to each process owner and/or process team as they work to design and control the process.

The preparation of an annual plan is in itself the end, not the resulting bound volume... To prepare and justify [a plan], people go through a lot of soul-searching analysis and juggling, and it is this mental exercise that is valuable.

Andrew S. Grove
CEO, Intel Corp.

spend the time with us to do things properly, and so you reap the harvest of your own lack of preparation…"

Abs interrupted forcibly. "And we don't have the time because we're rushing round like mad trying to fix the legacy of issues that you created for us last time!"

"Stop! Stop!" Lucy stood right in the middle of the room, her hands raised as though they could physically stem the flow of words and emotions. Abs and Deborah subsided, but both looked sullen, as though there were hundreds more things they wanted to say. Lucy looked round the room, and then let her gaze fall on Richard who took it as his cue. "I think perhaps if we took a short break. Be back here in ten minutes. No continuing of discussions. Okay?"

People nodded, slightly subdued, and filed out of the door. Richard walked over to Lucy. She had sat down on a chair in the corner, and as the last person left the room she dropped her head in her hands with a groan. "It's a nightmare!" she said. "I've never had to facilitate so hard in my life! Every damn cell seems to be a potential battle waiting to explode into its full bloody glory!"

"And every battle has become a truce of understanding and insight. Lucy, this is brilliant! Do you not see how far we have come in just one day? Have you not seen the people learning important points practically every five minutes? You can see the lights come on visibly. You can see the dawning realisations and insights in their faces. You can see issues being put to bed between the team that have festered unresolved for years. Can't you? Sure, when you focus on the protagonists, they seem to only reluctantly accept the conclusions. But each one has seen new things, and each time, we have reached a new conclusion; an agreement; a decision, where we have never had one before. The hard work that you are seeing is the result of people wrestling with themselves. But I've had the luxury of watching the others listen to the discussions, and I know that once people have had the chance to reconcile themselves to what they have agreed, they will be greatly enriched by what has come out of today!"

The words tumbled over each other, and Lucy was lifted by his enthusiasm. "Lucy, you are doing a brilliant job. Really! You may need to be a bit tougher as we get more tired, and maybe have more frequent breaks. But we really are moving forward. My team has insights and understanding now that will help us really transform this business.

At the conclusion of the discussions it is possible to calculate the relative importance of each of the processes to the overall achievement of the objectives. This is done by assigning values of nine, three and one to critical, major and significant symbols respectively,[1] multiplying each symbol by the weighting for that objective, and adding up the total for each process (see picture on page 84).

It is relatively easy to develop the QFD electronically, using either presentation or spreadsheet software.[2] However, in practice, creating a simple paper-based grid on the wall can free your projection equipment to focus the team on discussing the current cell.

Developing the grid of a QFD for your organisation can be tremendously rewarding, but it should not be undertaken lightly. Even when the discussions are well facilitated, it usually takes about eight hours to work objectively through every cell of a business QFD. Eight hours of joint awareness, new insights, shared understanding, as cell-by-cell the team explores how the business works. It could be the most profitable day your team have ever spent together.[3]

Or it could simply be eight hours of frustration, boredom and hobbyhorses. The difference will be in very large part, down to the disciplines of the discussion, and this brings us on to the second part of this chapter.

Ground rules

Agreeing ground rules at the start of a session can help to ensure the session remains productive. Suggested ground rules are:

 Be candid and honest

 Endeavour to keep to agreed times

 Everybody has an opportunity to speak on each issue

 Focus on the current task

 Only one person to speak at a time - no side conversations

 Everybody to remain involved with the discussion in hand

 Seek to understand rather than explain

 Have fun.

---

1 Other values can be used, but these values have proven the most useful in practice.

2 A preliminary example of a spreadsheet version can be found on the associated web-site (see Appendix 7).

3 See Appendix 15

Heaven sakes! I've learnt so much in just six hours. Essential, vital, critical pieces of knowledge about the business."

People were starting to drift back in and it was clear Lucy was not going to get her cup of tea now. But Richard had been better for her than a break. She felt ready to do what was needed to see this through.

As everybody reassembled, she prepared herself to recap, and to reset the ground rules, but before she could do so Abs interjected: "I just want to say sorry to the group. I was out of order there!" and was rewarded with nods and the odd muttered "S'okay!" And Deborah chipping in: "Yeah, me too!"

Lucy thought it was still worth resetting her contract with the group. "Okay, let's look back at how far we've come. We are now 78.6% of our way through the QFD." People smiled at her pedantic accuracy. "We have made great progress, but we are tired, and so I'd just like to remind you of the ground rules that have helped us so much in getting this far." She was about to run through them and abruptly realised this would be the kiss of death (or rather sleep) at this point in the afternoon, so she suddenly switched. "Which of them have you found most useful?"

People were momentarily thrown by the question, but then John threw in: "It's got to be the one about keeping things objective. It is so much easier to accept a point when you haven't had your ego tied to the alternative."

"No, I reckon it's the one about seeking to understand rather than explain," said Peter. "That point has been a real eye-opener to me, and it has really unpicked some previously entrenched issues."

"Oh, I'd go for the one about fun," said Andrew and drew further smiles.

"You would!" responded Susan, "but I think they've all been important. I reckon without the ground rules, we'd still be stuck on the second cell and fighting over the same piece of ground!"

Lucy saw her chance to pick it up again. "Okay, so if we're going to finish this before midnight, let's keep our focus on using them. Now back to the cell on the impacts of the Process of *'Developing products and processes'* on the objective of *'Reduce costs of poor quality'*."

Peter interjected here: "I think we've got confused again between processes and people. The question here is: Does our current process of taking

Establish clearly defined management processes and protocols

The meeting to develop the grid of the QFD is likely to be very intense. You will have a lot of new ground to cover with people who are uncertain of their new role, and still have unresolved issues from their old one. But the QFD meeting illustrates an important point about the role of management team members; that only a part of their role is described by the columns on the QFD. An equally important aspect of each member's role is how they work together as a management team.

The QFD meeting is not an isolated incident, and as your team struggles to get to grips with its new potential, there will be plenty of opportunity for conflict and confusion. If the meeting is unstructured and undisciplined, your team members will develop inappropriate means to assert their authority and gain influence over the proceedings, and as a result you will not get the best out of them. The most powerful and outspoken members will not always be the ones with the greatest potential to add value at any particular point.

When your argument has little or no substance, abuse your opponent

Cicero
Roman Statesman

The challenge is to establish processes and disciplines which ensure that people do not need to be outspoken to be heard, and which ensure that people can appropriately introduce and nurture their ideas and talents, even when they are not yet fully confident in them.

There are a number of tools which will help to develop those processes and disciplines. They are:

- session plans
- standard forms
- car parks
- general ground rules
- consensus reaching.

a new product idea and making all the necessary production changes to make it fly, irrespective of who does what within it, have an impact on costs of poor quality? From what's been said, one way or another, it seems to me that it has a massive impact. And unless we recognise that, we may not put in the necessary effort outside of this meeting to resolving the very important issues that were voiced earlier."

"Thank you Peter," said Lucy and then acknowledged another partly raised hand: "Andrew!" she said.

"Thank you, yes. I think Peter is right. Both the activities of *'product design'*, and of *'effectively altering production processes to deliver it efficiently'* sit within this process, and one way or another we end up with waste as a result."

At this three more hands went up. "Deborah, then Abs, then Peter again," said Lucy orchestrating the sequence.

And so the meeting continued. Richard thought the idea of having to raise your hand to speak, and then being ordered in a sequence of speakers, seemed a bit childish, but it had kept things calm and objective. The risk that an immediately relevant point might be delayed by the sequence appeared to be far outweighed by the order and fairness that it brought to the discussion. People were clearly listening for once and not simply biding their time to grab the floor before their neighbour, as so often happened in Richard's normal meetings.

The remaining cells went by easily, and by the end Richard knew that, even if the programme he had planned stopped right there, things would never be the same again. New insights had been gained, and people would inevitably do things with them.

Deborah and Abs had learned that handover of new products to production was a process, not just a stage in a project. And that it was the process that should be their focus for improvement, not each other.

Peter had been stunned by the potential impact of the finance, and in particular invoicing, process on customer loyalty, and the new opportunities stemming from that.

Susan was inspired by the leverage her new process on *'Supply line'* could bring to bear on *'Addressing new market areas'*, and no longer thought of it as 'buying', as she had when Richard first gave it to her.

Session plans

Meetings are often the most vital, the most time consuming, and the least well-planned aspects of management. While they are clearly a process, and have a desired output, the only form of process analysis and design applied to many of them is a scant, hastily written, agenda.

Time	Item/ description	Objective	Inputs	Process	Output

The 'session plan' is a mechanism to help plan effective meetings. Each meeting is broken up into a series of sessions, and each session has a defined objective, a clear process for achieving that objective, and declared inputs and outputs for the process. An example session plan for developing the QFD can be found on the associated web-site (see Appendix 7).

Although 'session plans' might at first appear to be simply a bureaucratic burden, their ability to drive people to think through what they plan to achieve with each session, and how they plan to do that, is immensely valuable. It is very common for people to initially resist using session plans, and then to become almost addicted to them.

Standard forms

Standard forms provide an excellent means for ensuring the right quality of preparation for a meeting, and for effectively communicating the outcomes of that preparation.

Used judiciously, well-designed forms (see the example on the right) can promote efficiency by guiding people through a well-considered process, and can help to ensure that the results are at an appropriate level of detail. One good form can save several iterations of misinterpretation and lost meeting time.

Process:			Process proposal
Owner:			
Team:			
Scope of process and probable sub-processes			

Outputs	Customers	Inputs	Suppliers

Process objectives:			
QFD	Related proc	Target	Measure

Business benefits:			
Likely strategies	Deliverables	Cost	

Assumptions/implications:

Management standards	Meeting schedule:

Stakeholders:

Andrew was clearly happy that the rest of the team had a far better understanding of the potential and importance of *'Provide and grow people'*, but he had also seen how he needed to extend his own view of training if he was to fully contribute to *'Reduce lead times'*.

John saw new potential for how IT was an integral part of the environment, and was enthusiastic about how he could have a real impact on lead times, resource utilisation, and costs of poor quality, though quicker and better informed decisions.

Richard had never seen his team so energised. He looked at the finished QFD on the wall, and realised that it was simply a representation of real change that had occurred today in his people. Only Daniel seemed to have been unaffected by it. His early attempts to control the meeting had been marginalized by the process, and so he had lapsed largely into silence, except to argue the case for his own processes. Richard thought Daniel was the one person in the room who had not learned anything. He could not recall once seeing Daniel's final vote differ from his initial one, in all 56 squares of the QFD. He had clearly not been swayed by any of the discussion.

Richard worried, not for the first time, that he should not have given Daniel the processes he had.

People were funnelling back into the room after the final break, and now it was Richard's turn to stand at the front. When everybody was seated, he thanked Lucy for taking them through the grid and then started to explain the next steps.

"So you now all have not only a process, but also a clearer understanding of its potential; a map of how it can support our objectives. And when Helen has typed them up you will have a transcript of all of the discussions that have taken place. So, what's next?"

The question was clearly rhetorical because Richard continued without breaking pace. He put up a picture on the video projector and said: "I want you all to think through the following questions for your process: What performance does it need to deliver to ensure we meet our Cylek UK goals? What performance is it delivering now? And what issues do you need to address to close the gap?"

Here he pointed at the picture on the screen. It was a sheet of paper with a number of questions and boxes printed on it.

'Car parks'

The 'car park' is a simple, but extremely effective mechanism for keeping discussions focused on their objective. It is simply a sheet of flipchart paper headed 'car park'.

When an important point is raised that is not part of the discussion it is common for a group to want to pursue the point even though it is not material to the objective of the meeting. Often they are worried that if they don't address it, it will get forgotten, and even if you do persuade them to drop the subject, it continues to occupy their thinking.

By listing such issues visibly in the 'car park' the group is free to focus on the task in hand, in full confidence that the issue will be revisited and addressed before the meeting finishes.

General ground rules

While they may at first seem a bit 'schoolmasterish', ground rules have the potential to vastly improve meeting performance. They provide a basis for the members of the team to contract between them what they deem appropriate meeting behaviour, and then to review and develop that in order to improve meeting performance over time. One senior IT group transformed its meetings from contentious battlegrounds to effective dialogue simply through progressively developing its ground rules.

Consensus reaching

Consensus reaching is a technique to reach an agreed conclusion from a range of different opinions. It is time consuming, and is therefore most appropriately focused on items that are likely to become contentious or entrenched.

"Lucy has developed a simple form to help you think though these questions, and she has undertaken to come round and help people when they need it." He looked at Lucy who responded with a simple nod. "I want the completed forms in this format within two weeks."

There was a sharp intake of breath and people shifted in their seats, and Deborah challenged: "I'm not sure that with our current demands and obligations that we can manage that, Richard." Abs chipped in: "We have to get our people on board, and some might be on holiday." Susan escalated the revolt with a more direct: "There's no way I can meet that!"

Richard held his hands up to quell things. Clearly he had been over optimistic. "Okay, okay! We'll use the meeting scheduled for a fortnight to examine progress then! But I'll need to have completed forms available for circulation one week before the following meeting in a month's time." The body language showed that people still thought this was tight, but not tight enough to protest over. "Okay. Thank you for your time," he said, "and see you tomorrow!"

Richard was euphoric. The sheer potential of the organisation; his ambition to progress; the designer instinct in him; seeing his ideas come to fruition, all combined into a sense of real excitement in him, like a kid on Christmas Eve, he simply could no longer keep still. As the last of his team left, he virtually bounced across the room. He wanted to move, he wanted to run, he wanted to shout! Lucy watched Richard's obvious displacement with a sense of great amusement. She could barely contain her laughter as he virtually pirouetted in the middle of the room, looking at all of the outputs, his face aglow. It was almost as if he didn't know what to do with himself.

He caught her looking at him, smiling indulgently, and bounded over to her. "That was so brilliant, I could kiss you!" He paused. "In fact, I will!" And he grabbed her in a great hug, and kissed her.

And then it happened.

He felt feelings of celebration change to feelings of desire. He felt a tight friendly embrace shift to simply holding, and a kiss intended for fun, for one fleeting moment was something entirely different. It lingered. Too long! He realised what he was doing. He knew it was wrong! He broke away, and broke the spell. His eyes locked on her face in a moment of uncertainty and panic. What had he done?

Lucy was looking down and away. So she had felt it too! Had she?

Consensus reaching is based on the premise that once everybody is in full possession of all the information, then a team view is likely to be more accurate than the individual view. This is clearly not always true, but within most management teams, only the most arrogant of people would claim their opinion should be taken over the opinion of a fully informed majority.

The key then, in consensus reaching, is to make sure that *all* the salient information is presented and understood by the whole team, and then to gain agreement to abide by the majority viewpoint before the vote is taken. It is also very important to separate points from personalities or ego. Consensus reaching is not perfect, but due to its openness, its conclusiveness, and its apparent fairness, it is far more effective than a free-form debate.

Meeting facilitation

The disciplines of the meeting processes and tools outlined in this chapter can make discussions significantly more efficient and effective in progressing the aims of the organisation, but only if they are used in a non-partisan way.

Groups tend to abide by the processes and tools where they believe they are being used fairly, but if they begin to see that they are being used selectively - say only when and if they support the manager's own agenda - then they are likely to disrupt and argue about the process, and make the meetings intensely inefficient by trying to adapt the tools to meet their ends as well.

Managers, particularly in the early stages of introducing change, cannot always afford to be non-partisan. During the initial meetings they may be the sole guardian of the vision in their group, and they need every opportunity to share, inspire and

Consensus reaching process

Each proposal will be presented in turn.

The proposer will make a brief argument as to why they feel proposal should be accepted.

The group will present an initial show of the 'Yes', 'No' cards to indicate their current agreement.

By invitation, the arguments for and against its acceptance will be heard in turn until the group is comfortable that all the main arguments have been heard and understood by themselves and their colleagues.

The group will confirm that it will be happy to abide by the majority viewpoint at this time.

A final show of the 'Yes', 'No' cards will be taken.

Richard turned quickly and spoke just a little too loudly. His tension showed in his words, "Let me help you pack away."

Lucy paused momentarily and came to her senses, quickly pulled back to the reality that Richard was now creating. "Yes that would be helpful". Too loudly? Too matter of fact? Yes, she had felt it too!

But felt what exactly?

Both embarrassed, they busied themselves in their tasks and did not speak. Flipcharts were folded, equipment put away, cases stacked, lights dowsed, doors shut and locked. They had run out of road. One of them had to speak.

Richard broke the silence. "I'll see you tomorrow," he said.

"Yes. Ten o'clock in your office," she said, turned and walked away.

Richard watched her go, his mind a confused mess of questions and part answers. They had originally planned another hotel meeting after the workshop just to wrap things up, but she had not mentioned it. Why? Did she feel the same thing that he had felt? Or was she simply embarrassed by what she saw as an unwelcome pass? Or had she just followed his lead, perhaps thinking he was embarrassed? Or was it because it was late?

And how did he feel? What did he want? Why had she cancelled the evening? He was clearly attracted to her, but was she to him? Had she responded? He felt she had. Was this nerves? Or self-protection? Or responsibility?

Responsibility! He thought about Laura, and about Nicholas. Yes, he would never do anything to put them at risk, they were too important to him. He had responsibilities, and he would always meet them!

On the other hand, Laura had become distant from him. She didn't take any real interest in his work. She was no longer interested in his plans and his schemes. He needed someone to share them with, and Laura just didn't seem to care any more. Did she really see him as any more than a meal ticket, a shelter provider and someone to share the chores? Sometimes he wondered.

A man needs more than that, he reasoned. A man needs someone who can appreciate the difference he is making, and who can stimulate and partner him to greater things. He needed that. He needed Lucy.

develop that vision in their people. Once this is achieved, the team can take responsibility for the urgency and impact of the project, and the manager can focus on ensuring the quality of the processes they use to get there. But until this is achieved, the manager may be very tempted to manipulate those same processes to ensure that the 'right' conclusions (in his or her view) are reached.

If this is the case, then the manager might consider using an independent facilitator (one without a fixed agenda of his or her own) to moderate the processes and tools within the group.

This need for an independent facilitator should, however, be seen as a purely temporary expediency. The reason for this is that, as people grasp direct responsibility for systematically developing the business, the manager's role must change to allow them space to do this, and to provide the necessary encouragement and facilitation. The prolonged appointment of an external facilitator is likely to confuse this transition, and impede the manager's own personal development.

In the next chapter we look in more detail at how people will grasp responsibility, and then in the following section we will explore how the manager's role must change to both support and accommodate their people's growth.

Common QFD pitfalls to avoid:

Looking at how the objective contributes to the process - it is the processes that deliver the objectives, not the other way round; you can't pull yourself up by your boot laces.

Seeing a process as defined by people rather than activity and output - just because your storeman completes an appraisal form doesn't automatically make 'people development' part of 'inventory management' - each person often uses, and takes part in, a number of different processes.

Not being absolutely consistent on the meaning of the symbols - define them clearly and visibly at the start, and refer back to the definitions whenever there is confusion.

Forgetting that impact on the objective can be positive or negative - it is as important to design out negative impacts as to design in positive ones - a critical contribution can be simply avoiding detrimental influences.

Letting the definition of the objectives and/or the processes drift - write them down clearly, refer back to them, and update them as the discussion progresses and new assumptions are made.

He would never leave Laura, he knew that, but men have affairs all the time don't they? Laura need never find out.

But supposing she did?

Richard remembered the turmoil and acrimony a past friend of his had been through and shivered.

Well it did no harm to dream about it then. And, as he drove home, his imagination played around the fringes of a full-blown affair with Lucy, and he did not try to stop it.

Encouraging commitment (Deploying the QFD)

The mechanics of creating the basic QFD covered in the preceding three chapters provide an effective framework for channelling the commitment of the management team to achieving the organisation's goals. But the mechanics do very little to fundamentally stimulate and encourage that commitment. Agreeing common goals, developing team roles, and establishing a common process, of themselves will not inspire passionate pursuit in all who hear it.

But implicit also in the three foregoing chapters was the fourth essential of teamwork: Encouraging people to throw their whole commitment into the work by providing opportunities for them to submit their own ideas and dreams for making the plans happen.

The mechanics provide the necessary structure for teamwork, but the way that the mechanics are implemented and used is what will either inspire commitment, or foster antipathy and resentment.

People become committed to things that they can understand; that they can see the need for; that they can contribute to; that they believe in; that they feel confidence in tackling; and for which they feel that they will be recognised fairly. The framework provides an opportunity for this to happen, but it is the relationships and interpersonal skills of the leader and the team members that will ensure it happens effectively. Commitment is born out of the ways in which people are recognised, included, talked to, listened to, and questioned.

Within the management team, the members may have been given these opportunities. But how do we ensure that the same opportunities to commit themselves will be given to the next layer of

When people are treated as the main engine rather than interchangeable parts of a corporate machine, motivation, creativity, quality, and commitment to implementation well up.

Robert H. Waterman
Management consultant and writer
in The Renewal Factor (Bantam, 1987)

Chapter 10

When they met the next day, everything seemed back to normal. For his part, Richard was too confused about things, and felt the risks were too high to progress things intentionally, but his mind continued to fantasise about how things might progress unintentionally. For her part, Lucy had been stirred by his kiss. She was attracted to him. There was something sincere and boyishly enthusiastic about him now she had got to know him. He was fun to be with, and he was attractive and in good shape. But he was married! And he was in England. And he was her client. She could resist him, and let's face it, resisting him was by far the most sensible course of action for her.

And so the next three weeks passed without further incident, and by the end of them, one could easily believe that nothing had happened.

Lucy busied herself with arranging meetings and attempting to support Richard's team with their process proposals. Some of the team seemed to resent her intrusion, and held her at arms length, but others welcomed her help and eagerly involved her in their thinking. The extremes were typified by Daniel and by Deborah.

Daniel's responses tended to be aloof. No, he had not made any progress. No, he did not want her help. No, he was not sure that he would meet the deadline, but that was between him and Richard Frewer. Thank you!

Deborah, on the other hand, had sought Lucy out on the day following the QFD work. She had ideas for involving her whole team, and wanted Lucy to help her to design and run a few simple workshops to build team commitment and to develop the process proposal. Deborah was like a sponge. She absorbed all that Lucy presented, and then drew out more.

Deborah was clearly very clever, and when she had bought into something she embraced it wholeheartedly, almost like a zealot. The combination left Lucy feeling drained, both physically and mentally, after every meeting. Lucy found the impact of this situation on herself difficult to comprehend. She had always imagined that working with someone like that would be energising and inspiring, but there was something about Deborah's style, something about how she drew control of

management and to others more junior? Their commitment to making things happen will be vital if the plans of the management team are to be translated effectively into actions.

In this chapter we will look at how that commitment can be harnessed through:

- creating process teams and drawing out their ideas and understanding[1]

- providing for the process team to make a commitment, and to gain the support it needs

- ensuring that debates remain objective and informed, and that contributions are recognised.

Creating process teams

The purpose of the process team is to support the process owner in designing, operating and managing the performance of their process.

The team will ultimately be the sole means of managing the process as a whole, and a lot of care needs to be exercised in selecting its membership. If the process is particularly large, the process team may well need to develop a number of smaller sub-process teams to manage sections of it. And if the process is particularly small, the owner may in fact be the only full time member of the process team - involving others only in those activities for which they have time.

Wherever practically possible, it is good practice to involve those people who run and administer the process. They are the people who have the most detailed information on the process; they are the ones

---

1 Some managers have the knack of asking for contributions and implying that they would fire anybody who made one. Organisations which have such issues regarding the manner in which managers communicate with their staff, would be well advised to address these before undertaking this work.

Managing by Design

all of the conclusions and decisions to herself, that actually worked the other way. However, she was at least making progress.

Like Richard with the top-level workshops, Deborah introduced her meetings and wrapped them up at the end. Everything else she handed over to Lucy to run. At least that was the model in theory. In practice, Deborah was very clear about what outcomes she wanted, and very vociferous in ensuring they were delivered.

Deborah had pulled together her process team from her existing management group. She had reasoned that whatever transpired from this would be the 'new way' of managing, and she wanted to make it absolutely clear to her people that this was not an add-on. This was not simply a project, or this year's management fashion accessory. This was 'it' from here on. Fail to change at your peril! She had also annexed Abs' Industrial Engineering Manager for her team. The proposal had not been well received initially, but Richard had stepped in and resolved it. Industrial engineering was part of *'Developing products and processes'*.

Deborah's first workshop was held barely a week after the main QFD workshop, and the whole Process Team attended. Deborah ran through all of the history to date in her introduction, and then handed over to Lucy.

Lucy stood in the middle of the room while people visibly recovered from Deborah's impassioned whirlwind tour of what had been happening. She took the few seconds pause to cast her eyes round the group. She had met all bar one person individually in the preceding week, so she had built at least some level of rapport with them, and she had thought out her strategies as to how to work with them. Her first step was to draw them out from under Deborah's shadow, so that they could build their own enthusiasm for the potential of this process.

"I wonder," she said, "what the potential is for *'Develop products and processes'* to really transform Cylek UK?" She paused for them to consider the implied question. She could see some of them beginning to think about it, but not everybody, so she pushed a bit more. "I've heard what the Cylek management team think about the potential. But I wonder what the people who really understand it believe?" She paused again, and looked around. One or two more seemed drawn into thought, but a few just seemed to be waiting for her to continue.

that need to be committed to implementing any change and making it work; and they are the ones who can help share the burden of process ownership. The process team should therefore include the key people in the management of the process, and may well include a key customer and/or supplier. But the team should in no way develop into a bureaucratic committee. The owner has the executive power, and if the means of involvement proves a barrier to progress, then the owner is responsible for resolving this.

Once the process team have been identified, every effort needs to be taken to engage them fully in their new role.

- Ensure they understand the background to what the company is trying to do.

- Develop their understanding of the QFD, and the role of process ownership.

- Inspire them with ideas of what process ownership means for them.

- Explain what is changing and what will remain the same.

Two other key aspects of engaging your team are: one, formally appoint them to their new roles[1]; and two, help them to develop their own vision of what is possible.

The closer you can align what needs to happen to what the team really wants to do, the more likely you are to succeed in managing the delivery of both. In tackling this, many people seem to start with what needs to happen, but unfortunately this tends to suppress or distort information on what the team really wants to do. It is almost as though our desires lose their validity in the face of expressed business need.

People don't resist their own ideas.

William Werther
University of Miami
in Nation's Business, March 1988

1   See section on formally appointing owners on page 120.

"What ideas could you dream up for transforming the performance and competence of Cylek UK?" She paused again and looked around. Her observations of how people were engaging with the question largely accorded with her perception of them from her one-to-one meetings. So far, so good!

"What we are going to do is to understand what Cylek UK's expectations are of us, and then to develop a proposal that will blow their socks off!"

"Why?" The question came from Tom Lewis, the Industrial Engineering Manager. Tom was Abs' right-hand man, and Lucy had the impression that he was even more pragmatic than his boss had been. She looked at him, waiting for him to continue.

"Why 'blow their socks off'? What possible commercial value is that? We have enough problems trying to implement hare-brained schemes as it is!"

One or two, Deborah included, distinctly bristled at this, but others seemed sympathetic to Tom's view. In hindsight, Lucy began to doubt the wisdom of her use of the phrase 'blow their socks off'. It seemed good and emotive at the time, but it clearly carried some baggage. But she could not afford to lose credibility this early in the proceedings by backing down on the phrase, so she frantically searched for a way to anchor its interpretation at a mutually acceptable level.

"Mmm," she said, "sort of like the Edsel, or the Sinclair C5?" She looked at Tom, and he responded: "Yes, and…"

But she interrupted him. "Or the Apollo moon landings, or the Millennium Wheel, or the personal computer?" Tom looked a bit less sure, and continued: "Yes, but…"

Lucy continued across him again. "Or the Cityrentable, or the MR3, or the Renewal Project?" she said, naming three recent disasters Technical had created for Production.

"Exactly!" chipped in Tom, seeing his point illustrated clearly. Others in the group were nodding.

Lucy continued: "Or the Plus K…" she said, naming a recent success that had been really radical. "Or 90% error-free production, or halving cycle times," she continued, listing things that production had been

Conversely, by starting with the team's desires, and developing a complete picture of them, it is possible to gain far greater insight into how the energy of the group can be best focused on the needs of the business. Starting with desires does not diminish the priority (in a business sense) of the needs, but it can inspire a greater collective will to address them as part of some larger intent. Addressing the immediate needs can be seen as the first logical step in a much longer-term horizon.

It is vital that we don't underestimate the importance of a collective team vision. A group of people who don't aspire to grasp the future, can only fear changes from the past. 'Change' only has negative value to them because they've not linked it to

Questions to inspire thoughts about vision

- To what areas of your customers' operations could your service provide additional impact; areas where your service is not currently used to its full potential?

- What are your customers' biggest blind-spots in the area of your service and offering?

- Where could you transform the operations of your customers over and above what exists now?

- What is the most outrageous thought you have in your head about how your service could develop?

- What is it impossible for you to do at this point, but if you could do it would make all your current projects obsolete?

- What sort of future for your organisation would you personally find so inspiring that you would move heaven and earth to get it?

anything positive. They can see the costs but not the benefits. If people are to embrace change it is vital that we inspire, nurture and develop a compelling vision within them. And if we start by building on and developing any personal vision they might have, we are likely to be far more successful than if we start with needs, and drive their vision back underground. Who knows, maybe their visions reflect opportunities that the organisation has not yet envisaged!

seeking for years. She paused. There was no interruption this time, and so she continued.

"Being radical doesn't inherently require that we suspend our common sense. To me 'blowing their socks off' cannot practically be achieved by hare-brained schemes. I, you, they, ... only have our socks blown off by people really understanding us and what we need. And by delivering simple, practical and previously unforeseen solutions which meet those needs."

"What we need to think through today, is what we believe will really make a practical difference to Cylek. Something that will begin to transform the way we do things. Something that we feel is worth investing the next year of our lives in. Something that is challenging, but will work. So let's start by understanding what our 'customers', Cylek UK, see our potential to be, and we'll carry on from there."

Lucy then proceeded to explain each relationship in the column of the QFD under *'Developing products and processes'*. She had developed the transcript of the original discussions into some simple slides to help with this. And when objections or reservations were voiced by the team, she noted them carefully on a flipchart to come back to later, and then moved swiftly on.

By the end of it, everybody seemed to be re-engaged in what was happening. She called for a coffee break so that they could share and build on that energy informally.

During break, Deborah came up to her "That was good!" she said. And Lucy waited for the 'but', for Deborah to come back on the way Lucy had bulldozed the group at the start. But it never came, and Deborah walked straight out for coffee leaving Lucy slightly puzzled. Had Deborah not noticed? And then Lucy realised Deborah had not. What Deborah and the group had seen was normal for them, it was Deborah's normal approach. Lucy smiled to herself, and shook her head, and got on with preparing for the group's return.

After the break, Lucy split the group into two syndicates, and posed each the question: "What performance should the *'Developing products and processes'* process deliver if it is to ensure Cylek UK reaches its goals?"

"You are to imagine that you are two rival groups competing for the contract to develop Cylek UK's products and processes. Imagine that everything will be outsourced to the winner, and that you have got to *win*! What

Another way of drawing out the team's vision is to present it with its process as a blank column on the QFD, and ask it to work through the potential relationships. This also provides an opportunity for reconciling the team's view with the organisation's view, by using the notes from the QFD grid session to supplement the arguments. The row developed by the management team can then be explained to the team as the customer's current expectations and understanding, and any differences from its own thinking can be pulled out and reconciled.

It does no harm for the team to understand that the top-level QFD belongs to the customer, and, as the supplier, it has no executive rights to simply change what it doesn't agree with. Business is not a democracy, and the differences in perception between the process team and the organisation represents either new opportunities for the process team (e.g. unforeseen potential), or areas where it needs to further influence the organisation's thinking (e.g. where there is room to improve the organisation's understanding of the process's potential).

Once the potential of the process is clearly understood, the team will be in a much better position to secure authority over it.

Where is the leverage to really make a difference?

Developing products and processes

Address new market areas	Business from new markets	> 34%	?
Provide excellent customer service	Customer retention	> 85%	?
Build leadership in platform technology	Innov. copied by compet'n	> 5 p.a.	?
Reduce production and delivery lead times	Production cycle	< 6 days	?
Maximise asset utilisation (incl. IPR)	Asset utilisation	> 55%	?
Reduce unit production costs	Cost of goods sold	< 70%	?
Build effective supplier partnerships	Supplier led business	> £80m	?

Developing a process proposal

When a 'successful' external agency bids for your business, particularly where that agency is a service supplier or consultancy, they take every effort to ensure that they can answer the following questions.

- In what ways does their offering meet your business needs better than their competition's (internal or external)?

Examples of specific outputs	Examples of generic measures
▪ Product range 'X'	▪ Consumer satisfaction
▪ Features	▪ Industry awards
▪ Sales of product 'X'	▪ Average product ranking
▪ Market position of 'X'	▪ Sales margin
▪ Meeting launch date	▪ Time to market
▪ Correction of production problem 'Y'	▪ Production satisfaction
▪ Meeting target date	▪ Unit production costs
▪ Within budget	▪ Average response time
▪ No lost production	▪ Support costs
▪ Adoption of technology 'XYZ'	▪ Machine down time
▪ Implementation date	▪ Innovations ahead of competition
▪ Sales generated	▪ Percentage revenue from new products

will you promise Cylek UK? What level of service will you maintain? What benefits will you assure us if we give you the contract? Use the column of the QFD to focus and tailor your offering, but don't feel you have to be constrained by it."

"What resources can we assume?" someone asked.

Deborah replied: "What we have currently, or less if you feel that is appropriate. Remember, cost savings are not only to do with our impact on the rest of the business."

"Supposing we can justify more?" someone else chipped in.

"If you are convinced we'd buy it, given our current situation, then put it in," replied Lucy. "But I suspect it will be an almost impossible sale in the current climate."

Deborah nodded in agreement.

The two groups split, one crowding into the area round the flipchart, and the other went off to use Deborah's office.

Deborah wandered over to Lucy. "I thought you were going to use that Competition Question exercise you used on us," she said, half as a question.

Lucy replied: "I could have, but I felt this would provide a more focused result. One that it would be easier to pick up and work with."

"Oh," said Deborah, nodding, but clearly reserving judgement.

Lucy smiled to herself again. Deborah's reaction had amused her. She liked Deborah, but she was glad she did not have to work for her.

The groups took to the exercise with real fervour. The element of competition drove them to be ambitious, but within the bounds of practicality. In her first visit to the groups, Lucy found she needed to push both groups away from specific products and process changes toward more generic statements of delivery performance. But she had expected that. People always seemed to drift towards tangible and specific examples. One group got it easily, but the other one, the one with Tom in, struggled. So Lucy asked: "Okay, what do you undertake to deliver in terms of service in three years' time?"

This question confused them. "We don't have any projects planned beyond eighteen months," one responded.

- How does their strategy and approach ensure that they can deliver their solution more economically than the competition?

- What are the interdependencies between both parties that are key to success?

The edge that the successful external agency brings is in the quality of understanding of the business need, and the effort they apply to developing a successful case.

Successful agencies apply this degree of rigour not because of any lack of experience and skills, but because they know it is crucial to developing the right answer. And if such rigour is appropriate for a professional external agency, how much more true is it for an internal one? How many internal teams can answer the questions posed above, confidently and accurately?

The principle that underpins process proposals is that our internal teams need to apply just as much quality thinking to what they are planning to deliver as the external professionals do. In developing a very clear and logical picture of *what* they are trying to do, *why* and *how*, they will inevitably build their commitment to making it happen.

The steps to developing the process proposal are conveniently described by the sections of the process proposal form[1]. This is expanded below.

Scope; sub-processes; outputs; customers; inputs; and suppliers...

...provides the opportunity for the team to clarify their understanding of the process role and boundaries. Where possible the

Contract bid exercise

One way of developing the team's vision is to get them to think radically about what the true potential of their process might be. What could they offer if they too were an independent agency offering this service?

Imagine you are an outside contractor, wanting this organisation to outsource this process to you. You literally want to win the work away from the internal team. What do you promise, in order to secure the contract?

Scope of process and probable sub-processes			
Outputs	Customers	Inputs	Suppliers

---

1   See page 140. A (correctly proportioned) proforma for the Process Proposal form can be found on the associated web-site (see Appendix 7).

"You will have!" replied Lucy.

"Yes, but we don't know what they will be!" challenged Tom.

"But is there any way you can describe how well you will do them, or the impact the benefits of them will have on our status or competitive position?"

"No, not really!" responded Tom belligerently.

"Then I expect you'll lose the contract," said Lucy calmly, "because your competitors can!"

Tom was about to respond, when Jack reached out and touched him on the forearm and said: "We could describe our performance in terms of time to market, unit production cost improvement, percentage revenue from new products - that sort of thing."

Tom subsided.

Jack was clearly on track. He was Deborah's Research Manager, and Lucy had got the impression from his interview that he could be a bit of a dark horse.

Arising from Jack's lead, the debate began to develop again. So Lucy quietly extricated herself and left them to it.

Deborah had gone off to answer some urgent telephone calls during the syndicate exercise, but she was back for the feedback. She sat next to Lucy as the groups stuck their outputs on the wall. Deborah scrutinised the flipchart sheets, and then turned to Lucy and said urgently: "They look a bit general! Where are the references to the new products we should be working on, and the types of projects we will have next year?"

Lucy's mind suddenly shifted up two gears as she wondered how to correct the forthright Deborah on something she clearly felt strongly about. It would have to be done quickly and quietly before she reversed everything Lucy had achieved with the team. But before she could get her thoughts straight to respond, Deborah was up on her feet.

"Excuse me! ...," she bellowed to get everyone's attention above the general chatter. Some of the colour drained out of Lucy's cheeks as she struggled frantically to think of how to intervene. This was the situation that her consulting nightmares were founded upon – the choice between losing all credibility by publicly backing down on something

team should write their purpose in terms of the difference their process makes to the organisation or its customers. For example *'Acquire and disseminate information to support the organisation'* carries a less challenging emphasis than *'Stimulate and guide the development of the organisation, through the acquisition and dissemination of information'*. The latter definition would require not only the fulfilment of the former, but would also continually encourage the process team to think ahead about how the process adds value.

The process scope should be defined primarily in terms of the activities the process encompasses. Here the process team can also describe how they see the process boundaries, and what flows across them. It defines the area within which the team will take responsibility.

The team can develop its understanding of this by reviewing the top-level process model, and through discussions with other process teams, especially those with which they share a common 'boundary'.

QFD objectives; process objectives; targets; and measures...

...provide the opportunity for the team to show how, in practice, it intends to support each of the QFD objectives for which their process has a relationship on the top-level QFD. It is important that the team fully explores the nature of each relationship and identifies process objectives and measures which reflect the unique contribution their process will make. In some cases the top-level objective and measure may be appropriate simply to adopt without interpretation, but often they will not, and in these cases the process team needs to think carefully about what exactly it is undertaking to deliver. There are a number to tools that may help with

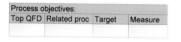

Process objectives:			
Top QFD	Related proc	Target	Measure

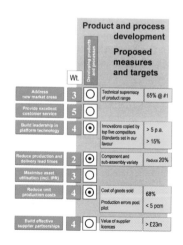

you have just pushed through, or humiliating a client in front of an audience of her people.

As the attention of the room was drawn to Deborah, Lucy had still not found an easy way out, nor decided which of the two equally unappealing options to take. She waited, her mind dreading the next words out of Deborah's mouth, but seemingly impotent to avert them. Her apparently limitless supplies of resourcefulness and confidence brought to nought by this 'no-win' situation.

Then Deborah asked in a much quieter voice: "Could someone please push the door to? We are about to start!" Then, with a smile at Lucy, she sat down again and whispered: "Got you good, eh?" She laughed, and Lucy smiled weakly back.

The outputs from both syndicates were excellent, and between them covered all the expectations posed by the QFD. Lucy encouraged the group by saying so.

Through subsequent exercises, the group then further refined the outputs into a list of six measures and targets which they wanted to propose to the Cylek UK board.

Deborah closed the meeting by outlining the next steps. And then she took some feedback from the group by splitting the flipchart into two columns, and heading one *'What Went Well'* and the other *'Room for Improvement'*. Lucy was impressed by the effectiveness of this simple device, and made a mental note to use the technique herself in future.

As they were clearing up, Deborah said: "Thank you Lucy, that worked really well! Oh, and sorry about my little joke. Jack mentioned the struggle you had in his syndicate, so I thought I'd play on it." Lucy smiled back "It's okay. I owe you one!"

Over the subsequent week, Lucy helped Deborah's team to work through the steps of refining their process proposal. The team was split into three groups in order to spread the load. The teams reported back just over a week later.

The first team made appointments to meet with all those departments and individuals they considered customers of their process. In each meeting, they outlined the objectives the team had agreed, and gained feedback

this: reviewing the Why-How chart[1]; the competition question[2]; or the contract bid exercise on page 158.

Intended business benefits...

...requires that the team think seriously about the benefits to the business of the objectives and targets they are proposing. It provides a challenge to think very carefully about the value of what they are undertaking, and of being able to describe it clearly in 'customer' terms.

Strategies; deliverables; and effort...

...requires that the team use its current experience to think through how it will begin to pursue its targets. This does not mean that they need to have done a full root cause analysis, and to have already decided detail solutions. But it does mean that broad strategies must be agreed (e.g. achieving delivery performance through a 25% reduction in downtime, or through a 50% reduction in production errors, etc.). Clearly the best tool to undertake this thinking would be a QFD between the process objectives and their defined sub-processes - see the diagram on the right.

Please note that strategies are best expressed in terms of delivering a change in performance of a critical success factor, not simply as activity. For instance, implementing email is not a strategy, but improving office productivity by 20% through the introduction of email is. Those who have email systems that have been introduced in the absence of clear performance targets, will probably have a much clearer understanding of the difference between the two.

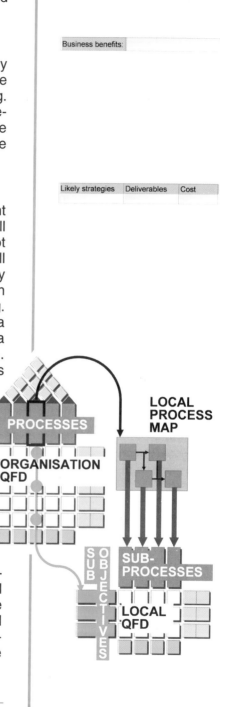

Business benefits:

Likely strategies	Deliverables	Cost

LOCAL PROCESS MAP

PROCESSES

ORGANISATION QFD

SUB-PROCESSES

LOCAL QFD

---

1   See chapter 2.

2   See chapter 4.

on them. It was surprisingly heavy going, not only in arranging the interviews, but also in disarming the cynicism from those customers they did manage to see. But they persevered and returned to the next meeting with the conclusion that their objectives were okay, but needed some additions.

"You'd think they didn't want us to improve," said Andrea, the team leader. "I had not realised how much cynicism there was!"

"What do you think causes their cynicism?" asked Lucy.

"Well, reading between the lines, I think that we've had a pretty poor relationship with them over the years. It was almost that we got on by tolerating each other, by doing just enough to prevent things falling over. They don't really believe that we will change."

"Do they want us to change?" asked Lucy.

"Yes, definitely, but they want us to focus more on them. They are worried that in pursuing our objectives, we will drop things that will screw up their work."

"Such as...?" prompted Lucy.

"Well, apart from those things that are already reflected in our objectives, the main thing appeared to be filling in the paperwork."

At this, there was a huge groan from the assembled group. Lucy looked round.

"Is this a common issue?" she asked the group.

"Are you kidding?" replied Jack. "It's bureaucracy city out there! They've got forms for everything. You can't even raise an eyebrow unless you've got a pink slip signed in triplicate!" His vehement outburst brought nods from everybody, except Tom Lewis.

Tom looked straight at Jack. "You just don't understand! You never have! It's your cavalier attitude to anything that doesn't benefit you, that has cost us hours of wasted work!"

Lucy stepped in quickly. She could see it getting out of hand. She wondered whether she could park the issue until later, but it seemed directly relevant to establishing a complete set of objectives. "Hold it! Hold it!" she interjected determinedly. "Whoooo! I bet we've been down this track a few times, haven't we?"

The intention is not to bind the process team to these initial strategies, but to ensure quality of thinking behind the target commitments.

Assumptions/implications...

...demonstrates the extent to which the team has fully considered the risks and implications of its current model of improvement. This section should challenge the team, both to look at the external impact of its processes, and to be pragmatic about external influences coming back in to the process. The potential problem analysis, right, illustrates one means of undertaking this work.

It is probable that working through this section of the form will encourage the team to reconsider its answers to earlier sections, but that is the main point of asking this question here - it is cheaper and easier to correct things on paper than in practice.

Standards; schedules; and stakeholders

...outline the team's understanding of the management and reporting disciplines they will employ in pursuing their goals. In many ways this is the final part of the contract, and states exactly to whom they will be accountable, how they will comply with reporting and management standards, and how often they will review their progress

Ensuring debates remain objective and informed

As teams work on the possibilities for their processes, and become inspired by the potential of their new responsibilities, it is all too easy for them to lose sight of reality. This can present two major problems. The obvious one is that their conclusions become impractical; the less obvious one is that it becomes more difficult to objec-

Assumptions/implications:

Potential problem analysis (the fun version)

Imagine that you are a group of saboteurs, intent on derailing the plans of the team

List out, down one side of a flipchart, everything you could do to make sure that the plan fails, or has disastrous results

...

Management standards	Meeting schedule:
Stakeholders:	

...

Then come out of role, and create a second list, on the other side, of all the ways that these things could happen accidentally

When you have finished, work through the second list and evaluate the probability and impact of these things happening on a scale of high, medium and low

Think out what you will do to avoid, remove, or cope with the high-risk items.

Jack nodded and Tom looked a bit sheepish, others smiled.

"I thought so, it seemed quite well worn to me!" Lucy continued. "Look we need to resolve this, but perhaps if we work through the other areas first, and then come back to it at the end?"

Lucy walked over and wrote the word 'Paperwork' on a sheet of flipchart paper headed 'Car Park'.

"Okay," she said, turning back to Andrea, "was there anything else that the customers wanted to add to, or change about, our objectives?"

Andrea thought for a moment and said "No, I think it all comes under paperwork one way or another. It's pretty much all about communication and fitting in with their systems." She looked around her team and they nodded back to her to affirm her conclusions.

"Okay," said Lucy. "What about the team that was looking into getting current data on the process performance measures?"

Jack stood up, walked to the front of the room, placed a view foil on the overhead, and switched it on. A list of the agreed measures came up on the screen.

"Like Andrea," he said, "this wasn't as easy as it looked. But let's go through them one by one."

Jack worked down his list of measures. His team had now put mechanisms in place for all but two of them, and had gathered enough historic data to provide an indication of current performance in about half the cases. Lucy was impressed. She could see why Deborah valued Jack so highly, but she wondered who had done his day job while he had done all this. She asked him at the break.

Jack looked at her slightly quizzically. "It only took three days!" he said. "The biggest issue was getting the team back together to approve it at the end."

"But, how did you find three days?" she pressed.

"I've got a good team," he said, "and we often do this. Deborah encourages us to simply opt out when we've got an important project, just like we would if we were sick or on holiday. We get to focus 100% on the task, and our people get used to taking the responsibility. And Deborah covers it if there is a real issue."

tively resolve conflict in the team and, as a result, some members may feel uninvolved and lose commitment. In other words, maintaining a grasp of the practical realities of the situation is crucial to maintaining the commitment you have worked so har to engender.

To ensure effective commitment, process teams need to maintain a practical reality-based bias to the discussions in three ways:

- mapping current reality and ensuring all proposed change is practically reflected within the map

- ensuring that customers review and provide feedback on the proposals

- establishing clear measures of progress.

These are explained in more detail in the following paragraphs. In the novel, Richard's approach to driving his people in these areas is fairly laid back, and he pays the price for it. In practice it is important to establish a clear and rigid timetable for doing this work, and for reviewing progress and performance against it.

Mapping current reality

Process mapping[1] is a hugely underrated tool in most organisations, perhaps because of the lack of emphasis on the 'design' side of management. A process map is simply a graphical logical representation of the flow of work, information and resources through the activities of the process. As with an architect's drawing, a programmer's flowchart, or an engineer's circuit diagram, the manager's process map provides the schematic representation of reality that is so essential to planning change and considering its implications. Even from the outset, the

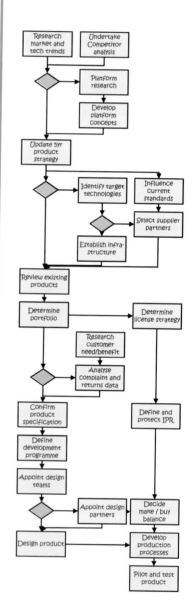

---

1 A basic guide to the protocols of process mapping is included on the associated web-site (see Appendix 7).

Managing by Design

Jack had a *'Why is this so strange?'* look on his face, but Lucy just shook her head and said "Amazing!" It was the sort of attitude she had spent years trying to drum into other clients to no avail.

Then a thought struck her. "But, if your people are doing your job, don't their own projects slip?" she asked.

Jack smiled. "We only ever allocate resource to 80% capacity," he said. "It was the first thing Deborah changed when she was appointed."

Lucy felt a 'Yes, but' coming on. "But, surely that lengthened all your delivery timescales?" she challenged.

"No, not at all," Jack replied. "We used to plan at 100%, and end up with 30-40% overruns. We now plan to 80%, and we get an average of 5% under-run. The business actually gets things earlier because we are better co-ordinated." Lucy smiled, and shook her head, and walked away.

The third group reported back after the break. They had been working on mapping out *'Develop products and processes'* into a flowchart of its constituent activities. A large roll of brown paper was fixed to the far wall and unfurled across the room. Literally hundreds of different coloured rectangles and lines adorned the sheet. And no sooner was it fully in position, than the debate started.

Lucy stepped in quickly. "Let us at least get an overview before we start on the detail." She nodded to indicate to Malcolm, the third team leader, to continue.

Malcolm quickly ran through the separate sub-process areas on the map to provide the overview, and then started to explain the detail. Lucy interjected again "Can I propose that instead of a large debate, that people take a good look at the map individually, and note any inconsistencies for Malcolm and his team to resolve after the meeting?" The group seemed happy with this and settled to the task. Lucy sat down on a table to watch.

After about three quarters of an hour, people had largely finished understanding the map, and noting the issues, and had sat down.

Lucy sensed it was time to return to the first issue of the meeting, but before she could do so, Andrea chipped in. "Can I just commend the mapping team on an excellent effort?" A few people mumbled "Yeah!" and somebody started a little clap which most people seemed to join in.

basic activity of developing the diagram provides practical insight as understanding is reconciled, waste identified and obvious improvement opportunities become evident.

Customer review and feedback...

...provides a basis for the process team to seek to validate their conclusions, before presenting their proposal back to the organisation as a whole.

In part, they will have done this at the broad level through reviewing their scope (see page 158). But clarifying exactly how teams plan to perform at those interfaces where their process meets with others, should help resolve any misunderstandings, and will help to reconcile the various process proposals from the outset. The best way to achieve this is through direct face-to-face meetings with customers and supplier processes. If at all feasible, these meetings could be through physically involving customers in the objective and target setting work, and similarly being involved in suppliers' goal-setting activities.

Establishing clear measures of progress

...provides objective evidence as to the effectiveness of the team in improving the process.

Measurement[1] proves a very emotive issue for many process teams. Normally this is because the measures identified require a lot of work to implement and maintain, and there is little confidence that they will provide significant value. Unfortunately, in many organisations, both of these arguments contain a significant element of truth. The effort required to implement the measures arises not only

Steps to implement process measurement

1. Identify measurement needs based on critical QFD relationships.

2. Explore measurement issues/ opportunities with customer processes.

3. Review existing measures.

4. Reconcile duplication of measures.

5. Identify missing measures or current weaknesses in measurement.

6. Develop/improve measures, and plan for implementation.

7. Implement and review.

8. Establish measurement routines and integrate into management process.

---

1   A basic guide to measurement can be found on the associated web-site (see Appendix 7).

Lucy stood up and said: "Yes, excellent effort!" and then continued: "In fact, I have to say that what I've seen today has all been excellent. I have been overwhelmed by the effort you have put in. In all honesty, I have never previously seen such a determined start to this sort of work, and I'm convinced you'll reap the benefits quicker as a result."

"We already are," Malcolm interjected, pointing to the map. "I've noticed three nonsenses in my area already, and my people are already now putting them right." Others nodded. There was a tremendous feeling of energy about the place. This was clearly a team that had grasped their future and were determined to control it.

Lucy started again: "But before we move on to 'Next Actions' and 'Wrap Up' we just need to tackle this item on the Car Park." She looked round at the group. Some of the energy evaporated. Swept away by the thought of conflict and unresolved issues.

Deborah stood up. "I am going to propose," she said, "that we add another objective of *'100% conformance to customer systems!'*" There was a shocked muttering around the room. Jack was about to explode in indignation, but subsided when Deborah looked at him, her face set. Even Tom looked surprised.

Deborah continued: "For as long as we feel it is okay to simply ignore another department's systems, we'll simply avoid the issue. Nothing will change, and conflict will continue with our customers. If we set this target, we'll have to either understand and acknowledge why they need the information, or help them to find a better way. I am set on this. I feel it is the only way to resolve a long-standing issue."

"But... but..." sputtered Malcolm.

"Spit it out Malcolm!" said Deborah, slightly mockingly, but not unkindly.

"It's going to involve us in hours of extra form filling!"

"Good," said Deborah. "I wondered how we were going to use the time we will save in arguments and conflicts with them over not filling in the paperwork!" A number of people sniggered.

She paused, and then looked more kindly at her troops. "For years we've ignored it, and things have just festered. It's time we took control of this issue, and we'll only do that if it's on our objectives!" Her tone was con-

because companies have invested insufficiently in this area, but also because important parts of the process are often missing[1]. Also, measures typically provide a lack of value because the information they provide is frequently not acted upon.

This unfortunate situation arises because the 'design' role of management has been long neglected in many businesses. As a result the 'control' role of management has been deprived of key objective data, and has been undertaken by managers getting personally and directly involved in the operations of the business. Without objective measures how else can a manager control crucial aspects of the business?

The solution to this issue is, unavoidably, to replace the missing investment. Accept that crucial things are missing and bite the bullet in replacing them. Success in implementing process measures requires the adoption of this simple mindset. But the consolation is that effective measurement alone can pay for itself even if it isn't integrated into the systematic management system. It is common for the provision of measurement data to drive up performance by 10%, purely through the focus and diligence it encourages, and it is very rare for the servicing of a measure to cost anything like 10% of your resources.

In many cases, effective measurement will provide the means to 40% improvement when integrated with the rest of your management system, and, once established, will consume less than 1% of your resources.

Administering measurement

One area that does need to be thought about in some depth, however, is the means by which the data for the measures will be collated. One key rule is that the incremental effort put into the measures should never be greater than the incremental benefits that are obtained as a result. So start by thinking simple, thinking samples, thinking existing data and thinking ease of getting hold of them. Then move away from this only where the increased accuracy and reliability is warranted by the benefits generated.

---

1   Predominantly documentation of the strategy and planning aspects.

ciliatory, and she was rewarded with nods, some reluctant, but most deter-minedly supportive.

"Good," she said, and looked back to Lucy to continue.

Lucy walked further into the middle of the room and looked at Jack. "Seems like you've got another set of data to collect," she said. And Jack smiled.

Summary

The successful transformation of your organisation will depend on effective teamwork both within your management team, and in the larger organisation. Harnessing the commitment, enthusiasm, and creativity of all your people is the key to making a dramatic and sustainable difference in your performance, and maintaining that rate of improvement over the long-term.

In this section we have reflected on how the process of QFD can help an organisation to establish the essentials of teamwork, through:

- reconciling the team's objectives into a simple set of very clear targets

- breaking the organisation down into very clear areas of responsibility, and formally appointing team members to those roles

- exploring the potential of every part of the organisation to work together and establish effective and fair mechanisms to practically encourage and support teamwork

- providing means for people to ally their own dreams and aspirations with the organisation's vision.

What can you borrow from this to improve the reality of teamwork within your own organisation?

....

....

....

....

....

....

Relevant materials available on the web-site to support discussion and application of the ideas in this section

Presentation materials in MS PowerPoint™ format:

  The concept of business processes

  Process ownership and its responsibilities

  Process visioning.

Basic Guidelines in Adobe Acrobat™ format:

  Performance measurement

  Process mapping.

Workshop exercises in MS PowerPoint™ format:

  Developing effective measures and targets

  Defining processes for the organisation.

Basic Templates in MS Word™ format:

  Session plan

  Process proposal.

Basic Tools in MS Excel™ format:

  QFD model.

Copies of key diagrams in MS PowerPoint™ format.

Section C

Lead and coordinate the implementation of QFD

Revolutions need directions and exemplary leadership, but not heroes. Heroes subvert the fact that change comes about by lots of people taking action.

Bill Harris

LEADING AND COORDINAT-ING THE IMPLEMENTATION OF QFD

Having clear goals and a commitment to deliver them is half the battle won. But it is only half the battle. What starts out right all too often grows warped and awry as confusion creeps in unseen and unchallenged. It is virtually impossible (and almost certainly uneconomic) to anticipate all eventualities from the outset, and yet these unforeseen, and only partially understood, issues can invalidate plans; put people into conflict; generate mistrust; erode commitment; and ultimately lose you your objective.

Because of this, it is vital that sources of such confusion are identified as soon as, or even before, they arrive. This section looks at how.

- Lead the change - ensure that your people continue to believe that this change is as crucial to your organisation now, as when it first started.

- Reconcile people's ideas with the overall strategy - ensure that all creativity and industry is harnessed efficiently to achieving the end goal.

- Manage upwards - build a commitment to what you are doing in those best placed to either support it or wreck it. Ensure that your plans are reconciled with the larger business.

- Drive a consistent approach - use common mechanisms to ensure everybody can demonstrate progress and communicate across the business.

Chapters 11 to 14 provide guidance in each of these areas.

"There … try it 'gain now, Mand!" came the muffled voice.

Colin could hear the switch being clicked, but there was no sign of life in the waste disposal unit.

"No good, Col?" asked Amanda as Colin extricated himself from under the sink.

"I think I'd use a choicer term than 'at if there weren't ladies present" he rejoined. And then continued, "Present company 'cepted of course!" - which earned him a damp cloth across the back of his neck.

"So what's next then?" posed Amanda.

"I'll get Susan ta sign a req. for a new one. Hold on a mo' though. 'Tain't 'er any more, it's John now!"

"Oh I can't keep up with all this changin'," moaned Amanda. "Like rear-rangin' the deck chairs on the Titanic."

Colin smiled to hear one of his favourite phrases thrown back at him. And then replied, "I dunno so much though. I reckon these changes'll do us some good."

Amanda looked sceptically at him.

"Seriously, Mand," he continued, "there's a new energy 'bout the place. Well at least in some quarters. Mind you 'is nibs'll 'ave to watch 'is back 'cos I reckon Matthews is after him big time from what I've 'eard."

"Ah well, Col," sighed Amanda, "if he wants to shape this lot up he'll certainly have his work cut out. I hope he's up to it!"

"Well, 'e ain't gonna do it from 'is office is 'e?" Colin replied, "an' 'ats where he seems ta be most times."

Leading the change

By far the biggest factor in the speed and effectiveness of transformation is the Boss. Where the change is actively driven from the top with clarity, focus and determination, it works. Where it isn't, it doesn't!

But where is the top? Who is the Boss?

In practice it is the person who has determined to take control of their area of the business. In some cases this has been the MD, in others the manager of a department, in others it has been the leader of a small team. But in every case, they have taken ownership of transforming how their organisation[1] worked, and what it achieved.

The need for the leader of the organisation to be persistent in driving the new ways of working cannot be overstated. Unfortunately, introducing a comprehensive systematic approach to management creates major tensions within the management team. This is because the concepts explained in the earlier chapters call for executive authority to be co-located with a clear systematic understanding of the business and its performance, and traditionally this has rarely been the case.

Traditionally, managers have often been free to make decisions without a comprehensive or accurate understanding of the real implications of those decisions on overall performance. Conversely, people who have worked diligently on developing quality processes to ensure performance have often had little authority to implement their conclusions. As a result, communication between these two groups has often been tense, resentful and fraught with misunderstanding and politics.

You can improve your own and your groups' productivity, whether or not the rest of the company follows suit.

Andrew S. Grove
CEO, Intel Corp.

---

1   This may be just one small part of a much bigger organisation.

Chapter 11

Lucy wandered down the long corridor, seemingly drained of her copious amounts of transatlantic energy. The last session with Peter had been a nightmare. It had been like pushing water uphill with a pencil. Every time she thought she had made some headway, Peter's arguments just flowed back round her to take him back to the position where he had started out.

As she turned the corridor, Richard almost knocked her over. He had his coat and his briefcase, and was clearly in a hurry to get home, or maybe somewhere else.

"Oh, hi Lucy … everything okay?" he flung out as he passed her. It was clearly just a pleasantry, not intended to get any response but an affirmative. Lucy was not in the mood to play that game. Her determined "No!" caused Richard to pause while he worked out what to do next to continue on his way. Richard thought an apology would work.

"Look Lucy, I'm sorry I haven't been around to help, but things have all got so urgent. I'll try and tie up a short meeting with you later in the week."

Lucy nodded resignedly. Her face looked clearly despondent and disappointed. Richard felt guilty. They had started to work this as a team, but he had just left her to it. He really ought to stop, now she needed help. He looked at his watch. Quarter past six. He'd promised to be home to baby-sit Nicholas by half past. His mind was torn by the two obligations. Perhaps if he just spent five minutes with Lucy, that would hold things for a bit. "Fancy a coffee?" he said brightly. Lucy nodded, and they walked back to his office.

No sooner had they got though the door, than Lucy started in on him. "Richard, we had an agreement. You would spend time with each of your managers, to establish clearly what you expected of them, and I would then follow up and help them to meet your expectations. You were to create the tension and I was to supply what was needed to fill the gap."

Richard turned back to Lucy from the coffee maker, a cup in each hand. "Lucy," he cut in, "I'm sorry, but there have been all sorts of issues that have cropped up over the last week. I never foresaw any of them. But

The reasons behind this are inherent in the way that many organisations perceive management skills. Executive authority is often vested in those who can fire-fight well, and who are able to juggle the complex, uncertain and stressful demands of business in their head and regularly deliver a competent solution. Such work is normally seen as intellectually challenging, with high kudos, short-term gratification, and attracting the authority and status to make a real impact. Conversely, the job of developing quality processes is often given to people who are more methodical and systematic in their approach. It can be a thankless task, with hours of painstaking analysis often being rejected on the basis of a five-minute opinion from someone with 'executive authority'. As such it often attracts people who are either single-mindedly wedded to the logic of this approach, or who lack the talent to make progress in any other way.

The net result is that, corporately, decisions have often become distanced from information, and talent has become distanced from method and system.

The logic of systematic management is to reconcile these key competences into a body which collectively takes real responsibility for performance.

The task of reversing years of tradition, and resulting self-interest, must not be underestimated. Amongst the talented and authorised are not only those who have allowed their more methodical side to be suppressed, but also those who never had a methodical side in the first place. While the former group may simply need time to redevelop their systematic skills and to adjust their previously successful working patterns accordingly, the latter group often fight a determined rearguard action of delay and refutation. A rear-guard action that, due to the nature

How well aligned are management and quality improvement in your organisation?

Who practically engineers (designs, tests, monitors) the processes in your organisation?

....

....

....

To what extent are their decisions based on clear and objective analysis of performance?

....

....

....

To what extent do they have executive power to implement change and resist disruption?

....

....

....

Bold objectives require conservative engineering.

James E. Webb
First Administrator of NASA

I made clear to all of my management staff what they were to deliver at the workshop, and I reinforced it last Thursday, at the management meeting."

Lucy interrupted: "And to what extent did they commit to delivering them?"

"Well, Deborah was practically effusive," replied Richard, "she…".

Lucy interrupted again: "And Daniel? And Peter? And Abs?"

Richard lapsed into silence.

"Richard," Lucy continued, "some of your managers have really taken to this. Deborah is brilliant, and Susan and Andrew aren't bad. But, with others, I feel that they just haven't bought into it, and I have no authority to make them do otherwise."

"You mean they're rejecting it?" challenged Richard.

"No I don't mean that!" replied Lucy. "I mean that they are ignoring it. And they are rejecting me. I am only of value to them if I have the answer to something they need. If they don't believe they need to do it, and they don't, I am simply an irritation to hold at arm's length. And that is very frustrating. Look Richard, all this was your idea. I just got on board to help. But you seem to have dumped it and run. And I can't actually do the bits you have to do!" There was real anger and frustration in her voice.

Richard resignedly looked at his watch again, then looked back at Lucy. She was looking at her lap. He pulled out his diary, and looked under tomorrow's date. Packed full of appointments, and the next day the same. He picked up the telephone and pressed a button. There was a pause. And then someone picked up the other end.

"Hello, Gloucester 494739!"

"Hello," replied Richard in his most apologetic tone, "look, sorry Dear, something has come up…"

But that was as far as he got. The line went dead. She had hung up. What was the matter with her? It was only a damn meeting with friends!

Lucy, sensing a shift from the normal, looked up at Richard's face, full of surprise. Richard blinked, looked down at the desk and replaced the receiver. "Well!" he said.

of what is being attempted, often plays on the sympathy of your whole management team.

Unfortunately there is no easy fix for this, just the dogged, relentless, and sometimes lonely task of:

- establishing clearly what is required of your direct reports

- seeking to plan and develop mechanisms to reinforce the use of the QFD

- maintaining the vision of the 'new way of working'

- monitoring and reviewing progress

- identifying and addressing behavioural and organisational issues

- coaching and guiding people in fully exploiting the new ways of working

- making time to do all of the above.

These points are covered in more detail through the rest of this chapter.

Establishing clearly what is required of your direct reports

This can, in large part, be achieved by the assignment of separate and discrete process responsibilities to the members of the executive team.

If the business is to be run systematically, the executive team, as the key decision making body, must focus on 'processes' as the context for all of its decisions. For this reason, it is important that process responsibility is awarded to all members of the team. Failing to do so runs the risk of either disenfranchising some members as the management of the business becomes more and more systematic, or remaining unsystematic as those same members fight to retain their 'voice'.

In the most successful implementations of the systematic approach, the executive

Behind an able man there are always other able men.

Chinese proverb

Lucy guessed what had happened, and felt guilty for her part in it.

"Look Richard, I'm sorry! We can do this some other time…"

Richard glared angrily at her, and then caught himself. It was not her fault. He slumped, and then sliding his coffee to one side he said: "Come on, let's work this through over dinner. It appears I've got damn all else to do this evening." And he picked his briefcase back up and strode toward the door without waiting for an answer.

Over dinner, Richard had understood the depth of the problems Lucy was encountering with Daniel, Peter and Abs, and he had developed a strategy to pick up with them and re-emphasise their need to grasp this properly.

The first course of Moules Marinière and Cocquilles St. Jacques had been focused on the issues and what needed to happen. Over the fillet steak and the Père Noir they had been on the same side once again, dreaming dreams and scheming schemes. And over the crèpes and the ice cream they had been friends, simply relaxing and enjoying each other's company.

As Richard left after coffee, it seemed the most natural thing in the world to give Lucy a friendly goodnight kiss. And as he walked out to the car he felt good, but he also felt some of that chemistry he had felt at the end of the QFD session. He reflected on it happily as he drove home, content in his fantasies, but never letting them stray to the point they became complicated. He felt terrific!

His contentment lasted until just a few seconds after he had set foot inside his front door. He was actually smiling when he turned the corner into the lounge. But one glance at Laura's face reminded him of Laura's abrupt termination of their phone call, and informed him that his current facial expression was a big mistake.

Laura, already charged with the feelings and frustrations that she had built up over the preceding three hours, first found herself incredulous, and then very rapidly intensely angry at Richard's apparent disregard, and even mirth, over leaving her so let down.

body comprises experienced managers, each of whom has a process responsibility, and who collectively reflect a comprehensive balanced picture of the total organisation as processes.

This arrangement should be formally reinforced by establishing clear job descriptions and appraisal targets based on the responsibilities of process ownership. It should also be informally reinforced by ensuring that questions and challenges arising out of *specific* issues, focus on drawing out the *systemic* and *process* implications.

Other ways of ensuring a clear picture of what is required include:

- opening a discussion on the management behaviour that will be necessary to guarantee delivery of the QFD targets,[1] and then collecting the conclusions into an agreed contract within the management team

- publishing a standard of management values[2]

- developing guidelines and checklists for individual managers to use in undertaking their work.[3]

Seeking to plan and develop mechanisms to reinforce the use of QFD

If your organisation is new to the systematic disciplines, then it is very likely that your current mechanisms (meeting agendas, policies, procedures, practices, etc.) reinforce the old ways of working, even if only by association. It is important that these mechanisms are identified, reviewed and developed to make use of, and fully support, the systematic approaches that have been introduced.

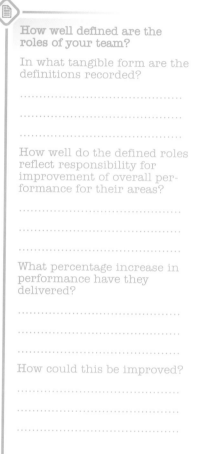

How well defined are the roles of your team?

In what tangible form are the definitions recorded?

....

....

....

How well do the defined roles reflect responsibility for improvement of overall performance for their areas?

....

....

....

What percentage increase in performance have they delivered?

....

....

....

How could this be improved?

....

....

....

If you do what you've always done, you'll get what you've always got.

Source unknown

---

1 This can be done by using the scales on page 72, or perhaps the questions in Appendix 4.

2 Perhaps based on the table on page 68.

3 Relevant materials are included on the website.

Gripping both arms of her recliner she virtually threw herself out of the chair towards him, pausing momentarily to grab a book off the table which she launched at his head. He ducked quickly, and brought himself upright to find himself looking directly into Laura's furious face.

Too shocked to respond, he backed out into the hall under Laura's ferocious verbal tirade.

Laura found that she could not help herself as she vented her frustration on her husband, but as the pressure inside her ebbed, tears flowed freely, and finally, resignedly she continued in a quieter voice. "You just don't understand what it is like for me, Richard. You just don't. And to be frank you just don't care, so please don't pretend you do!" And she turned and walked away. He heard her footfalls on the stairs as she made her way to bed.

Richard had not really understood how important this evening had been to her. It had transpired that this was the first time she had been invited out by people since they had moved to Gloucester six months go. She had seen the first rays of sunlight in this new, alien, and lonely environment, and now she felt she had seen Richard callously block them out, stilling the small emerging seedling of her new social life.

Richard had been aware that Laura had been taking Nicholas to the local Church on Sunday mornings. He had welcomed the opportunity to get some work done. But he had not realised what it meant to her. Apparently Laura had started going to Church because she was intensely lonely, and felt that it would be a good way of meeting people. The people there had been friendly, but it had taken time for Laura to build any sort of relationship, because Nicholas had been so demanding during the coffee at the end of each service. She had felt that she was getting somewhere when one of the women had said she and some friends were going out for a drink, would Laura like to join them? She had suggested a baby-sitter to Richard, but he had been adamant that he would get back, and then he did not.

Richard had tried to be realistic. "There'll be other invites," he said. "Oh, you're so sure are you?" she spat venomously. And looking at Laura's face he saw a sense of despair that he had not seen before. No, he was not so sure!

In some cases this may require additional mechanisms to be developed, such as a QFD-based planning cycle, routine coaching sessions, and any other forum you require to fully reinforce the approaches we have outlined.[1] It will also require you to establish a clear plan for the implementation of the agreed management approaches within the process teams.

Where there has been agreement of what needs to happen within each process team, but no agreement over when, progress has proven to be very variable. In some cases the rate of progress would mean that it would be unlikely that the process team would be making systematic improvements within two years. Clearly this is unacceptable - but without a clear and agreed plan it is far from uncommon.

The plan[2] should set out clear deadlines for:

- establishing clear and agreed performance targets for the processes

- implementing measures within each process

- setting up regular management meetings to review performance (both at the process level, and collectively at the organisation management level)

- delivering the first systematic process performance improvement.

As one recent reviewer of the novel put it:

"We had very firm goals and deadlines for QFD development - we used the process health checklist early on - very effectively. Later on we had strict timetables for quad charts and review. I think these are vital for setting standards and expectations and to keep all the teams moving at least at a minimum pace. It is the leader's job

---

1   More is said on this in Section E.

2   An example of such a plan can be found on page 437.

The morning sun streamed into the meeting room as Richard sat waiting for the last of his team to arrive. Despite his promises to Lucy, Richard never did make the time to push his managers on their process work. He had intended to, but a major customer crisis, and an urgent demand for a three-year business plan, pushed any ideas of scheduling meetings with them right out of the window. He had planned to raise the issue when he met them as part of the existing schedule of meetings, but invariably his mind was on other things at the time.

And now he had a sense of foreboding about how this meeting was going to develop. He glanced at Lucy's grim face, and could read clearly in her expression her forecast of how things would turn out. She sat quietly. This was Richard's meeting, not hers.

In his mind, Richard cursed himself for not being more disciplined, and he temporarily lost himself in a 'devil and angel' debating session:

"I should have prioritised my time better…"

"But you couldn't have been expected to foresee the crisis…"

"Then I should have rearranged some other things…"

"Oh, come on! These are senior managers – they shouldn't need you to wet nurse them…"

"But on things like this they always have."

He was broken out of it by the arrival of Susan who muttered an apology and sat down. Richard looked around the room. Peoples' faces seemed to reflect Lucy's recent assessment of their progress. Deborah was clearly alert and enthusiastic, Daniel looked sullen, Susan looked interested and slightly apprehensive, Peter had distracted himself with some figures he was looking over.

Ah well, once more into the breach dear friends! Richard stood up. "Welcome everybody. Thank you for being prompt. Our objective today is to review the process proposals you have developed, and to check that, collectively, they will ensure that Cylek UK will achieve its objectives. Now we did arrange to circulate the proposals before the meeting, but I have only received three of them, and so I am hoping that the remaining proposals can be presented before we start."

to beat this drum right from the start. In the novel Richard does this far too late. Thankfully we didn't make that mistake."

Maintaining the vision of the 'new way of working'

Whenever anyone attempts to create change they introduce a tension to pull people into the new way. Unfortunately that same tension tends to pull both ways, and the change agent often finds his or her energy sapped by the continual pull back to what existed before. And yet that tension is vital to success. So it is important both to anchor yourself, and to erode the foundations of those you are seeking to change.

Anchoring yourself can be achieved by surrounding yourself with constant reminders of your vision, and renewed evidence of progress. It is vital that you spend a few minutes at the start of every day reinforcing clearly in your mind exactly what you are trying to achieve.

Having lost sight of our objective we redoubled our efforts.

Duke of Wellington

Eroding foundations is best achieved by a 'burning platform'. This stresses your compelling need to change; providing a constant reminder of why remaining the same would be injurious and possibly fatal.

Displaying constant reminders of both, visually, audibly, and by implication (e.g. progress graphs) will help tremendously in driving change - both in your people, and in yourself.

Maintaining and reviewing progress

We ask questions all the time about what is important to us - it is natural! People

Daniel interjected: "Well it can hardly be before we start, Richard, since we have already started!" Good old Daniel! Offence is the best form of defence!

Richard just took it on the chin, and continued: "Thank you, Daniel. I will choose my words more carefully. We will start the meeting with a presentation of the proposals that people have not yet seen. So who would like to start?"

Daniel interjected again, "Richard, we ought to discuss the previously circulated proposals presented first. I for one have a few questions on them." Richard checked himself, and noticed that a few others were nodding in agreement with Daniel's suggestion. He fancied that the nods were from people who had not actually done their proposals. Putting off the evil hour, perhaps?

Richard wondered whether to challenge this. He felt he was losing control of the meeting. He was all geared up to confront those who had not done anything, and he felt he needed to reassert himself. But, on the other hand, it would be good to recognise those who had put the effort in, and it would provide an example of what was required. He replied, perhaps a trifle silkily, "Thank you Daniel. That is a good suggestion!" He pulled out the three proposals he had received and looked at the one on top. "Susan! Could you take us very briefly through your proposal?"

Susan gave a quick overview of her proposal, and then answered some simple questions of clarification. She was about to sit down again, when Daniel waded in: "Susan, how can you both reduce inventory levels and improve your service levels to the shop floor, as you have proposed here? That is impossible!" He looked at Abs for support. "Abs already has a lot of problems with shortages, and reducing stock levels can only make it worse. Isn't that right Abs?"

Richard felt a sinking feeling. So Daniel's strategy was to tie up the meeting in debate. And very cleverly. He had picked on a common prejudice and sought an ally who would be most swayed by it. Not only that, but his ally was someone who had failed to address the issue in the past, when he ran the process. Abs had a vested interest in arguing this one through.

Richard stepped in quickly. "At this stage I would like to focus on getting an overview of the proposals. We can note any reservations, and deal with them later."

develop a picture of what's important to us by the questions we ask and how we focus on their answers. And if we don't ask questions, people naturally assume it is not important.

So, is the progress that your people are making on implementing their plans important to you? And do your people see that?

A clear programme of reviewing progress on a regular basis establishes the importance of that progress to you; both by the time you invest in it, and by the quality of the questions you ask.

Identifying and addressing behavioural and organisational issues

Similarly, picking up on issues of progress, and doggedly examining everything the manager is doing to ensure that the programme is brought back on track, serves to further reinforce the message.

It is also important to pick up on behaviours that reinforce the wrong value set. This is most clearly evident in interchanges in meetings, where people's ideas may be put down, or other forms of politics may be prevalent. The behaviours of your managers to each other, and to their staff, establish the values of the organisation. Every deficiency in this area is an opportunity for you to reassert the new value set, whether inside meetings, or privately outside.

As part of a review of their implementation of QFD, one company asked its staff the question: 'What is important to your manager?' The results made depressing reading.

To address this issue, the comments were collated onto separate sheets of flipchart paper and pinned around the room. One

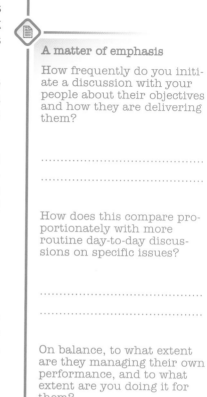

Daniel was not to be put off so easily. "But this is a very important issue, Richard!"

Richard was just about to respond, when Susan stepped in quickly. "Thank you, Daniel. We're aware that this is a difficult problem to tackle, but we also know that it is in wrestling with these apparently conflicting goals that we can add real value to the process. We have undertaken some initial benchmarking in the industry, and some literature surveys, and currently our inventory levels are 70% higher and our service levels 40% lower than the average of top quartile companies in this area."

Richard was sure his jaw had dropped. Wow! Susan really had done her homework. But he noticed that Daniel was about to weigh back in, clearly only temporarily stunned, and he had to stop this here.

"Thank you, Susan. But I'd prefer to leave the detail discussions until later. Excellent work by the way! And now, Andrew, can you take us through yours?"

Andrew presented the proposal of the *'Provide and grow people'* process without incident; as did Deborah for *'Developing products and processes'* immediately afterwards.

Richard had been impressed. He had enjoyed the sense of his team grasping their responsibilities and rising to the challenge. But now he tensed himself for the inevitable conflict. "Okay," he said, "they are the ones we have already seen. Who is next?"

There was a short pause, and then John stood up. He pulled a number of sheets of paper from his file, and proceeded to pass them round the room. "Sorry I didn't get these out before the meeting," he said, "but I was still working on them last night!" He waited until everybody had got a copy, and then started on a rambling explanation, probably because his proposal had not been particularly well thought out.

Richard let it go. He felt he had bigger issues to deal with in that meeting.

When John had finished and sat down, Richard looked meaningfully at Daniel, then at Peter, and then at Abs. Abs stood up. "I haven't had time to put our proposal into the same format as everyone else, but I can run through our goals if you would like?"

Richard nodded.

sheet for each senior manager but with the names removed.

The managers were offered one point for each of their colleagues that they could correctly identify, and ten points for their own (it was a large group). Most managers got practically all of them right, despite being appalled at the results.[1]

When we sit down to think about it, we are all aware of the impression we create. We need to take responsibility for managing that impression, in order to ensure it is the one we *want* to create

Coaching and guiding people

A valuable means of picking up on behavioural issues in private is through organised coaching sessions. Good managers recognise their scope for improvement, and welcome the opportunity of someone helping them to think through their approach. Poor managers often don't recognise their scope for improvement, but if that is the case, coaching is even more crucial.

Establishing a programme of regular one-to-one coaching sessions, and using them to help managers establish and pursue their own performance targets, can prove a major accelerant to the adoption of systematic management approaches. Not least for the opportunity that these sessions provide in encouraging and supporting managers to undertake similar sessions with their own people.

Making time

All of the above represents a considerable burden of time, and yet what we have addressed is purely and simply 'the leader's role'.

Questions to begin to stimulate individual members of your team in rethinking their role:

What mechanisms do you employ to ensure that the needs of your customers are kept in the minds of your people?

What evidence do you have that the objectives of your area are clearly and accurately aligned with the practical aspirations of your staff?

By what means do you objectively monitor and manage the performance of your area of responsibility?

How have you validated any performance measurement you have undertaken, and on what basis have you decided on improvement targets therein?

What improvements have you made to the performance of your area, and what process did you employ in making them?

How will the performance improvements you have made to your area be retained and built upon after you have moved on?

What do you see as the relative merits of viewing research work in 'project' and in 'process' terms?

What do you see as the essential features of an organisation if it is to ensure success in continuously and systematically improving performance?

---

1   See page 443.

Abs then launched into a quick listing of all the current production performance targets. Clearly he had not thought at all about developing them, and Richard suspected that he had not even convened his process team to discuss it.

Richard wondered how to tackle this. He suspected that if he let it go, Daniel and Peter would just follow suit and attempt to present any current departmental targets as being the process proposal. On the other hand, he did not want to have a go at Abs in public. Abs was really an earnest and generally conscientious manager, but he lacked confidence. It would be unfair of Richard to take him down, just so that he could properly deal with Daniel and Peter. He decided to suspend judgement, but to make it clear he was doing so.

"Aren't those your current departmental targets, Abs?" he asked.

"Yes they are," replied Abs. "I felt that they still represented what we are trying to do."

"Mmm," replied Richard. "Well, I have a lot of reservations with that approach, but let's leave it for a minute and get a quick overview of the last two proposals."

He looked expectantly at Daniel, and then at Peter. They looked at each other, and then, by some unspoken consent, Daniel looked back at Richard and took up the baton.

"I haven't done a process proposal. I have had other more pressing priorities that required my attention."

So, now it was clear. Daniel was going to brazen it out. Richard's adrenaline was pumping. Perhaps it was wrong, but he felt none of the compassion he felt for Abs. When Richard looked back on the meeting, he realised that he had spent all of the time while other proposals were presented, just waiting for this point. He focused on Daniel.

"Daniel. Were you not clear on what was required for this meeting?"

Daniel replied: "As I said, I had other priorities."

"But you did not approach me to resolve them, or to inform me of the issue?" The tone was of a question, but it was rhetorical. They both knew the answer. But Daniel had a different tack.

It is probably the case that, as leader, you spend a lot of your time endeavouring to do all this anyway. The problem is that, more often than not, the mechanisms behind this work are rarely the most efficient, or the most focused.

For instance, you may spend time at meetings with one or two of your subordinates, without properly clarifying your role in helping them to develop theirs.

In practice, senior managers often find their diary is full of activity that could be delegated (eventually), or could be developed into a process, or could be subsumed within the activities of 'Leading the Change'. Making time to lead, then, is a matter of refocusing[1] existing activities:

- analysing how you spend your time currently, and deciding what needs to change

- looking at your forward diary and workload, and reconsidering how you will approach it

- developing and applying a routine for deciding how to tackle any new work that comes to you

- establishing a plan for undertaking the work required by the 'top-box' role

- monitoring your progress and developing your approach still further.

More detailed guidance on this matter will be found in Chapters 18 and 19, after we have considered the influence of personal values on our role and responsibilities.

In the next chapter, we look at how the leader needs to coordinate the responses of his or her people to the challenges they have been set.

There's no telling how far a person can go if he's willing to let other people take the credit.

Robert Woodruff
CEO, Coca Cola

---

1 A simple program for thinking through these steps is available on the associated web-site (see Appendix 7).

Managing by Design

"Well certainly Lucy knew. I assumed she was co-ordinating all this and would have informed you. Didn't she?"

Neat shot, thought Richard, slightly flummoxed as how to respond. Yes she did know. Yes she did inform him. Damn!

Richard did not answer. He looked instead to Peter, who simply shrugged and said "I'm in the same boat as Daniel."

Richard looked round at the whole group. He felt deflated. "Okay, let's take a coffee break," he said. "Back here in fifteen minutes."

Proposal reconciliation

The key advantage of QFD is the basis it provides for breaking down the objectives of the organisation into logical practical elements. These provide opportunities for ownership and creativity at every level of the organisation.

However, sometimes the ownership and creativity results in process development charging off in the wrong direction. Given the level of discussion and guidance provided by the QFD, this might at first appear unlikely. Yet the capacity of the human mind for losing sight of its objectives, when caught up in enthusiasm over the possibilities (or concern over the issues), is a constant source of amazement for anybody concerned with setting those objectives.

And even when managers endeavour to ensure that the learning from the top-level QFD is pursued faithfully, misinterpretations and subtle differences in emphasis, easily creep in.

The issue lies in the freedom given to the process teams. Instead of deciding the performance required of each process team and defining that explicitly - a process in which ambiguity can be avoided - the management team state what the organisation is to achieve, and allow the process teams free rein in considering how they will support that. The result holds far more potential for ensuring commitment and innovation, but greater risks in misinterpretation.

In a practical sense the process proposal is the key means for ensuring that those misinterpretations are addressed at the earliest stage. The diagram on the next page illustrates how this is achieved.

- The organisation establishes a set of clear goals which represent their aspi-

Chapter 12

As people walked out, he sat back down in his chair and waited for Lucy to come over. She did so, and sat on the edge of the table.

"Difficult," she said, commiserating with him. There was no recrimination in her tone, even though he felt he deserved some. In fact, he felt he deserved lots.

"So, what do we do next?" he asked. "We surely can't run the next session while we are missing three proposals."

"Well…," said Lucy, "it could be run, almost at a 'draft' sort of level, and there would be value in it. It could even provide a flying start to Daniel and Peter in developing their proposals."

"So what do you reckon?" he asked.

"Carry on as we planned for today," Lucy replied. "And then think about how it changes the rest of this programme at the end." She seemed clear and upbeat about it, and this lifted Richard's spirits.

"Okay!" he said, and they wandered out to join those having coffee.

After the coffee break, Lucy introduced the next steps for the meeting. She started with a question.

"How do we know that, if we focus on, and succeed in, delivering all the process objectives, that we will necessarily ensure the top-level Cylek UK objectives will be met?"

The group thought for a moment, and then Andrew proposed: "Because the grid of the QFD links them together!"

Lucy said: "Fine! And if I put down a hundred dollars, sorry I mean a hundred pounds, who will bet me that delivering the objectives we've seen here today will guarantee Cylek UK's objectives will be met?"

There was silence for a moment or two. Then Andrew defended: "But we are missing objectives from some of the processes."

Lucy replied: "Yes, but even supposing we weren't, would they necessarily add up?"

ration for the business over the coming year.

- Process teams consider their role in meeting those aspirations, through the context of the QFD, and are invited to tender their proposals to support the organisation.

- The process teams' proposals are then reviewed by the organisation to ensure that they collectively ensure the organisation's success.

- When the proposals are approved (possibly after some negotiated adjustments) the process teams are commissioned to take responsibility for delivering what they have promised.

The first two bullet points above have been covered in Chapters 2, 7, 9 and 10. It is the third and fourth bullet points that we shall explore in this chapter: how should the management team consider and approve each proposal?

Essentially there are two questions that the management team should reflect upon when reviewing the proposals.

- To what extent does the proposal represent a carefully considered ambition?

- To what extent does the sum of all the proposals deliver what the organisation needs?

Depending on the answers to these questions, three supplementary questions may arise.

- Do we need to prioritise our efforts in moving forward?

- Should we adjust our aspirations in the light of the proposals?

Daniel answered: "No!"

"Right!" confirmed Lucy. "But if we are literally going to focus on delivering the process objectives, we had better make sure they do add up. We had better make sure we are confident that delivering the process objectives will ensure our top-level objectives are met."

Lucy paused to check that everybody was following, and then continued: "That is what the next activity is all about. We have each worked out what we need to do in our own processes, and we now need to make sure that we have let nothing drop down the cracks in-between."

Andrew repeated his concern: "But we are missing objectives from some of the processes!"

Lucy looked at him. "Yes, it would be better if we had them all, but in doing it this way we can get some pointers as to what they will need to deliver. And we can also provide useful feedback to the processes which have made proposals." This seemed to mollify the team's concerns.

"Okay," said Lucy, "I'm going to split you into two syndicates, and you will each take one row of the QFD.

"What I'd like each syndicate to do is to list out the Cylek UK objectives, measures and targets for that row, and then list, underneath that, all of the proposed process objectives that you believe contribute to achieving it. Look through all the proposals, but obviously focus on those that have a strong relationship as identified on the QFD. Everybody okay so far?"

Most nodded, and Deborah summarised: "You want us to produce a list of all the process objectives that have anything to do with our top-level objective?"

"That's right," confirmed Lucy. "But then I want you to ask whether the sum of your list will practically guarantee your top-level objective."

"How do we do that?" challenged Peter.

"Well, by experience and discussion. At the end of the day, this is probably your core expertise - evaluating whether you have done enough to meet your objectives."

"So there's no special tool for this?" asked Deborah.

- How do we need to equip the processes to enable them to deliver what they have promised?

In the rest of this chapter we look at how these questions can be tackled.

To what extent does the proposal represent a carefully considered ambition?

Process proposals represent an opportunity to shine. They represent the opportunity to identify previously unforeseen potential, and to harness the enthusiasm and commitment of the process team to use that potential to best leverage the organisation toward its goals.

However, for some, they may represent the opportunity to coast. They may represent the opportunity to set lazy goals that require little more than the continued application of current practice.

Whichever route is taken is likely to reflect either on the ability and/or the attitude of the process owner, or on his or her understanding of what is required.

In respect of the latter (the understanding of what is required), it is very beneficial if each manager responsible for developing a process proposal is given an opportunity to think through what a high-quality process proposal might look like.

The checklist on the right outlines some questions that may be reflected on in evaluating the quality of a process proposal. In practice, though, it is often more effective to ask the management team what criteria they would use to evaluate the quality of process proposals presented to them. The debate serves both to guide people's ideas on what is required, and to normalise the expectations of the group. In one case a company went as far as using

Evaluating process proposals

Have the most appropriate people been appointed to the team?

Does the proposed scope of the process reflect a suitably forward-thinking perspective?

Have the boundaries of the process been set through discussion with neighbouring processes?

Are all important relationships on the top-level QFD listed, and do these correlate with the QFD itself?

Have the top-level objectives been appropriately translated into process objectives?

Do the proposed measures and targets reflect a proactive sense of the process' potential?

Do the targets represent significant but realistic improvement?

Are the targets supported by well-considered and practical strategies?

Is there clear evidence of thinking through the business case, in terms of benefits and costs?

Does the proposal reflect a balanced and thorough consideration of the potential risks?

"No, not really," replied Lucy. "Any tool I can think of would be really very cumbersome. But I promise you that when you get into this, you'll find that it's not difficult to do."

"Supposing they don't add up to the top-level objective?" challenged John.

"Ah, that's step four," replied Lucy. "What you then have to do is to work out what additional process objectives you need, and which process is best placed to own them. This step will provide very useful input to the processes that haven't developed proposals as yet."

Daniel looked uncomfortable at this, and challenged right away. "But supposing we don't agree with the objectives that the syndicates dream up for us?"

Richard just stopped himself from responding: "Well you should have done a bloody proposal in the first place!" and it occurred to him what a deep level of resentment he was harbouring against Daniel. He began to worry whether it was showing, and whether it was counter productive.

Instead, Lucy responded: "You will have the opportunity to consider them and propose alternatives, if need be."

"And if we don't want to do that?" Daniel interjected belligerently.

Lucy cast a very quick glance to Richard, but continued with hardly a pause.

"Well, if the sum of the process objectives will not ensure the top-level objective, then we will need to reconsider our aspirations for the top-level objective." she said.

She stood up and started speaking quickly to move the process on past the interjections. "The final step, is to see whether any of your list of process objectives is ultimately superfluous in ensuring the top-level objective, and to feed this back to the group. That will enable the process team to prioritise the objectives they have set themselves. Is everybody clear?" she asked.

"Mostly, yes," replied Susan, "but that only covers two rows. Do we repeat the exercise for the other rows?"

"Exactly!" confirmed Lucy.

the defined criteria to award a prize for the best proposal presented.

If, however, a poorly crafted process proposal is due to the ability or attitude of the manager, this is first and foremost a coaching issue. For this reason it is best addressed by the leader, who should take it up directly and individually with the process owner in advance of the proposal being presented to the management team.

To what extent does the sum of all the proposals deliver what the organisation needs?

Having ensured the quality of thought and commitment applied to individual process proposals, the next issue is whether the proposals collectively deliver what the organisation needs.

The means of determining whether the proposals collectively deliver the top-level objectives is essentially subjective, since it relies heavily on understanding the relationships and weighing up probable outcomes. Therefore, it benefits from involving the whole management team in the discussion. However, for reasons of efficiency, it is often preferable to undertake an initial review, objective by objective, within syndicate groups, and then approve the conclusions in plenary.

A process for reviewing the proposals is shown on the right.

There are three possible outcomes to this question of whether the proposals deliver what the organisation aspires to.

- The proposals meet the organisational needs.

- The proposals fall short of the organisational needs.

- The proposals exceed the organisational needs.

Process for proposal review

1. Take each objective, one at a time, and write up clearly the measures and targets, and any other criteria that you believe are key to the objective.

2. Then work through the process proposals, starting from the critical and moving to the significant, and flipchart from them, all the intended achievements that will materially deliver the objective.

3. Clarify which are the priority actions to ensure that the objective is met, and mark them clearly (and which process) - lean toward the 'preferred (high-scoring) processes' if possible.

4. Identify what (if anything) is additionally required to guarantee delivery of the objective, and the process to which you feel it should be assigned.

The syndicates worked progressively through the rows of the QFD. Most of the team accepted proposals to further develop their process objectives with good grace, but Daniel, predictably, did not.

However, rather than compromise the top-level QFD objectives, Richard listed these 'unresolved issues' in the 'Car Park' and said he would pick them up with individuals outside the meeting. The hidden meaning behind Richard's words stood out like a beacon to everybody, but Daniel chose to ignore it, and the meeting progressed largely without incident and finished almost on time.

Overall, Richard viewed the meeting as a success. Those who had developed process proposals had received valuable feedback, and refined their proposals to focus on the priorities for Cylek UK this year. Those who had not developed proposals, now had some useful guidance on what to focus them on. And, despite the issue with Daniel, Richard felt even more confident about achieving the top-level goals.

As people filed out of the room, Richard simply put away his pen and proceeded to mechanically pull down the flipchart sheets from the wall and stack them together. Lucy looked on. She felt the meeting had gone well under the circumstances, but wasn't sure what Richard felt about it. He had seemed rather matter-of-fact through the meeting, with none of the excitement and enthusiasm that he had shown in the previous meeting.

Lucy was concerned about this change in his manner, and that he appeared to be ignoring her. Did he view the problems they had had in the workshop as her fault? Did he feel that something was wrong in how she had facilitated the meeting?

To her, the contrast in his manner was plain, and she wanted to make sure that any resentments Richard might be harbouring were out in the open. She raised the matter by illustrating it directly. "No kiss this time? I must be losing my touch in workshop design!" The words were out of her mouth before she had fully thought through the possible ramifications.

Richard, whose mind over recent days had regularly strayed to thoughts of Lucy and that kiss, was thrown off guard by the dilemma of opportunity and risk. On the one hand, he knew she meant nothing sexual by the question. On the other hand, here was an opportunity, and the thought

In practice, all three cases are possible, not only within the same QFD, but even within the same objective on the QFD; for instance where the objective's achievement demands a combination of strategies.

Where the proposals are seen to meet the requirements of the organisation, clearly it is only necessary to confirm the process teams in their intention, and ensure that their resource needs are fulfilled.

Where the proposals fall short of the organisation's needs, the nature of that shortfall needs to be identified, and the appropriate process charged with adopting responsibility for it. In practice, this proves fairly easy to agree within the meeting, and for the process owner to sell back to the process team afterwards.

Do we need to prioritise our efforts in moving forward?

Where the sum of the proposals exceeds the organisational need, there is the opportunity to prioritise process improvements, and relieve the pressure on some to concentrate resources on others. Whether this is done within processes or across processes depends largely on the extent to which they hold resources in common. For instance, where process resources are largely independent, then prioritising within a process helps the process team to focus their resources better. But where key personnel and resources are shared between processes it is preferable to prioritise some processes over others.

To some extent it may be desirable to identify the priority processes before the teams review whether the objectives will be met. This is particularly important where there is not enough resource to improve all processes equally. By indicating the preferred priority processes,

Example of proposal review

Increase turnover by 30%

Sales process: Secure sales of £140m

Manufacturing process: Increase productivity to 85%

Purchasing process: Increase supplier reliability to 99%

Sales will ensure business is available

Purchasing only need to maintain supplier reliability at the current level

Manufacturing will only support a throughput of £115m with this objective

Purchasing needs only to achieve 97% reliability

Manufacturing need an objective related to increased capacity

of kissing her appealed greatly. But he knew it would be too forced, too contrived, and he knew he could not carry it off. He liked playing on the edges of flirting, on the edge of possibilities, where he did not have to commit himself. If he was to kiss her now, he was sure he would be making a statement. The tension of the moment rose up inside him. Shit! It was all too complex!

Mentally he brushed the whole thing to one side, and focused back on the workshop.

"No your touch seems just fine to me!" and immediately he felt back on safer ground. "Come on, let's get a coffee. We can tidy up later."

As they sat over two Cappuccinos, down in the coffee bar, Richard visibly relaxed. While Lucy was distracted, administering to her coffee, he took the opportunity to run his eyes over her. She really was quite stunningly attractive. Richard wondered what the contour of her thighs would feel like under his hand. He wondered what she wore under her skirt, he thought he could spot the tell-tale bumps of suspender clips. The thought overwhelmed him momentarily, and he shook his head to clear it and get back to reality.

Lucy saw him, and gave him a quizzical look. Covering quickly, he responded: "Are you finding it cold down here too? I think I'm in a draft".

"No, I'm fine," Lucy replied. "Do you want to move?"

"No, it's okay," he said. "I'll live!"

She stirred her coffee some more, and then said: "Richard, do you mind if I give you some feedback?" She looked up toward him, as she finished the question.

Richard was taken unawares, he braced himself wondering what was coming. Was Lucy going to pick up on his behaviour to her? In trepidation, but with a tone that he felt conveyed casualness itself, he said: "No, that's fine!"

Lucy smiled. She caught the tension in his voice, but decided to take the words at face value.

groups that find the sum of their proposals more than meet their objective, can bias their conclusions toward the priority processes. In this way, all teams will tend to relieve pressure on the same set of non-priority processes. This may appear to be putting the cart before the horse, but priorities need not be cast in stone and they may be easily reconsidered as conclusions emerge.[1]

Should we adjust our aspirations in the light of the proposals?

In some cases, it may not be possible to agree changes to proposals in order to meet the organisation's needs. This could either be due to personalities or practicalities.

In the event of the former, it is up to the leader to address the issue, either off-line, or within the meeting.

In the event of the latter, it may be necessary to reconsider the appropriate objective so that it more accurately reflects what is practical.

There is no real issue in doing this, and the team will feel more free to set challenging goals if they know that there is an option to reconsider those goals once the means to deliver them have been fully explored.

The means to review the top-level objectives would be to consider what the sum total of the process proposals would deliver (if they cannot be improved) and then to set the top-level target at that point.

The 'clothes-line' approach referred to earlier in Chapter 7 can be easily modified to achieve this. People can use the 'clothes-line' to debate and reach consensus on how much collective impact the proposals will have.[2]

1   For an example of this approach, see page 458.

2   For an example of this, see page 449.

Managing by Design

"It's about how you respond to Daniel. Sometimes you give the impression that you are fixated on him. That your responses to the group are almost tailored for Daniel's benefit." She stopped and looked at him, waiting to see how he responded.

Richard exhaled. He had not realised he had been holding his breath. Daniel! He was beginning to have the same thoughts himself. He decided to be honest.

"Yes," he paused momentarily as he thought about how to continue. "I have to admit he seems to occupy a lot of my working thoughts. It seems like a constant battle having to either stay one thought ahead of him, or let him have his way. I really don't know what to do about it."

He had been looking down at the table as he spoke. Now he looked back up to Lucy's face. She had a small amount of Cappuccino froth at the corner of her mouth that caught his eye, and as she spoke back to him, he followed the contours of her lips and he wondered what they would taste like. What they would feel like to kiss them properly. Lucy had stopped speaking. He became aware that she was waiting for a response.

"Sorry? I'm not sure I got all of that!" he said.

"I said," replied Lucy, "could Daniel's reaction be in part due to the way you treat him? Do you think that you might influence Daniel's behaviour by your expectations of how he will behave?"

Richard's brow creased. He thought that she had just used psychobabble on him. He had always thought she was beyond that. He was disappointed and slightly annoyed. It showed in his response.

"Ah, the classic rationalisation! The guilty are simply products of the innocents' inability to treat them properly! Is that what you're saying?"

Lucy felt affronted. "No, it wasn't! I know Daniel is a problem of his own making. I'm just very slightly concerned that he might be dragging you down with him. That you might end up playing his game rather than your own."

Richard's face showed he was vaguely appeased so she continued. "Do you not find, sometimes, that you end up being drawn away from your normal behaviour in order to deal with how Daniel might behave?"

Lucy waited for Richard to nod and then continued: "Daniel's normal mode of operating appears to be conflict and politics, and that is where

If at the end of the debate, the net performance gain is considered insufficient to meet what the business needs, participation in that conclusion will at least provide extra impetus to the process of reconsidering more ambitious performance improvements. One technique for this is to physically move everyone to the desired target level on the 'clothes-line' and ask the question: "What barriers would have to be removed for you to perform at this level?"

How do we need to equip the processes to enable them to deliver what they have promised?

The secret of success is simple. You work out what you want. You work out what it costs. Then you pay the price in full! That's it; that is all there is to it.

But often companies are held back from success because they fail to accept this simple principle.

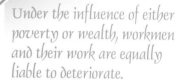

Under the influence of either poverty or wealth, workmen and their work are equally liable to deteriorate.

Plato

Once the process teams have their proposals agreed, it is vitally important that they have their resource needs met, or the shortfall will be borne in lost opportunity or hidden costs.

If, on the other hand, you feel that your people always overestimate, then it would be good to reflect on Richard Branson's answer to the question of success. He replied, "I find people I can trust. And then I trust them."

The hardest knife, ill-used, doth lose its edge.

William Shakespeare

The best way to get your people to stop including margins in their proposals is to stop making them need to!

Commissioning the proposals

It would be easy to say to the process teams "Get on and do it!" But that misses a tremendous opportunity to reinforce the whole ethos of what has been done:

he appears to be drawing you. Into his own territory, where he is more than able to fight you!"

Richard thought about this for a while. He could see the truth in her point, but he could not see what he should do about it.

He thought about what his normal mode of operating was. It was about visions, and coaching, and supporting. He really could not see that working with Daniel. And it would take so much time. Time he did not have.

After about a minute he finally said: "I can see you have a point, but I'm going to need to think about it further."

"Good," said Lucy. "Now, some news! I have the impression that Cyrus will be paying us a visit shortly, to see how all this is going on!"

Richard exhaled noisily, and responded: "Are you sure?"

"Well, nothing is confirmed," said Lucy, "but he phoned me last night, asked how things were going, and said he was going to speak to you to arrange a visit. He normally makes a visit when I get about a couple of months into the work, but of course all the other projects have been in the US, and relatively easy for him to get to. I feel quite honoured that he's continuing it, even though I'm right over here!"

Richard was quiet. He looked a little crestfallen.

"Look Richard, this is actually a terrific opportunity. Think about it! If you are going to make QFD really hum in the future, you've got to get Cylek to be a whole lot clearer on their priorities. And you could also do with them giving you some slack on corporate initiatives while you get things going. What better champion could you wish for in your corner than Cyrus. And as for me, I want him to buy into the approach we've taken here. I want other parts of Cylek to benefit from this, and he's the one who can make that happen."

Richard could see her point. "Okay, it's not quite as bad as I at first thought," he conceded.

"Bad?" she exclaimed. "It's brilliant! But we are going to have to think our way through how we present things to him. The whole thing has got to be stage managed!"

Richard nodded. "But my diary is still horrendous," he said.

- for the leader to thank the team for its proposed performance

- for the process owner to reinforce the importance of what has been agreed

- for the team to understand the next steps, and how the quality of its service will be reviewed

- for people to feel a vital part of the organisation's future

- for the systems[1] to be adjusted to reflect the new agreement.

The activity of commissioning the proposals represents a real opportunity to reinforce what you are trying to achieve. If the proposal was from an outside contractor, it is very likely that the contract signing would be a formalised affair, and for very good reason.

The effort in commissioning an internal proposal should be nothing less!

For when the ancients said that a work begun was half done, they meant we ought to take the utmost pains in every undertaking to make a good beginning.

Polybius
Greek Historian

---

[1] Systems might include ISO 9000 documentation, local mission statements, or other procedures or quality definitions.

"Well, how about another evening session?" she suggested. "We need to do some more planning on the workshops now anyway." The thought of another evening at Lucy's hotel appealed to him. In fact it might turn out to be several evenings.

"Fine," he said, "how about tomorrow night?"

"That suits me," she replied. And then after a short pause she continued: "But when are you going to find time to chase up on progress? Particularly Peter's and Daniel's progress?"

Richard looked at her. It was a blank, neutral look. He was clearly not seriously engaging with the question, so Lucy continued with the initiative. "Why don't you invite Daniel out for a quick drink tomorrow evening. Draw him onto your territory, and try to move things forward there. If you suggest the hotel for 5.30 pm, then we can begin our meeting straight after. Say 6.30?"

Richard felt trapped, but he conceded. He could not think of a worse way to start the evening. He hoped Daniel would not be able to make it.

Managing upwards

So far in the book, we have largely ignored the context of your management system: the corporate chain of command within which it may only represent one part.

If you are lucky (?) you may either be the owner of your business, or have a very sympathetic boss or board of management, who are keen to let you get on and manage your organisation in your own way.

If you are even luckier, the corporate framework, of which you are part, has already embarked on QFD, and you are undertaking this work as part of fulfilling the potential of your 'process' within that.

But if, as is most likely the case, you are breaking new ground in your company, and your boss, quite reasonably, is concerned to ensure that your new approach will deliver, then you need to develop a strategy to build and sustain that confidence.

Such a strategy is likely to include the following elements.

- Selling your plans as a vital step in grasping the future of your business.

- Developing commitment to your work in this area.

- Getting approval for how this work will, and will not, interface with the corporate framework.

- Agreeing the criteria by which your work will be judged a success.

- Integrating key corporate strategies into your work.

- Introducing the approach to other parts of the business.

- Gaining concessions and support in those areas where you most need them.

The manager who supports the boss - the manager whom the boss can rely on and trust - is the one who will be given the most freedom and the least supervision.

Mary Ann Allison/Eric Allison
Vice President, CitiCorp/Financial writer
in Managing Up, Managing Down
(Simon & Schuster, 1984)

Chapter 13

The freak heat-wave boded well for a surprisingly pleasant weekend, providing the promised storm could do something to reduce the humidity. Unfortunately, the sudden change in the weather had caught the Cavendish Hotel off-guard. The heating system appeared to be running full blast. A dishevelled and clearly overheated barman had informed Richard that they were waiting on maintenance, and would he like some extra ice in his drink. The low sun, streaming through the conservatory, created flickering patterns through Richard's gin and tonic. It oscillated intriguingly on the teak counter, as the sparkling liquid rocked from Richard placing it forcibly on the bar. He looked at his watch. Five fifty-five. Where was Daniel? The heat did nothing for his temper.

He mentally allowed Daniel another five minutes, and when he did not show, he slung back the last of his gin and tonic and went upstairs in search of Lucy. He knocked lightly on her door.

"Come in," she said. The door was ajar. Richard pushed it open. Lucy stood by the dressing table in a bathrobe.

"Richard!" she said in surprise. "Sorry, I thought you were a cold refreshing drink."

Just then, Richard was aware of someone beside him. He turned and saw a waiter carrying a tray with a large bottle of mineral water, a bowl of ice, and a glass. The waiter looked expectantly at him, so Richard took the tray and turned back into the room. "Voila!" he said. "Abracadabra, and lo, I have become a cold refreshing drink." He walked into the room and placed the tray on the circular table with a flourish.

"You're early!" she accused.

"Yes. Daniel, bless him, didn't show. So I've been getting hotter and madder for the last thirty minutes."

"Yes, it is hot," she replied. "I'm beginning to wish I hadn't asked for a room facing west. Help yourself to a drink. I've got another glass somewhere."

- Understanding how you will handle concerns and criticism.
- Establishing the means to report progress.

In this chapter, we look in more detail at the 'upward' responsibilities of leadership, and at how the above elements can be worked out in practice.

Selling your plans

The first step in a successful strategy to 'manage upwards' is to convince your bosses that the steps you are taking are clearly the right ones.

If your organisation is undertaking this work as part of a larger initiative on QFD, then the key mechanism for achieving this is your process proposal.

While this might seem obvious, the influence of the process proposal is far more subtle than we might at first give it credit for. To this point, it is entirely possible that you may have seen the process proposal as simply the means to reply to the needs of the organisation. But that is to fail to realise its full potential.

The process proposal provides the means for you to earn the full confidence and support of the business for your most ambitious schemes. Intelligent wording of the proposal can convince the business of your arguments, earn you the resources you need, and buy you the right to get on with it without interference.

Think of the process proposal as the application form for the job you most want in the world - and you will probably get it!

If, on the other hand, you are pioneering the application of these approaches within your organisation, the selling job is both more important and more difficult.

No living being is held by anything so strongly as its own needs.

Epictetus
Roman Stoic philosopher

Selling your plans

In attempting to sell your ideas to your boss, it is worthwhile reflecting on the quote above, and thinking through the following:

What are your boss's dreams for the future?

....

....

....

....

....

And what are the issues that keep him or her awake at night?

....

....

....

....

....

How can your plans make a difference in these areas?

....

....

....

....

....

....

Managing by Design

He looked round the room, everything was in disarray. "I'm sorry! I should have phoned up first!" he apologised. "I'll go, and let you get dressed."

Lucy turned from sorting out her hair, and smiled at him. "It'd've made no difference," she said. "The phone doesn't work. Nothing in this place seems to. I'll get dressed in the bathroom while you cast your eye over my outline thoughts for Cyrus's visit, then we can go and get some dinner."

She walked over to the bed, and Richard went to close the door.

"Don't," she said urgently. "Leave it open. I've been carefully cultivating that little bit of through draught. It's the only respite I've got. Come over here and look at my plans." He could see that the bed was covered with sheets of flipchart paper. "Sorry about the mess," she said. "I was getting a bit enthusiastic." Richard sat on one side of the bed, while she sat on the other and flicked through the various bits of paper.

Lucy was right about the heat. Before five minutes were up, Richard had discarded jacket and tie, and was undoing his shirt cuffs.

Lucy ran through the last sheet of paper, and then stood up and said: "Right, you have a read of those, and I'll get dressed."

Just as she did so, there was a knock on the door.

"It's open," said Lucy.

Daniel walked in. He had arrived late, and the desk had directed him up. He stood just inside the door, and cast his eyes around, and then gave Richard and Lucy an old-fashioned look.

Richard looked affronted, but Lucy laughed.

Daniel started to bluster "Yes, well…" Clearly he was about to make something of the situation.

"Oh, come on Daniel!" said Richard. "Use your eyes. This is work. Nothing is going on! Lucy invited you in, for crying out loud!"

Daniel looked around the room again, and took in that the bed was littered with work. He could see that he was making something of nothing, but retained his scowl anyway.

Your task is to build sufficient confidence in your bosses that they provide you with enough latitude and support to enable you to make it work.

The first step is to take the initiative. There is a world of difference psychologically between selling a new idea, and justifying your position.

A formal presentation[1] covering:

- the business threats and opportunities that your organisation is facing, or will face over the coming months/years

- what your organisation needs to deliver if it is to fully grasp them

- how that translates into challenging performance targets

- the dormant potential of the organisation and how it can be mobilised in pursuit of those targets

- why this requires a change in the management approach (linked to an exploration of the current issues in the management approach)

- the logic of the new ways of working, and its associated benefits

- your plan to deliver this, and the progress you have made to date,

will do much to demonstrate the quality of your thinking, and the rightness of your approach.

You may recognise that the content to support those headings, falls naturally out of the work of the preceding chapters.

As marketers, we have to bring our vision down to a useful level.

William Olsten
CEO, Olsten Services Corp.
in Success, February 1988.

If you can't tell me something about your business I don't already know, you probably aren't going to surprise our competitors either.

Anonymous CEO to division heads
Hickman and Silva, Creating Excellence
(New American Library, 1984).

---

1 An outline presentation template is available on the associated web-site (see Appendix 7).

"Come on, let's get our drink and leave Lucy to tidy up," said Richard, standing up. He picked up his jacket and tie, and ushered Daniel out.

The drink with Daniel was far from satisfactory. It was clear from the outset that Richard was not going to win Daniel over to his vision of the future. Richard got the impression that any vision of the future acceptable to Daniel would not have Richard anywhere in it.

The meeting terminated, almost predictably, with Richard explaining, in no uncertain terms, that he required Daniel to deliver a complete process proposal to his desk by this time next week.

When Lucy came down to dinner, Daniel had long since gone. And Richard was sitting morosely at the bar. She walked up silently and sat down beside him. She looked stunning in a figure-hugging black dress. Richard looked her up and down.

"Wow!" he said. "Are you trying to convict Daniel of his prejudices?"

Lucy simply said: "No, it just happens to be the coolest outfit I've got with me." Then she paused and added: "You're not telling me that Daniel seriously thought something was going on up there?"

Richard shrugged. "No, not really, but I think he was seriously surprised when he first walked in the door."

Lucy laughed as she remembered the surprise on Daniel's face. "I'll go and check they've got a table," she said.

While she was gone Richard thought about her words. She had said "… going on up there" not "… going on between us". Strangely, Richard felt some hope at her choice of phrase, it sustained his fantasy. He took the time while she was gone to wonder whether she wore underwear under her little black number. He couldn't see any lines showing, and suspected she did not.

When she returned, Richard told her that he'd spoken to Cyrus earlier that evening. He was coming over next week. He would be with them for the Thursday morning, and was then catching a 2pm flight to Paris from Bristol.

"That'll be perfect," said Lucy.

Developing commitment

Your goal in selling the plans for your work is to develop a sense of partnership with your bosses. At the very least, they should believe that what you are doing should be done, and to give you their blessing for that.

They may not be convinced that this is the right approach until it has delivered physical results. But they should at least be convinced that the approach should be tried and evaluated, and that you and your organisation are clearly the right place to do this.

You are far more likely to gain the support and latitude you need if the company feels that you are a visionary who is piloting a new approach on its behalf, rather than seeing you as a bit of a maverick who has yet to learn the error of his or her ways.

The key to success here, is to arrive at a point where it is their decision to pilot the new approach and make it work, and you are simply the foresighted and capable agent who will do this for them.[1] How you do this depends on the relationship you have with your bosses, but it is probably worth exploring the issues with them at a point where the QFD has been defined, but before your people are committed to deliver the results.

The more QFD is seen as a joint project with your boss, the more latitude you are likely to gain in applying it.

Would you persuade, speak of interest, not of reason.

Benjamin Franklin
American statesman

Possible questions to answer in gaining agreement on QFD

What are the limitations of the organisation's current approach to planning and management?

....
....
....
....

How does a QFD based approach overcome these?

....
....
....
....

What are the organisation's main concerns and reservations likely to be?

....
....
....
....

How will these be answered?

....
....
....
....

---

1   Nice trick if you can pull it off!

It did not take Lucy and Richard long to work out how best to play Cyrus's visit. Richard wanted to get the business part of the evening out of the way as quickly as possible. The humidity in the room, combined with Lucy's good humour and her stunning figure, made it easy for Richard to allow himself to get distracted.

Richard fancied that he could actually see beads of perspiration breaking out on Lucy's chest, and he wondered what they would taste like. He could almost imagine the saltiness on his tongue. Then he began to imagine Lucy's breasts set free from that figure-hugging dress. He imagined further, his mind dwelling on and relishing each image as he watched her across the table, and he began to find himself increasingly uncomfortable and had to move to rearrange himself.

Truth be told, they both had a lot in common, and they both enjoyed each other's company. And the heat, and the wine, and the odd unguarded innuendo had their effects on each of them. But, despite the banter, it dawned on Richard that Lucy had been holding a line which meant that things could not just develop accidentally-on-purpose, and that any pass would be very clearly and explicitly, exactly that. And when it came time to make a move, Richard found that he couldn't raise the stakes high enough to simply put himself on the line. The risk and implications of rejection were just too much for him to contemplate. And so, with a feeling in the pit of his stomach that Richard thought he had left behind in the school playground, he reluctantly gave Lucy a simple goodnight kiss and headed for home, thinking of what might have been if only he had been a bit more adventurous.

Cyrus arrived at 8.30 on Thursday morning, complete with entourage. As per the plan they had developed in Lucy's hotel, Lucy sent the entourage on a factory tour with Abs, and siphoned Cyrus off into a separate meeting room, where Richard awaited them.

As Cyrus entered the room, his eyes were drawn to the far wall. An interwoven montage of diagrams, matrices and graphs drew his gaze. He was intrigued, but mindful of protocol, he turned quickly to Richard, and they shook hands.

"Cyrus, welcome to Gloucester!" said Richard by way of opening the conversation. He had met Cyrus only once before, briefly during his round of final interviews. Truth to tell, he felt slightly in awe of this man

Getting approval for interfaces

Achieving a partnership with your bosses will make it far easier to gain concessions on conforming to the corporate framework.

The latitude that you are most likely to need in implementing the new approaches is freedom from having to know and justify the specific reasons for the latest isolated incident, to the nth level of detail, within hours of it having happened.

At one time, a manager of a thousand-person-strong organisation used to regularly get demands from his boss to explain individual system crashes in isolated but critical parts of their organisation. This happened typically twice a week, and took up a lot of his and his people's time in simply finding the information. How much better to be able to answer: "Yes, we are currently at an average of 1.8 of those a week. The trend is declining at 23% per month. The main reasons are illustrated on this graph and I have teams tackling the top three, which represents 72% of the issue."

Photograph: Courtesy Forster Photo

Unfortunately, if this response is counter-cultural, it may not be seen to be as constructive as it clearly is. It is therefore very important that the expectations of your bosses are managed from the outset. They need to believe that you are still in control when things don't happen in quite the same way as they used to previously.

Other examples of interfaces that you may need to agree concessions on, include:

- Lengthy departmental reports
- Old and out-of-date measures
- Involvement in corporate initiatives
- Existing procedures and standards
- Aspects of corporate policy.

who held a large part of his career, his future, and his security in his hands. He hoped it did not show.

Cyrus smiled easily, "Thank you Richard. It's nice to be here. How ya doin?"

"Fine," replied Richard, "as we hope to demonstrate! We felt it would be useful to give you a quick overview of what has been happening, as a context to the rest of your visit. Is that okay?"

"Shoot!" said Cyrus.

Richard indicated a chair at the table, and Cyrus took this as his cue. He pulled the chair out and sat down. Lucy followed suit. And Richard walked over to stand beside the montage on the far wall.

"What you see here," he began, "is the result of our efforts to plan our business goals into the operation of the Gloucester facility."

Richard glanced at the neatly arranged, professionally prepared sheets, and looked back at Cyrus. He expected him to be impressed by the amount of thought and preparation that had gone on. He did not look it. And when he spoke, he did not sound it either.

"Really?" he responded, a touch of sarcasm was evident in the tone. "Most places seem to achieve the same thing much more simply. You know the odd meeting, the odd set of written objectives. That sort of thing!"

His eyes held Richard's in a piercing stare. Richard was now on the back foot. He had expected a bit of breathing space to get into his stride. But clearly Cyrus was more direct and blunt than that. Lucy should have warned him.

Richard struggled to think how to respond to this. Clearly, Cyrus could not see the need for this level of thinking. That was what Richard needed to address first. He decided he had to take some risks, if he was to regain the initiative.

"Yes they do. Providing the goals aren't too onerous. You know the odd 5% here and there." He had deliberately taken a sideswipe at the Cylek common goal setting approach. He continued: "Or where you suck out the future health of the business to deliver more challenging targets. But where is the skill in delivering 5%, when your business is capable of delivering 50%? Where is the challenge in saving 2% of your costs, when

Agreeing success criteria

So, that is what you want of them. What are you offering in return?

Gaining a clear agreement with your bosses on how they will judge the success of your work is an important part of your contract with them.

One place to start is simply to ask them the question directly. For instance, what proportion of your ambitious performance targets do you need to achieve for them to consider the approach successful? Does it have to be all of them, bearing in mind that they are probably in excess of what was originally requested? Or does it have simply to be in excess of the original request?

This is a point where you might usefully reflect back upon your own objectives for this work[1], and consider how they might figure in the success criteria.

Make sure that whatever you agree with your bosses as the success criteria are explicit, and that they are reflected in your own job description and personal objectives.

1   See page 11.

Exploring success criteria

What expectations does your organisation have for you and your team to justify yourselves?

....
....
....
....
....
....
....
....

To what extent do these over-play or underplay the real concerns that the organisation should have?

....
....
....
....
....
....
....
....

What information really reflects whether you are in control of your responsibilities and achieving your potential?

....
....
....
....
....
....
....
....

you routinely waste 20%? Achieving 10% of your potential can almost be delivered by luck and goodwill. Achieving 100% of your potential, without compromising the future, requires careful thought and planning."

Cyrus had lost some of his aggression. Richard fancied that he was considering the points in a new light. But the cynicism was still there. "So what you're saying is that this will deliver me 50% improvement?"

Richard realised that this was where 'the rubber hit the road' with Cyrus. The Old Man was not impressed by theory. He took a flier. "Over the next two to three years, without any shadow of a doubt!" he replied. Cyrus sat back in his seat and eyed Richard carefully. Lucy looked at Richard wide-eyed in surprise. This was not in the script.

"So how does it work?" asked Cyrus.

Richard started with the Why-How chart, and how the objectives were set, and then moved on to explain the top-level QFD and some of the insights that had arisen from it. He then drew Cyrus's attention to the measures and targets.

"You will see that the targets we have set ourselves for the remainder of this year, while reasonably ambitious in 'normal' terms, are significantly below the 50% we aspire to."

Cyrus raised an eyebrow, indicating his wish for Richard to continue, and implying that he was watching carefully and critically. Lucy had been wondering, ever since Richard had made the 50% claim, how he was going to handle reconciling this bit.

"There is a good reason for that."

A second glance caught Cyrus and Lucy frozen in their previous facial expressions. Richard continued with hardly a pause. "Whatever targets we set ourselves have to be owned, and believed in, by both the management team and the organisation as a whole. At this point, many of them are still thinking from an incremental mindset, but working through this goal setting process has begun to change that. As an example of this we can look at the work done by the *'Design and develop products and processes'* process."

Richard indicated the outcomes of the work Lucy had been doing with Deborah, which had been stuck below the main QFD.

Integrating key corporate strategies

As the work in your organisation progresses, the rest of the business is not likely to remain standing still. Increasingly this means corporate initiatives of one sort or another:

- Business Process Re-engineering
- Focusing on the customer
- Balanced Scorecard
- Environmental Stewardship
- Business Excellence Model
- Investors in People, etc.

It is unlikely, unless you gained agreement at the outset, that you will simply be allowed to opt out of them. Yours may be the only valid case amongst 49 excuses, but it is not likely to be seen that way.

Unfortunately, corporate initiatives are often applied as blanket formulae, with little consideration for what individual organisations may already be doing. Resistance is often assumed to be laziness or complacency, and is not tolerated.

It is better then, to evaluate how the new initiative can be integrated into what you are already doing, and how what you are already doing can be integrated into the initiative.

Fortunately the systematic approach to management accommodates virtually every reasonable initiative known to management. Because it is comprehensive and focuses on the responsibilities of effective management, other initiatives often either fit within it, or emphasise one of the elements of it (see right).

In these cases it is relatively easy to use what is proposed to augment your own

How popular initiatives fit with the systematic model (also see Appendix 6)

Initiative	Element
Business Process Re-engineering	Process
Focusing on the customer	Purpose
Balanced Scorecard	Predict
Environmental Stewardship	Purpose
Business Excellence Model	All aspects
Investors in People	People

"You can see that Deborah Lewis has already got her team thinking of more radical objectives, for instance 30% reduction in design to market time. I am confident that our performance this year will actually exceed these performance targets, and build their understanding, and their confidence, to pursue even more radical targets next year. You will get your 50%, but I have to take my team with me in order to deliver it. And that is why it's a two to three year goal."

Cyrus did not look fully convinced, but he appeared to be giving Richard the benefit of the doubt. Lucy looked impressed with Richard's quick footwork. So much so, that she had become convinced that 50% was not only possible, it was the only way to go. If you could not design a business to perform 50% better, you were clearly not seriously trying.

Cyrus spent the next ten minutes probing the detail of the diagram with Richard, and with each answer, he became more and more comfortable. Finally came the question Richard had been expecting from the outset.

"So where does all this fit into the objectives you agreed in your budgeting process in December?"

Richard reached into his file. He pulled out the original fax he had received last Christmas. It had always looked a little jaded - the standard jagged font, and the typical black lines from a poor signal - but the intervening months had been less than kind to it, and it now looked positively scruffy. He stuck the fax up beside the rows of neatly typed objectives for effect.

"We believe," Richard explained, "that the objectives you set us for this year, will not only be fully honoured by pursuing the plans shown here, but that the additional thought we have put into them will ensure that they are guaranteed, and exceeded, and that the excess performance will reveal itself in customer benefits, market benefits, and cost benefits."

A wry smile played on Cyrus's lips. The showmanship had not been lost on him, as he compared the soiled fax he had sent four months previously with the inexorable logic of the QFD process. He knew that his goal setting process had been anything but rigorous. It had taken two hours as part of a larger meeting, and had been based solely on what the market and the money markets were likely to expect.

On the other hand, he felt that Richard had gone to the other extreme. But time would tell, and he would give it enough slack to enable him to make that judgement more objectively. He had one more card to play.

approach, or to demonstrate conformity with what you are already doing.

The biggest danger arises when the new initiative represents a new objective on your QFD, as for instance environmental stewardship might.

Where the initiative represents a clear change in operational goals or practice, this needs to be carefully evaluated against the QFD, to see how it fits into the current strategy. The conclusions and implications from this evaluation then need to be reflected back to corporate management.

The Managing Director of an operating arm of one huge multinational successfully controlled all corporate proposals for a two-year period in this way. He would demonstrate a clear grasp of the implications, through using the QFD, and then schedule the intent for the next rewrite of the QFD.

Introducing the approach to other parts of the business

Because of the visible success of this approach, it is easy to get swamped with requests to help introduce it to other parts of the business. In the case of one organisation, they almost came to resemble a consultancy more than a manufacturing concern.

If your response to these requests is not managed very carefully, the danger may be that your own organisation will take its eye off the ball.

Encouraging your staff to get involved in other implementations can be a tremendous boost to them. It can help to recognise and reward their efforts, and raise their profile in the business as a whole.

He turned to Lucy. "This is a bit off of your normal track." The implied question hung in the air.

"Yes, well, I'm not the architect of this one. I wish I had been. But to misquote Oscar Wilde, I'm sure I will be next time!" Cyrus smiled at her, slightly paternalistically, and she continued: "Seriously Cyrus, it's a terrific process, and it has so much potential for us, for Cylek as a whole. I've never seen anything like it before, but I know it will work, I've already seen it doing so. I want to help Richard prove it here, and then I want to put it into the rest of Cylek. Once the others have seen what it can do, I will be so much in demand I'll have to double my fee rates."

Cyrus laughed. "If it does all you say it will, I'll double them for you! But it surely can't be all roses. What isn't going so well at the moment? Where are your problems?"

Cyrus caught the pause, the quick exchange of glances between Richard and Lucy. The pause lengthened, and he knew they were going to be honest. They were clearly thinking through how to phrase it.

Lucy had decided to stay quiet. It was up to Richard as to what he would say. How open he would be.

After what seemed a long time, Richard looked back up at Cyrus. "Well, this example of how the QFD deploys down into processes." He pointed at Deborah's outputs. "It has to be said that this is by far the best example. Others are working hard to catch up, but some just don't seem to be bought into it at all."

Richard paused again, wondering how obvious his own failings in this area were to others. "Pushing this approach is bringing me into conflict with some of my staff. I believe they don't want the transparency that the process brings. They don't want the clarity of issues and the real measures of performance that may invoke additional responsibilities on them. I am concerned that, at least subconsciously, they hide their weaknesses, and don't want to be exposed!"

Cyrus seemed to look right through Richard and merely sounded "Hmmm."

Richard replayed the last line in his mind "… they hide their weaknesses…" and felt curiously exposed to Cyrus gaze, almost like Cyrus was saying "… and you don't?" Richard found he had started to shuffle

However, the requests are likely to come in while you are still building on your early success, consolidating the approach, and taking on even more ambitious goals. It is vitally important that you balance the needs of the larger business, and the recognition of your people, with the needs of your own organisation.

One way of doing this is to have a set budget of time for your staff to do this work, and to focus your support on those parts of the business that are most integrated with your own. In this way you maximise your chances of the approach having a dramatic, growing, and lasting impact on the business as a whole.

There is one further quality check you should apply before offering support. Only do it for those parts of the business that would do it even without your help. Their leader will need that sort of determination if they are to stand any real chance of being successful.

Gaining concessions and support

Perhaps the most disabling event facing a team using QFD to transform their business, is a budget cut - whether that is represented in terms of a reduction in finance, or a recruitment freeze, or a block on planned capital expenditure. It is vitally important to the achievement of your goals that you do all that you can to protect your team from these risks. Your work will ultimately generate major improvements in efficiency, which can be realised through cost savings if required, but only if you can invest the resources to do it properly.

In seeking support for any further funding or investment that your plans need, ensure that the implications of cutting that investment are fully understood. Your financial backers will be more used to traditional management approaches, where

slightly. He caught himself, braced himself, and moved quickly on. "But I recognise that I will need to address this!"

Cyrus stood up abruptly and said "Thank you for that. I like the way your thinking is going, but I want to see some more for myself. I have to leave at eleven, perhaps we could get back together at a quarter of eleven, once I've had a chance to look around and speak to some people."

Richard nodded and Cyrus continued: "Can you direct me to Daniel Matthews' office? I promised to drop in on him while I was here."

Richard's heart sank. But, hopefully without it showing, he said to Cyrus: "I'll walk you over there."

"It's no problem," said Cyrus, "I don't want to keep you." Clearly Cyrus did not want a chaperone. His tone said it all.

"It's okay," said Richard. "I've got to go back to my office. I can drop you off there on the way."

At ten forty-five exactly, Cyrus walked into Richard's office. Richard looked up abruptly from what he was doing.

"I won't beat around the bush, Richard," Cyrus started. "I have strong misgivings over what you are doing here, as it appears do a number of your staff. Some are concerned that it will cause the company to take its eye off serving customers. Others feel it is onerous and bureaucratic. I am concerned that you may get so wrapped up in the theory that you drop the ball in practice. But..."

He had run through his speech without taking breath, but here he paused, and allowed his features to soften. "I appointed you to this position because you're young and you have different ideas. I feel I need to give you a chance to prove yourself. But I have to admit to being concerned about the possible downsides." Here he held his hands in a gesture of supplication. "I can only give you a limited window to deliver in. Cylek UK is currently under-performing. We missed budget last year, and the last four months' figures show a steady decline. I expect you to meet the performance targets agreed in December for this current financial year, and to have made significant and sustained progress towards this within the next three months. Within that timescale you have a free hand to make your approach work. We will continue to fund Lucy's support for your

the level of investment of management time in thinking out the future is far less, and where the major management focus is on handling the unexpected. Your enterprise is different, and needs to be treated so. Involving your bosses in understanding what you are doing may help you to establish this in their minds, and to stack the deck in your favour.

Handling concerns and criticism

Unless you are extremely fortunate, unforeseen issues will arise, and things won't go exactly according to plan. Some of these things will become visible to your bosses, either in your own reporting, or in the responses of customer organisations.

How you handle those concerns will be a key factor in your continued autonomy.

It is politically naive to assume that claiming that the problems are being addressed at the systems level will deflect all criticism. People trust and respect people who are like them, who talk their language. Accordingly, if your bosses are detail freaks, demonstrating that your knowledge is ahead of theirs will do much to establish your credibility. And then moving to the systemic solution will do much to convince them of your values.

Managing upwards is as much a game of psychology as it is of strategy.

Reporting progress

Having gained approval, support and even commitment for what you are doing, it is now important to maintain it.

Effective selling is not a one-off activity, but an ongoing process of relationship and confidence building. This is true whether the sale is being made outside the organisation for money, or inside the organisation for support.

Criticism has few terrors for a man with a great purpose.

Benjamin Disraeli
English Prime Minister

work for those three months, but we expect results. I'm sure I don't need to clarify the alternatives for you."

The last words were spoken firmly, but not unkindly. Richard nodded.

"Apart from that, I have to admit to being excited by what you are attempting here! I want to see you succeed! Make it work Richard, for both our sakes!" With that Cyrus turned on his heel and was gone.

Richard looked down at the papers on his desk, and wondered what to do next. He had not expected the visit to go like this. Lucy and he had hoped for so much more from it. They had not allowed for failure. Their mistake. He became aware of someone watching him from the door, and he looked up to meet Lucy's empathetic gaze.

"He's always been one for the grand exit," she said. "Are you okay?"

Richard just looked at her and wrinkled his nose slightly, a sort of facial shrug, and sat down in his chair. Lucy walked further into the room, looking more intently at him, as if trying to assess the damage.

"Were you seriously expecting more?" she asked him.

He shrugged again. "Well, more time would have been nice!" he suggested.

Mirth was clear in Lucy's voice. "Richard, you're from R&D, and from the UK. Cyrus is from Sales, and from the States! You have different concepts of time! You got about as much from him as you were going to get! Seriously!" Richard shrugged again.

"So, what else did you secure from him?" she asked.

Richard looked up quizzically. "What do you mean?"

"Well," she continued, "if you've got your key people meeting a three month timetable on this, there is no way you can conform to the budgeting timescales or the Oroto project, without extra resources. Did you get concessions on those?" Richard went quiet, and Lucy closed her eyes momentarily as she thought of a more positive constructive response than the one that had just occurred to her.

After a few moments of silence she continued: "Okay, we'll deliver performance improvements in three months that exceed his expectations, but that will mean we need to clearly rethink our plan for this, and the implications for people's time. That will tell us exactly what the con-

A key means of building that relationship and confidence over time, is the reporting process you use to keep your bosses appraised of the situation and your progress.

The report provides a real opportunity for you to demonstrate that you know what is needed, and that you are doing everything to deliver it. Accordingly, the report should present the following.

- A summary of progress against the factors that your bosses see as important. There will be deficiencies on occasion, but if they hear it from you first, it will demonstrate that you are 'on the ball'.

- A clear and demonstrable grasp of the reasons behind any failures or short-falls, and foresight that potential risks are being considered and managed in the most appropriate way.

- Evidence that risks and issues are being addressed according to a clear schedule; and what your bosses can expect to see as a result, and when.

The key goal in your report is that your bosses should be left in no doubt that you understand, and that you are managing the situation better than they would themselves.

cessions we need are, and we can justify them against the improved levels of performance we are proposing. Okay?"

Richard remained quiet. Still thinking. So Lucy concluded: "Okay, I'll get on with the plan" and lifted herself out of her seat. The abrupt movement seemed to bring Richard together to a point of resolve.

He looked up, his expression firmer. "Yes, that's a good idea. If you can draft it this afternoon, perhaps we can review it this evening?"

Lucy was a bit taken aback by the sudden change. She smiled briefly, said: "Fine!" and left.

Driving a consistent approach

If, as a result of working through the preceding chapters, the process management team is now clear on what it needs to do, is there any need to address 'how' they do it?

The answer to this question is a resounding "Yes!" and for a number of reasons.

- A rigorous approach is required to ensure that the results are delivered.

- A systematic approach is required to ensure that the results are sustained.

- A consistent approach is required to facilitate communication and learning.

- A common approach is required to enable the above to be achieved economically.

In practice, the management approach adopted by the process teams in driving and developing the performance of their processes has proven the major determinant in the ultimate success of QFD in transforming organisational performance.

Where managers have failed to change their approach to management, progress has not been delivered. But where managers have been required to adopt the systematic principles outlined in Chapters 4 and 5, progress has been inevitable.

It is therefore incumbent on the leader to guide, support, encourage, and drive their people to adopt an effective approach to managing their process performance.

But Chapters 4 and 5 outline a general concept, not a tangible system. For the concepts to be of use to working managers, they must be interpreted in a practical system. They must use one common, simple and practical system; which managers can adopt and operate together,

The prime occupational hazard of the manager is superficiality.

Henry Mintzberg
McGill University School of Management
in The Nature of Managerial Work
(Harper & Row, 1973).

Chapter 14

The plan Lucy had developed was very tight.

Delivering clear performance improvement in three months required that all of Richard's team devote significant chunks of their time to implementing the new management approach and making it work.

Deborah had actually done most of the work for her process already, but the time she had consumed in doing so was quite daunting. Lucy had estimated that Deborah had put in at least 80 hours personally, and that her team had probably spent 600 man hours between them, in attending workshops and undertaking their actions. Richard knew that persuading some of his other managers to invest similar amounts of time was going to be a full-time job for him. And it was time he did not have.

But he also knew that without investing the time he would not meet his targets, and that would mean he was out of a job. These next three months were all important. He would have to work every waking hour to survive. Surely Laura would understand.

But Laura was determined not to understand. She did not believe it would only be for three months. She felt that she and Nicholas had sacrificed enough of Richard. She felt that the job had already taken an unfair proportion of Richard's time, and now, greedily, it was demanding what little she had left of it. Richard found himself vacantly staring at the chair she hurriedly vacated before slamming the lounge door behind her.

Richard felt sick. It was all so unfair! He was only doing this for the family. Yes, sure, he got a kick out of being successful in his career, but really it was so that Laura and Nicholas could have the lifestyle they deserved; so that they had some security in their lives. Laura would understand eventually. Until then the die was cast. Richard would focus all his energies on the job, and then Laura would see that, three months later, he would be as good as his word.

Richard called a meeting of his management team to debrief them on Cyrus's visit. He explained the three-month deadline and presented Lucy's plan. There was an audible intake of breath when the plan appeared on the screen, and this developed into muted murmurs when

without confusion; and which the leader can consistently require of all his or her direct reports.

Expectations of process management

So how should we interpret the principles of Chapters 4 and 5 into a practical effective system at the process level? What should we expect from our process owners in pursuing the aspirations agreed in the QFD?

We should expect that:

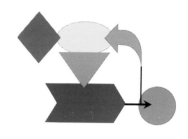

How well do you do these things currently?

 the process is operated according to its design, and procedures are followed accurately

 performance of the process is measured, particularly with regard to customer service and satisfaction

 performance is reflected against the agreed targets at all levels of detail to evaluate progress against forecast

 unexpected gaps and issues are identified and prioritised, responsibility for addressing problems is assigned, and the team learns from its performance

 problems are tackled through a defined discipline, and changes are made to plans and projects as appropriate

 processes are modified and standardised to ensure consistent performance improvement.

he explained that they would each need to invest an average of about 700 man hours over the next two months.

The murmurs grew, and culminated in an explosion of words from Abs. "This is insane! Where do we find that sort of time? Production will fall over!"

Richard countered quietly: "Abs! It's two-and-a-half people for two months. It is not that bad!" Abs pursed his lips and shook his head.

Peter joined in the fray. "Richard, that is three man years of effort across our eight processes. It is the equivalent of 4% on our manpower costs over two months. We can never justify nor sustain that!"

Richard countered again: "But, over the year, it is less that 1%, against a 10% performance improvement. That would meet anyone's criteria for project payback!"

"But that assumes this hare-brained scheme is actually going to work!" Daniel expostulated. "Full house," thought Richard, who had been wondering when Daniel would see fit to enter the fray.

"Okay! Here are the facts of life: I have been charged with delivering this. I am charging you with delivering this plan. I want to know how each and everyone of you intends to meet these milestones, and your requirement for additional support to enable you to do so. This is a reasonable request of people at your level of seniority. I shall expect your plans on my desk by close of play on Friday, and I will be making appointments to meet each one of you personally next week, to discuss through the implications. Full stop. End of meeting."

There was silence. And then gradually, under Richard's gaze, people closed their files and trooped out of the door. Richard realised he had overdone it when even allies like Susan, Andrew and Deborah avoided looking at him, and left as sullenly as the rest.

When everyone else had left, Lucy said: "Richard, that was a bit harsh. You don't have to fight them all you know. Most of them are on your side."

"Oh yes!" he snapped back. "And that's how it looked to you did it?" His tone was sarcastic.

Lucy said quietly: "Yes, it did! But you did not give them a chance to say so."

Process management is the practical engine that harnesses the potential of the business to the clear aspirations of the goal-setting process. The six principles that underpin effective process management are reflected in the diagrams on the preceding page.

- Ensure a clear understanding of 'purpose'
- Establish a winning 'philosophy'
- Harness the best from your 'people'
- Develop through the 'process'
- Seek the ability to 'predict'
- Continuously strive to 'perfect'.

In this chapter we explore in more detail what these principles mean in practice.

Ensure a clear understanding of 'purpose'

It is very easy for people to get wrapped up in the task they are doing, particularly where the task is technically challenging, and this can cause them to lose sight of the customer and the real purpose for their work. In extreme cases the technical challenge can become the primary reason for their efforts, and the customer can simply become somebody who confuses the issue and distracts them from it. When this happens, relationships break down and the work quickly becomes irrelevant.

It is therefore vital that the focus on customers is maintained as consistently as the technical interest. To achieve this requires an ongoing programme of awareness, customer contact and recognition.

However there is a real danger that such a programme may become bureaucratic, mechanical and even trivial: a matter of going through the motions without having any real effect. For this reason it is important that the programme is anchored in

Anticipated evidence of 'purpose':

- Data from having explored and understood the current situation

- Clearly defined strategies for building or maintaining customer focus

- A milestone plan for how the strategies are to be delivered

- Minutes of meetings; data on progress; plans on display etc. reflecting that the strategies are in active use

- 'Customer familiarisation' and other training sessions/material

- Involvement of process staff in customer activities

- Customer visits and surveys (or interviews)

- Workshops on how to better support process customers

- Prominent visual evidence of customer satisfaction targets, trended performance, and future actions for improvement.

Richard was just about to argue, when he realised that the only people who had spoken were Abs, Peter and Daniel, and that it was Daniel who had done just enough to push him over the edge. A well-timed, emotive blow to his area of weakness: The unproven nature of QFD. He closed his eyes, silently cursing himself. He had played right into Daniel's hands like the marionette he was.

Lucy could see Richard's thinking loosen, by the shift in the tension of his body, so she continued: "May I make a suggestion?" Richard looked up into compassionate blue eyes; he felt both stupid and safe. He nodded dumbly.

"Don't wait until next week. Go round your allies now. Let them know you appreciate them. Do it quickly, before one of them does something drastic."

There was something in Lucy's tone that gave Richard the impression that she knew something she was not letting on. He looked at her enquiringly.

She knew what he was asking, but she just said: "Well some of them have had a rough ride over the last year or so. They are very good people. Very 'marketable' people. But they've hung around. And they have supported you in this. If they feel that you don't appreciate that, well, they might just have a better offer developing!"

Richard nodded. He had got the message. "I'll start this afternoon," he said.

A bit of humble pie went a long way with most of his team, but it took time out of his day. Time from other things. Time he had to make up in the evening.

The office around him was deserted. He had just finished signing off the paperwork for the new security procedures. He looked up at the clock on his wall, ten to nine, and his heart fell as he thought of going home. When Laura did not ignore him, it was because she wanted to have a go at him. It was a choice between silences or rows, and arriving home at this time of night would probably secure him both.

He rose heavily from his chair, and slid a few reports into his briefcase. He closed it, and then heading for the door, he stopped, shook his head

reality through effective measures of customer satisfaction, with prominent displays of current performance to reinforce its importance to your organisation.

Establishing ambitious targets for the measure will then drive your staff to seek deeper and more creative relationships with your customers.

 ## Establish a winning 'philosophy'

Appropriate targets can play a large part in driving the behaviours of your staff, but it is rarely enough to write out the objectives from the top-level QFD, hold a workshop, and stick the results on the wall or in a memo.

For objectives to be powerful enough to direct the full energy of the organisation in a consistent and shared direction they have to become part of the day-to-day fabric of the organisation. They should be explicitly and regularly repeated in explanations, rationales and general routine. In this way, the *why we do things* becomes clear, consistent and explicit.

But words are rarely enough in themselves - they are drowned out by the actions people see around them. If person 'A' (who 'toes the line') is not recognised while person 'B' (who doesn't) gets a promotion - then toeing the line becomes clearly not the 'sensible' thing to do.

The manager needs to understand exactly what behaviours are seen to be valued within his or her organisation, and how. The manager must then determine how these differ from the behaviours needed to support the objectives, and adjust the value set (who gets rewarded and why) to support this.

Anticipated evidence of 'philosophy':

- Explicit precise definition of the process objectives

- Process objectives demonstrably linked to the company objectives

- Prominent displays of objectives and why they are important

- Up-to-date displays of progress (measures) against objectives

- Personal and team objectives clearly linked to the department objectives

- Regular progress reviews against the objectives

- Proposals, new initiatives and all management communication reference the objectives

- Objectives are a major explicit part of the appraisal process.

and returned his briefcase to the side of his desk. Who was he kidding? How was he going to do any more work? He was totally bushed.

He headed down the stairs and out into the evening chill of the car park. He wondered exactly what his reception at home would hold for him tonight. Nicholas would clearly be in bed. His best hope was that Laura would be too! Either asleep or feigning it!

But when he got home, the house was not only in darkness, it was empty. Panic flooded through Richard. He felt like someone had pulled a plug on his insides. He felt cold. He felt scared. He felt angry.

He rushed from room to room, but no-one was there. Nicholas's bed was not slept in. He rushed into his own room and threw open the closet doors, fully expecting to see Laura's clothes missing. They appeared to all be there. But then again, she would not have taken them all.

Where had she gone? Where had she taken his son? To her parents? He would telephone them now!

He rushed to the telephone, and snatched up the receiver. And his eyes fell on the note beside it. It was to him. It was Laura's writing.

Coldness gripped him tighter. He looked at the note unseeingly. He had imagined this happening. If he was honest, he may even have wanted it on occasion. But the harsh reality was worse than anything he had considered. He forced himself to look at the note. To read it.

"Richard, Nicholas sick with a fever. Have gone to Casualty. Come as soon as you get in. If, of course, you can spare the time. Laura". The note was terse, but at least they had not left him.

Relief rushed in, and he realised how silly he had been. Of course, they could have been anywhere. Next door, or at a friends perhaps. He had built up demons in his mind. He had been victim to his own paranoia. He re-read the note, and the relief was replaced with concern.

His son was in hospital!

He rushed back out of the front door, and leapt back into his car and started the engine. As he moved off, he realised he did not know where the hospital was. Still, if he headed for the town centre he could always ask directions from there.

Harness the best from your 'people'

Only part of the value set is reflected in the formal reward system. The vast majority of it is reflected in the 'development' people receive, both at your hands, and at the hands of their colleagues. Sadly, when managers think of development for their people, their minds often tend toward formal training courses.

But in practice, most of a person's development arises through:

- being exposed to a series of challenges and new situations/roles
- receiving advice and support on the job (e.g. coaching)
- adopting strategies and frameworks to fulfil the role effectively
- learning from the result by observation and feedback.

This rarely happens most effectively and efficiently by accident. Instead, the manager needs to actively plan these opportunities and experiences for his or her people, matching their development to the improvement opportunities that are likely to arise in their department.

In this way the manager can achieve a balanced strategy: ensuring that the problems and issues that arise are used in the optimum way to develop both departmental performance, and personnel competence.

Develop through the 'process'

Of course, development becomes a lot easier to plan when the processes people need to be developed in are clearly understood. The key to this understanding is process mapping.

Within most objective professions, schematics are used whenever change is

Anticipated evidence of 'people':

- Active and agreed development plans for each person in the process

- Active use of appraisal system to guide people's development

- Measures of progress in fulfilling agreed development plans

- Analysis of competence growth in process staff

- Effective teamwork training programme

- Defined programme of personal and team coaching

- Records of coaching activity for each subordinate and team.

Things were not totally straightforward, and when he eventually walked into Casualty it was almost ten o'clock. He saw Laura by herself in the far corner of the waiting room, and rushed towards her. He expected her to be pleased to see him, but the cold glare he received stopped him in his tracks.

"Where have you been? Four hours we've been waiting here! He's been sick twice, and they still haven't seen him." At this she gestured to a play area on her left, and Richard glanced round to see his son, pale and listless, distractedly fiddling with a yellow wooden block.

"I'm sorry," he said turning back to her. Her look in return carried only hostility. Was she blaming him for this? Were hospital waiting times his fault? He turned away and went over to sit on the floor by Nicholas. When he looked back over at Laura, she was determinedly looking away.

The doctor, when they eventually saw her, three-quarters of an hour later, was apologetic and deeply tired. She explained that they had been dealing with a serious smash on the M5. She was sorry for the delay. Richard could see that she had been doing her best, her young face was drawn and her hair was all over the place.

He said: "That's okay, we understand." This drew a snort of derision from Laura.

The doctor turned to Nicholas, and forced a more sing-song tone in her voice. "Hello little man. My name is Doctor Jane, and we're going to see what we can do to make you better. Where does it hurt?"

Nicholas did not reply, and when Laura left a long silence, Richard felt he had to step in. "He's been vomiting," he said.

Laura snapped around. "Oh yes, and you'd know, would you?" she said angrily.

Richard looked at her pleadingly. "For crying out loud Laura, you explain things then!"

"I was just about to," she said. And then turning to the doctor: "He's running a temperature of 103 and isn't keeping anything down. He's even bringing up water. And there's traces of blood in it!"

The doctor appeared to take the parental spat in her stride. Perhaps she was used to them, saw them all the time. She simply picked Nicholas up, and said: "Would you come this way?"

considered or problems are to be explored, because they help people to think through the implications and consequences. This is especially true when such thinking is being undertaken by a group, because the schematic is especially helpful in explaining one person's reasoning to another.

Business lends itself to such schematics. The processes by which business is undertaken can be mapped in terms of flow diagrams, and this has proven invaluable to many organisations.

Process maps are the main vehicles for ensuring that:

- people follow the proven and optimum path

- there is a basis for redefining the ideal

- deviations can be identified and the consequences of change, evaluated

- performance issues can be tracked back to operational defects

- improvements are maintained over time.

 Seek the ability to 'predict'

Measurement is probably the single most potent factor in ensuring business improvement.

The mere act of feeding someone with information on the performance of their work makes them responsible for that performance - and companies have demonstrated this time and time again whenever they have established clear performance measures: "What gets measured, gets done".

However, for sustained improvement, the discipline of measures needs to be supported by the discipline of problem-solving. Rigorous analysis of the issues that preclude us from our target perform-

Anticipated evidence of 'process':

- Clearly defined interfaces for the process (see Chapter 10)

- Overall schematic of the process (process diagram), showing how its sub-processes link together

- Process maps readily accessible and used to guide people in the process

- Records of official projects to improve the process, and updates to the map

- Minutes of process management meetings, to review its operation.

Anticipated evidence of 'predict':

- Measures of performance of the process: rate of output; timeliness; quality; customer satisfaction; unit cost

- Meetings to identify trend and performance issues, analyse causes and agree actions

- Graphs of performance against target, on display

- Use of problem-solving tools such as Pareto, etc. to analyse and solve performance issues

- Documented use of problem-solving processes.

After some time of checks and questions, they said they needed to keep Nicholas in for observation, but not to worry, it was simply routine. She was sorry that they had no facilities left for Laura and Richard to stay with him, but it would be better for all concerned if they went home and got a good night's rest and came back in the morning, since Nicholas was sedated anyway.

Richard drove most of the way home in silence, but as they turned into their road, Laura finally exploded:

"What was that all about? How would you know what the matter with him was? You're never here to know! We're outsiders! We're no longer part of your world, part of your damn agenda! Don't you dare, ever dare, presume to answer for me ever again! You just don't know!"

Richard was caught off guard by the tirade. He had been nursing a grudge all the way home too. He vested it in self-defence.

"Look, you may have problems with me, but don't bring others into it! You ignored the doctor's question. That poor young woman had clearly had a really tough time. The last thing she needed was a sullen cow playing: 'You're the doctor, you figure it out!'."

He did not see it coming until it was almost too late. He flinched to the right, as the back of Laura's right-hand crashed into the side of his mouth, cracking his lips across his teeth. He braked hard, held up his left hand, and raised his left leg to ward off further blows. The car stalled in the middle of the road. And Laura, poised to strike again, turned, stepped out of the car, and stormed off towards their front door.

Richard closed his eyes, and mentally counted, but his mind was anywhere but on the numbers.

He could taste the blood in his mouth. He could feel his lip already beginning to swell.

Finally, he undid his seatbelt, reached over and closed Laura's door, restarted the car and drove up into their drive.

Laura had disappeared inside the house, and when he put his key in the lock he found it would not work. She had put it on the latch. He was locked out.

ance should be followed up by successful solutions, and predictable results that ensure we can be confident our performance will fulfil our commitments.

Continuously strive to 'perfect'

The primary concept and purpose of systematic management, is to free management thinking from the routines and responses that trap it in the bottom box. But 'the price of freedom is eternal vigilance'.

The challenge is to continuously identify areas where we are beginning to become prisoners of our own thinking, and also new opportunities to think differently.

There is plenty of material to help in this process - in books, papers, seminars, journals, other companies, customers, suppliers, the ideas of colleagues, study groups, think-tanks, consortia, etc.

It is only by remaining alive and awake to the constant stream of opportunities these materials provide that we will prevent our current solutions to *'Systematic Management'* from becoming future issues that systematic management will need to solve.

How can the role of the process manager be reinforced?

The battle to establish management in its proper role is long and arduous, but is unavoidable if your organisation is to fully reach its potential.

But only part of the battle can be won logically. The main fighting is actually done at a subconscious level through:

- reinforcing the management role through your questions
- modelling the management role through your approach

Anticipated evidence of 'perfect':

- Persistent pursuit of relentlessly increasing performance targets

- Workshops, in which the role of the department is reassessed, and clear performance targets are defined

- Prioritisation of improvement areas

- Regular meetings to monitor progress and address issues

- Annual in-depth review of progress

- Comprehensive audit of the current situation in the department.

He looked at his watch. It was almost two in the morning. He really could do without this. He rang the doorbell, and waited. He could hear movement in the house. He tried again. And again. Then he bent down and spoke through the letter box.

"Come on Laura, let me in." There was no reply.

"Laura, please." Still no reply.

"Laura, come on, let's not be stupid about this!"

He heard movement in the house, and Laura was on the other side of the door. She brought her hand down hard on the letter-box flap, forcing it shut and almost trapping his thumbs. Richard stood up.

"Laura, be reasonable."

This time she answered. It was half a sob. "Sod off! Go and take your precious time, and give it to that bloody doctor. You clearly prefer her to me. Go and see if she'll have you!"

Richard was shocked. That was so unfair. How could she say that? What had he done? He had not even glanced at the doctor.

Richard stepped back a few paces, and looked up at the front of the house. He wasn't really sure why. Perhaps it was that he sensed people were beginning to look at him through their darkened windows and he didn't want to create a floorshow for them. Perhaps he was trying to find another way in. He stood trying to look nonchalant for a few more moments while he weighed up his options.

He didn't feel that Laura in her current state of mind was likely to relent, and he couldn't face the looks of his neighbours if he spent much more time trying to argue his way in.

With a brief shake of his head, Richard gave up, turned around and got back into the car. He paused for a moment and then started the engine and drove off.

Richard spent what remained of the night at the Cavendish. He did not know why he picked that hotel, it was well out of the range he would normally be prepared to pay for a room. Perhaps it was because he was feeling so sore, and felt that being near Lucy might help. Perhaps. Perhaps it was something else. He was not sure any more. He felt under

- developing the appropriate management skills through training and coaching

- rewarding and recognising the correct management behaviours

- tackling incorrect management behaviours head on and ensuring that nobody profits from them

- ensuring the resources for managing systematically

- using meeting structures that reinforce the correct management approach

- using evaluation and appraisal models that assure the correct management approach.[1]

The importance of establishing a systematic process to ensure that the goals of the QFD are delivered, and delivered sustainably, cannot be overemphasised. Without the disciplines reflected in this chapter, the goals on your QFD will remain a pipe dream.

Unfortunately, most of the onus for ensuring that the QFD is pursued objectively and systematically rests with the leader, and this has major implications for his or her time.

In past implementations of QFD, time has proven to be a key factor in ensuring a successful result. Investing time in the right things for the right reasons is crucial to making QFD work effectively for you, and for this reason the whole of the next section is devoted to helping you think this through.

Men don't plan to fail – they fail to plan.

William J. Siegel
VP, Printz-Biederman Manufacturing Co.
Sign on desk

---

1 A system for evaluating the adoption of systematic approaches in management can be found on the associated web-site (see Appendix 7).

Managing by Design

attack from all sides, and he felt that Lucy was the only friend he had to share it with.

He was close to despair.

Summary

Your leadership of the change will ultimately prove to be the single biggest factor in its success. In this section we have explored what this means in practical terms.

The time, attention and quality of thought that you invest in:

- Establishing clear expectations of your management team, and addressing any shortfalls of behaviour against that

- Reconciling the commitments made within the organisation, with the goals it is intending to achieve

- Ensuring that you gain the support and protection you need from those to whom you, and your organisation, report

- Establishing an effective and consistent approach to delivering the performance targets that have been agreed,

will either guarantee the results you need, or will allow your implementation to founder on conflict, confusion and ignorance.

What changes could you make in your own personal approach to ensure the success you need?

....

....

....

....

....

....

....

....

Relevant materials available on the web-site to support discussion and application of the ideas in this section

Presentation materials in MS PowerPoint™ format:

Developing process proposals

Template for 'managing upwards'

Process management.

Basic guidelines in Adobe Acrobat™ format:

Time management

Self assessment vs. systematic approach.

Workshop exercises in MS PowerPoint™ format:

Process proposal reconciliation.

Basic templates in MS Word™ format:

Session plan for process-management meetings.

Basic tools in MS Excel™ format:

Quadrant chart template.

Copies of key diagrams in MS PowerPoint™ format.

Section D

Developing a greater personal effectiveness

Philosophers are adults who persist in asking childish questions.

Isaiah Berlin

DEVELOPING A GREATER PERSONAL EFFECTIVENESS

The work described in the earlier chapters will greatly accelerate and amplify your efforts. You will find your organisation becoming more exciting and effective, and your people taking more responsibility for making it so.

But success brings imbalance, and new tensions. The more powerful the tool, the more skilled you need to be at using it, and the more careful you need to be in putting it to one side, or in encouraging others to use it. Success in implementing QFD will have massive implications on you personally.

This section is aimed at helping you to think through those implications, and how you will:

- maintain a balance between your professional life and your personal life

- ensure that what you are doing does not consume you (and your identity)

- align what you are achieving with your personal vision and values

- reconsider and adapt your role such that your people can best grow into their new responsibilities

- ensure that your diary matches up with what you need to be doing

- face up to the need for hard decisions, when they are the only practical solution.

These points are further expanded in Chapters 15 to 20.

"You're chipper tonight, Colin. Won the lottery or something?"

The whistling and the floor polisher stopped simultaneously as Colin looked back to see who had spoken.

"Ah, good evenin' Mister Matthews, an' you ain't so down in the mouth yersel'."

"Every cloud has a silver lining Colin," Daniel replied a trifle smugly. "Speaking of which, I understand you're retiring soon."

Colin wasn't too sure how to take this final comment, given the context, but he decided to play it straight. "Pretty soon, just a month ta go." And then he spotted an opportunity for mischief, "Always providin' you can keep us in business tha' long!"

Daniel ignored the slight note of sarcasm in the reply. "You won't know what to do with yourself when you leave here!" he challenged.

"Ha!" replied Colin in indignation. "Tha's what you think. Mary an' me 've bin preparin' for this for the last ten-year. In fact the 'ull is gettin' delivered next week an' Mary's already made a start on the sails."

Daniel gave him a sceptical look.

"True as I'm standin' 'ere Mr. Matthews. Life's gotta be more than fix this, fix 'at, an' 'eres yer paycheque. In fact if I weren't so 'appy at 'ome I don't reckon I'd be 'alf as good at my job 'ere. Mary keeps me straight an' 'elps me to see things for what they are!"

Daniel smiled, then he made his excuses, and bid Colin good night. And as he walked down the corridor he reflected, a trifle ruefully, on Colin's last few comments.

Balancing work and home

A key intention of promoting the techniques explained in this book, is that they will free up your time so that you may achieve a better balance between home and the office. But there is a very real danger that the increased clarity, and the exposure of issues will, if anything, drive people to spend even more time at work.

Man is essentially teleological; that is he or she tends to automatically gravitate towards what he or she thinks about most, and most clearly. The principle is used a lot in 'success' literature, where people are called to visualise a clear and detailed picture of what they want to happen. The concept is that we attune ourselves to be more receptive and responsive to habits and opportunities that are in line with that vision.

In clarifying goals for your organisation; in breaking them down to motivate and align your people; in exposing issues so that they can be addressed effectively; the intention is to make the job of management easier and more effective. As a result you will free people to achieve what they really want, and to reduce the burden of entrenched meetings and last minute panics.

The irony is, that the very things that make the job easier and quicker (so that it occupies less of your time) also make you want to spend more of your time doing it.

That might sound bizarre, and you might be inclined to reject it out of hand. But consider: most of us want to achieve; we want to be needed; we want the praise and admiration of others; we want to win!

To some extent, even a confused picture of business can supply most of these needs. But if, as we intend, the changes you make:

I have never yet heard of anyone on their deathbed, saying that they wished they'd spent more time in the office.

Rob Parsons
Author of 'The sixty minute marriage'

The Achiever is the only person who is truly alive.

George Allen
American Pro Football Coach

Chapter 15

The alarm went off at 6am.

Richard woke, feeling like death warmed up. An inner emptiness, a deep dark void, seemed to confuse and disorient him. But gradually the pieces of the night before fitted back into his reality.

He sat on the edge of the bed with his head in his hands. What a bloody mess. His son in hospital. His wife playing Mae West. His career about to end. And with nothing clear and resolved about any of it. He looked up at the ceiling and railed into the white emptiness: "Bloody hell! This is just so bloody unfair! How is anyone expected to cope with all of this?"

He paused briefly, as if half expecting an answer, and then hung his head. After a moment or two he rose, and simply got on with things. He did not know what else he could do.

The face that stared back at him from the bathroom mirror he barely recognised as his own. Dull eyes and drawn features seemed to complement the ugly redness of his swollen lip. He probed the lip gently, amazed at how sore it still was, and wondered whether claiming he had opened the car door into it would prove a plausible explanation. He tried it out in the hotel car-park to check the authenticity of his excuse.

He arrived back at the Hospital just before seven, and asked after Nicholas. He was directed to a waiting room. Laura was already in there waiting. He went over and sat beside her. Nobody said a word. Perhaps they could maintain some semblance of normality at least.

Nicholas had had an uneventful night. But the doctors felt they needed to keep him in for a few days. He woke up when they walked into his room, but quickly fell back to sleep again. The nurse suggested Richard and Laura leave him and come back around lunchtime. Laura asked if they had a quiet area, or a chapel she could use, and the nurse indicated it was down the hall.

As they walked out together, Richard tentatively broached the subject.

"I'll pop in at lunchtime, and then again at five. Do you want me home this evening?"

- clarify what you really want to achieve and make it more vibrant and accessible

- build a real spirit of teamwork and interdependence

- deliver what others may only have dreamed about,

then business may fulfil your needs more than your home life.

This becomes particularly true for those of you with families, particularly at certain stages of your family's development when:

- you may be beginning to become confused about your role, except possibly as a source of finance

- family members are becoming more independent and are pursuing different, and often unclear, goals

- you are starting to feel that there are no really clear worthwhile goals left to achieve in your personal life.

The danger is that work may become the only place where you can truly be what you want to be. Particularly if in the bid to support your family materially you have been drawn away from being able to invest spiritually in your family and friends.

So what are the alternatives?

Well, you could simply put up with things as they are, and allow more of your energy and dreams to be invested in your work. But the danger is that you lose your depth and personality. The only relationships you would be engaging in are those prescribed by the organisation and its protocols. Added to which, some of you would be denying the responsibilities you took on in marriage and childbirth, and the costs of that are enormous.

Or you could keep your business objectives and their deployment muddy. But

How much of an issue is 'balance' likely to be for you?

Where do you...	Work	Home
Have the clearest goals?	☐	☐
Achieve the most?	☐	☐
Get most recognition?	☐	☐
Feel most in demand?	☐	☐
See most possibilities?	☐	☐
Have greatest fellowship?	☐	☐
Find your mind most active?	☐	☐

He who fights with monsters might take care lest he thereby become a monster.

Georg Wilhelm Nietzsche
German Philosopher

"Suit yourself," was all she said.

Richard never did make the lunchtime slot, but he got back to the hospital for five. He discovered that Laura was back in the chapel. She had spent the whole day either at Nicholas's bedside or in the chapel. Richard spent five minutes with Nicholas watching the boy sleep, then he braced himself for another blow-up as he went to find Laura. He thought she would be furious about him missing the lunchtime session, and felt the privacy of the chapel would be a safe place to face it.

As he walked through the door he was struck by the peacefulness of the place. Laura was kneeling on a mat, her eyes closed, her hands clasped in front of her, facing a candle and a large wooden cross. The flame burnt steadily without flickering. Richard hadn't really believed in religious things since his teenage, but he knew it brought Laura comfort.

Richard moved stealthily into the room, and went and knelt beside her, waiting for her to emerge from her prayers; hoping that, in mirroring her posture with his own, he might ameliorate some of the anger she would focus on him.

He was really surprised when, still in an attitude of prayer, she reached out and took his hand and held it tightly. For a moment he wondered if she really knew that it was him. But then she turned, and smiled sadly at him, blinked and said quietly: "Sorry, Richard."

The apology took him by surprise; he hadn't been expecting it. Sure he felt Laura was in the wrong over her behaviour last night, but it wasn't like her to apologise in this way, particularly given that he had missed the lunchtime session. For a moment he suspected some elaborate charade, but when he looked in her face he could see that she was sincere. The impact of his wife's honest apology denuded his own guilty thoughts of their validation, and made them stand out in stark contrast. And he found himself unable to meet Laura's open gaze, and had to cast his eyes downward.

Laura continued to look at him, and then said: "Nicholas is still sleeping. Would you please stay here with me for a while?" Richard nodded slowly and Laura continued, her voice barely above a whisper, stretched by some inner tension. "Would you pray with me? Would you ask God to look after our son with me?"

that would be to miss out on so much potential and fulfilment.

Or, you could invest as much time and energy in thinking through your personal life, as you do your business life.

Attempting QFD with the family is not what is being advocated here. Anyone with normal teenagers and a typically idiosyncratic spouse could see that they would not get past step one, and would be more likely to end up wearing the flipchart than writing on it!

But using the tools personally, to rethink your role, would be a good start. And as you become clearer about your impact on the lives of your family and friends, so your personal goals and values will become clearer.

Your personal QFD is unlikely to be as complete or as logical as your business QFD, and you would be brave beyond reason to pin it up on the wall, but that is not the point. It is the questions that arise from doing the QFD that provide the insights and the growth points, not the neatly drawn diagram on the page.

Think about it:

- What relation does your *Sunday afternoon walk* have to the *maturity and values of your eight-year-old son*?
- Or how could *spending time with your friends* help you to *influence the society you live in*?

Your personal QFD will contain scores of similar question for you to explore and find new opportunities and potential within.

QFD could really enrich the thought you put into your life - both your personal life, and your work life - and get a better balance for both.

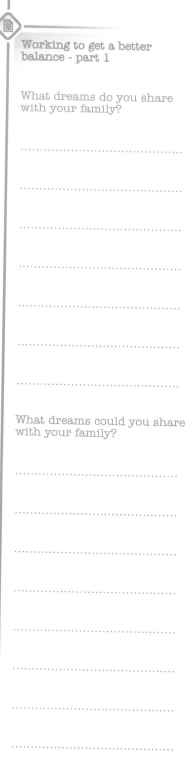

Working to get a better balance - part 1

What dreams do you share with your family?

....

....

....

....

....

....

....

What dreams could you share with your family?

....

....

....

....

....

....

....

Still reeling from the apology, and from his own unresolved reaction to it, Richard was having problems assimilating this new request. Laura had never asked him to pray before. She knew he didn't believe in God, and anyway, even if you did believe in God, surely prayer was a private thing. But kneeling there in the chapel, and not daring to look back into Laura's sincere green eyes, he simply nodded dumbly. To him it seemed the easiest course of action.

As Laura turned and bent her head in silent prayer, Richard followed suit, and kneeling there in the stillness, Richard found a strange quietness steal over him. His questions, concerns, challenges, and embarrassment seemed to evaporate from him as he knelt and held his wife's hand.

Afterwards, they walked to Nicholas's bedside, still hand-in-hand. Strangely bound by a common experience of peace, prayer, and a steadily burning candle.

When they left the hospital at eight, Richard suggested Laura leave her car and they pick it up in the morning. They drove home together, feeling closer than they had felt in months.

Nicholas's illness was diagnosed as complicated viral infection that evening. The consultant had seen them as they were about to leave, and explained that Nicholas was out of real danger, but that there was still an element of risk, and that they would need to keep him under observation until they were confident that it was fully under control.

For the rest of the week, hospital visits anchored Richard's day at either end. Most of the time, they would sit by Nicholas's bed, but sometimes Richard would join Laura in the Chapel; simply to be with her, to show her support.

Richard loved his son deeply, but the time at the hospital was giving difficulties in pursuing the plans at work. And regularly he would find his mind wandering to the issues back at Cylek. He was finding it difficult to kneel beside Laura in an attitude of prayer, and would tend to stand up after a few minutes and step quietly around the sparsely furnished room, being careful not to disturb the one or two others who were also using the room.

Richard felt guilty that he could not, even at a time like this, keep his mind focused on his family and in particular Nicholas. But he rationalised

The next four chapters continue to develop this theme of your personal relationship with QFD, in four different ways.

- Chapter 16 looks at personal identity, and its impact on the ultimate benefits that you derive from QFD.

- Chapter 17 looks at how Why-How charting can help you to examine your personal identity more clearly, and can help you to build links between who you are at work and who you are at home.

- Chapter 18 looks at how the lessons from your personal life can be reapplied at work.

- And Chapter 19 looks at how you develop your personal QFD, and its implications for managing yourself and your time.

The intention of this book is to equip you to successfully transform the performance of your organisation by implementing QFD, but your personal effectiveness is vitally important to both that success, and to the impact of that success on you as an individual. These chapters will help you to think these things through effectively and to prepare for them.

However, before you move onto those chapters, you might like to take a little time to think through the following questions.

- When someone asks you socially: "What do you do?" does your answer reflect your work or your personal life? Why?

- Do you tend to feel more guilty about allowing your personal life to intrude into your work time, or about allowing your work to intrude into your personal life? Why?

- Where do you fit on a scale from 1 to 10, where: 1 is 'My personal life is purely a means to enable me to relax and refresh myself so that I can pursue my work'; and 10 is 'My work life is

Working to get a better balance - part 2

What for you are the most important things in the world?

....

....

....

How does what you do at work impact on them?

....

....

....

How does what you do at home impact on them?

....

....

....

....

Does this reflect a balance that feels right to you?

that it was probably because there was so little he could usefully do, while work was crying out with needs he was far better equipped to fulfil.

But while he was at work, he found that his ability to concentrate was suffering. As debates progressed interminably, he was more prone to allow his mind to wander to Nicholas than he was to step in decisively to resolve them. He could sense himself missing vital opportunities to progress things because he was not equipped to deliver the incisive conclusion at the time it was needed.

His mind was in turmoil, and his workload appeared to be building and building as unresolved issues took up more and more of his time.

He spent most of Saturday, physically beside his son's bed, but mentally in the pressures and confusion of his factory. By six o'clock he had realised that he was doing nobody any good, and, with some degree of trepidation, he broached the subject with Laura.

"Laura, I need to go into work tomorrow!" he said gently.

She looked at him, a little quizzically. "But it's Sunday!" she challenged.

"I know… It's just that things have been falling behind. I haven't been able to concentrate on things there, and they are likely to go seriously wrong if I don't do a bit of preparation for Monday."

She looked at him incredulously. "But surely other people can do those things. They aren't dependent on you are they? For heaven's sake your son is seriously ill, surely they can't expect you…" She faltered as Richard's gaze dropped into his lap in resignation, and she realised that, to all intent and purposes, he felt they really were dependent on him. She reached across and put her hand on his shoulder. "It's okay," she said.

He looked up again. "I'll make sure it's not for the whole day."

Laura nodded and said, "One thing though, I'd really appreciate it if you came to Church with me before you go. It's important to me. Could you do that?"

She had been wondering how to broach the subject of Church since the time they had prayed together in the chapel. Richard would expect her to go to Church on Sunday, as she had for the past few months, but she felt he would baulk at the idea of coming along himself.

purely a means to enable me to fund the projects and activities in my personal life'?

Are the answers to the above questions the balance you want in your life? And if not, how could developing a clearer focus for your personal life change this?

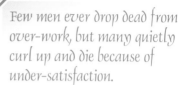

Few men ever drop dead from over-work, but many quietly curl up and die because of under-satisfaction.

Sydney Harris
American Journalist

And yet, Church for Laura was more than a Sunday Social. She had come to feel a presence around her; a presence which had been supporting her through Richard's neglect and Nicholas's illness. But she was growing increasingly concerned that this experience was yet another source of separation between her and Richard, and as her dependence on it deepened through Nicholas's illness, she wanted more and more for it to be an experience she could share with her husband.

Richard's request to work on Sunday had opened up an opportunity, and now she was taking it.

As for Richard, he was clearly puzzled. Going to Church was the last thing he felt like doing, and he wanted to challenge Laura on her request. But as he struggled to find the words, he realised that accepting would be the easy way out. It would only be for an hour, and so little of the last week had been normal anyway. He nodded his assent, and Laura nodded back, almost as a seal of confirmation over their agreement.

Personal values

The more surely and quickly you are able to deliver your goals, the greater your responsibility for ensuring those goals are the right ones.

I think therefore I am! Does this mean that the extent of my existence is dependent on the quality (or otherwise) of my thinking? Perhaps if we do not think enough, our existence may tend to be simply the extension of somebody else's thinking? A tool driven by their ideas and their view of the world?

As you become a more powerful tool, shouldn't you examine more carefully the ideas and values that you are driven by?

There is a risk in any section like this that the reader ends up being told what to believe. The intention here, however, is not to provide answers, but to stimulate questions which you need to answer for yourself. Of course, simply saying that is in itself suggesting that 'responsibility' is a valid and acceptable model. However, in this case, it is a fairly safe and reasonable one.

Stewardship

Depending on your world-view, the human race has either been appointed stewards of the world in which we live, or, by dint of our own strengths and superiority, we have taken stewardship of the world. Either way, our position in the world establishes us as stewards, and we carry the authority of stewardship, which we exercise for good, or ill. The world: socially; physically; spiritually will become what we make it (at least in the short term).

Every choice we individually make, and everything that we do, affects the world in some way. Every time we make a selection, or speak out, or demand, or praise,

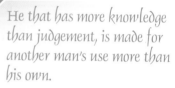

Is it progress if a cannibal uses a fork?

Stanislaw Lec.
Polish Aphorist

He that has more knowledge than judgement, is made for another man's use more than his own.

William Penn
Founder of Pennsylvania

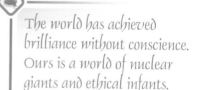

The world has achieved brilliance without conscience. Ours is a world of nuclear giants and ethical infants.

Omar Nelson Bradley
Permanent Chairman
Joint Chiefs of Staff
Armistice Day speech, 1948

Chapter 16

The Church service lived down to Richard's worst expectations.

He walked into the Church self-consciously, almost as if he was trying to project an air of "I'm here for someone else, but I'm okay and I don't need this sort of emotional crutch". It was a look that he hoped would ward off all but the most determined approaches. It largely succeeded, except for one or two women to whom Laura introduced him.

The service was printed in an old red book, and was turgid to say the least. A series of old fashioned words, their meaning made obscure by their convoluted phrasing, and responses spoken lifelessly without any apparent emotion or sincerity. Hymns, with familiar tunes, but with sentences twisted and distorted to such an extent that Richard missed out entire verses while his mind struggled to make sense of the first line.

He wondered, not for the first time, what Laura found so appealing in this strange ritual. He could not imagine that, if a God really existed, he would hide himself in such tortuous rhetoric. A 'living God', as they claimed that he was, would surely not leave his people with such meaningless cant. He accepted that the words might possibly have some underlying relevance if you dug down deep enough, but looking at the faces around him, he was not sure that many of them had found it.

They sat down for a reading from the Bible. The reader was good. He might have been a classical actor in his heyday. He spoke with expression and made the words come to life. All of a sudden, Richard found himself captivated. Here was someone for whom the words really had meaning, and the meaning echoed in his voice, and in his hands, and in his expression, and even, Richard fancied, in his soul!

And the words had meaning for Richard too. They seemed to echo in the areas of his life that he kept shut in a darkened room. They raised questions at him that he did not want to face. Questions about integrity, and values, and life choices. Questions about who we really are. And then, without warning, the speaker appeared to look directly at Richard and said: "For what is a man profited, if he shall gain the whole world, and lose his own soul?"

or criticise, or purchase, or ignore, or support, or use something, we are either exploiting our rights of stewardship, or exercising our responsibility for it. The sum of our collective decisions is the major influence in the world today. Our small, even minuscule, part in stewardship will build up and compound with millions of others for good or ill.[1]

And, as leaders of our organisations, our impact is greater still. We do have a real responsibility to re-examine what we are trying to do. To challenge some of the myths and fuzzy thinking that abound, and to begin to deliver a result that we feel really will begin to change things for the better.[2]

We have a responsibility to at least face up to exploring what our view of steward-ship is, and what it means.

Making a difference

What difference do you want to result out of your time here on Earth? Do you have a purpose for your life? What do you invest your time (work and personal) into?

You will almost certainly be doing some-thing that adds value somewhere. It is highly unlikely that anybody entirely hedo-nistic and self-centred would have perse-vered anything like this far with the book. So what actually are your values?

- Community?
- Justice?
- Humanity?
- Learning?
- Truth?

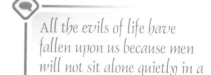

All the evils of life have fallen upon us because men will not sit alone quietly in a room.

Pascal

For evil to triumph, all that is required is that good men do nothing.

G.K.Chesterton.
Author of the 'Father Brown' stories

---

1   An excellent exploration of this is provided in Patrick Dixon's book 'Futurewise', published by Trafalgar Square, in January 1999.

2   Whatever your considered opinion of 'better' is.

Richard was stunned; the words seem to have been spoken directly at him personally. He blinked and looked back at the speaker, expecting him to have stopped, and to be pointing directly at Richard, exposing him before this room full of strangers. But the speaker had moved on; had swept his gaze over others in the congregation.

However, the speaker had changed forever in Richard's eyes; he had been transformed from a crusty old curmudgeon to something altogether more sinister. Richard felt discomfited, and he could feel his heart beating faster. He felt like he had been 'found out'.

As the reading finished, the reader closed his book and walked back to his pew. Richard felt fearful that he should look at him again as he sat down, but he did not. Instead the preacher began his sermon, and Richard found himself letting out a breath he had been holding. He had not realised how nervous he had been. He knew he was just being stupid, and reflected ruefully on how superstitions can even get to sane, rational, fully-grown men.

The preacher was talking about his own experience, and Richard was surprised to find that he had worked in merchant banking before he had been ordained. Richard began to feel more comfortable.

But after two minutes preamble, he then said to the congregation, "I want you to think about the phrase 'For what is a man profited, if he shall gain the whole world, and lose his own soul?'." And despite all his rationalising, Richard felt the fears he had just swept from his mind come stealing back over him once more. Richard stared directly at the vicar, half expecting him to turn and glare back at him.

Richard then looked sideways at the man who had done the reading, to see if he was looking at him, but he was looking expectantly back at the vicar. Richard felt like he was caught in some '60s B movie, waiting for the trap to spring.

He looked back as the preacher continued his sermon. He kept on expecting the look, but the look never came, and then Richard felt he was being deliberately ignored. What was this? What was happening? There had to be a rational explanation. Had Laura arranged this? Was he part of some macabre game?

He looked at Laura, but she was rapt in listening to the preacher. However, sensing Richard looking at her, she turned to glance at him.

Whatever your values are, whatever you hold dear, you will be more effective if you are clear about them.

Is business any different? Is your organisation simply a means for you to fund your personal life, or does it represent the opportunity for you to progress your values more directly?

There is a serious risk of misinterpretation here. What is being advocated is not the subversion of business to your personal ends. Rather it is the alignment of your values with your role in achieving the goals of your organisation and vice versa. It is about the power of integrity.

The business context

To explore this further, let us consider the context of business. At its simplest, a business is a symbiosis between three stakeholders:

- the shareholders, or owners of the business
- the employees, and the local community
- the partners (customers and suppliers) of the business.

It exists to trade and convert what each of these stakeholders has into what another needs in return (see diagram on the right):

- shareholders provide capital in exchange for some security of return
- employees provide ideas and effort in exchange for wages and development
- trading partners provide revenue in return for service and vice versa.

The business needs to invest the capital into facilities, which the employees can use to develop and supply services in return for revenue, which is repaid to the shareholders and employees. If it does all

Her look of interest changed to one of concern, as she could see the worry in Richard's face.

"What is it?" she whispered urgently. "Are you okay?"

Richard nodded dumbly, and looked back at the preacher. He was just being silly, and anyway Laura was not that good an actress. But what was going on?

The preacher continued talking, and drawing out questions about identity, about who we really are, about being true to ourselves. The very things Richard himself had been thinking about during the reading. He then began exploring the sort of person we need to become if we are to successfully pursue wealth and fame and power, and Richard began to hear a description of himself spoken from the pulpit.

An irrational fear of exposure gripped him tighter, as the preacher spoke about focus, and compromise, and selfishness, and then he went on to surmise that, while we may be seen as successful, we have often distorted our inner selves so much in straining for such things, that it is then no longer us who is there to enjoy them. That, in pursuing the big things, we so often lose the pure, innocent, unabashed joy we need to really appreciate them. And what excitement we gain from them, is therefore transitory and quickly swept away in the next pursuit.

Finally, the preacher finished by saying that success is working out who we really are, and then trying to be that to the best of our ability.

"For me," he said, "it means: what do I make the role of vicar, rather than what does the role of vicar make me? What does it mean for you?"

At the end of the service, Richard was subdued. But once outside the Church and back in the car, Richard sat with his hand on the ignition and challenged Laura. "Have you told them about me? Did they know that I was coming here with you today?"

Laura looked back at him, clearly puzzled by his manner and the forcefulness of the questions. "No. Why would I? What's brought this on?"

"Have you not spoken to anyone in the Church about our difficulties?" he pressed.

"Richard! No!" she said emphatically.

these efficiently, then everyone is happy to continue and build on the relationship. If it does it inefficiently, one or all three parties migrate to other relationships and the business dies.

If the organisation is super-efficient at these things, the business develops a discretionary power of its own. It develops a 'surplus' over that needed to satisfy the needs of all three parties.

- It has delivered a return to the shareholders, which meets their fair expectations, and secures their continued involvement.

- It has delivered opportunities, rewards and salaries to the employees, which meets their expectations and secures their continued service.

- It has delivered service to the customers and custom to the suppliers that meets their expectations, and secures their continued loyalty.

- And it has generated additional wealth, which is not required simply to maintain the status quo.

The 'big question'

So what does the organisation do with this additional wealth that it has generated? Conventional thinking might see it as naturally the due of the shareholders. They are, after all, the legal owners of the business. This is the concept that underlies 'managing for shareholder value': the goal is to maximise share growth to outstrip other businesses.

But why? To what end? Does delivering the additional wealth directly to the shareholders provide any additional benefits to the organisation? Or are they likely to be, as a result of this unexpected windfall, more expensive in terms of their future expectations? And given the impact of dividends on share price, are the share-

A business that makes nothing but money is a poor kind of business.

Henry Ford
Founder, Ford Motors Inc.

Richard inherently felt this was wrong. Whether he agreed with Church or not, surely, at the very least, it was about listening to each other's problems and praying over them. He looked disbelievingly back at her.

She sensed his confusion. "I've only been going for a while, and only to the services. I've not yet felt close enough to anyone to talk about any problems we might have. Richard, what is this? What is going on?" she asked urgently.

Richard could see she was telling the truth and felt mollified. But he was still confused.

"Well, did you suggest the reading for today?" he asked.

Laura stared into his urgent face and a light dawned. "That reading really got to you, didn't it?"

"Well, did you suggest it?" he pressed, not responding to her question.

A small smile played on Laura's lips. "Richard. No! All the readings are defined by the Church calendar. I think you can see them listed in the thick green books in the pews."

"So you knew that was the reading for today?" he accused her.

"No, I didn't," Laura said vehemently. "I never look in the book. To me, as to 90% of the Churchgoers you'd meet, the reading is a total surprise."

Richard seemed to accept this. Laura continued: "But if you felt that the reading was meant specifically for you, you would not be the first to attend Church for the first time and feel that bits of the service were written for you personally. Many people feel that way. It is the way God works sometimes."

Richard put on his most sceptical face.

"Come on," said Laura. "Let's prove this one way or another," and with that, she stepped back outside the car and headed back toward the Church building.

Richard paused for thought, and then followed her. When he came in through the door, she had the lectionary in her hands at the day's date, and pointed triumphantly to where it said *'Matthew 16:13-28'*.

"There you are," she said.

holders at the end of this transaction the same ones you started out with?

And anyway, other stakeholders have played just as big a part in generating the surplus; do they not have some claim on the benefits?

For instance, it might be better to invest it in your employees. In developing their numbers, or their skills, or their attitudes and motivation, or in improving their community and environment.

Alternatively you might invest it in your business partners. To improve the quality and impact of the services you provide, or to develop new products.

And both of these investments have the potential to improve your effectiveness; to increase your efficiency and help build more 'discretionary surplus' for the future. Both of these investments, managed properly, provide ultimate benefits for your shareholders, not as a one-off windfall, but as a sustainable long-term return.

In a partnership shouldn't the spoils benefit all parties? Is it really a partnership?

The role of vision

This might sound academic. You might feel that you are not in a position to call the shots. But even though your shareholders or parent organisation are the legal owners of the business, you are not powerless in how you influence the distribution of the wealth you have created.

But if you want to have a voice, you have to have a vision!

It is the vision that defines the partnership, and it can be a partnership if there is a common goal, a common vision, to pull all three parties together.

There is something sick about a person whose only interest is money. And the same can be said, I think, for the company whose sole goal is profit.

Richard J. Haayen
CEO, Allstate Insurance Company
in Nation's Business, March 1988

Richard looked at the page, and Laura continued: "Shall we look it up in the Bible?" But Richard shook his head. He had the Church notice sheet in his hands, which listed the same reading. He folded up the piece of paper and put it in his pocket, and headed out of the door slowly, a puzzled look on his face.

Laura knew better than to press, and simply followed him at a distance. But at the Church door, she turned and looked back at the Altar Cross. She felt in her heart that the presence she had come to know, and so desperately wanted Richard to share, had begun to make its existence known to him. A well of gratitude seemed to spring up within her, and, with watering eyes, she simply whispered: "Thank you!"

Richard went straight off to work after dropping Laura at the hospital. They had not said a word the whole journey.

During the afternoon, Richard found himself repeatedly distracted by thoughts of his soul, and his identity, and what they were. Had his career moulded him in its image?

By five o'clock, he had made little progress in his thinking in any area, and he prepared to return to the hospital. He noticed small traces of panic building up in him. He had so much work to do, and was becoming increasingly less able to do it. He felt he could scream. He looked up at the ceiling and, though he felt foolish, he felt he just had to say it: "Look, if you're there, and I'm not agreeing that you are, just give me a break will you?"

Back in the hospital he looked in on Nicholas sleeping peacefully, and then carried on to look for Laura in the chapel. But, as he entered the room, he realised she was not there, just an older woman leafing through a Bible on the lectern. She looked up at him as he walked in, and he smiled back at her.

He was about to turn round and walk back out again, but thought it might convey a bad impression, so he walked to the back of the room, sat down and waited quietly. After a few minutes the woman left, and Richard walked over to where she stood and gazed down blankly at the Bible text. He grabbed a handful of pages and let them pour out of his grip one by one to the other side of the book. His heart seemed heavy, and he was

You have to be able to paint a picture of the future that is big and bright and powerful, which people want to be part of, and which they feel confident in. You have to be able to explain to your shareholders why retaining their money will enable you to build a future for them that is better than anything they are likely to achieve by taking the additional wealth to themselves. And if you are already delivering to them what they were expecting, they are very likely to listen to what else you have in mind - you have already proven your worth.

The point is, implementing the approaches outlined here will generate more output for less resource, more impact for less cost. It will generate a 'discretionary surplus' for your organisation.

That additional wealth can be absorbed by the shareholders, or it can be used to leverage the future of the organisation. But it can only be used for the latter where there is a clear, ambitious and compelling vision for what that future is.

Creating a vision

People are not motivated by money. People are motivated by vision. Money way well be needed to pave the way to that vision, and it may also be an indicator that the vision has been reached, but money is not the vision itself.

The challenge then is to develop a vision that your people, your shareholders and your business partners can believe in.

And the closer that vision parallels your own value set the more effective and compelling you will be in selling it to other people.

The first thing is to be clear on what your values are, and then to understand how your work provides opportunities to influ-

The role of vision

Three workmen were laying stone blocks on a building site. A stranger, watching them for a while, noticed that they were undertaking the task with totally different levels of satisfaction and effort. So after a few minutes he went to the least happy builder and asked: "What are you doing?"

The man replied "Me? I'm just laying blocks, one atop another like so!"

The stranger then moved on to the second builder, who seemed reasonably content. "What are you doing?" he asked.

"Hey!" replied the builder, "We're building this huge wall, its going to be a fair size when it's finished."

Moving on, the stranger came to the third builder, who looked positively joyful, and asked the same question.

The builder replied, "We are building a huge cathedral that will be the most magnificent building to be seen for miles around, and it will stand for centuries - and my name will be written on its walls."

about to do it again, when his gaze caught the words "What good will it be for a man if he gains the whole world, yet forfeits his soul?"

Goosebumps came up all over him.

He looked at the top of the page *'Matthew 16'*.

He scrabbled in his pocket for the Church newsletter. He folded it out, smoothed out its creases, and read the words *'Matthew 16:13-28'*. He felt cold, as his mind struggled for an explanation he could accept.

And then it found one.

Of course, it was the reading for today. Probably no end of people had looked at it. No wonder it fell open there.

Some of the panic left him as he assimilated this rational explanation. After all, what else could explain it?

Well it could also be coincidence. There were only 2,000 pages in the book. Every so often, someone would accidentally turn up the right page! Wouldn't they?

Strangely comforted by being back in control of his own world, he re-read the words on the page: "What good will it be for a man if he gains the whole world, yet forfeits his soul?" and as he read them he knew in his heart, without any shadow of a doubt, that they were meant for him, whatever his head might say!

He returned to the back of the chapel, sat down, held out his hands, and let his head fall into them.

He was not sure how long he spent there. Sometimes thinking. Sometimes throwing up arguments to challenge the plausibility of a super-natural being that hid in coincidence. Sometimes reviewing his life. Sometimes considering who he really wanted to be.

As he poured over his thoughts and ideas, he gradually became more accustomed to the idea that he really was not the person he really wanted to be. That he had lost some of himself in recent years. And as he accepted this, paradoxically he became more calm and resolute.

He could still regain himself as the person he could respect and admire from the inside as well as the outside. It was simply a matter of being entirely and unambiguously clear on whom that person was.

ence them. At first the links might seem a little tenuous, but it is possible to find the means to link almost any situation with your value set, and to do so profitably.

And as we recognise our work as an extension of ourselves, rather than the other way round, we become better at it, and more committed to it. We develop a passion that can win others over to our vision as it strikes personal chords with their own value sets.

So what do you want your organisation to achieve? If you really can't personally identify with anything, then you are probably in the wrong job, and you should get out of it. If, however, you can see real opportunities to shine, to add real value, to make a difference, then you should grasp it and pursue it.

Work can profitably be a meaningful activity. The unquestioned assumption that additional wealth is automatically the due of the shareholder is quite often the major factor in people seeing their work as simply the means to fund their lives and their purpose, not to be their lives and their purpose. You have the opportunity to break that paradigm to the benefit of all parties. But if you are bored with your organisation, why should any of your people be any different?

I desire so to conduct the affairs of this administration that if at the end, when I come to lay down the reins of power, I have lost every other friend on earth, I shall at least have one friend left, and that friend shall be down inside of me.

Abraham Lincoln
Sixteenth President of the United States

Managing by Design

And then a thought struck him.

He had been through all this before. For the company. If QFD could work for that, then surely it could work for him.

As if energised by the thought, he launched himself out of his chair and headed out of the door.

Clarifying your purpose

In the preceding chapter we looked at creating a compelling vision to transform your organisation. But there will be some who are reading this who will feel that such vision is not for them. Do you feel that way? Do you feel that 'great purpose' is a nice concept, but wholly impractical for you?

Perhaps so, perhaps you feel that you do not have such freedom. The biggest barrier to purpose is lack of freedom.

But the biggest cause of lack of freedom are the walls we build around ourselves. Are you free? Or do you have self-imposed limits which you have ceased to question, challenge, or even to recognise?

In this chapter we look at this question, and how, if we do have such limits, we can identify them and break through them. We will look at:

- the concept of paradigms, and how they can cause us to limit our thinking

- Why-How charting, and how it can help us to identify hidden rules and limits in our lives

- Why-How dangers - why you might not want to do this

- congruence - what you might achieve if you do.

The concept of paradigms

There is something called 'pike syndrome' after a story of a pike placed in a large tank with a glass partition half way along it. After a day of constantly banging into the partition the pike changes its swimming patterns to avoid it. Then the partition is removed, but the pike swims as though it is still there. For the pike, the other half of the tank has simply ceased to exist.

Why, in all the plenitude of God's great universe do you choose to fall asleep in this small dark prison?

Rumi

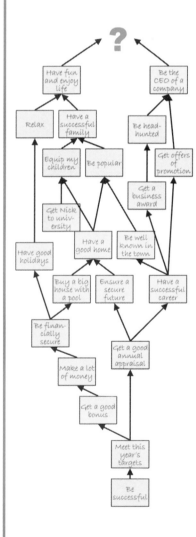

Chapter 17

The small crumpled sticky-note arced across the room to hit the far wall, and join a number of similar yellow balls around the base of the waste paper bin.

Richard did not see it complete its trajectory. He did not care if it was inside or outside the bin. He was too wrapped up in the frustration that was his own personal Why-How chart.

The clock on his windowsill showed the time at 2am, and the sheet of paper in front of him was littered with the rudiments of a Why-How chart. Two seemingly unlinked triangles had grown on the page.

The small crumpled yellow balls had been Richard's repeated attempts to bring them together. The two halves of the diagram, barring one or two sparse lines, were defying all efforts to bring them together under one purpose. As far as Richard could see, he was essentially two totally different people. One, the right-hand-side triangle, which made business more efficient and sustainable. The other, the left-hand-side triangle, which provided for his family and endeavoured to develop Nicholas into a good person. And nowhere, in either of those two people, could he really see anything that made him 'him'.

Who on earth was he? What made him who he was? What was his purpose? Why? Why? Why?

Richard banged the table in frustration. Was he really just some machine that made the world go round? Was that it? He hated the thought that it might be.

He pushed the paper to one side. It was so late. Perhaps that is why he could not think straight. Resignedly, he got himself ready for bed, and crawled in beside Laura. He was so tired.

And yet sleep would not come. He had questioned his own identity, and now his mind was frantically searching everywhere for an answer. For a brief moment, he envied those who could simply say their life was about 'serving God', but since he did not believe in God, that would not work! And even if he did, he still saw the answer as a cop-out.

Pike are fairly dumb creatures. Humans are far more intelligent, and so our glass partitions have become more sophisticated, even to the extent of renaming them 'paradigms', but they work the same way. The problem with the walls of our personal prison is that we do not even realise they exist.

But we can see them in other people, and we recognise them in phrases like 'I can't do that!' or 'That's not me!' or 'I'm too…'.

That is not to say we should not recognise boundaries and obstacles. But in the case of boundaries and obstacles we make a conscious choice based on judgement, and we can re-evaluate them when conditions or aspirations change. They play an explicit part in our goal setting and in our values, and as such they provide guidance rather than limitation.

Paradigms on the other hand can limit our thinking without us even realising that it is happening. Essentially a paradigm is an unquestioned pattern of behaviour or thought. Often this pattern has developed as a helpful framework for dealing with something, for instance organising a meeting or handling an argument. They can provide familiar routine and comfort in the face of uncertain, complex and important tasks, and as such they can be extremely valuable.

The danger comes when they become the only way to tackle that task; when they become ritual rather than reason; when they become an alternative to thinking rather than a means to support it.

Unchecked, paradigms allow a sense of community to become racism; objectivity to become bigotry; faith to become superstition; and past wisdom to become the walls of our current prisons. Paradigms can be very useful; they can stop us continually banging up against obstacles that

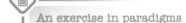

An exercise in paradigms

Without taking your pen from the paper, join all nine dots with 4 straight lines.

•   •   •

•   •   •

•   •   •

But there had to be an answer somewhere. There had to be some goal which would make both halves of his life meaningful. The question cycled endlessly in his mind, and gradually there came a dawning realisation. At first he fought it, rejected it, it was too heinous to contemplate. But once conceived, it could not be unthought, and it kept coming back, stronger and more forceful with each encounter. Richard physically shook his head as if to throw it from his mind, but he could not. It hammered on the doors of his conscious, and eventually, too weak to resist, Richard gave it entry, and sat looking balefully at it.

One reason underpinned both sides of his Why-How chart. It had remained hidden for years, because it loved the darkness. But Richard had demanded it make itself known, and now it stood there four-square in Richard's mind, defying him to do anything about it.

The one thing that held his life together was… His own selfish vanity!

Richard fought frantically to unseat the conclusion. And he challenged it with the things he had done for Nicholas. The thing sneered at him. "Why?" it asked. "For him? Or for you? Was it not so you could be proud of him, and boast of him to others? Was it not so he would love and admire you?" And as Richard thought back over the last year or two, he found it almost impossible to identify one thing that he had done solely and simply for Nicholas. Even his choice of Christmas presents had been things that he felt would develop Nicholas's mental abilities above those of his contemporaries.

As Richard thought of Nicholas and what he wanted him to be, he saw Nicholas growing to be like him, and he knew the thing was right.

He did not even attempt to challenge it with regard to work. Even he could see the fingerprints of 'his vanity' smeared all over it.

In despair, Richard conceded the truth. The one thing that was truly 'him' had emerged, and Richard hated it. He fell into a black sleep, with his last thoughts being that he really had grown into the sort of person he least admired.

He awoke with a start on Monday morning, his pulse racing, and a sense of panic rising within him. He felt strangely uneasy, as if waking from a bad dream, but if there had been a dream it had slipped irretrievably from his memory.

are still there. But when they continue unquestioned, beyond the point when the obstacle should be removed, they become a liability. They become the main limitation to you identifying and pursuing your true potential, and thus your real purpose.

But paradigms are rarely seen from the inside as such boundaries, even though they are. They are more often areas where we have given up thinking and exploring. They are often expressed as objectives or goals (often not very specific ones) where the reasoning behind them is not fully thought through. Examples that are most common, and you may therefore recognise in your past, are:

- I want to be rich
- people need me to guide them
- promotion and advancement is always good
- being proved wrong is bad
- I have got to win people's admiration
- I want to know everything
- be totally independent.

Of themselves, the principles may not be wrong. But the problem comes when they become an unquestioned, and even unconscious compulsion; something that we don't even realise is driving us.

Personal Why-How charts

Undertaking a personal Why-How chart helps you to identify these paradigms, and to question them, and, where appropriate, to move on past them. Mapping out the Why-How chart for yourself is very similar to the process we covered for the organisation in Chapter 2.

1. Start by listing out, on individual yellow sticky-notes, your current personal objectives. These are the things you want to be or achieve

Try not to become a man of success but rather try to become a man of value.

Albert Einstein
German Physicist

And then he remembered last night, and, unbidden, a phrase he had read some time in the past stole into his mind: 'I have seen the face of the enemy, and the enemy was me'.

A sense of hopelessness and depression overtook him. His insides felt leaden, and he had a strange urge to burst into tears. But he resisted, and mentally shook himself. His mind sought for something to fix the breach, to eliminate the unwanted disturbance in its routine. "What is a soul anyway?" he asked himself. "And you don't believe in God, so phrases from scripture clearly have no relevance!"

For a few moments, the barrage of his self-doubts were alleviated, and he felt better. But then he realised that his rationalisations did not actually change anything. God, or no God, he had still allowed himself to become someone he was deeply disappointed in. Yes, the scripture may have been the trigger, but the conclusions were very clearly his own. He turned and buried his face in his pillow.

When the alarm went off, he was still thinking things through, but he felt calmer. He seemed to be handling the issue almost academically as he went through the motions of washing and dressing. The issue came quite simply down to this: he was no longer the person he wanted to be, and he would change! He was not sure exactly how he would change, but he was confident he could.

And yet, for some strange and obscure reason, the decision to change did not come easily to him. It was almost as though his old self retained its grip, and said "Come back to me, it's more comfortable here, and I can make your real dreams come true!"

But by the time Richard and Laura reached the hospital that morning, something had already begun to change in Richard. It was almost as though becoming aware of the problem diminished its hold on him. As though bringing it into the light caused it to weaken, to begin to recede.

He could look at Nicholas, and focus on him being a separate human being, and not an extension of himself. He could see someone with his own life to lead, his own mistakes to make. He tried to think back. Did he really see Nicholas as a reflection of himself, to be managed and developed so that others could applaud Richard's fathership? He was not really

across all areas of your life. They could be to do with:

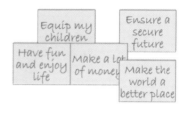

- possessions and material wealth, including where you live
- attainment of certain standards, prizes or membership
- capability, skills and competence
- impact on others, and how you affect them, relationships
- impact on the environment, and changes you bring about
- spiritual goals and your personal journey.

Try and develop a balance across all areas of your life:

- yourself
- your work and career/vocation
- your family and home
- your community
- your leisure activities and clubs.

When you have listed as many goals as you can, you should group any that clearly go together, and then lay them out on a large flat wall covered with sheets of flipchart paper, so you can see them all.

2. Take the first goal that you want to work with, and ask yourself the question "Why do I want to do this?" If the answer lies in another sticky-note, then place it above the one you are working on, and link them by an upward pointing arrow. If the answer is a new goal or objective, write it on a new sticky-note, and link it by an upward pointing arrow. Then ask 'Why?' of the new objective and repeat the process. When you have got as far as you can with that chain, pick up the next sticky-note and work with that one. Challenge yourself to be clear and explicit on your goals, and do not be afraid to rip vague ones out and replace them.

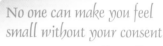

No one can make you feel small without your consent

Eleanor Roosevelt
American author and humanitarian

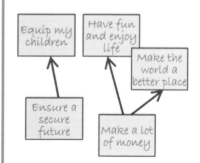

sure, but he realised the more he thought about it, the more he seemed to be polarising his memories and recasting his history.

One thing he was sure of, was that by concentrating on Nicolas as a discrete individual, he felt the love he had for the boy rise within him. As he focused on the boy's struggle to make sense of his future, the pain and delight that he would face, and what he would need to help him get through, he felt that same love grow and threaten to overwhelm him. He loved the feeling. It seemed to give his own life a new depth and intensity, the contours seemed sharper and the colours brighter. This was what really mattered. He thought back over what his life had brought him so far, over the trappings of success that he had so eagerly pursued. And yet ...

How long was it before the Jaguar became just 'the car' or the dwelling of their dreams had deteriorated to just 'the house'. He thought of the time that Nicholas, eager to become involved in his Dad's ritual washing of the new car, had watched with joy Richard's splashing of the foamy sponge over the bonnet, and then picked up a rock and copied him. A key step in Nicholas's development, and Richard had only seen the scratches. He had favoured the emblem over the reality, the material over his son. He was wracked with the guilt his new insight bestowed on him, and he held Nicholas's hand and tears dripped on the sleeping boy's bed.

Later in the morning, back at work, he sat in his chair and looked around his office, and thought over the last six months. Was this really success? Externally, it looked like every picture he had ever had of success, right down to the sleek rosewood desk, the brass fittings and the executive trappings. Viewed from the outside he had a beautiful home, a luxury car, went on exotic holidays, and had the respect and admiration of 800 people.

Viewed from the inside: he had a house of turmoil and conflict which he never got the chance to enjoy; he had a car which he only got to drive in the dark or in the rush hour; his supposed holidays were frequently interrupted with work, or with thinking about problems; and he had the resentment and distress of 800 people.

In retrospect it seemed strange to him, but he had never really evaluated it from the inside before. Just how had he been sold this picture as success? Exactly whose screenplay was he acting in?

3. Continue to work through the sticky-notes one by one, even those that are already linked together, until you have them pulled together into one diagram. Be prepared to redraw the diagram when it gets too confused.

4. Enrich the diagram further, by asking "Why else do I do this?" to pull in further links. When you are confused as to which is the more important objective, ask yourself which you would give up for the other.

5. Where you have separate parts of the diagram, which cannot seem to be pulled together, this may indicate that you haven't delved deep enough into your motives, and you may need to persevere with asking "Why?"

6. When you have finished mapping upwards, look at some of the higher-up objectives and think about whether you could deliver them in other ways. Use this exploration to challenge some of your earlier objectives. Ask also, whether the lower-down objectives really do supply all that is needed to achieve the higher-up objectives, or whether other things are necessary.

Dangers of personal Why-How charting

But please be warned that developing a personal Why-How chart is not easy. Some paradigms protect us from aspects of ourselves that we literally don't want to face. If you think you are really not ready to be honest about your motives, then please do not attempt the Why-How chart. If you do, you may either unearth something you will find difficult to handle, or more likely you will fudge certain parts of the chart to make them more palatable, and you will waste your time on an exercise for some mythical being who is not really you.

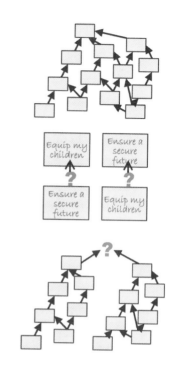

We must not cease from exploration. And at the end of all our exploring will be to arrive where we began and to know the place for the first time.

T.S.Eliot
English Poet

He physically shook his head in disbelief that he could walk this far down a blind alley without realising it. Did he really think that it got any better further along? He closed his eyes, sighed deeply, and slowly, almost imperceptibly, shook his head again.

So where had it gone so wrong? Had it always been like this? Was there never a time when he was really successful?

He thought back. There was a time when he had really enjoyed work, a time when he had been merely a design engineer for Ektracom. Sure, even then he dreamt about getting promoted, getting a company car, what he could do with the money. But they were not the things that had driven him most. What had made him happiest, and most content, was the feeling of making a real difference within his team. Of cracking a difficult design problem, and seeing his colleagues' faces delight in moving forward and doing something worthwhile. He remembered the highlight that he treasured most, of being in a shop and hearing a customer ask for the specific product he had designed because: "… I know somebody who reckons this thing has totally changed the way he does business." Wow! He lived on that for months!

It was strange. He had not felt successful then, because he did not earn enough money; he had a second-hand car and other people got to tell him what to do, even when they were wrong. But work was fun then, he shared it with friends who wanted the same things he did. And the car may have been second hand, but Laura and he had had such good times in it, they had been everywhere. He could still remember that Escort storming over Ditchling Beacon, and the time it had left that MG for dead at the lights. That was some car, you could do superb handbrake turns in the snow. Even Laura loved it. Mind you she had loved everything then, and so did he. They had talked for hours about things that really mattered, and how they would like to make them change. Looking from the inside, that felt far more like success than this did.

Sure they had had tough times, but they had got through them together, whether it was with the team at work, or Laura at home. They got through the tough times because they had a common goal. They were going to make things better. It did not matter whether it was a new product, a different way of working, helping their friends through a tough patch, campaigning against hospital closures, or dreaming of a family. They were going to make things better. It was the joy of fellowship, in that goal of making things better, that had been the springboard for so many happy times. That was success!

If a Why-How chart does not cause you to wrestle with yourself then you probably are not being fully honest in your answers.

However, you are a lifetime project, and you do not have to complete the plans in one evening. Work through the Why-How chart at a pace that suits you, and do not worry if it remains incomplete. The objective is not to complete the diagram; the objective is to develop new insights and understanding, which will help you to refine your values and your purpose, and to open up new opportunities for achieving them.

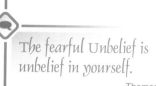

Publishing your personal Why-How chart

Once you have completed your personal Why-How chart, you may be tempted to share it widely with other people, perhaps by pinning it up on a wall.

Don't do it!

Your personal Why-How chart is exactly that - personal.

Other people will be unlikely to see or interpret it the same way you do, and any thought that you may at some time share it could limit your openness and honesty in completing it.

Congruence

Probably the best way for testing your Why-How chart is to work through it with a good friend. Somebody you trust, and who is not afraid to say "Hold on, how does that fit in with what you said last week?"

In this way we can be tested for congruence. Congruence is achieved when what

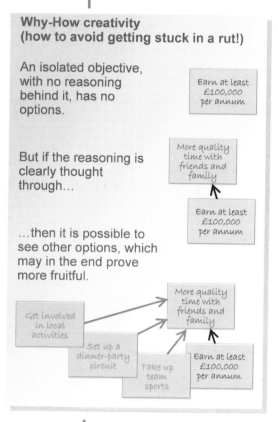

Why-How creativity (how to avoid getting stuck in a rut!)

An isolated objective, with no reasoning behind it, has no options.

But if the reasoning is clearly thought through...

...then it is possible to see other options, which may in the end prove more fruitful.

Managing by Design

He felt quite light headed thinking about it. But he could not live in the past, and bringing his thoughts back to the present had quite a sobering effect on him. He could not just jack it all in and go back to being a designer. And anyway, Laura would never go back to living in a flat. His shoulders sagged a little. Laura, Laura, Laura, what happened to you? What happened to us?

And then he smiled, quite unexpectedly, as a thought suddenly popped into his head. "Is this a mid-life crisis?" It was almost as though part of him had been detached observing his thinking from a distance, and posted the question. He was amused to think of himself as experiencing a mid-life crisis. He was only 34! Is this what they felt like? Is this why men jacked in job, wife and family and ran off with a student to become a beach bum in Marbella. For the first time he could see the attraction. He thought of making love to Lucy on a deserted beach in the setting sun, with no concerns for any business plans or school fees. And sighed a deep contented sigh.

Surely that would feel like success. Wouldn't it?

But no! Not really! Not for long! Richard was beginning to think that people either put into the world, or they took out of it, and if more people took out than put in, then the world got worse. He had responsibilities. He was just getting to grips with addressing himself as a vain glory-seeker; he was not going to fall into the trap of being an, equally shallow, pleasure seeker. No, whatever he was going to do now needed to be something that would enable him to feel that his life had value. That in some way shape or form, the world would not have been a better place without him.

When, late in the evening, he at last pulled his personal 'Why-How' back in front of him, he felt far better equipped to complete it. He felt foolish placing at the top of his chart 'to make the world a better place', but it was what he truly wanted to see himself doing. It was for him, a better sense of his identity; of who he really wanted to be.

He looked at the words he had placed at the top of his chart, and inwardly squirmed. He felt embarrassed by them. They seemed naive and unsophisticated. He imagined how embarrassed he would be if anyone else saw them. He wondered whether to strip the newly written yellow sticky right back off the chart, and replace it with something that appeared more deeply insightful, and less open to cynicism and ridicule.

we believe is entirely consistent with itself, and entirely consistent with our behaviours. An example of a congruent person is one who thinks a healthy body is key to enjoying life, has reconciled that to match up with their models of what they really enjoy doing, and who gets pleasure out of healthy eating and regular exercise.

Congruence can be achieved in all areas of our lives and congruent people tend to be immensely powerful and persuasive. They walk the talk and believe in what they are saying.

Is that important to you? Almost certainly, if you want to lead a congruent organisation. Part of the transformation of your organisation is the logic that we have covered in the preceding chapters. But a far bigger part is the leadership of someone who is absolutely clear on what is to be achieved, why it is to be achieved, how it is to be achieved, and has fully reconciled his or her life and behaviours to making it happen.

Leaders are leaders only if they have followers. Followers become followers because they are inspired and enthralled by a clear picture of the future, which they fully believe will become reality. They are attracted to people with vision and energy. And, vision and energy come from developing a well thought through purpose, and resolving clearly how it is to be brought about.

Anyone can change the world. All you need is faith and a plan of action.

Ernesto 'Che' Guevara
Bolivian Radical

An exercise in paradigms

One possible solution to the nine dots exercise is mapped out below:

Managing by Design

But what could he replace them with? The truth of the matter was, that no matter how twee it sounded, he really did want to be someone who made the world a better place. It was as simple as that.

He considered ruefully, how easy it was to wrap self-centredness and materialism up into sophisticated intellectual language that gave the author an air of wisdom. But that anything to do with simply 'being good' sounded foolish and uneducated. It was almost as though language itself was stacked in favour of him retaining his darker side. Perhaps it was simply that 'goodness' did not need to hide behind intricate arguments and sophisticated concepts. And anyway, why did he need it to sound sophisticated? Exactly who was he trying to impress? Was this not just 'vanity' trying to get in through the back door?

The more he thought about it, the more content he became with the simple straightforward words that left him nowhere to hide. He would just have to brazen it out.

The next day at work, he was even more confirmed and confident in his chosen path, and he had begun to work out the implications it had for his role in Cylek UK.

Richard had concluded that to make things better, really make things sustainably better, he needed to make himself dispensable. If the bits of 'betterness' depended on him being there, then they would stop when he stopped. There had to be something residual in 'adding value', or you couldn't be sure that you really had. He reflected on this for a while, and felt this was more like he would like to be. Developing the company so it could almost run itself.

Maybe he would not make himself fully dispensable, just dispensable for holidays, weekends, and the hours between 5 pm and 9 am. That would suit him just fine. Then in the hours from 9 to 5 his role could become one of developing structures and approaches for others to run the business, rather than to run the business himself.

In hindsight, he felt that the QFD his team had already developed would take him a long way towards this, but that he needed to develop his role with each member of his team to enable him to take a position that was commensurate with his new strategy. He would start with Susan.

Reconsidering and re-evaluating your role

Where your personal Why-How chart relates to your personal life is a matter between you and it. It is not the remit of this book to explore any further in that direction, except inasmuch as it clarifies or affects your understanding of your role within your organisation.

Where your personal Why-How chart relates to your business life, you have hopefully developed new insights into your management role.

It is likely that one of four things have transpired in exploring your role as it relates to work.

- You have merely mapped out the status quo, and have gained no new insights into your role, or

- you have concluded that your work life is incompatible with your personal aspirations, and you need to reconsider your vocation, or

- you have recognised that it is the detail of the job[1] that particularly inspires you, and that managing it is an unwelcome overhead, or

- you have reinforced your view that your role lies in leveraging the potential of your organisation, and have seen new possibilities in how you might do that.

In the case of option one; you are clearly of a fairly fixed mind, and are unlikely to gain anything more from reading this book, but you are to be commended with persevering with it thus far.

In the case of option two; it is well to recognise when we are in the wrong place.

No one can do inspired work without genuine interest in his subject and understanding of its characteristics.

Andreas Feininger
Photographer

---

1   For example, technical aspects, or dealing with people, or solving puzzles.

Chapter 18

"Wow, I've never seen tulips that colour!" Susan bent low over Helen's desk to get a closer look at the vermilion and green marking on the flowers that virtually obscured Helen completely. "So, what's this then, a secret admirer? You're a dark horse Helen!" she said looking up, and across the flowers, to a slightly reddened face.

"Yes, thank you Sherlock!" Helen replied in a mock tart tone.

"Who are they from then?" asked Susan, and then more quietly, "or aren't I to ask?"

Helen moved her head toward Susan's conspiratorially, and covertly jabbed her finger toward Richard's open office door, her eyes opening wide as if to say: "You'll never believe it!"

Susan mimicked Helen's expression, and then tilted her head as if to say: "Well, what do you know!" straightened up and winked.

"Perhaps he's got some for me too!" she said quietly as she turned towards Richard's office for their recently called meeting.

"Susan, thanks for making the time!" said Richard, coming round his desk and ushering her towards the meeting table.

"That's okay. I wanted to talk to you about a few things anyway and it's practically impossible to get hold of you these days." She paused momentarily as she sat down, and then said: "And by the way, where's my flowers?"

Richard smiled at her joke, and she continued in mock indignation: "No. I'm serious, Richard. I want to know where my flowers are!"

Richard leapt at the first response to let him off the hook. "I thought John bought you your flowers!" he said.

"Oh they're those sort of flowers are they?" Susan retorted with narrowed eyes and a knowing nod of the head.

Our background and environment can lead us unquestioningly into places where we can never feel at home, and while you feel this way you will be unlikely to achieve your potential. It might be good to start talking with people who can help you think about your next steps.[1] If you stay doing what you are doing, you will struggle to find the energy to implement what you have read in these pages.

In the case of option three; sometimes people get drawn into management because they are good at what they were doing, and they appreciate the recognition, status, money and power conferred by the promotion. But they never really get inspired by thoughts of organisation design, and redeveloping things to deliver lasting improvement. They are inspired by the short term and the detail, not by the long term and the big picture overview. As a result they tend to manage by making detail decisions to keep the show on the road. Perhaps this book might inspire them to see management in a new light, and might provide them with tools and methods to make it more appealing. But if not, then they would be better to be honest with themselves about their motivation, and reconsider whether they are doing the job under false pretences. Fortunately for them, very few of them are inclined to pick up a book like this in the first place, so we can relatively safely assume that you are probably not in this category.

In the case of option four; your personal Why-How chart probably reflects (at least in part) your role in achieving lasting performance through others, rather than through yourself. It was for you that this book was written, and you will be the most likely group to understand why so much

> *Most people perform essentially meaningless work. When they retire that truth is borne in on them.*
>
> Brendan Francis
> American Writer

---

1   One place you might start is with your manager, or alternatively you could look at www.whatevernextltd.co.uk

Richard looked shocked. "No, they're not!" he said, and sat back in his chair.

Susan laughed, to show she was only joking, and then said, smiling: "You be careful! That's how rumours start!" and then quickly continued with: "Now, I need to talk you through some rapidly approaching capital and contract purchase decisions," and started to draw some sheets from her file.

Richard placed a hand on her file to stop her, and said: "Hold on, before we get lost in the detail, tell me about your progress on the QFD."

Susan stopped in her stride, and said: "Sorry. I assumed this was to go through the purchase approvals, I haven't brought my QFD papers with me."

"That's okay. Just give me a general overview, an update on where you've got too. I spend so much time in the detail, I rarely get a chance to speak to the team about the strategic things."

Susan looked aghast. "Richard! It seems that the only time I get with you, these days, is all on the strategic things. Meeting after meeting. But, when I need to get your input on critical operational decisions, you're like the Scarlet Pimpernel. I can never get hold of you!"

Richard looked abashed, and the office went silent while he looked at the gaping hole in his new strategy, and Susan thought of what to say next.

Susan was right of course. The only times he had seen her recently was at QFD meetings, and at a recent Cylek worldwide conference on site utilisation.

"Sorry, Richard," said Susan, taking in Richard's obvious confusion, and reading it as due to her outburst. "I was out of order!"

"It's okay," said Richard, hastily. "You've made a very good point, and I think I would get a lot out of it if we could talk it though together. I promise I'll ensure the detail is addressed before you leave. Is that okay?" Susan nodded.

is freely given away within it. You understand what it means to add value.

You understand that success lies in
investing your time in your people and
systems so that they can achieve, and
continue to achieve, great things. But this
almost certainly presents you with a
dilemma - a 'Catch 22' situation. You need
time to develop your people and systems,
but your current working practices tie you
up in numerous activities that preclude you
from doing this. Developing your people
and systems will free off your time, but at
the moment they are not sufficiently
developed and you don't therefore have
time to develop them.

If this is your dilemma, then the challenge
is to find mechanisms and tools that can
help you to develop your people through
the activities that you are already doing.
This chapter illustrates four mechanisms
to help you do that:

- Top-box
- Managing the monkey
- Developing your people's vision
- Drawing out the systematic.

Top-box

The top-box tool is a simple mechanism
for identifying opportunities to delegate
some of your current activities and
involvement to your people, and for planning out how you will do it.

Take, for example, a review meeting with
a customer. Perhaps one at which one of
your team is already in attendance, but at
least one where a member of your team
may be invited.

The top-box acronym (see diagram over
the page) helps you to think through your
role, and how you can develop your team
member to take it over.

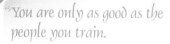

You are only as good as the people you train.

Lonear Heard
President, James T. Heard Mgt Corp
in Black Enterprise, September 1987

Susan expected Richard to go back to the QFD, but he did not. Instead he asked: "These capital and contract purchase approvals, what does my working through them with you add to the process?"

Susan replied quickly "Well, your advice and insight mainly!"

"Really?" queried Richard. "Is that really so?"

Susan paused this time, and thought more carefully before replying. "Well, you do have advance knowledge of Cylek initiatives, and of other budgetary commitments. Your review of purchase proposals does help to ensure that the things I don't have foresight of are taken into account."

Richard thought for a moment. "So, actually, all you need from me is an understanding of whether these commitments will create any budgetary conflicts?"

"Yes," replied Susan. "Basically, that's it!"

"But each time I've done this before with Abs, we've waded through all of the contract details to ensure that we weren't going to get caught out."

Susan waited silently.

Richard continued: "Do I not need to do that?"

"David Comber told me it was part of the process. He said you always check through the terms."

"Yes," said Richard, "I do. But does it add any value?"

Susan shrugged. "I don't know. Have you ever changed anything in the terms of the contract?"

"Gosh no! David's much better than me at that. He's fully qualified and I only skim through for obvious errors. I thought that all contracts over £25k had to be approved by the MD?" Richard left it hanging as a question.

"They do," replied Susan. "That's Cylek policy. But surely you're approving the sum, not the details of the contract. We've got paralegals like David to do things like that."

The following is an example of how it works in practice:

T: You might discover that your involvement is because you are particularly skilled at handling the customer

O: You might conclude that your Sales Manager should also have those skills

P: By chairing the meeting you can keep an eye on what is happening, and provide support to your Sales Manager through the process of the meeting, and some coaching

B: As your Sales Manager becomes more adept, you can pass over more of the role of the chair to him or her, and perhaps make guest appearances for specific items

O: You could then take the opportunity to review the purpose of the meeting, and to establish your Sales Manager's role in leading it

X: You can schedule a separate meeting with the customer to check that things are progressing to his or her satisfaction.

T	Test: Test why you need to be involved in this activity.
O	Opportunity: Identify the opportunity to develop others.
P	Plan: Plan how you will bring this about.
B	Back-off: Back-off to allow your people to develop.
O	Officialise: Make the changes official.
X	X-Check: Check that things are continuing to work out.

The challenge is to use top-box[1] to reflect on all of your activities, and to find new ways to develop your people through them, by coaching them, and by changing the nature and format of the meeting to make better use of the opportunities.

1   A form to help you to think through 'top-box' can be downloaded from the associated web-site (see Appendix 7).

Richard thought for a while. "I find it difficult to accept that in signing this off I'm only responsible for the budgetary implications, especially in these days of liability and litigation."

Susan nodded. "True, but you can't be an expert on everything. Surely your responsibility is to ensure that I, as the process manager, employ a competent contracts officer and establish the systems to assure the quality of his work. Perhaps your signature is a sign of your confidence in Cylek UK's systems."

Richard smiled and nodded. He liked that concept. "And do our systems ensure the quality of these contracts?" he posed back at Susan.

Susan thought for a while. "I don't know yet," she said. "I haven't evaluated them fully."

Richard smiled again as he thought of his next step. "Well, until you have, you can do the double checking of the contracts, and I'll sign to say I've got confidence in you."

Susan pursed her lips tightly, and then nodded to affirm the agreement, but her eyes smiled. For her it was the logical solution.

"That was fun," said Richard enthusiastically. "Now, what value can I add to the next item on our agenda?"

Richard had scheduled meetings with three more of his managers that day. Daniel predictably was not among them. The earliest Daniel could deign to see Richard was on Friday, the day after tomorrow.

But the meetings he did have planned for the day went well, and in every case, he not only managed to find ways to move the processes forward, but he also managed to divest responsibility for undertaking some of the less productive aspects of his old role.

In his meeting with Deborah, he managed to resign from the monthly tedium of the *Product Development Stage Gate Review Committee*, in exchange for a regular walkabout through the design department.

Managing the monkey

One of the books in the *One Minute Manager* series is entitled *The One Minute Manager meets the Monkey*.[1]

The principle of the book was to avoid taking other people's monkeys (problems) on your back. Your people can come and seek your advice and guidance on how to deal with the monkey, but the monkey stays on their back. In this way you do not tie yourself down with extra work, and you can use the monkey to coach and develop necessary growth in your people.

An example would be when a subordinate comes into your office to tell you that they can't source a vital component and so a critical piece of work will be delayed. The temptation may be to contact other people, and call a meeting to resolve things, but in doing this the monkey becomes your monkey. An alternative approach would be to ask your subordinate: "What do you see as your options for handling this, and what guidance can I provide you in taking it to the next step?"

Avoid the initial temptation, make it clear that when they leave your office they will take the problem with them, and ask what advice or guidance you can give that will help them to deal with the problem.

Developing your people's vision (aligning their goals)

Part of every leader's role is providing the big picture to reconcile troops who are operating from smaller pictures.

Ideally, this is a proactive, visionary drive on the part of the leader that serves to

Give a man a fish and you feed him for a day. Teach a man to fish, and you feed him for life.

Source unknown

---

1   The One Minute Manager books are an excellent easy to read series for anybody seeking to refocus their time on developing their people. The One Minute Manager Meets the Monkey, Blanchard, Onken and Burrows, Fontana, 1989.

And in his meeting with Andrew, he traded an exciting new role of using QFD for strategic competency planning, for the boring old role of chairing the *Salary Review Committee*.

The only meeting that proved anything less than delightful was his meeting with Peter.

Peter looked over the top of his glasses, clearly exasperated, and with exaggerated emphasis, carefully explained: "Richard, Finance is about control. It is about policing other people's decisions. It is about auditing and authority. You cannot simply devolve responsibility for finance to individual process owners without creating anarchy and chaos. The finance process has to be executed within the finance department by trained financial people. Anything else is irresponsible. It simply isn't good stewardship."

Richard was quiet, thinking Peter's points through, and how he would tackle it.

Into the silence, Peter added: "You would be losing money hand over fist!"

Richard tried another tack. "Peter, supposing you ran the R&D process, just for the sake of argument, you wouldn't let it be financially irresponsible. Would you?"

"No! But I don't, and my point is made clear if you just look at how R&D overrun their budgets year after year. They got hold of some spurious theory that a 5% delay is more costly than a 50% overspend, and see it as carte blanche to ignore our financial controls".

Richard was momentarily distracted by the red herring "That theory is not spurious. You can do the maths yourself!"

"Yes, yes. But my point is, that individual process owners seem congenitally unable to manage their finances responsibly without us standing behind their shoulder."

Richard sat back for a moment silently cursing himself for allowing himself to lose the initiative over the theory of new product funding. He

guide all actions thenceforth, but that is rarely the case in practice, particularly where the troops fall back to focusing on their bit of the picture.

The more parochial and narrow the picture that the troops have, the more time that the leader must spend using his or her understanding of the big picture to make adjustments, to provide detail, to resolve conflict, and to build links between the small pictures. For some leaders this can take up a vast amount of their time.

But if the troops have a picture of their role which is not parochial, which embraces the big picture and establishes visionary links to their colleagues' roles, then the call on the leader's arbitration skills is far less. The more your people can grasp a proactive vision for their role, the less they will depend on you to guide them.

Clearly QFD provides a good foundation for doing exactly that, and yet there are many cases where process owners focus on control rather than influence.

The challenge for the leader is to take every issue that needs his input to resolve, and to use it as a learning point to help stretch his or her people's visions, and through that, their grasp of responsibility.

Drawing out the systematic

By developing your people's vision you begin to draw them out into considering the systematic impact they can have on the business, and the people around them.

Another means of doing this concerns how you approach problems that come for your attention. If you have a very busy workload, you could be forgiven for simply ensuring that the problem is resolved, but that misses a tremendous opportunity to

Questions to inspire vision in service processes

What activities do you currently undertake?

What could others do as part of their work that would reduce this load or improve its quality?

How would taking on this work provide them with new opportunities or other benefits?

What would they need to do the work efficiently and to the best of their ability?

How could you service them in this?

paused, reflected on what he was trying to achieve here, and then started again.

"Okay, supposing you did run the R&D process. What would you do differently that would ensure responsible financial stewardship?"

Peter thought for a moment. "Well, there are a number of things. I'd certainly ensure that project managers reviewed expenditure as an essential part of each project review. I would tighten up their financial forecasting. And I would include a budgetary review at the start of each monthly meeting so that we were absolutely clear on what our current financial position was."

"So why do you think they don't do that?" interjected Richard.

"Well, for a start they just don't seem to appreciate the importance of it. They don't realise the implications on the rest of the business. And secondly, I don't think the project managers actually know how to manage their project costs. At least they have never shown any indication of the ability."

Richard interjected again "But if they did, that would make your job easier, right?"

"Oh, like you wouldn't believe it!" said Peter.

"Okay," said Richard, "but what about other areas of the business? Should they adopt a similar approach too?"

"What, you mean HR, MIS, Production etcetera?" asked Peter.

Richard nodded, so Peter continued: "Undoubtedly!"

Richard then postulated. "But we would want some consistency in the approaches they took to doing this wouldn't we? So that we had confidence in their approach, and could easily improve it, if necessary?"

He looked at Peter who nodded, and said: "Yes, absolutely".

"So we couldn't leave each process a totally fee hand to develop their own?" challenged Richard.

"No-o-o," agreed Peter hesitantly. He was beginning to have an inkling of where this was going to end up.

identify how the processes can be improved to provide a lasting solution. The Check Sheet[1] (below) helps explore an issue to draw out the systematic learning that is possible. It is very useful in ensuring that 'monkeys' are handled effectively, and that the conclusions your people reach make a systematic and lasting difference, not only to the organisation, but also to calls on your time.

The specifics:	Looking at the system:	Looking at prevention:
What happened?	How could you categorise this with similar incidents?	How can we prevent these incidents?
When did it occur?	How frequently do they arise? What is the trend?	What should we do to monitor and manage this?
Who was affected?	Who are those most vulnerable to such incidents?	How should we bring our customers on board?
How were they affected?	What is the total impact of these incidents on our business?	How can we minimise the impact in future?
Why did the incident occur?	What are the most likely causes of these incidents?	What can we do to further reduce the risks?
Where did it start?	In what locations, conditions, etc. do they mostly occur?	How can this learning be used elsewhere?

1   The check sheet can be downloaded from the associated web-site (see Appendix 7).

Richard continued: "So, we really need one group which can develop an efficient and effective approach, and then sell it to those who need to use it. You know; really get their buy-in and commitment to it!"

Peter just sat there looking at Richard, with a wry smile on his face. "And I suppose the best home for such work would be within the finance process?"

"You know," said Richard, tongue firmly in cheek, "I'd never really thought of that. But yes, you're right, I suppose that would be the best home. Thank you, Peter!"

Designing your role

Over the preceding five chapters, we have begun to develop a picture of the leader's role (your role) in moving the organisation forward, and what that means.

How you use 'yourself' will be the major factor in your success in transforming your organisation through QFD. The extent to which you congruently lead, inspire, expect, resolve, design, challenge and support change will in large part determine how effectively it takes place.

In this, you have a difficult and complex task ahead of you, and a vast range of options as to how it might be undertaken. How do you best configure those options to make the difference you need?

A thought. If QFD works for designing an organisation, can it also be applied to effectively designing the 'role' of the leader? Can it be applied to designing you? That may be an awesome thought, and one that you might find difficult to contemplate. But at one level you are the sum of your actions and behaviours, and your impact on the organisation is determined by those actions and behaviours.

In the past, people have used QFD successfully to gain real insight into their role, to balance their time, and to redesign their activities to maximise their impact on the organisation.

In this chapter we will consider how the process for developing an organisational QFD can be adapted to develop a personal QFD. It is done by:

- developing objectives, measures and targets

- identifying the main activities to deliver them

- exploring the potential of each activity

Chapter 19

Richard felt inspired by his success during the day. In fact, he viewed it as his most successful day ever. He felt energised and released. He felt like the butterfly newly evolved from the caterpillar. He felt great!

Back at home that evening, he felt ready to start on developing a QFD for his new role. He was going to design the new him. The world was his oyster.

He looked long and hard at the Why-How chart he had developed for himself and wondered where to begin. He had only written it two nights ago, and already it seemed out of date. Could he have changed that much in just two days? He began to feel that he would need to rewrite the whole thing. The original chart seemed so wrong, had he just wasted his time?

And then he remembered that it was the original chart that had woken him up to the real issues in his life. Far from being a waste of time, it had probably been the most pivotal exercise in his working life. It was only out of date because of the work that it had done in him.

But, it was still out of date. And frankly, there was something in him that balked at the idea of going through it all again. He felt his energies were pushing him to do the QFD now - that was where his enthusiasm lay.

So be it. He would attempt a QFD, knowing he could always repeat the whole process later. It was almost as though his subconscious was eager to reveal new things, not to consolidate and refine the old.

"After all," he rationalised, "this whole process is about new understanding developing, not about getting stuck in the detail and paperwork."

Content that he had justified his approach, he pulled a new pack of yellow stickies in front of him. His pen poised, he glanced back at the old Why-How chart for inspiration.

He decided that he would initially focus on his work role. He felt that would be easier. He was not fully sure that he could reconcile his role as MD and as family man into one homogenous whole, at least not yet. He felt that he needed to do a lot more thinking on his role with his family, before he was ready to attempt a QFD there.

- calculating the ideal balance of time.

Developing objectives

The objectives of a leader should not be confused with the objectives of the organisation that he or she leads. In many companies this subtlety has been overlooked and it is not uncommon to find that managers have simply had their departmental objectives copied directly, and exclusively, into their personal objectives. This lack of thought is pure laziness on the part of the organisation, and unfortunately tends to focus the manager into the 'bottom box'.[1]

A good organisation should be able to deliver its objectives whether the manager is there or not. The manager's role is therefore to ensure it is a good organisation; and one capable of taking on even more demanding objectives in the future.

So what might the objectives of such a manager be? Typically if the manager's role is about developing the capability and performance of the department, they might include:

- improving the competence of staff
- ensuring the quality of processes
- developing efficient use of information
- sustaining a rate of improvement
- building strategic partnerships for the future
- establishing transformational values.

These are clearly a long way from *'Increase throughput by 10%'* or *'Reduce costs by 5%'*, and yet they are the very things that will deliver that sort of improvement sustainably.

To be truly motivated, one must make personal commitments.

William G. Dyer
Bringham Young Unidersity
in Strategies for Managing Change
(Addison-Wesley, 1984)

---

1   See Chapter 3, and the closing pages of Chapter 8.

There were too many unresolved questions in his private life: too many areas that he did not want to explore too closely; too many decisions to make. Somewhere at the back of his mind he knew it was because he was being irresponsible and selfish, but he did not feel ready to let go of his fantasies yet, and he knew in his heart that they would not survive in the light.

Anyway, he had to start somewhere, and what was wrong with starting where he felt most encouraged to do so.

He started by listing all of the differences he wanted to bring about from his time at Cylek. Sticky note, after sticky note, fell onto the pile in front of him, covering topics from rate of growth to management competence, from the influence of the Gloucester facility to the quality of the systems being used.

He scribbled on, occasionally glancing out of his study window into the streetlight outside, until at last his ideas dried up. He checked back onto the original Why-How chart, to see if there was anything he might have missed, and hastily scribbled two more notes. And then he gathered all the notes back in front of him.

As he reviewed the notes, it struck him that what he had written seemed to fall into two camps. In the first camp were all his ideas about what Cylek would achieve: how it would grow; how its role would develop; the control it would exert over its markets; the impact it would have on its customers etc. The second camp contained his ideas about how Cylek would be: the approaches it would take; the quality of its people; the motivation and culture of the place etc.

He was struck by how similar the items in the first camp were to the QFD they had developed for the business itself. Most of them were much more far-reaching than on the existing QFD, but he could easily imagine them on future QFDs.

And the more he thought about it, the more he began to reflect that maybe these things weren't his role at all.

The idea sounded almost heretical at first, and he pushed it away. He could almost imagine Cyrus's face if he told him he did not see it as his job to 'grow the business'. But the more he played with the concept, the more he began to see the truth of it.

In developing your own personal QFD, you might use elements of these as a basis for thinking through your own objectives, and add in any others that are specific to your situation and the point you are starting from. It is useful to reflect on your Why-How chart, if you have developed one, to ensure that you have considered all of your objectives.

It should be remembered that the departmental objectives must be delivered, and the manager is responsible for ensuring that the department achieves them, so they do need to feature as a measure of the manager's performance. But the expectation is that the manager delivers the objectives through the organisation, and not in spite of it.

It is important, also, that the manager develops measures and targets for his or her other objectives as well. This helps to clarify what the objectives mean, and what they do not. Until someone has worked out clearly how they could measure 'growth in direct report competence' they really do not know clearly what they mean by it. Targets further help this clarification. A good question to bear in mind is "What level of performance is the threshold between success and failure, and why?"

Identifying activities

Having developed a clear and comprehensive picture of the objectives, the next step is to think through the mechanisms by which they are achieved.

In the case of the manager, these mechanisms are clearly the activities of their working week.

But in developing the columns of the personal QFD, it is important that they don't simply reflect what the manager is already doing, but also what he or she should be doing, for instance activities which support:

Managing by Design

It was not the coach's job to ensure that his football team scored more goals in each successive game. It was the team's job to do that. It was the coach's job to build the vision for that in the team; to grow their confidence in achieving it; and to help them to develop their approach to ensure it was delivered. If the coach leapt onto the pitch to make the crucial scoring pass, all hell would break loose. The coach added value because he made himself dispensable. Each and every match, the team had to deliver on their own.

Perhaps then, the MD's job could be seen in the same way.

Perhaps, thought Richard, his job was to ensure that his management team caught the vision for business growth and made it their own. Perhaps his job was to achieve the items he had listed in the first camp, solely by what he achieved through the items he had listed in the second camp.

He thought for a moment, a puzzled look on his face, and then he hastily flicked through the sticky notes he had in the second group, and added two more: *'Ensure a shared and compelling vision for the future of the business'* and *'Ensure determined objective pursuit of the vision'*.

He sat back. He felt slightly nervous about his conclusion, but the more he thought about it, the more he was sure it was the right one.

Growing the business was his management team's job. And the more he saw it as his, the more inclined he would be to step into the detail, second guess their decisions, and end up doing their job for them. After all, that's what had been happening when you boiled it all down. And while he was doing that, who was doing his job: of ensuring commitment to a common vision; of broadening and deepening his people's perspectives; of improving their game?

He thought back on his day, on how much he had achieved, and he knew he was right to think this way.

After grouping the sticky notes from the second camp into six distinct objectives for his role, Richard then proceeded to list out all of the activities he undertook in his role. He had initially favoured listing out only those activities he felt he should do, but then reasoned that this would be a more objective way of re-evaluating his time. And after all, even if his current activities remained valid, he might get new insights into the objectives he should bear in mind when undertaking them.

- personal growth and development
- staff growth and development
- improving the organisation
- focusing the organisation.

A good way to start the list, is to flick through your diary and your calendar, and copy out separate activities on individual sticky-notes, so that they can be grouped later if appropriate.

The list can be further augmented by looking back over your objectives, and identifying other activities that you need to consider if the objectives are to be met.

It is quite common to end up with 40 or 50 activities and, unlike the organisational QFD, a lot of personal QFDs have over 20 columns. However, where activities clearly do overlap, it is best to group them together, or they will distort the end result. You should aim for between 20 and 30 activities to get sufficient detail in your conclusions.

Finally, you should recheck your activities to ensure you know exactly and specifically what you do in them, to make sure they are not vague and nebulous.[1]

Exploring potential

As in developing an organisational QFD,[2] the grid between the objectives (rows of the grid) and the activities (columns of the grid) provides a tremendous opportunity to explore how each activity can contribute to the objectives, and to discover new and previously unforeseen potential for leveraging current activities to achieve more - the QFD equivalent of 'work smarter not harder'.

Amid a multitude of projects, no plan is devised.

Publilius Syrus
Roman writer

---

1   'Coaching sessions with my people' is clear, while 'Developing staff' could mean anything as an activity.

2   See Chapter 9.

By 10.30 he had grouped his activities into a number of management processes, and had drawn out the grid of his QFD. He looked at the clock on his windowsill, and then back at the empty grid of his QFD. He knew if he started it now he would not finish until he early hours, and yet he did not want to delay.

He stood up, and stretched, and decided to make himself a cup of tea while he made up his mind. As he stepped out onto the landing, he heard the muted sounds of sobbing downstairs. Quietly, he stole down into the lounge, and gently sat down beside Laura, a look of concern on his face.

"Whatever's the matter?" he asked. "Come on now. He's okay now. They said we could bring him home tomorrow didn't they?"

Laura turned a tear-streaked, distraught face towards him. He held out his arms, and she collapsed into him. "Oh love!" he said, "what's the matter?"

She shook her head, and pushed tighter into his chest, as if defying him to lift her head up like he always did. He just held her more tightly, and after about a minute he said: "Won't you tell me what's the matter?"

Laura straightened up. "It's okay. I'm okay now," she said wiping her eyes.

Richard took one of her hands. "Please tell me," he pleaded.

Laura looked into her lap. "Oh I don't know. It's just … well it's just I'm so scared of losing you both," she said. And again her face puckered up and the tears came. She looked away.

"Oh Laura! Laura!" said Richard, moving in closer. "It won't happen. Nicky is better now. He was never really in any serious danger. You heard the doctors."

Laura looked back at him slowly and asked: "Yes, I know, but what about you?"

Richard looked down into his lap. He felt Laura's stare upon him as she waited for him to respond.

He made a decision. He was a man of integrity.

Still gazing at his knees, he began: "I'm sorry Laura. I know I've been working too hard. I know I've asked too much of you. Taken too much

The cells should be considered individually, to identify the potential of that activity to move the objectives forward, using the definitions on the right. The process is likely to be much quicker than for the organisational QFD, because the debate is less. Often people undertake personal QFDs on their own, or with one other person to act as a sounding board. The diagram below shows an example of what your finished personal QFD might look like.[1]

- ⦿ **Critical:** (9 Points) Process is fundamental to progressing the objective
- ○ **Major:** (3 Points) Process is key to achieving the target performance
- △ **Significant:** (1 Point) Process will significantly contribute to the result
- **Blank:** (0 Points) Process will not significantly impact on the result

Example: Personal QFD for a senior management role

Objective	Wt.	Thinking in the 'top box'	Reading journals and books	Being mentored by others	Attending events & training	Customer visits & job shadow	Customer reviews	Planning with the customer	Implement 'SLA's with partners	Establish vision for change	Establish performance targets	Business planning workshop	Resource planning	STC cascade	Social teambuilding activities	Report process performance	Review process performance	Problem solving	Develop process strategies	Manage resource plan	Set individual perf'ce targets	Establish personal devt. plans	Review team performance	Coaching direct reports
Ensure business plan delivered	4	O			△	O	Θ	△	△	Θ	Θ		△	O	△	Θ	△	O	Θ	O	△	O	O	
Develop partnerships for success	3	△		△	△	O	O	O	O		△	O		△	△	△	O	△	△	△		△	△	△
Ensure systematic management	5	Θ	△	O	△	△	△	△	△	O	Θ	△	O	△	△	O	Θ	O	O	△	O	O	O	Θ
Review/address performance	4	△					O	△	O	△	Θ	△				Θ	Θ	Θ	Θ		Θ	Θ	Θ	O
Ensure goal & strategies to deliver	4	O	△	O	Θ		△		O	O	△	O	Θ	△	△	△		O	△	Θ	△	△	△	△
Build customer vision & our role	2	Θ	O	O	△	O	Θ	O	O	O		△	△		O			O			△			O
Increase management contribution	5	O			△		△	△	△	O	Θ	△	O	O	△	O	O		△	△	△	Θ	Θ	Θ
Develop personal competence	3	△	△	Θ	△	△		△		△	△	△			△	O	△	O		△		△	△	△
Ranking		112	18	87	18	27	45	92	49	81	146	114	34	23	41	76	168	80	122	53	114	110	118	130
Calculated																								
Minutes per week (or)		144	29	161	30	50	61	130	70	96	169	156	38	32	51	86	212	92	163	62	120	124	133	153
Days per year		13.8	2.8	15.4	2.9	4.7	5.8	12.5	6.7	9.2	16.2	15.0	3.7	3.0	4.9	8.3	20.3	8.8	15.6	5.9	11.5	11.9	12.7	14.6

When the grid is complete, the scores can be added up in the usual way[2] and used to assess what balance of time should ideally spent on each activity.

Calculating the balance of time

The scores at the bottom of a personal QFD reflect the relative importance of each activity to progress the personal objectives (your personal objectives).

---

1   The QFD shown above is a real example from one of my clients. It was developed in Excel™ and so the bulls-eye symbol differs slightly from the standard. The Excel™ template is available from the associated web-site (see Appendix 7).

2   See page 84 on how the QFD is scored. The template described in footnote 1 performs these calculations automatically.

for granted." Here he looked up into her eyes, as if to confirm his words. "But you've got to believe me. I will never leave you. Never."

Laura continued to gaze at him for a while, and eventually, slowly, a contented smile formed in her eyes, and she fell back into his arms.

"Well, that about wrecks the QFD grid for tonight," thought Richard.

During Thursday, Richard managed to get his meetings with Abs and John, each of which proved fairly successful.

And at 5pm he and Laura collected Nicholas from the hospital.

By 7pm Nicholas was in bed, Laura slouched beside him on the beanbag, both fast asleep.

Richard closed the door on this scene of contentment and retired to his study to complete his QFD.

When he had completed the grid at 9pm, he had problems accepting what it told him.

According to the numbers at the bottom of the grid, he needed to spend over half his time coaching, developing, monitoring and inspiring the members of his Management Team, if he was to efficiently pursue his objectives.

His current biggest activity of sitting in at meetings, warranted less than 5% of his time, and even then the focus had shifted - emphasising the use of the meeting to develop the role of his subordinates, rather than get involved in the detail.

To be frank, the result frightened him. The change was too great.

He began looking frantically for where he might have got the weighting or the maths wrong. He tried altering some numbers to bring it into better balance. But each time he did so, he was not happy with the changes he had made.

By 11pm, he had made no further progress, but was becoming resigned to the fact that the QFD was right, and it was tradition that was wrong. Still, it was a very bold step!

One way of looking at this, then, is that the time you spend on each activity should be in proportion to its importance; in other words, in proportion to the scores at the bottom of the grid.

If you calculate what this means in practice, you may be shocked by the extent to which your current time allocation is out of kilter with the relative importance of the tasks to your objectives. If you are shocked, then you are far from alone.

If you wish to calculate what the scores in your personal QFD reflect in terms of time spend, then you can follow this procedure. The total scores at the bottom of each column should be added up into a grand total. This grand total equates to 35[1] hours/week or 220[2] days/year.

The ideal amount of time allocated to each activity should therefore be:

$$\frac{\text{Column total}}{\text{Grand total}} \times 35 \frac{\text{hours}}{\text{week}} \left(\text{or} \times 220 \frac{\text{days}}{\text{year}}\right)$$

This provides a useful guide to what your diary/calendar should look like.

When you have calculated the ideal time for each activity (days/year in terms of calendarised items, hours/week in terms of regular items), work through your diary and list up what you actually spend.

Please be realistic here. If you could have used a meeting for coaching, but did not, do not list it as coaching! Facing up to the facts frees you to make a choice - it is denying the facts that constrains you.

Having listed up ideas and actuals, pragmatically work out what you can change,

---

1   Remember we are trying to work toward an ideal rather than perpetuate poor practice.

2   If you are not a full-time manager, you may need to adjust these numbers.

Resignedly, he closed the door, roused Laura from her recumbent vigil, and went to bed.

Lucy scanned the numbers at the base of Richard's personal QFD.

"I see what you mean," said Lucy, "but actually I suspect it's right. I've long thought that the reason managers end up so busy, is because they don't put enough investment into their subordinates and their systems. I'm afraid this just panders to my prejudices. Sorry!"

"But surely it can't be practical. Can it?" challenged Richard.

Lucy looked at the QFD again. "Well, only this week, you were telling me your theory of dispensability and adding value. You tell me!"

Richard shook his head and moved away. Theory was one thing. Putting it into practice was something different entirely.

Lucy continued to pour over the QFD.

"You know, this is really something!" she said. "It really is a terrific tool. There are enough insights in this little grid to fill about fifty management textbooks. Have you tried to develop one for your life?" she asked as she turned to look at Richard.

Richard turned back. "Almost," he said, "but I came up with objectives of integrity, fidelity, responsibility, and worried that it might cramp my playboy style." He laughed, but it was a forced laugh. Lucy went quiet.

Richard eventually broke the silence. "I will do a QFD for my life," he said quietly, "and I know it will tell me things I don't want to hear right now. I know I've not been as good as I could be. In fact," he paused and he looked down, "I think I've been pretty crummy. But all that is going to stop. I know the sort of person I want to be, and I'm going all out to be that person. It's just that it's a big pill to swallow. You know?"

He looked back up at Lucy, his mouth creased in a sad but determined expression, his eyes appearing to hold a new depth of understanding.

They stood quietly staring at each other for but a moment. Each confident that something deep and meaningful had passed between them. Each reaching out to the other, their eyes affirming that special, shared experience. Each holding some small sense of regret. And in that look, their

and plan them back into your diary and calendar as clearly defined activities.

Please remember, however, not to be driven by the numbers. If you are really unhappy with them, look back into your QFD and reconsider your assumptions. If all of your assumptions are right, and yet you are still unhappy with the conclusion, it does not mean have to revise your diary. Although you might consider making a few minor adjustments in line with what you feel is practical.

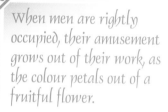

When men are rightly occupied, their amusement grows out of their work, as the colour petals out of a fruitful flower.

John Ruskin
English essayist

relationship changed, and they felt a different, deeper closeness to each other.

At that moment, they truly became friends.

"Anyway," said Lucy, breaking the moment, "I thought you had a meeting with Daniel now?"

Richard looked hurriedly at his watch "Gosh, yes, gotta fly!" and with that he grabbed his file and rushed out.

Making hard decisions

As people work to implement systematic approaches in their own area to support the achievement of the QFD (see list right), your championing and support will be key to their enthusiasm and commitment. But managing systematically does not suit everyone. The responsibilities and disciplines involved make sense and are valuable to those who take their responsibility seriously. But there are many others who:

- prefer to make their decisions freely

- do not want to look too deeply into their own approach and motives

- enjoy conflict and panic

- are fearful of being exposed by anything systematic

- enjoy picking and choosing an approach which suits them rather than the task

- have tied their self-image to their experience and intuition.

To be fair, there are elements of this in all of us, but for most of us, our desire to make a real difference, and our degree of self-honesty, is enough to keep all of these things (largely) in check.

For some, however, they consciously or subconsciously value how they appear more than what they are: they value living comfortably in a lie above achieving something worthwhile through wrestling with the truth. Any systematic approaches to management are a threat to them, and all they see is extra work, loss of freedom, a diminishment in their power and the potential to fail at it.

This, once again, is partly true of all of us. But some feel it so strongly that they fight a rearguard action. Initially this is only passive resistance, but eventually it can develop into full-scale rebellion.

Steps to local implementation

1. Develop process objectives/proposal.

2. Map the process and its sub-processes.

3. Establish performance measures.

4. Develop the local process QFD.

5. Appoint sub-process owners / assign responsibilities.

6. Establish local management process.

7. Initiate focused improvement projects.

Chapter 20

If the meeting with Peter had been taxing, the meeting with Daniel was frankly impossible.

Any attempts at drawing Daniel out, were met with stormy, reserved excuses and rationalisations. Daniel seemed determined not to let anything slip, and was very reluctant to engage in anything that might be seen as dialogue. Richard felt like he was banging his head against a brick wall, and getting nowhere. In the end, he resorted to just drawing out the basic facts.

"Daniel, exactly what progress have you made against what was agreed at the last meeting?" asked Richard.

"I don't remember any agreement," replied Daniel archly.

"Okay, against what was demanded at the last meeting," clarified Richard.

"Richard, I've told you how busy we've been here."

"Daniel, I want a straight answer. Where is your implementation plan? And what progress have you made?"

"We haven't been able to do a plan!" Daniel replied defiantly.

"But you are aware that you were required to deliver one to my desk last Friday," challenged Richard.

Daniel remained stonily silent, and just glared malevolently back.

"Okay," said Richard, "we are both here together. We've got the time now. Let's develop a plan." Anger was evident in his voice as he stood up and moved to the flipchart in Daniel's office.

He scribbled the word 'Plan' at the top of the page, and then looked back down at Daniel. "Have you any suggestions for what should go on this plan Daniel?"

Daniel just stared back, and curtly replied "No!"

"Okay," said Richard, "let me suggest the activities that seem to be on most everybody else's plan." And he wrote up seven activities required

On the evidence of the implementations to date, you can be assured that, as you work to establish these ideas into your organisation, you will face this. How you react to it will in large part determine the success of your entire implementation.

Jack Welch faced up to this situation in parts of GE, and included his conclusions within his annual report.

He explained that GE employed four types of people. These can be explained by a simple grid, like the one on the right. In his annual report (see right) he made it clear that the values and processes of the organisation were more important than the short-term results.

Conversely, a major steel producer, who had embarked on a Total Quality (TQ) programme in four plants producing different steel products, did not see things that way. The demands on the steel plants, which were at the same location, varied widely over the year. Historically the plants regularly found themselves either overloaded or with idle labour. As part of the TQ programme it was agreed that they would move labour between them as demands fluctuated. One plant manager embraced the concept wholeheartedly, and regularly provided staff to the other plants. However, when he was short of staff, the other plant managers claimed they could not spare anybody, seeing instead the opportunity to use them on internal projects.

Still, culture change takes time, and so the single plant manager persevered. But then he saw his bonus for output performance go to his three colleagues, who had made their output with his people. He left the company shortly after.

Sometimes the type three manager under performs precisely because the type four manager is not sharing the values.

GE's four types of managers:

Results Yes	**Type 4** Rejects values and delivers results	**Type 1** Espouses values and delivers results
No	**Type 2** Rejects values and doesn't deliver results	**Type 3** Espouses values and doesn't deliver results

Excerpt from GE Annual Report

In our view, leaders, whether on the shop floor or at the tops of our businesses, can be characterized in at least four ways.

The first is one who delivers on commitments - financial or otherwise - and shares the values of our Company. His or her future is an easy call. Onward and upward.

The second type of leader is one who does not meet commitments and does not share our values. Not as pleasant a call, but equally easy.

The third is one who misses commitments but shares the values. He or she usually gets a second chance, preferably in a different environment.

Then there's the fourth type - the most difficult for many of us to deal with. That leader delivers on commitments, makes all the numbers, but doesn't share the values we must have.

This is the individual who typically forces performance out of people rather than inspires it: the autocrat, the big shot, the tyrant. Too often all of us have looked the other way - tolerated these "Type 4" managers because "they always deliver" - at least in the short term.

Continued on next page...

to implement things in Daniel's processes. He then drew a three month timescale along the top of the page, and looked back at Daniel.

"So when do you propose to complete this first activity, Daniel?" challenged Richard.

Daniel shrugged, looked up at the ceiling for a moment. Then said: "Let me see." He ostentatiously pretended to flick through his diary, and then glared back up at Richard and growled: "Not within that timescale!"

Richard closed his eyes and composed himself. He had known from the outset that it would come to this eventually. He had rather that it happened after the business results had started to improve, so that he could at least be a bit more sure of his own position. But now it was clear; there was only the road to the inevitable available to him, and there was nothing to be gained now by further conciliatory attempts. The only thing left for Richard, was to issue an ultimatum. He looked Daniel straight in the eyes.

"Your performance to date in implementing these changes has been unacceptable. Your progress has been negligible, and your excuses do not reflect any more difficulty than your colleagues have had to face, but they are much further ahead than you in this. I am giving you formal notice that I expect to see the first three steps listed here," he pointed to the flipchart, "all complete within the next four weeks. I expect to see a well-developed plan to that effect presented at next week's management meeting. And I will be entering a note of this conversation in your record."

Richard closed his file, and Daniel eyed him malevolently.

Then Daniel replied, in cold measured tones: "I will comply with your request. However, I reiterate my warning that these changes will adversely affect our customers, and I will submit a letter to that effect, to you, in writing."

Richard turned around and left. They had been though this spurious 'damage customer relationships' argument a number of times, and Richard could see no point in, yet again, replying to this clearly bogus claim.

He would wait for the letter and reply, point by point, in writing. He hoped that would be an end to it, but he strongly suspected it would not. Frankly, he wanted Daniel out, and he was now only concerned about

In implementing systematic approaches to management, similar effects can occur:

- resources can be withheld
- measures can be manipulated politically
- information can be used against those providing it.

And sometimes the rewards for doing them are nothing to do with the leader; they are simply inherent in the existing systems and culture.

As you begin your implementation, you will have some committed allies, some entrenched rebels, and probably a majority on a scale in the middle. If you allow the rebels to score from your allies you will lose the middle ground.

Exhortation and logic will not be enough. The inherent unfairness in the system and culture will need to be compensated for. Rebels must be dealt with in such a way that the middle ground realise that you are serious and determined.

For many managers who embark on the work outlined in this book, handling such resistance is the toughest part of the task, and one that they are typically least inclined to tackle. As a result they send out mixed messages about how serious they really are. Their severe dislike (perhaps even fear) of conflict, delays them from taking action, until such action becomes inevitable and distinctly unpleasant for all concerned.

Vacillation and delay will only exacerbate problems of this type - they really do not diminish over time! The longer you leave the floor to the insidious influence of your opponents, the more they will establish their power base, and the more drastic will be the action you have to take to tear it down.

Excerpt from GE Annual Report ... continued

And perhaps this type was more acceptable in easier times, but in an environment where we must have every good idea from every man and woman in the organization, we cannot afford management styles that suppress and intimidate. Whether we can convince and help these managers to change - recognizing how difficult that can be - or part company with them if they cannot, will be the ultimate test of our commitment to the transformation of this Company and will determine the future of the mutual trust and respect we are building.

It does not do to leave a live dragon out of your calculations, if you live near him.

J.R.R. Tolkein
English professor and popular novelist.

how long it would take, and what damage Daniel could do in the meantime.

Richard discovered exactly what damage could be done, within a week of his meeting with Daniel. The shattered glass of the crystal decanter lay all around him. The sparkling reflected light seemed to mock the dark depression in his heart. It seemed to jeer at his sense of unfairness and betrayal, and he imagined Daniel's smirking face in every piece.

The door had shut quietly, and he straightened, lifting his head slightly backwards he stared, unfocused, at the line where the wall met the ceiling, and opened his eyes wide in order to absorb back the pools of liquid forming in front of his eyes.

He breathed in deeply and held himself, and clenched his jaw, sensing himself on the precipice of collapsing into a sobbing rage. He braced himself until the moment passed, and then let the air out of his body slowly.

His shoulders slumped, and, as he closed his eyes, a single tear rolled down each cheek to the corners of his mouth. There, the saltiness seemed to both comfort him and bring him resolve, and in a single determined movement he brought both hands up to wipe the tear tracks away.

He leant forward, grasping the back of the dining room chair, and looked sideways out of the window, but his mind was focused on pictures of what had just transpired, and of the scenes that must have led to this point.

The decanter had been her wedding present to him, and while the aim had been wild, the projectile itself had been chosen with care. It was intended to represent the way she felt he had shattered her love for him. It was an act of finality, and, in keeping with slamming the door, it clearly indicated that Laura felt there was nothing else he could do or say. Their marriage was over in her mind!

But he had not done the things she had said. He was innocent. Yes, okay, he had thought about them, he had played with the ideas and images in his mind, and he had even loosely dwelt on plans as to how these things might be brought about. But HE HAD NEVER ACTUALLY PHYSICALLY DONE ANYTHING. He had, at least as far as the law was concerned, remained faithful to Laura.

It is far better to take clear, consistent and timely steps from the outset, to keep control:

- stamp on inappropriate behaviours
- recognise the need for off-line discussions
- modify and use the reward system
- use the disciplinary process.

Stamp on inappropriate behaviours

Imagine the following. John, a member of your management team, puts up an excellent transparency covering the performance measures of his area at your management meeting. The slide has been well thought out, using colour to emphasise certain points. It is the first time one of your people has done anything like this - reports are normally verbose, text based, and handed round.

John is very keen though (perhaps a little too keen, even sycophantic) and while his slide is excellent it has a little logo in the right hand corner that looks really naff.

As the slide goes up, Steve, another of your team, remarks "Couldn't you have put some fairy lights on it John? It's Christmas next month!" People laugh, and Angela chips in "He's just after brownie points for his Christmas bonus!" John smiles back a little ruefully, and continues his presentation.

Fairly normal interchange; fairly trivial; fairly harmless, so you let it go. But think for a moment. What has happened here? Who is setting the 'norms' for behaviour in your group?

Humour is an excellent device for helping things to flow, for smoothing things over and for taking the awkwardness out of situations. It can leave effective messages

Reviewing behaviour

What inappropriate behaviours exist within your management team?

....

....

....

What desirable behaviours are lacking within the team?

....

....

....

What factors allow this situation to continue?

....

....

....

Managing by Design

He had been hanged, without trial or jury, on the wicked, malicious mischief making of one man. Anger burned within him. He was furious at the injustice. He raged at the cynically unfair timing of it. At precisely the time he had determined to focus himself on Laura's love and support, at precisely the time he had allowed himself to become vulnerable to what it meant to him, it had been wantonly destroyed, vandalised. In his mind's eye, he could see Daniel celebrating his success, and he hated him with a blackness he had never thought possible.

He thought it strange how the anger and hate was overwhelming the sense of loss in him, he began to feel guilty that at the time his marriage was in tatters, he was more consumed with his enemy than with his wife. More consumed with hate, than with love and compassion. He forced himself to think about her, to imagine her pain and despair when Daniel Matthews spun his web of lies.

He imagined the moment when Daniel came calling, he visualised how the conversation must have gone:

"Laura, I'm so sorry to come calling on you." "Hi Daniel, come on in." "Oh you poor, poor girl," and the pitying eyes.

He could imagine Laura, thrown and confused by this turn in the conversation, and then he could imagine the poison dripping, as Daniel ripped open the wound and pretended to embalm it.

"I'm so sorry, I don't even know how to begin, but I just know if it was happening to me, I'd want someone to say it."

Richard did not know if those were the exact words. He did not know if they were said slowly with mock compassion, or in an agitated rush. But he could image the cold ripping feel of the knife in his wife's stomach. He could imagine the numbness and the energy draining from her, as Daniel told Laura about her husband's hotel trips. And he could imagine the sheer black despair as she felt the bottom ripped out of her world, as Daniel manufactured the details of the affair, the betrayal.

He heard the final words again, he saw the decanter come spinning by his head, and he saw Laura's suffused face and angry mouth as she yelled, half sobbing.

"Don't lie to me, you bastard! Don't cheapen me any more! Daniel saw you in bed, he saw the messed up covers, he said you were undressed. At least do me the final courtesy of telling me the truth … please!"

without being disruptive. We often don't realise its power. But in leaving messages, it can have its dark side as well, and in smoothing things over it can reinforce a culture that you no longer want. And all too often, humour will be the main weapon of the cynic and the rebel, gradually eroding the values you would like to establish.

Point-scoring, in any form, has to be dealt with. And often, in dealing with it, you will be working against the current culture. You have the last word, and you need to ensure that the norms being developed in the interchanges of your team are the norms that you want.

Unfortunately, this will mean that, as you emphasise the positives to redress the balance and you pick up people on comments that are just a little too acrid, you may appear a wet blanket. You, who can be as witty as the rest; you, who enjoy a laugh with the team; you, who have your own reservations about the cheesy nature of certain aspects of the slide; you have to forgo belonging in order to create the new norm. You have to publicly stake your position and credibility with what is right, rather than what is popular; and by doing so consistently, gradually make popular what is right.

The need for off-line discussions

Some issues can be addressed within the meeting by ensuring balanced discussions, establishing your own view, and reinforcing the ground rules. But often, especially when the unwanted influences are subtle, it is best to tackle the issue outside of the meeting on a one-to-one basis.

This is particularly easy if you have established a routine of coaching your people - observations at a meeting can be fed into

Culture is a pattern of basic assumptions - invented, discovered, or developed by a given group as it learns to cope with its problems of external adaptation and internal integration - that has worked well enough to be considered valid and, therefore, to be taught to new members as the correct way to perceive, think, and feel in relation to those problems.

Edgar H. Schein
Massachusetts Institute of Technology
in Organizational Culture and Leadership
(Jossey-Bass, 1985)

Many of those who were ahead of their time, had to wait for it in none too comfortable quarters.

Stanislaw Lec
Polish Aphorist

The last word had been almost begging. It had mirrored the look in Richard's eyes. He did not say a word, he just stared at her imploringly, praying against hope, that she would see things as they really were. His only weapon, the truth, impotent against Daniel's lies. He was too confused to say anything.

It seemed like an eternity that they had stared at each other, their faces pleading what the other person could not give, until Laura looked down in resigned despair. Convinced her husband's silence was his final cowardly insult to compound her betrayal, she had walked out of the room, a broken woman.

He imagined her pain and emptiness, and his rage and anger took hold once more, for just a few seconds, and then, almost taking him by complete surprise, his body collapsed under him, and he fell to his knees, and he wept bitterly.

He did not know how long he knelt there. He just stayed where he was. He could not think of where else to go, of what else to do. It all seemed so hopeless.

Then he heard the door open again, but he did not look up, something in him did not dare, he did not know what to think, he did not know what to hope. He heard the footsteps, ever so soft, coming round the table, and he heard them pause at the edge of the broken glass. He did not understand, he did not know what to make of it, but a faint glimmer of hope flickered dimly inside him. He clenched his eyes tight shut, and for the first time since he could remember, he prayed for real. He prayed silently, but in his heart, impassioned pleas fought each other to merge into one yearning whole. And then the footsteps continued, and he felt Nicholas's small arm lay itself across his shoulders. This small, silent act of trust and love broke his heart, and he fell to the floor sobbing uncontrollably, while his three year old son, with the wisdom of ages, simply clung to him. At that moment he knew, no matter what it cost him, he would not let go of his family, he would not give up his wife and his son! He would give up anything and everything else, but not them! And he felt himself pleading to God. Full of remorse for his past blindness and stupidity, he bitterly pleaded that God would help him to keep his family. And as he lay there, in his son's small arms, the strange calm that he had felt in the Chapel settled over him once more.

the next coaching session - but it is also possible to do it through more direct feedback.

Rebels do have to be dealt with fairly. This is not only for ethical reasons, but also for the impact on the rest of the team. If a rebel can illustrate that they have been dealt with unfairly, they can elicit enormous sympathy from their colleagues. Each issue has therefore to be fully understood to ensure that it is not a landmine.[1]

Whatever you build has to be built on firm foundations. Flaws can so easily be exploited to bring the whole thing down.

Modify and use the reward system

Formal reward systems are an excellent way of tackling behavioural issues. They can be examined to see which types of behaviour they encourage, and then modified to encourage the right behaviours. It is vitally important that your rebels are not seen to benefit over your allies when the time comes for appraisals, pay rises, and bonus payments.

Use the disciplinary process

Finally, it is likely that you may need to invoke your disciplinary procedures. You would use them for financial irregularities. Not using them for operational irregularities says that we are not really serious about this. If somebody can do their job exactly as they feel like, what value is the employment contract anyway?

You do not have to fire people, but failing to show you are serious from the outset makes it far more likely that you ultimately will. When we realise there is only one

Feedback process for tackling a participant's poor meeting behaviour off-line:

Re-emphasise what you are trying to achieve in terms of the meetings

Re-establish his or her personal role in bringing about that achievement

Explore how he or she fell short of that role in the last meeting

Illustrate the implications of that on yourself and others

Clarify the standard you expect him or her to achieve at future meetings

Ask what help he or she needs to contribute at that standard

Listen to expressed concerns and take them on board

Clarify the options available to him or her, and their consequences.

Anyone who thinks there is some good in everyone hasn't interviewed enough people.

Anonymous personnel director

If you've got them by the balls, their hearts and minds will soon follow.

Charles Colson
Special Assistant to President Nixon
The Watergate Tapes, 1974

---

1   Landmines are issues where the rebel has allowed himself or herself to appear at fault, but where they can later demonstrate they have behaved reasonably - please note: this is not paranoia - it does happen!

He sat up, looked into his son's bewildered, but loving eyes, and hugged him like he would never let him go.

Richard walked into the kitchen, slowly, quietly, almost reluctantly. He stood with his back to the wall. She sat hunched over the kitchen table, her back to him.

As he had put Nicholas back to bed, his resolve had deepened. He would trade everything he had, for his family back. He felt more comfortable that she was looking the other way, it made it easier to start.

"I have been stupid. I have lied. I have cheated!"

He spoke these things slowly and softly into the silence of the room. Laura stayed as she was. She did not appear to tense or release. He continued: "I was physically attracted to Lucy. I toyed with the idea of an affair. I allowed myself to get into situations where we were alone, in places where we never should have been."

He paused, and swallowed, and continued more quietly, but audibly: "I fantasised touching her, and taking her to bed." He stopped again, and stared intently at Laura's shoulders, but they remained in their same neutral position. He continued, barely above a whisper: "And at one point, I actually planned to do it, to betray you for her". He could see the shoulders tense this time, he could see her brace herself against the pain.

"But I swear, on all that I hold dear, I have never, ever, had any sexual contact with any other woman except you." Her shoulders remained tense, and he realised how Clintonesque that sounded. He felt a sense of panic rise up inside him, but he fought it back down. He could not lose it now.

"I had planned to, and I am so, so sorry for that. But before it happened something inside me changed." And he told her shoulders about that time in Church where he had become so confused over the reading, and about how his thinking had changed, and the decisions he had made. He then explained that he would give up anything and everything for her if she would keep him.

way to go, it is amazing how well we take to it. But as long as people can see that not going that way could still be a viable option, some of them will waste a lot of time, energy and self-respect in resisting it.

If you know that there is no alternative to being systematic about managing your organisation, it is kinder to make the same truth absolutely clear to everyone else.

So, does this suggest the end of empowerment, involvement and getting the best out of people? Absolutely not - quite the opposite. But what it does say is that if you hire a man to bake bread, he can deliver it round, square, with currants, or pink with purple stripes - but he had better not insist on delivering bacon instead.

And on that note, one key aspect of the system to sort out early on, is exactly what your managers are contracted to deliver. If your contracts are not right then you are going to struggle from the outset.

An organization with an indispensable man is guilty of management failure.

Harold S. Hook
Chairman, American General Corp.
in Forbes Magazine, October 19, 1987

The room had not changed from when he had walked in. But he had said all he could. The die was cast, and all he could do now was leave her to her thoughts, and hope, and perhaps pray, that they would come right.

Richard lay motionless in the darkness of their bedroom. The night stretched on endlessly, as he fretted about his future. Their future. Every time he glanced at the clock, expecting to see an hour had passed, the hands showed barely the passage of a few minutes.

It was now almost four in the morning, and once again, as he had done each half hour previously, Richard considered going downstairs to Laura, and almost immediately rejected it from his mind. She had to think this through on her own, he had to give her the time and space to do that. But he hated the uncertainty. Waiting for his future to be decided gnawed at his insides, and the worry made him want to do something. To do something more than simply lie there waiting. He was aware of his feelings wavering between panic and despair, and felt powerless to do anything about it.

He sensed movement at the door to the bedroom, and braced himself physically, determined not to make the first move. The shadows in the room seemed to darken slightly, and he was aware of Laura seating herself on the bed beside him. He listened intently for her breathing or any noise that would indicate Laura's state of mind. The moment drew interminably, and then Laura spoke, her voice normal but with a hint of resignation, as though she knew that Richard was awake and listening to her.

"Just get it sorted Richard. That's all I ask. It can't go on like this!" And with that he felt her lie down on her side of the bed. He knew she was facing away from him. He knew that was the end of the matter, for tonight at least. Her meaning was clear to him. He had to sort it out quickly, or give it up, and Laura was trusting him to do that, period. End of conversation.

Summary

Implementing QFD represents a substantially different and inherently more intensive way of working. As such it will have a major influence on your life both inside and outside of work. This change can be very disruptive if it takes you unawares.

It is therefore very important to prepare yourself for your role in ensuring that you manage QFD and not vice versa.

- Be explicit in considering your personal life, and avoid the temptation to think of your life as two distinctly separate situations.

- Be clear on who you are, and what that means for what you do.

- Understand the impact of paradigms and break out of those that imprison your thinking.

- Explicitly change your role and your activities so that you can be what you need to be to transform your organisation.

- Don't delay or avoid tackling the issues that prevent change from happening. Being is more important than appearing.

What can you take from this chapter to rethink your role in making change happen?

....

....

....

....

....

....

....

Relevant materials available on the web-site to support discussion and application of the ideas in this section

Presentation materials in MS PowerPoint™ format:

   Developing vision.

Basic tools in Adobe Acrobat™ format:

   TOP-BOX planning form

   'Drawing out the systematic' checksheet

   Personal evaluation form.

Workshop exercises in MS PowerPoint™ format:

   Developing a personal QFD.

Basic tools in MS Excel™ format:

   Personal QFD template.

Copies of key diagrams in MS PowerPoint™ format.

Section E

Adapting management practice to fully exploit QFD

The art of progress is to preserve order amid change and to preserve change amid order.

Alfred North Whitehead

ADAPTING MANAGEMENT PRACTICE TO FULLY EXPLOIT QFD

The tools and ideas expounded thus far have tremendous potential to transform an organisation. But if the management forums and traditions that surround them were designed to support the old style and practices of management, then that transformation is likely to be short lived.

The old forums will continue to ask the old questions and thereby reward old behaviours of evasion and politics. The key to getting QFD to drive real change is to ensure that your management mechanisms focus on facts and objective evidence from a systematic perspective.

Your management processes will either be made consistent with QFD, or they will corrupt it. Accordingly, it is vitally important that:

- management meetings are designed to efficiently review performance against the targets, and that they are structured to reinforce analysis and objectivity

- people are required to tackle their problems and issues in a disciplined and systematic manner to ensure that they do not recur or cause (political) problems elsewhere

- potential conflicts and issues between processes are identified early on, and mechanisms put in place to ensure that they work together effectively

- management reporting concisely and accurately reports progress against what has been agreed, and reflects the quality of management being applied to that progress.

How this can be practically achieved is explored in Chapters 21 to 24.

The trolley crashed into the table, spilling tea from the two mugs, and forcing Jack and Colin to look up from their bacon sandwiches. Amanda struggled to get the errant vehicle back on track, and shouted over her departing back, "Sorry dears, it's on its last wheels 'n' we can't get the main taynents!"

"S'alright Mand, no 'arm done," said Colin.

"What on earth is a 'taynent'?" asked Jack.

Colin looked up in surprise, and then with hardly a flicker replied, "Ah, I forgot. You're not a real engineer, you're a sparky!"

Jack gave Colin a glowering look as if to say "Get on with it!"

"Well a Taynent is the bush tha' guides the castors," Colin continued. "The main one's a sort o' cup …"

He held his hand cupped upside down to illustrate, and looked up to make his point and caught the 'I wasn't born yesterday' look on his breakfast companion's face.

Colin smiled and said, "Maint'nance; she meant maint'nance".

"Oh," said Jack, and then laughed.

"Speakin' o' which," continued Colin, "do you reckon they'll maintain all 'em changes they've bin puttin' in place round 'ere?"

Jack shrugged, "It seems the right thing to do, and most people are behind it."

"Ah but 's no good puttin' new wine in old wineskins!"

Jack look confused about this bacchanalian turn in the conversation, so Colin continued, "There's no point in puttin' people in new roles if yer gonna ask 'em all the old questions. It's the culture tha's gotta change in this place, not the job titles."

Systematic management meetings

The vast majority of management work takes place in meetings: team meetings, one-to-one meetings, project meetings, review meetings, problem-solving meetings, customer meetings, telephone meetings, virtual meetings, etc. Practically anything that a manager wants to do will involve communicating with somebody about something. It is in the nature of the manger's role. The manager effects his or her role through other people. His or her effectiveness is in the impact that he or she has on the behaviours, knowledge and attitudes of those people.

And yet, for many managers, meetings are seen to be the things that get in the way of them doing their work. Meetings clutter up their diaries, tie up their people, and stop them from doing their job. But if their job is 'meetings', then it is not meetings per se that are the problem. It is the design and purpose of the meetings that is the real issue.

Meetings are a crucial element in reinforcing the conclusions of your QFD, and in ensuring that it is pursued effectively. In this chapter we look at how this is to be achieved, by:

- exploring the problems of typical meeting structures

- reconsidering what managers need to achieve with their time, and the role of meetings therein

- proposing a more effective structure for management meetings.

The problem of meetings

Consider for a moment, your own work. Is it that you have too many meetings, or is it that the meetings that you have are not

Culture and meetings

The form of meetings often reflects the culture (the implicit behaviours and values of an organisation) and vice versa.

What culture do your meetings reflect?

....

....

....

....

....

....

....

Chapter 21

In his office, early the following morning, Richard was clearly finding it extremely difficult to settle to anything. He would sit in his chair behind his desk barely long enough to rearrange his papers in front of him, before launching himself back into pacing the length of the room again.

Several times he had punched the first two or three digits of Daniel's internal telephone number, only to replace the receiver heavily, and slump back in his chair counselling himself to bide his time.

A very large part of Richard wanted to explode violently in front of Daniel, to scream at him, to strip him of his job, and in large part to smack him in the mouth.

But another, calmer, more rational part of Richard realised that this was exactly what Daniel wanted. Daniel wanted Richard to act while he was still in a position of weakness. He wanted Richard to cross the line, to cause his personal indiscretions to affect his business decisions, to act rashly, and to do it while Daniel still held the upper hand politically.

This calmer, more rational part, was encouraging Richard to see how he could hurt Daniel most by biding his time, appearing unaffected, and slowly inexorably ejecting him on the terms of Richard's choosing. And slowly, surely, gradually, it brought Richard to a point of calm, almost cold, determination.

By the time he reached the first item on his schedule, there was no indication that any inner turmoil had ever existed. In fact, Richard was beginning to feel quite positive about things.

Today was the day of the first management meeting to review process performance, and Richard could almost savour delivering Daniel a written warning as a result of a continued failure in performance. Yes, Daniel was going down, and Richard would not give him the satisfaction of knowing what hurt he had caused him and his family.

Lucy was his first visitor for the day. As she had promised, she had mapped out a standard format for future management meetings. She had split the meeting into two halves: the first half mechanically reviewing

efficient in progressing what you need to progress?

Is too much of your time taken up in meetings per se, or is too much of your time taken up in discussions within those meetings where you cannot really offer or learn anything new?

Unfortunately, our experience of meetings is that they are inefficient and, as a result of handling this issue inappropriately, managers tend to make the situation worse not better.

The diagram below illustrates a common picture of the causality of inefficient meetings and the problems that arise in practice. We lose time because:

- we keep revisiting and going over old ground
- people have not prepared or done what they have promised
- some discussions are only relevant to one or two people
- people lose concentration and stop listening
- the process is not focused on clear goals
- we do not agree and confirm clear actions
- people are not realistic about commitments
- people cannot remember what was agreed.

Concern over vital items slipping

Schedule vital actions as meetings

Little time to fully think things through

Difficult to make time to do tasks

Failure to complete actions

Difficult to prepare for meeting

Little time to communicate

Incomplete preparation

Difficult to design the meeting

Actions are not clear

Poor documentation of meeting

Go over old ground again

Chase actions

Need for another meeting

Inefficient meetings

Use meeting to complete actions

New loads on the diary

Extend remit of meeting

Meeting results in new actions

Extend length of meeting

Hold meetings to complete actions

Problem not fully resolved

Extend membership of meeting

Desision to hold meeting

Meeting overruns

New issue arises

People lose concentration

progress and performance, and highlighting any issues; and the second half giving opportunity for more in-depth discussion on selected topics.

Richard was puzzled. "Why separate the review from the discussion?" he queried.

Lucy smiled. "It makes the meeting more efficient."

"What? Covering the same thing twice makes the meeting more efficient?" Richard sounded incredulous.

Lucy saw this was not going to be quick, so she sat down. She thought for a moment about the best way to begin.

"You know those Cylek Performance Review meetings you attend in Houston?" Lucy paused and waited for Richard to nod acknowledgement, then continued: "They start off reviewing performance, and then an issue comes up. What happens?"

"Well, we debate it until we've got some clear actions, I guess!"

"And what process do you use?" queried Lucy.

Richard shrugged. "I'm not sure really, we just work it through until someone's appointed to take it away."

"And how long do you allow for that discussion?" continued Lucy.

Richard shrugged again. "As long as it takes I guess."

"Think back, Richard," challenged Lucy, "exactly how useful is that debate?"

Richard thought for a while, and then smiled. "Well, it gives me a chance for a snooze," he replied.

Lucy smiled back. "And then you return to the review, until the next issue?" she queried.

"Yes, that's about it," Richard agreed.

"And how do the debates at the end of the meeting compare with the ones at the start?" asked Lucy, already knowing the answer.

"Well, we're often rushed toward the end, so they either tend to be delegated out, or we just agree something quickly," Richard answered.

Meetings are often inefficient. And here is the paradox - we make them more inefficient because we seek to have fewer of them. Because they are fewer, they become longer and more general. Because they are longer and cover more points they have greater membership. And because of all of this they become less specifically relevant to what you need addressed, and thus more inefficient.

Added to which, knowing that the meeting is likely to be of little value to us, we fail to do what is necessary to ensure that it is more efficient. We resent preparation time, and we also tend to see meetings as an opportunity to complete our actions and get other bits of work done with the people who are there. This saves us time but introduces inefficiency for some others, so they start doing the same thing. Very soon it becomes institutionalised and nobody even realises it is happening - they just complain about meetings.

Meetings are 'good'. They are a vehicle for management effecting its role more efficiently. It is their poor design and subversion that proves 'bad'. And by seeing meetings as 'bad' we tend to adopt and introduce the very behaviours that make them so.

Meetings as a vehicle for management

The efficiency of meetings is directly related to the efficiency of the management time spent within them. So let us start our consideration of how meetings can be better designed, by considering the efficiency of management time.

Essentially a manager's time can be invested in a number of places as can be seen in the diagram on the next page.

Ideally management time is invested in enabling the skills and processes of the

The tragedy of the commons

A story is told of a piece of common land allotted to villagers for grazing their livestock. The land could support two animals per household, but after a little time some people started grazing a third animal. Seeing that some people were benefiting in this way others followed suit, even though it was against the rules. After a while those grazing two animals began to notice that their animals carried less meat, because grazing was harder, and so they introduced a third animal, simply to maintain their due. Before long the common land became overgrazed, and most of the animals died.

"And are the issues at the end less important than the ones at the start?" queried Lucy.

"Sometimes," Richard replied. "But not usually. I guess it depends on whose perspective you're seeing. Often it is the UK issues that get left to the end of the day."

Lucy paused, and then said: "A meeting to review performance has a different dynamic and uses a different process to that needed to effectively understand and resolve issues. The review is objective, clinical. It should briefly and appropriately observe all areas of performance, and list and prioritise the issues that arise from them. It should be comprehensive and balanced." Richard nodded and waited for Lucy to continue, which she did.

"Resolving the issues, however, is something that is most efficiently achieved with a process that is specially designed to do exactly that. The amount of time each issue gets should not be dependant on when it occurs in the meeting. And how can you prioritise where you will spend the time, until you know what all the issues are. Added to which, it may be that not all members of the group need to be involved in all the discussions."

Lucy noted that Richard was not trying to argue, so she continued. "If in our meeting, we swiftly and clinically run through the review, we can then work out the best approach, and use of our time, in addressing the issues that have arisen. That is what I'm proposing with this meeting format."

Richard thought for a moment. Lucy was often right about these sorts of things, as bizarre as they seemed at the time. He sighed: "Well, I have to admit it sounds good in theory. Let's try it out and see how it works in practice!"

Richard had fully expected a showdown with Daniel, but he was disappointed. Daniel was the model of propriety. His plan listed all the relevant activities for the implementation, with scheduled dates for completion all within the next two months. True, none of his tasks were complete yet, but the first three activities were all scheduled within the deadline Richard had given him. Richard could not find fault with him anywhere. Daniel was clearly keeping his nose clean on the work front, and biding his time. Richard could see that Daniel wanted to provoke him

organisation to ensure that everything can be handled efficiently to the customer's satisfaction. Of course, if this is not possible, then the manager may get drawn into specific tasks - tasks that the process does not allow others to do with sufficient confidence. Some managers mistakenly believe this is the management role.

If there are too many such tasks (possibly because of issues in skills and processes that are not being systemically addressed) then the manager may not be able to do the work as well as he or she would like, things go wrong, and the manager is drawn into sorting them out. This is often a major source of overload, and can be so severe that the manager no longer has time to move back into the first box to sort things out systemically.

If the workload is too great, the problems continue until things fall apart in crisis. At this point everything becomes urgent and critical, and the manager has no time to think of longer term strategies such as inspiring, equipping and developing his or her people and processes.

But the problem of time is not solved by avoiding these 'management' tasks. These 'management' tasks are the only things that have the potential to solve the problem of time.[1] The further the manager moves down and to the right of the diagram at the top of this page, the less

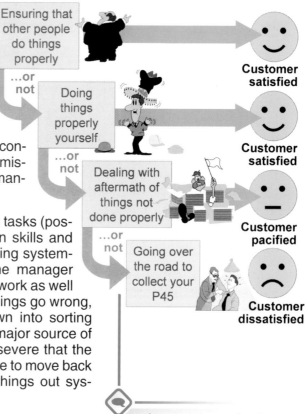

Investing management time: Where does it go?

Ensuring that other people do things properly

...or not

Doing things properly yourself

...or not

Dealing with aftermath of things not done properly

...or not

Going over the road to collect your P45

Customer satisfied

Customer satisfied

Customer pacified

Customer dissatisfied

Whoever admits that he is too busy to improve his methods has acknowledged himself to be at the end of his rope.

J Ogden Armour
President, Armour Meat Packing Co.

Problems cannot be solved at the same level at which they were created.

Albert Einstein
Nobel Laureate in Physics

---

1   This is not technically true. Failing to resolve issues through management can ultimately solve the time problem. But then you might find you end up with all too much time on your hands!

to unreasonable behaviour, while giving no legitimate excuse for it in terms of his work. But he was convinced that Daniel could not keep this up. He just needed to wait a little longer to nail him. Still, Richard could wait.

Lucy's format for the meeting worked well. With some forceful facilitation, she had ensured all the issues were written in the 'Car Park', and the review section had passed by quickly and efficiently. Within half an hour, the whole team had got a comprehensive and accurate picture of the progress and issues.

"Okay," said Lucy, "we now have a list of the issues we need to address if we are to make progress according to plan. Some of them seem to be quite similar, so perhaps we can group these and address them together. Any suggestions?"

Lucy linked together those issues that the group felt could be considered as a unit, and then asked for nominations for those things best tackled outside the meeting. Several items were suggested, but when it came to assigning responsibilities for taking them forward, there appeared to be a marked reluctance from 'some quarters'. However, Richard quickly appointed people if they proved too bashful.

"That leaves us these three items," summarised Lucy, "and I propose we use the remainder of the meeting to make some headway on these. Are there any proposals on which order we should tackle them in?"

"'Lack of time' seems to be the one that is the biggest issue for us," suggested Andrew, "and the least easy for us to resolve individually. I would certainly value us spending time on resolving that one." The room seemed to nod in unison, but Richard groaned inwardly. He was just about to challenge the proposal, and expound that it was largely a matter of individual priorities, when Lucy asked the group if anybody could suggest a process for tackling the issue. Richard held his peace, he was intrigued as to what possible process could be used, and waited to see what transpired.

Clearly the group were equally intrigued, because they all went silent. Lucy looked around the group eagerly, and Richard was beginning to think that he would have to pipe up after all, if only to help Lucy out of an obvious hole, when Lucy spoke out again.

influence he or she has per unit of time that he or she spends.

Similarly, if management meetings are drawn down and to the right of that same diagram, managers have to invest more and more hours in each and every one of them, to have anything like the effect needed to keep their business on the rails. But that is exactly where most managers tend to draw those meetings if left unchecked. The pressure on their own time, of having to resolve the details because they have not developed the system, will cause them to take every opportunity to draw the meeting into isolated short-term specifics, and to progress their detailed agenda at the expense of other's more strategic thinking. And this side-lining of strategic thinking will happen because their short term issues are inevitably more urgent.

This in itself is a vicious circle, inasmuch as it often precludes items from the agenda until they become crises in their own right. And so, poor meeting design can allow a handful of 'reactive' managers to pull the whole organisation down into the same boat.

The design of effective management meetings

The key to solving the issue of time is to get managers to see that the time problem exists **because** they have not been fulfilling their 'management' role, which manages time efficiently. And that this 'management' role is not an extra burden; it is the solution.

Selling people this view of management is perhaps the most difficult part of the whole implementation of systematic approaches. And even when people accept it logically, there still remains a

> Whoever would change men must change the conditions of their lives.
>
> Theodor Herzl
> Austrian journalist and Zionist leader

"Normally, for this sort of issue, a company would use a standard 'Problem-solving process', but I know we don't actually have one here."

"That's because we never have problems, only disasters in the making," quipped John.

"Yes, like getting our air conditioning serviced by 'The hole in the wall gang'," retorted Abs, alluding to the recent problems with temperature control that had seen him handing out ice creams on the shop floor.

"Thank you, Mister Softee!" John retaliated.

"I don't want to get drawn into introducing a whole new process this afternoon, you'll be relieved to hear," continued Lucy, "but can I propose that we perhaps do the following." She moved to the flipchart, skipped a page, and proceeded to write in her large neat capitals.

"Firstly, let's get a complete quantified understanding of the issue. Secondly, we will identify what the main causes of 'lack of time' are for us. And thirdly, we will try and identify some potential solutions to those causes."

Richard was beginning to feel a bit uncomfortable. This seemed like the long way round. The answer to him was devastatingly clear: people had to get their priorities right. He wondered whether to interject at this point. In the end he decided not to. Lucy had rarely let him down so far, he needed to have more confidence in what she was doing. He let it go.

"I don't imagine that we will fully solve this issue within this meeting," Lucy continued. She had spoken seriously, but drew a few sniggers at what people thought was clearly a ludicrous alternative.

"No! But ...," she paused, clearly serious, and waited for the group to settle down and recognise that maybe she intended to go further than they clearly felt possible. "I do intend that we deliver a clear brief to whoever takes this forward outside of the meeting."

Some of the group were clearly confused by this woman who appeared to be seriously suggesting the resolution of an insoluble problem. Lucy waited for them to make up their minds, and was rewarded with a slightly subdued, but clearly attentive, audience.

Lucy flipped over to the next clear sheet of flipchart paper, and posed the first question: "So, how much time are we actually short?"

large lag before they take it on in their hearts and behaviours.

But 'excellence is a game of inches', and each manager has at least the opportunity to establish new norms and effectively prove the point. To do this two things need to be considered.

Firstly, to make meetings more efficient we need more of them; but shorter, more focused, with less people. The end result will be more meetings - but individuals will actually spend less time in meetings.[1]

Secondly, we also make meetings more efficient by having different types of meetings.

The systematic model reflects six different types of meetings, each of which have different formats and membership, and some do not even feel like meetings at all.

1. There are review meetings, which are simply to ensure complete understanding of progress/ performance, and to identify the issues involved. They are quick, clinical and objective to the point of being almost 'cold'. Most of the work and communication is done and circulated before the meeting.

2. There are planning and goal setting meetings, such as developing the QFD and cascading it. These are strategic and seek to draw out and align people's aspirations with the needs of the business (see Section B).

3. There are problem-solving and change-making meetings where small groups meet to resolve issues and

(2) Planning and goal setting

(5) Team development

(1) Review

(3) Change

(6) Operational

(4) Customer and contracts

---

1   Actually, this is not true. Managers will spend less time in those meetings, and then put this time into yet more focused brief meetings to progress the other parts of their role that they do not currently have time for.

Managing by Design

Richard challenged: "I don't think we are tackling the right question. I have one hundred and ninety-six hours in my week, and frankly I don't want any more. I just want to use them differently."

There was a pause while people worked out the sense of this. Lucy was concerned that Richard might have just thrown in a huge red herring, but then, on a hunch, decided to go with the flow.

"Say some more, Richard," she encouraged.

"Well," mused Richard, "what I mean is that, one way or another, too much tries to fit into my week. That is what I see as the problem. There is too much for me to do!"

"I think Richard has a point," supported Peter. "I certainly don't want to have any more time to spend here. I spend more than enough time here already."

"Perhaps the problem is that our jobs are too big?" posed Susan hesitantly. Her face almost showed a cringe, as she waited for people to react to what she had said.

"Or that we're trying to do too many jobs," chipped in John, keen that Susan should not lack support.

Daniel saw an opportunity. He took it. "No! I don't think that is the case. My job was manageable until I got all this QFD stuff dumped on top of it."

He purposefully avoided Richard's eyes, and looked to Peter and Abs for support. Abs obliged. "I must admit the QFD has created a whole extra workload." Daniel nodded sagely in response, and then looked to Peter for a follow-up. Peter merely nodded non-commitally.

Richard felt his anger rise. But Deborah stepped in first. "Wait a minute," she challenged. "All this 'QFD stuff' as you call it: the target setting; process management; setting up measures; process meetings; coaching etc. That is our job! It is probably most of the other things that we do, that should be seen as the extra workload. Planning and controlling the performance of our processes IS the manager's role. All of the other stuff we do isn't really management stuff at all!"

Daniel looked at her darkly. "So top-level customer meetings, saving crucial contracts, attending Cylek worldwide sales meetings, ensuring we have money coming in to pay our salary. That is not management?"

effect changes in the organisation's processes.

4. There are customer/partner meetings to explore the needs of the relationship and to seek new ways to provide a better service.

5. There are team and individual development meetings, which explore group and personal issues, and seek to develop relevant attitudes and skills in people. These include training sessions.

6. There are also 'meetings' where people engage simply with the operational process and progress work as their job defines. Picking up the 'input' from one person and providing 'output' to another.

Each of these meetings is quite different, and has different objectives, membership, process, formats and environments. Although each takes place at all levels of the business.

Our problems often begin when we try to combine these into a single 'one-size-fits-all' meeting, in order to 'save time'. Unfortunately the lack of clarity and focus on what process and approach to use at any point leads to confusion, disengagement, misunderstanding, and many of the problems that many of us are all too aware of. Separating out the meetings (even as different sections within one larger meeting) and designing them appropriately, is key to resolving these problems.

In some cases this is fairly easy: meetings of type 4, 5 and 6 are often the best defined and least overlapping meetings within an organisation, and many other texts concern themselves with these areas.

Meetings of type 2 have already been covered in the earlier chapters of this

The length of a meeting increases in direct proportion to the square of the number of people present and awake.

Anonymous

Managing by Design

It would have been difficult for Daniel to get any more derision into his voice if he had been playing Voldemort, but Deborah stood her ground. "No! Frankly no!" she said. "They need doing. They often need doing by someone senior; sometimes even someone as senior as us. But when we do them we're not 'managing' the process, we are simply 'operating' it. And if after doing our proper job of 'managing' we find we simply don't have time to do that 'other stuff', we had better make sure we develop and manage the process to make sure it gets done in some other way!"

Her eyes fixed on Daniel all through her delivery. She matched his tone with hers, and Richard felt an insane urge to cheer her on. His spirits continued to rise as Andrew joined in.

"Deborah's right." Andrew looked around the group, determined not to focus on Daniel. "All too often we fail to place enough emphasis on developing our people to do these things, because it is somehow easier to do them ourselves. But that does not make it our job to do them."

Deborah, grateful for Andrew's support, continued: "I would go further. I would say that doing those non-management tasks should be seen as a failure. A failure of our management process. A failure to develop the systems and people to ensure they are done effectively within the process."

This last comment was too much for Peter. "Excuse me," he interjected, "that may be fine for those of us with the luxury of 35 minions to do M'lady's bidding, but I have a department of three people. Are you seriously proposing that I should dump all the work on them, and go and play golf for six hours a day?"

Deborah coloured slightly. She felt she had overstated things a bit in retrospect, but she could still make the point. "No I don't," she replied, "but in your case, you really are fulfilling two roles, and while the one that is purely 'management' as opposed to 'specialist' may only be part time, it is still vital that it does not allow the process to dump more work on you than is absolutely necessary or efficient."

Peter appeared mollified, and Lucy saw an opportunity to move on. "Okay, so how would we state the problem?" But Daniel, sensing the tide turning against him, made a concentrated push.

"This is rubbish! Are you seriously proposing that I should abandon high-level skills and responsibilities such as negotiation, selling and execu-

book,[1] and we will move on to meetings of type 3 in the next chapter.

Our concern in this chapter is meetings of type 1; meetings that are intended to review progress/performance and identify issues therein.

The model for undertaking these meetings is illustrated in the diagram on the right.[2]

The primary objective of the process management meeting is simply to ensure that performance is improving to plan, by monitoring performance against that plan, and setting new plans in place to address any shortfall.

- Current overall performance of the process is briefly reviewed against forecast.[3]

- Shortfalls against forecast are highlighted without discussion.[4]

- Progress on actions is reviewed, and where delays in completion explain the current shortfall, this is marked up against the highlight.

- Sub-process management reports are very briefly reviewed, and where sub-process performance issues explain the process performance shortfall, this is marked up against the highlight.

- Shortfalls without explanation are then addressed, and actions set to investigate and address them within the sub-processes.

- Issues of performance, either on completing actions, or in terms of the quality of sub-process management,

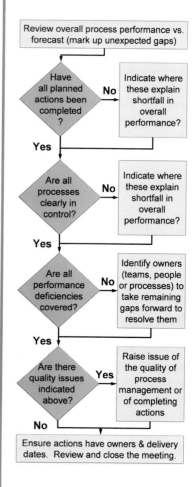

---

1 See Section B.

2 A session plan for the meeting is included on the associated web-site (see Appendix 7).

3 'Forecast' should represent the estimated improvements in performance, period by period, which will ensure the targets are achieved within the agreed timescales.

4 This is simply achieved by identifying them, and writing them up on a flipchart, with space in between or to the right to capture further commentary and proposed actions.

tive judgement, for the mechanical dreariness of simple clerical activities such as measurement and record keeping? You have to be out of your tiny tree!"

Despite the rudeness of Daniel's tone, Richard could see that his point had found a sympathetic ear with a number of people in the room. In fact, even he had been affected by it. Was he really condemning his management team to a life of drudgery? He was sure he was not, but he was temporarily lost for a response.

The room was silent, and Daniel sensing he had won the initiative plunged on. "Fair enough, if you are so sure that this bookkeeping overhead is so necessary, and I have to admit I remain unconvinced, then give us each a team of clerks to do it, and let us get on with the real business of leadership!"

This brought a couple of nods, and some rueful glances. Deborah just looked angry. Richard wondered if he could be so wrong; he felt a sense of disquiet rise up in him. But Lucy remained calm, her face a picture of serenity and confidence. Richard felt a bit better when he saw this, and the momentary nervousness was replaced by anticipation of how Lucy would deftly turn this whole thing round.

Daniel was now clearly looking at Richard to respond, as were most of the rest of the group. Richard felt uncomfortable again, and hoped Lucy would cut in, which, after just a few moments, she did.

"You raise two very good issues there, Daniel. Do you mind if I take them in turn?" Lucy paused briefly, but continued quickly. "Let us leave to one side, just for the moment, the question of how boring the proposed management role might be, and focus first of all on the question of who does it. Suppose, for the moment, Deborah was to delegate all of this Process Management activity to Malcolm Carter, while she invested her experience and skill into the next generation of web-based modem development. I'm sure that our future range of web-modems would be commercial winners. But whom would we best invite to the meeting that managed the performance of Cylek UK? Who then could provide the best insight into how our approach to product development should evolve? Who would be best placed to talk about how the business should transform itself? Should it be Deborah, with her head stuffed full of technical profiles and protocol analysis? Or should it be Malcolm? After all, it would be Malcolm who had the firm grasp of the implications of any Cylek policies on the potential of the development process to outpace

are addressed. (These may need to be dealt with outside the meeting if there are specific issues with individual performance.)

The meeting can be very brief if everything is clearly under control, and information is circulated in advance. The key to the success of these meetings lies in people doing what they should do, and communicating their progress on it, before the meeting.

If all actions are completed, all issues can be related to processes, and all process owners are doing what they should do, the active meeting can be over in 15 minutes. If everything is happening as it should be happening, the meeting does not interfere. Why should it?

But if performance on completing actions is poor, or process ownership is weak, or the logic of the QFD is flawed, the structure of the meeting ensures that something is done about it. What the meeting is essentially reviewing is the quality of the management process. And it is the management process that controls the performance of the organisation, not this meeting.

The design of the meeting is intentionally spartan. There is no place in it to do anything apart from understand the factors affecting performance, and to assign responsibility for addressing them.

This does not preclude scheduling a more discursive meeting to directly follow the management meeting and pick up the issues, but it does require that the whole picture is objectively and completely understood prior to delving into specific areas.

It also provides the opportunity for more appropriate people to be involved in addressing the issues. In many cases this

Once somebody asked me to identify the single most useful management technique that I learned through my years of managing. My answer was: the practice of regularly scheduled one-to-one meetings.

Andrew S Grove
CEO, Intel Corp.

our competitors. And it would be Malcolm who fully understood the scope for improving the quality of information supplied to production. Frankly, it makes little sense to separate management decision making from management information."

Daniel could sense the point slipping away from him, and quickly countered: "I don't agree. Malcolm could keep Deborah informed so that she could fulfil her executive role. We'd then use our best people more efficiently!" Some more nods greeted this.

Lucy continued her challenge: "Then, are you suggesting that Deborah is so sharp, that she can provide a higher quality of input based solely on an occasional update, than Malcolm could based on extensive experience of the detailed planning and analysis of the department's operations?" Here Lucy turned to Deborah and asked: "What do you think Deborah? Could you?"

Deborah smiled. "Not a snowball's chance in hell!" she said.

Before Daniel could interject again, Lucy continued deftly: "But that still leaves us with the issue of boredom."

Here she paused, leaving Daniel to wonder whether to go back over the last battle, or fix his sights on this new one. Before he had made up his mind, she continued: "If you think that this systematic approach to management is going to be anything less than intensely stimulating, challenging, and at times frightening, then you still have a very impoverished view of the role. But that is hardly surprising, because we're only just getting started, and all you've managed to focus on so far are mechanical things like measures, but there is much more, so much more." Here her eyes assumed an almost mystical, far-away quality, and she proceeded to explain.

"Do you know the implications of letting your customers flag up incorrect items on invoices and not pay for them? One quarry company did this, and transformed their business, dramatically improving both sales and profit. Does that surprise you?" She had the group's attention. "Or can you anticipate what impact it would have if you allowed your people to select which manager they wanted to work for?" She heard a noticeable intake of breath from the group and continued: "One big fabric manufacturer in the States does this very successfully.

"Could you improve your overall performance by 50% in 12 months? Would you even know how to start? Soon, every ounce of your expert-

will be the team looking after the process[1] that is giving problems.

It is important to note that, within the process management cycle, there is no room for isolated initiatives and improvement projects; there is no place to simply measure project progress! This is not an oversight. All too often, when improvement projects are established outside of a targeted performance gain, they fail to achieve their full potential. The principle that underpins the management cycle is that projects only exist in relation to a measured shortfall in performance, and that progress only exists in relation to a forecast improvement in performance. Within this, projects can be controlled as normal, but they are managed on their impact, not their completion.

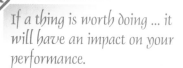

If a thing is worth doing ... it will have an impact on your performance.

---

1   'Process' here refers to a whole process or any part of a process.

ise and intellect and experience will be harnessed in using a complex set of information to make lasting, irreversible and radical changes to this business, and frankly you had better be up to the task! Because I am here to tell you, that I could never see it entrusted to some boring pedestrian cleric. And if you're not able to anticipate your customers' thinking, to inspire your people to previously unthinkable heights, to draw out abilities that they never thought they had, and to efficiently harness that into a radical and earth shattering strategy, then you are not going to make it!"

She finished to silence, and looked round the group. Richard and Deborah looked as if they wanted to applaud, but most looked a little shell-shocked. Except Daniel: he looked incredulous, and increasingly angry.

"Drivel!" he exclaimed. "Unadulterated Yankee bullshit!"

Everybody looked shocked now.

Richard was the first to break the silence. "Daniel, I think you owe Lucy an apology. I suggest, that if you can't keep a civil tongue in your head, you leave the meeting".

"That suits me fine. I can't listen to any more of this," said Daniel. He swiftly picked up his pile of papers and left.

The room seemed stunned.

Richard stood up. "Sorry you all had to witness that. I will pick up with Daniel after the meeting, but for now, if there are no further objections, I suggest we continue with our problem-solving - after a short ten minute break to catch our breath."

Coffee was a fairly muted affair. People sensed a wind of change, that things would not, could not, remain the same, but appeared unsure of where their colleagues stood on this. The incident with Daniel seemed to cast a cloud of uncertainty over the whole proceedings. But for reasons only he himself understood, Richard felt distinctly up-beat.

Tackling issues
(Pursuing the goals)

To this point, practically everything you have read in this book has been about establishing and cascading a coherent set of goals through the organisation by:

- identifying the organisational objectives from the business context

- clarifying those objectives with unambiguous targets

- cascading them into the logical elements of the organisation

- enabling people to make local commitments which support them

- maintaining their currency by means of measuring progress against them

- regularly reviewing and reinforcing them by means of focused meetings

- reviewing and reconciling them against your personal goals

- establishing an appropriate management role in meeting the objectives

- resolving and removing alternative goals and agendas.

Implementing all these ideas, takes us to a point where everyone should be totally clear on what they are tasked with achieving, at least at the management level. This alone is likely to deliver performance benefits, purely by the level of focus and clarity that is achieved. It is not uncommon to see performance improve by tens of percent simply because people are more continuously aware of the importance of the goals and the active interest of management in them.

But the intention of clarifying the goals was not simply about increasing the pressure, it was about clarifying where change needs to occur, and about providing guidance in effecting that change.

We never seem to have enough time to do things properly, but we can always find time to do them twice!

Source unknown

Chapter 22

When, at last, people had regrouped, Richard felt he needed to know where they stood before proceeding with the rest of the meeting. When he rose to his feet, silence descended almost immediately.

"Daniel raised some important questions before coffee. His recent behaviour, while regrettable, does not diminish their validity, and I feel it is important that we don't simply gloss over them. Daniel's questions are pertinent to the whole issue of time management, and before we proceed any further I would like to hear others' views on the track we are taking." Richard remained standing, and looked around the room.

As he expected, Deborah was the first to speak. "I still hold to the views I expressed earlier. What we have done over the past few months has really opened my eyes on what management really is. I therefore think this discussion, of how we focus more time in this area, is crucial, and that we should continue it, with or without Daniel."

Richard noticed clear nods of agreement from John, Susan and Andrew. Peter and Abs appeared more subdued, their eyes cast downwards. Richard waited in silence for one or other of them to speak.

Peter was the first to do so. In a very measured, voice he delivered his typically well-considered reply.

"What we are trying to do here seems to make a lot of theoretical sense, and I find it difficult to fault the logical arguments put forward as to why we should do this. But…" Here Peter paused, marshalling the sequence of what was to follow in his mind. "I have three major reservations about what we are attempting here. The first, is that what we are attempting is unproven, and I feel that we are taking an unreasonable level of risk in being in the vanguard of applying these techniques. The second, is that the implementation of these techniques is creating conflict and pain within the management team, and I am concerned that continuing to force things forward could cause us to lose some very valued colleagues. The third, is that I, for one, am not sure that I really have the ability or inclination at my age, to adopt an approach that is this different from what I normally do." Here Abs was nodding in agreement, and Richard also noted that Andrew and Susan were nodding as well.

The engine for change is a clear gap between the newly adopted goals, and the current performance. But the process of being objective and analytical should not stop at this point and give way to prejudice and fancy.

Imagine a discrete activity (manual, machine, or computer), which has a new goal of 500 outputs a day over current performance of 380. The reasons for the new goal can be logically determined from our top-level strategy and our QFDs. (Possibly through a top-level QFD linking to a process QFD, and then in turn to a sub-process QFD.) We now need confidence that the solution will be analytically evaluated against what is needed, and will be objectively selected as the best option. Unfortunately, in practice, the danger is that the team on the ground will simply go with the first idea that seems to work, and implement it without much further thought.

It is possible that the team has hit upon the perfect solution, and thus it has achieved the objective quickly and efficiently. But experience demonstrates that in practice this is very unlikely to be the case. For every lucky break cited by the fire-fighter, seven disasters can be cited by those involved.

- The project became embroiled in politics because different power bases saw the problem differently.

- Only the symptoms were tackled; the real issue continued to cause new and more complex problems.

- The solution was clearly a pet-idea, and far from being the best option, and real opportunities were missed.

- The ultimate cost and time of the solution outweighed the benefits, and left people suffering far too long.

All progress is based upon a universal innate desire on the part of every organism to live beyond its income.

Samuel Butler
English novelist

"Thank you for your candour, and your clearly thoughtful contribution, Peter," said Richard sympathetically.

Even though Richard had been a touch patronising in the delivery of his response, others nodded in agreement. It seemed that the whole group accepted the validity of what had been said.

Richard continued "To be frank, I am not sure that I can answer your reservations, but I would like to make the following points. The first is that, while the combination of tools we are using may be unique, the individual tools are well proven. All the tools do is present us with information and understanding. What we do with that information and understanding, is down to us. We are not ceding control to some inanimate system; we simply take what the system tells us into account, as we make our decisions in the normal way. Is it really a risk, to see things more clearly?"

He paused to allow the group to assimilate what they had heard, and then continued. "The second, is that I very much regret the conflict and pain that is arising from this work. But I believe that QFD is incidental to that. I believe that any major change of approach, in us as a management team, would create such conflict and pain, just because we are who we are. The truth is, we have fundamentally different views of how to do things, and whenever we have a choice, we have an argument. Look back before QFD and you will see it is true!"

Peopled nodded, so Richard continued: "Any major change creates conflict and pain in us. But major change, whether QFD or something else, is clearly necessary. Our performance shows clearly that we cannot continue the same as we were. Our choice is not whether we change, but whether we change ourselves, or have someone else do it for us."

He paused again as he formulated his third point. "Finally, I am aware that the new approach may not suit everybody, but I make this pledge to you now. If you will cooperate with me, unstintingly, to make this work, I will provide you all the support I can, including my time. And if, at the end, you feel the new role does not suit you, we will work together to find a new role better suited to you, without any loss of status or pay."

Richard looked around the room, and finally he looked at Peter, who said: "I don't think you can say any fairer than that Richard. I am on the bus." And then Richard glanced at Abs, who simply nodded his assent.

- The implementation was poorly managed and people were not really sure what they were doing.

- People were oblivious to the fact that the problem was continuing even after the project had finished.

- Things drifted back to the way they were some time after the project was completed.

The above issues are all too common in the core of companies. And the problem is that the approach people often take to make change in practice, takes little account of preventing these things from happening.

The situation is changing, however, and many companies have introduced clear processes and disciplines for solving problems efficiently and permanently. These work by:

- clarifying, by means of data and objective analysis, the component whose performance is responsible for that deficit, and what performance is required

- seeking and exploring a wide range of options to meet that performance (including best practice both inside and outside the company)

- selecting the preferred solution objectively based on experimentation and analysis of its performance

- carefully project managing its implementation, to clear quality, time and cost targets

- re-evaluating performance to ensure that the problem is fully resolved

- ensuring the performance is managed and maintained by integrating it into the relevant operating practices.

From the above, it is clear that good problem-solving processes work by ensuring that the objectives remain clear even in the detail of the analyses and decisions.

Richard felt a cheer go up in his head, and could barely contain his fist punching the air.

Lucy stood up as Richard sat down, taking this as her cue to continue. "It looks like we won't get time now, to tackle all three of the issues on our Car Park this afternoon, but I propose we use the remaining time to bottom out, as far as we can, this issue of time. Is that okay?" The group was clearly in agreement, and so she continued: "So how do we state the problem?"

"How about 'Too many operative issues place demands on our time'?" suggested Deborah.

"I think I see where you are coming from," said Abs, "but 'Operative issues' - what on earth are they when they are at home?"

"Well, you know," said Deborah, "doing the detailed work itself, and sorting out problems that have arisen".

"How about calling them 'Operating routines and problems' then?" suggested John.

Lucy felt the phrasing was still a bit oblique, but people seemed to be in agreement, and so she wrote on the flipchart: 'Too many operating routines and problems place demands on our time', and then asked: "Right, who can quantify this?"

The group went quiet, and looked puzzled, and then Susan suggested: "Well, how much extra time do we need freed off? Deborah, you are further down this road than the rest of us, how much time do you feel we need to spend on this new approach?"

Deborah thought for a moment. "Well, it is not so easy to answer that question, because it depends on where you draw the line between what we call the new approach, and what we should have been doing anyway. The new approach does not really change what we should do, more how we do it. For instance, we should all have been spending time setting our objectives, refining our strategies, developing our people, improving our processes, measuring our progress and learning from problems, and I'm sure that we all have been doing these things, however inadequately." She paused to check that everyone was with her so far, and then continued: "But to do all of these things properly, will require that I devote at least half my week to them." There was an audible intake

There are a lot of good problem-solving processes about, and if you already have one that effectively achieves all of the above established in your organisation, you would be well advised to reinforce it as an essential element of your work to establish systematic approaches.

If, however, you do not currently have such a process, it is vitally important to the sustainability of your improvements that you develop one, and that you equip your staff to use it. The following is offered as a possible approach that you could adopt or adapt as necessary.

PROBLEM

PROBLEM is a simple seven-step methodology for ensuring that problems are solved systematically. It is based on an easy to remember acronym, so that it can be used readily as the need arises (e.g. in discussions) but it is also supported by sophisticated checklists where a more rigorous application is required.

- PROFILE the exact problem to be tackled.

- Analyse the ROOT CAUSES of the problem.

- Identify and evaluate your OPTIONS for tackling the root causes.

- Develop a solution package to BALANCE short-term and long-term costs and benefits.

- LAUNCH the project to implement the solution(s) and manage its fulfilment.

- EVALUATE the outcomes to ensure that the problem is fully addressed.

- MAINTAIN the result by ensuring that all policies and practices are updated to reflect it.

A range of materials to support this model are available on the associated web-site (see Appendix 7). What follows is a basic

Profile   Collect
Root cause data
Options
Balance
Launch
Evaluate
Measure   Maintain

of breath. "For my particular area, management requires at least 20 hours per week."

The group were quiet, assimilating this information, and Richard was glad that Daniel was not around to react to this.

Lucy picked up the initiative. "Okay, so in terms of hard numbers, the demands on our time are 20 hours a week too much?" Some of the group nodded, others still appeared subdued, so Lucy checked: "Does everybody agree with this?"

John looked up. "I guess I do. I just hadn't realised the full extent of what we were talking about. I guess we are just coming to grips with the extent to which we haven't been doing our jobs. I can't argue with what Deborah says. I know I should be doing all those things. I know they will lead to success. And I know that to do them properly would take me at least half my time. Yes, I guess I'm 20 hours a week short!"

Lucy looked around at the others, and Peter chipped in: "My process is somewhat smaller than most of yours, so I'm not sure that 20 hours isn't an overestimate for me. But if you find me 20 hours, I'm sure I can use the remainder profitably."

"What are the sort of things that intrude on those 20 hours?" asked Lucy. "What do they get taken up with? Let's try and make a list of all the things that we will need to reduce or avoid, if we are to get those 20 hours back. Then we can get a more practical look at what we are talking about." She flipped to a new sheet of flipchart paper and stood poised with her pen.

Abs said: "Well, I know the biggest time taker for me, is when something goes wrong that has implications for our delivery promises. You know the sort of thing: supplier failures; machine breakdown; forecast inaccuracy; paperwork mistakes; design errors." He cast a dark look at Deborah.

Peter chipped in: "A lot of my time is taken up in meetings and video conferencing. There are a lot of corporate forums where I'm expected to be present."

And so the list grew: sorting out conflict between departments; completing reports and other paperwork; meetings to sort out issues; customer reviews; special project committees looking at the corporate initiatives; meeting suppliers; IT system crashes; management meetings; cascade

outline of each step within the PROBLEM model.

Profile

The goal of this step is to arrive at a clear definition of a workable and owned problem, which everyone involved understands and is based on hard facts rather than assumptions and opinions.

The three main elements in achieving this are as follows.

- Firstly, to identify the detail of the problem area. What process and groups of people are involved; what is the current output of the process and what should it be; and who is going to own both the problem and its solution.

- Secondly, to understand exactly what is happening at present, by flowcharting the current activities and practices.

- Thirdly, to establish - at the outset - what measures are going to be taken to verify whether or not any improvement has been made.

Root causes

The next step in the PROBLEM model, is to establish the most probable root cause of the whole problem. Achieving this is done in two distinct parts:

- Firstly, a comprehensive range of potential root causes is identified, using a variety of 'opening up' techniques such as brainstorming and fishbone diagrams.[1]

- Secondly, these potential causes are analysed and verified with data to separate the causes from the symptoms, and to establish the cause or causes which have the biggest impact on the problem.

---

1   A basic guide to the tools employed in problem-solving is provided on the associated web-site (see Appendix 7).

It isn't that they can't see the solution, it is that they can't see the problem.

G. K. Chesterton

The question is one of fighting the causes and not just being satisfied with getting rid of the effects.

Ernesto 'Che' Guevara
Bolivian Radical

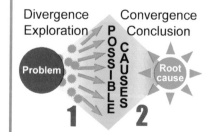

briefings; recruiting staff; design reviews; disciplinary issues; reading junk mail; responding to e-mails; staff personal problems; checking on subordinates …

As the stream of suggestions dried up, Lucy concluded: "So, it is out of this list that we need to save ourselves 20 hours a week. Step two, what are the main causes of these activities imposing on our time?" She turned to a fresh sheet of paper.

Peter was first out of the blocks. "Well, in my case, it is because I don't have anybody else to do them," he said.

"Mine too," said Abs, "I'm the only one who can make the decisions on making late shipments. No-one else has a full enough picture." Lucy had written up on the flipchart 'Resource limitations' and 'Lack of people with complete overview'.

And gradually, this list grew too: Process failures; lack of competence in subordinates; corporate policy; customer expectations; lack of investment in prevention; carelessness; system errors; poor communication; lack of awareness of implications; poor decision making; lack of empowerment; poor checking; bureaucracy; inefficient systems; inefficient meetings; poor completion of actions; people not doing things when they say they will; lack of preparation; corporate demands; politics; people saving time by dumping the problem on others; poor e-mail behaviours; poor staff selection and development; poorly designed systems …

Eventually the suggestions began to slow, and Lucy took the opportunity to bring it to a close. She was fairly confident that the list had the most relevant issues on it.

"It's a sort of Catch 22," said Deborah. "This list of problems causes us to lose the time that we need to prevent these problems from happening in the first place."

"I'm not sure that's quite true," argued Andrew. "I'm not sure that we can do anything about Corporate Policy."

"Even if that were true," retorted Deborah, "and I'm not sure that it is, look at the rest of the list. Systematic improvement of our processes and our people addresses a large number of those issues. Doesn't it?"

Options

Having determined the root cause(s) we now need to identify a range of possible solutions which would eliminate the chosen root cause or causes, and which reflect an understanding of best practice.

This 'Options' step is a real opportunity to ensure that the organisation is developing creatively through the adoption of innovative ideas and techniques for opening up our thinking.

There are a number of possibilities to ensure that this happens. These include brainstorming sessions, the use of creative design tools, undertaking a literature survey on the subject, visiting companies with similar processes and seeing what they do, and canvassing the opinions of others.

Balance

The range of possible options are evaluated, and those selected are pulled into a balanced solution. 'Balanced' here implies that, in pulling together a solution package, benefits need to be balanced against cost, opportunities need to be balanced against risks, long-term effects need to be balanced against short-term ones, etc.

As with identifying the most probable root cause, this is a process of gathering and using data to weigh up which solution to implement. There are a variety of tools that help the team to think this through, including QFD itself.

When the solution has been identified, the means of its implementation is agreed. This is then pulled into a complete forward plan with appropriate milestones to enable its effective management. Successful implementation depends on accurate planning. This includes providing

If you do not expect the unexpected, you will not find it.

Heraclitus
Greek philosopher

No matter how complicated a problem, it can usually be reduced to a simple comprehensible form which is often the best solution.

Dr. An Wang
Founder and CEO, Wang Laboratories

There was a general assent to this, but then Peter reminded the group: "But the essential feature of a 'Catch 22' is that there is no way out of it!"

"Well let's call it a Catch 21 and three-quarters then," retorted Deborah, irritation beginning to show in her voice.

"Peter's got a point though," sympathised John. "The link may be there, but breaking it is not going to be easy. It is almost like we'll have to borrow time on account."

"It strikes me that we have two options," suggested Susan. "We can cut ourselves a bit of slack and invest it into that list to generate even more slack, and simply keep the cycle going. Or we can simply stop doing what is on that list, and put up with the consequences until we have our new management system running properly."

"Sort of like cutting ourselves a lot of slack, and investing it?" countered Andrew.

"I suppose so," agreed Susan. "The risk of cutting ourselves a lot of slack might be that we can't survive the consequences. The risk of just cutting a little slack might be that it takes too long."

"If we are going to make this work," said Richard, "time is something we just don't have. We deliver improvement starting next month, or this process stops dead in its tracks!"

Lucy, concerned that the discussion was beginning to lose its way, stepped in to bring the process back on track. "It seems we are moving onto thinking through our options, but before we do that, can I just confirm with the group that this list really does represent the causes of the stated problem?"

The group looked back at the list and muttered their general agreement, so Lucy continued. "So, we now need to tackle the third step: generating options. But before we get too deeply into discussion, let's try and identify all of the possible options. I've already heard Susan suggest: 'Stop doing the operational bits and accept the consequences', and also 'Slowly address the issues on the list'. Are there other suggestions?" She flipped to a clean sheet and wrote them up.

The list grew gradually: pretend we're on holiday two days a week; hire in some management cover; appoint a stand-in from among our subor-

for all the resources likely to be required when the 'new' way of working is in place.

Launch

During the 'Launch' step, the problem team maintains a watchful eye on progress against their original plan. Any deviations to the plan are considered from three perspectives.

- Can the deviation be corrected?
- Does the deviation have any knock-on effects on other parts of the plan?
- Does the deviation imply further similar problems in the future?

The team not only addresses the deviations as they become aware of them, but also uses them as new data to help them in predicting and preventing future problems in the plan.

Evaluate

Once the implementation of the solution is complete we now need to 'Evaluate' its effectiveness, to ensure that it has not been compromised by unresolved issues and variable application.

In this, the penultimate step, the measures that were identified in the 'Profile' stage are used to check that the performance gap is fully addressed, and that no unfortunate side effects have been generated.

The 'Evaluate' step is also the point at which the team reconsiders its effectiveness, and clarifies the 'learning' that is available to it in improving its own performance (both collectively and individually) and also the performance of future problem-solving teams.

It does not matter how small you are if you have faith and a plan of action.

Fidel Castro
Cuban leader

What gets measured gets done.

Anonymous

dinates; subcontract the work to some consultants; address the issues permanently - don't just fix them; create consequences for not doing this; don't respond to cc e-mails; take each of these issues as an opportunity to develop our people …

Lucy fought hard to avoid debate, and encourage new contributions, until she felt they had listed all they were going to. She then asked the group to individually stick a red sticky dot against their two favourite suggestions. When the group had sat down again Lucy reflected on the picture that had emerged. There were two winning suggestions each with four dots - these were 'Stop doing the operational bits and accept the consequences' and 'Pretend we're on holiday two days a week'.

"Wow, we are Gung Ho!" exclaimed Lucy. "Looks like we're up for drastic action!"

"Well, Richard pointed out that we don't have time for anything else," said Susan.

"Aren't those two things really the same?" enquired Peter. "One is just one way of doing the other." People agreed that he was right.

"The next most favoured suggestions," continued Lucy, "were 'Hire in some management cover' and 'Appoint a stand-in from among our subordinates' with two dots. And finally we have 'Address issues permanently' and 'Use issues to develop our people' with one dot each. It seems to me that what we have here are separate aspects of a complete solution" she proposed.

The others looked at the flipchart some more, and finally Susan responded: "I think you're right. But is it feasible? Can we actually do this?"

John retorted: "Can we afford not to?"

Abs asked: "Would you support hiring-in management cover, Richard?" and everybody waited for the answer.

"Yes, I would," he replied. "But you'd better make sure that you're not just creating more work for yourself by taking on outsiders."

"I was actually thinking that it would allow me to get Stephen to deputise for me, and then the management cover could be for him. It's what we usually do when I go on holiday," submitted Abs. Richard nodded approval.

Maintain

The purpose of this last step, is to ensure that the implemented solution becomes the new way of working and that the problem, as defined, remains permanently fixed.

Achieving this normally requires that any existing procedures are modified and that new sets of standards and guidelines and measurements are established. It also usually requires training and education for all those involved in the change.

Linear and non-linear thinking

There is a danger, particularly in light of the current vogue for 'non-linear' thinking, that the problem-solving approach of identifying specific root causes may be seen as too 'linear'!

But before you conclude that, you might like to consider the following points.

1. A solution should efficiently meet the problem as defined. To move outside of this remit is to solicit and encourage effort in areas that have not been guided and prioritised by your planning.

2. If you want a non-linear solution, you should set a non-linear goal that is focused on the strategic needs of the business. This will ensure that the failing 'components' are broadly defined and that the options are innovative and radical.

3. The QFD provides all the scope you need to be non-linear, but within an objective and disciplined framework. It helps to ensure that your non-linear efforts (which can be resource draining and risky in the initial stages) are focused in the areas where you will get greatest benefit.

"There is a flaw in our thinking though," challenged Deborah. "If we dump our work on those who work for us, how then do we free them up to get them involved in this process?" The group went silent. It was almost as though she had poured water on the glowing embers that were just about to burst into flame.

Richard pondered for a short while. "Actually, at this stage, I am less concerned about that. They have been involved in the decisions to date, and I don't think they'd be too bothered if you shouldered the burden of the next steps. You can always consult them where appropriate. And if you need them any more involved, at least you will have the time to think through how you do it. I am willing to fund an extra twenty contract heads over the next four weeks, if you need them." Richard concluded. "But, if I'm to get away with it, I need you to focus your new management approach on our real current performance issues." The group nodded assent.

"Can I just check what we're actually going to do with these two days a week?" queried Abs.

Richard nodded. "The way I see it, you are going to ensure your implementation plans are fulfilled. You are going to work, one-to-one or in groups, with the people who will deliver progress and performance, and you are going to ensure that it happens."

Lucy was not sure that was quite the way she saw things, but it was close enough, and it seemed to have the backing of the group.

"Tomorrow afternoon I will be going through a few tools and approaches with Deborah," Lucy announced. "But anyone else is welcome to join us. I am sure you will find they will help in what you are about to do!"

"What sort of tools?" asked John.

"Mainly tools that help in solving problems and in delegating tasks," answered Lucy.

"Sounds great," responded Abs. "What time?"

"Two o'clock," Lucy replied. "But if anyone can't make it, I'd be happy to run additional sessions."

There was a general murmur of assent, and a few diaries and organisers were flicked open and consulted.

4. Even solutions defined by non-linear thinking can (and should) be refined and improved in linear ways.

5. Sometimes we espouse concepts like 'non-linearity' not because they are right (even though they may well be) but because it seems to absolve us of the need to be disciplined and objective in executing our responsibilities. Be 'non-linear', but first examine your real motives, and second do it within a responsible framework.

"Before we get too far into the detail though," Lucy continued, "can I just check that everyone is in agreement with our conclusions on the first Car Park item?" People were, so Lucy moved on.

"Before we launch into the second, then, I believe that Richard wants to say something about it."

Richard stood up, and started talking as he walked round to the front of the room. "Yes. This was the issue of poor communication between processes, and tripping over each other's initiatives, or not getting necessary support from each other. Could everybody make a session on Thursday afternoon at 4.30pm? It will only take about an hour, and I promise you will find it worthwhile."

There was some debate, and eventually it was pulled forward to 4pm. Then Lucy proposed a way to take the third item forward, and then closed the meeting.

The roof

The structure of QFD, and the way that the grid is developed, does much to ensure that the various parts of your organisation work together in harmony. The various teams and individuals within a QFD framework:

- understand the overall picture, and where each part needs to contribute

- are conscious of how they can negatively impact the business and damage the efforts of other parts of the organisation

- have agreed their final objectives with their colleagues on the management team

- are equipped with a model to see the implications and impacts of their decisions.

QFD goes further than any other goal-setting tool to ensure that this is the case. And yet it is still possible for conflicts and confusions to arise in practice.

The roof of the QFD takes the need for the organisation to work together in harmony one stage further. It provides a means for each process to reflect on its relationship with each other process, and to decide on how it will communicate (or not) to ensure it remains in alignment with them. In this chapter we:

- look at how the roof of the QFD works to achieve this

- consider a practical mechanism for working through the roof with your team.

How the roof works

The roof of the QFD maps out intersections between each process (see right). The point marked on the example is the intersection between process B and

[Intra-organisational conflict] exists because as groups become more committed to their own goals and norms, they are likely to become competitive with one another and seek to undermine their rivals' activities, thereby becoming a liability to the organisation as a whole. The overall problem, then, is how to establish high-productive, collaborative intergroup relations... The basic strategy of reducing conflict, therefore, is to find goals upon which groups can agree and to re-establish valid communications between the group.

Edgar H. Schein
Massachusetts Institute of Technology

Chapter 23

Richard was a model of calm rationality when he went to pick up with Daniel after the meeting. He knew that would unsettle Daniel more than anything else. Not that he was expecting a lot from the meeting. He realised that he did not yet have enough to fire Daniel safely, and he fully expected that Daniel would have calmed down by now, and would recognise that he stood no real chance of pushing his position. In the event Daniel acted it out exactly as Richard imagined he would: minimal (but sufficient) acquiescence with the conclusions; maximum restatement and justification of his position and behaviour.

But Richard felt more and more confident that it was simply a matter of time.

Later, over a beer in the adjacent pub, Daniel confided to Peter "It's him or me, and I'm absolutely determined that it's going to be him!"

Peter looked concernedly at his friend. "Don't do anything stupid, Dan. He's no mug, and even though he's on the final countdown, I would not be surprised if the old man cut him some more slack. I think he is going to be around for a while, and even though I don't like what he is doing, I'm beginning to think it really can work."

"It won't work!" replied Daniel with final certainty. "Rely on me. It won't work!"

Peter looked at Daniel more closely. They locked eyes, and Peter said finally: "Dan, I meant it. Don't do anything stupid. "

"Too late for that now, and anyway, what's stupid is appointing that pillock in the first place," said Daniel with venom. He picked up the remains of his pint, slung it down his throat, and simply got up and left Peter sitting there.

When the management team arrived on the following Thursday afternoon, they found the room empty except for four tables in a line, and

process E, as you can see if you follow the lines of intersection down.

Each intersection can be examined to see how the processes are likely to impact and influence each other, and the conclusions mapped onto the grid.

Processes are potentially in synergy if, in pursuing their individual objectives, they are likely to have a positive impact on each other's work.

Conversely, processes are potentially in conflict when such pursuit is likely to have a negative impact on each other's work.

If, however, they are unlikely to affect each other, the intersection should be left blank.

The purpose of working through these is to provide an opportunity for each process to decide what communication they need with each other process.

For instance, if they are in conflict, they may want to consider a periodic review of what each one is doing, or a regular bulletin of planned changes.

Or, if they are in synergy, there may be a case for developing a number of joint projects that will benefit both processes.

A list of some of the possible communication mechanisms that might be considered is shown on the right.

Options to consider for communication:

Formal meeting between teams

Formal meeting between owners

Formal meeting between selected team members

Written communication

Informal discussions

Part of another meeting

None required.

eight chairs, placed one each on opposite sides of each of the first three tables, and on each end of the fourth.

"Please, take any seat," encouraged Richard, "and I'll explain what we're doing when we're all here."

When the last person had arrived, Richard said: "Okay, as agreed at the last meeting, we are here to plan out the communication between each of our processes, so that we can be sure we don't keep tripping over each other. You will notice the strange seating arrangement. This, as I will explain later, will give each of us the opportunity of discussing our communication needs with every other process owner, so efficiently that we will be out of here by 5 o'clock."

Richard moved over to the flipchart, and flipped over to a strange triangular grid placed on top of the process names on their QFD.

"Let me introduce you to the roof of the QFD," he said, a little melodramatically. "The roof of the QFD is normally for recording potential interaction between the mechanisms. We are going to use it to record whether our processes are likely to be in conflict or synergy with each other, and thereby what communication needs we have between each of them. Very shortly, you will be having a discussion with another process owner, probably the one opposite you at the moment, and together you will be answering three questions."

Here he flicked over another sheet to the three questions.

"Firstly, you will need to agree whether, if both processes were to ruthlessly and independently pursue their objectives, they would create problems for each other, or whether they are likely to move each other forward. If you are likely to create problems, then you are potentially in conflict, and need to keep each other informed of developments and possible implications so that you can avoid any serious issues. If you are likely to move each other forward, then there is some potential synergy between your processes, and you should communicate occasionally to identify any common projects that you might undertake. The first step, is to agree whether you are in conflict or synergy, or neither. You can then mark the roof of the house, where your processes intersect, with a cross for conflict, or a circle for synergy, or leave it blank. Okay so far?"

John stepped in quickly with a question. "Can you give us a practical example of conflict and synergy, Richard? Just so we can check we're understanding right!"

Mechanism for developing the roof

It is possible for the roof to be thought through and developed by the management team as a whole. But this proves time consuming, and is often fairly tedious. It is difficult to take an interest in communications you have no part in.

An alternative mechanism, which proves efficient and fun in practice, is to set up an exercise where each process owner can meet each other process owner, one-on-one, and decide between them the relationship and the communication needs.

The diagram on the right shows the seating set-up for the exercise. 'n' is the number of processes rounded up to an even number. If there is an odd number of processes, there is no one in the stationary seat at the top of the diagram (labelled 'n'), but on every turn one process will still sit out at that table.

The example on the right shows the seating arrangements at the start of the exercise for nine processes.

All process owners move one seat round the cycle every five minutes. This keeps discussions focused and the energy up, and stops those who are discussing a blank cell from getting bored. The diagram on the right shows an example pro-forma[1] for process owners to complete for their discussions.

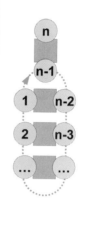

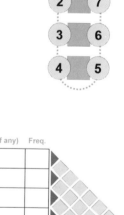

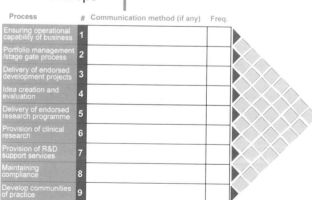

Process	#	Communication method (if any)	Freq.
Ensuring operational capability of business	1		
Portfolio management /stage gate process	2		
Delivery of endorsed development projects	3		
Idea creation and evaluation	4		
Delivery of endorsed research programme	5		
Provision of clinical research	6		
Provision of R&D support services	7		
Maintaining compliance	8		
Develop communities of practice	9		

---

1   A copy of the pro-forma is available on the associated website (see Appendix 7).

Richard thought for a moment, his hands clasped together under his chin, his lips pursed, and his eyes fixed somewhere around John's knees.

"Okay," he said, "if Peter's process, *'Stewarding assets and resources'*, had an objective to save ten percent of overhead costs, and Andrew's process, *'Providing and growing people'*, had an objective to increase average competence by ten percent, then you could imagine that they might spend a lot of time arguing over the training budget. As such their objectives might place them in conflict, and they would clearly need to have regular discussions about their plans and strategies. Yes?"

"Probably," said Susan. "But, if Andrew's focus on competence was targeted at making overhead activities more efficient, then maybe they would not be in conflict?"

"Quite so," agreed Richard. "Two processes are not inherently in conflict or synergy. It depends on the detail of the objectives they've set themselves, and how they interpret them. That's why we need to have these discussions."

"And what would be an example of synergy?" asked John.

"Well, if we stick with Peter and Andrew, then synergy might be achieved if Andrew set an objective to reduce absenteeism by fifty percent. You could then imagine that Peter and Andrew might want to set up joint projects in this area, or at the very least involve each other in the specification of those projects."

Some people were nodding, others were clearly still thinking. Daniel was gazing out of the window. Deborah looked troubled. "Hold on," she said. "Andrew could have both the objectives you mentioned for his process."

"Ye-e-e-s?" said Richard cautiously, waiting for Deborah's point.

"So would he then be in conflict, or synergy?" Richard was momentarily stumped. He had not come across this situation in using QFD for product design. He thought quickly.

"Well, both! Peter and Andrew would need to communicate in both respects!"

"You didn't mention that as an option," said Deborah, slightly suspiciously. "What symbol do we use for that?"

Each process owner:

- marks the agreed relationship against the other process
- agrees whether any communication is necessary
- considers whether any existing forums could be used or adapted for this
- agrees any new forums or mechanisms if necessary, and their frequency
- moves on to the next discussion.

A compound picture of the relationships can be stuck on the top of the QFD diagram if required, for completeness.

If in the course of working together, process owners find the need to review their communication needs with other process owners, for instance if a new objective develops, these can be simply be agreed between process owners, and updated on the QFD.

Most of the professors appreciated it when you washed off the blackboard but not Dr. [Albert] Einstein. Every morning he'd burst into tears. Way I see it, I had a job to do, and I was bound and determined to do it right. He wasn't the only perfectionist in the university business.

Garth Peterson
Former janitor, Princeton University

	Wt.	Customer support and order management	Develop new business	Producing and distributing product	Maintaining the supply line	Developing products and processes	Providing an effective environment	Providing and growing people	Stewarding assets and resources	Measure	Target
Address new market areas	3	○	⊙	△	⊙	○		△		Business from new markets	> 34%
Provide excellent customer service	5	⊙	△	⊙	⊙	○	○	○	⊙	Customer retention	> 85%
Build leadership in platform technology	4		△	⊙	○	⊙	△	⊙		Innov. copied by compet'n	> 5 p.a.
Reduce production and delivery lead times	2	⊙		○	⊙	⊙	⊙	⊙	△	Production cycle	< 6 days
Maximise asset utilisation (incl. IPR)	3	○	○	△		○	⊙	△	⊙	Asset utilisation	> 55%
Reduce unit production costs	4	○	△	⊙	○	⊙	⊙	○	○	Cost of goods sold	< 70%
Build effective supplier partnerships	4		△	⊙	⊙	○	○	○	⊙	Supplier led business	> £80m
Ranking		93	53	165	150	135	112	99	122		

Richard felt that Deborah has sussed that he hadn't been prepared for this, but he continued gamely: "We will mark that with a combined cross and circle like this." He drew one on the board. He looked back at Deborah, and she smirked at him. Yes, she knew! Ah, well.

"Okay. The second step!" announced Richard. "The second step is to agree with the other process owners, what level of communication you will need. Here are some examples of what you might consider."

He flicked to the third sheet of flipchart paper. "As you can see," he continued, "they range from regular formal team meetings, to simply copying each other with your project plans. It really is up to you to work out what is appropriate. Any questions?"

There weren't any questions, so Richard continued: "The third step is to write it up on your proformas, and agree to any initial meeting dates that you might need. Is everybody okay with that?"

"Proformas, Richard. What are they?" asked Peter.

"Oh, sorry! I've still got them here. I'll hand them out now. When you have your meetings, fill in your conclusions against the process you were meeting. And at the end of all your meetings, you can update this roof I've drawn on the flipchart. Now! As to how the discussions will take place. Your initial discussion will be with the person sitting opposite you, and then, after five minutes, you will move to the next seat as indicated on this diagram."

He flicked to another sheet of flipchart paper, which showed a simple circuit with one person remaining fixed. "I am going to temporarily look after the *'Developing New Business'* process for this activity. Is everybody clear on what is going on?"

"Five minutes isn't long, Richard," challenged Andrew.

"Yes, you will have to watch your time and remain focused. But I'm sure that if, on occasion, you can't finalise your discussion, you can always finish it off outside. Lucy will give us a one minute warning, and move us on as required. So let's start. The first five minutes begin now."

Process management reporting

As has been explained in Chapter 14, process management routines are the engine that harnesses the potential of the business to the clear aspirations of the goal-setting process.

The nerve centre for this cycle is the process (or sub-process) management meeting. It is here that the performance against forecast is presented, and issues are prioritised and assigned. It is also this meeting that reviews if all other parts of the cycle are working on time.

The quality of the process management meeting lies in the objectivity and systemic nature of its decisions. Key aspects to explore, when assessing the quality of a team's work at this level are as follows.

- Are they focusing on the right objectives and are those objectives unambiguous and comprehensive. Do the objectives clearly relate to the QFD at the next level up?

- Is current performance against the objectives clearly understood, and have resulting gaps been prioritised?

- Do the team have clear plans in place to address the performance gaps systematically, and have they forecast how these plans will affect performance, over time, to meet the objective?

- Is progress against the forecast regularly and accurately measured, and are performance deficits or trend issues clearly identified?

- Are all major performance deficits or trend issues analysed objectively, systemically and systematically using appropriate problem-solving tools?

- Have these analyses been used to modify current improvement plans or to define new ones?

The professional's grasp of the numbers is a measure of the control he has over the events that the figures represent.

Harold Geneen
CEO, IT&T

An individual without information cannot take responsibility; an individual who is given information cannot help but take responsibility.

Jan Carlzon
Ex-CEO SAS

Chapter 24

Richard was not really sure why he had gone back to the Church on Sunday. Laura had not asked him to come, but she seemed pleased that he had. For the most part, he felt that he had got a lot out of the last visit, and the curmudgeonly reader, and wondered whether he would get another insight this time round. Part of him felt he was honour bound to fulfil the bargain he had made in prayer amongst the shards of the crystal decanter.

He was surprised by how different the service was. The building, the congregation and the vicar had not changed, but the door-person had given him different books than on his previous visit - larger and more colourful.

The whole tone of the service seemed lighter and more informal. The wording of the hymns and responses seemed more immediate, more accessible. People around seemed more at ease, and less stuffy, and there were children present too.

Richard was beginning to wonder whether they had fallen victim to some marketing consultant. Heaven knows they could do with one, he thought.

The reader had not been as inspiring as on his last visit, and the sermon seemed largely to pass him by. It seemed more focused on the hoards of children who had been invited to the front of the Church.

By the time the last hymn was called, he was beginning to think he had wasted his time. He flicked through the hymn book to the song headed 456, and thought: 'Thank God it's not a long one'.

He recognised the title though, and his thoughts were confirmed by the introductory tune. He knew this song. It was by Sinead O'Connor. He liked this song, but he had never sung it, and the thought of it being murdered by the Derby and Joan club and the cast of St. Trinians, filled him with dread.

But when the singing started, it was strangely haunting and serene. He concentrated on the words:

Make me a channel of Your peace.
Where there is hatred let me bring Your love;

- Do all planned actions have clear owners and timescales defined, and has some form of risk analysis been undertaken?

- Is performance on completing actions reviewed and systematically improved?

Process reporting

If the process team is clearly in control of its performance, and is handling issues diligently and effectively, then there is little point in interfering with their work. If, on the other hand, the process team is not in control, and/or issues are not being properly addressed, there is clearly a need for guidance and support. The key lies in knowing quickly and accurately into which category the process team falls.

Unfortunately, conventional reporting is an easy place to hide and obscure real issues, and talk up failure into a virtue.

Quadrant chart reporting overcomes this problem by requiring that the process team map out, on one sheet of paper: the salient aspects of their performance; trend against forecast; analysis of shortfalls; and their action plan to address those shortfalls.

If process management routines are the engine that drives continuous improvement, then the quadrant chart acts as the transmission, wheels and tyres; galvanizing improvement through clarity and objectivity.

Quadrant charts, as their name might suggest, are a single sheet of A4 paper, divided into four quadrants. These quadrants contain all the pertinent information on how the process is being managed.

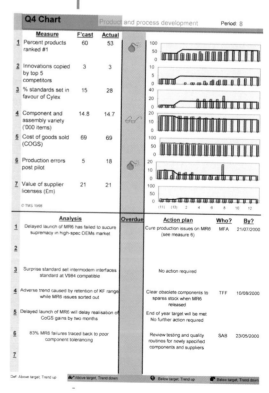

where there is injury, Your pardon, Lord;
and where there's doubt, true faith in You.

Oh, Master, grant that I may never seek
so much to be consoled as to console;
to be understood as to understand;
to be loved, as to love with all my soul.

Make me a channel of Your peace.
Where there's despair in life let me bring hope;
where there is darkness, only light;
and where there's sadness, ever joy.

Make me a channel of Your peace.
It is in pardoning that we are pardoned,
in giving to all men that we receive;
and in dying that we're born to eternal life.

As he listened to the singing, he felt a strange yearning open up inside him; an emptiness that he could not fully describe, or explain.

At the same time, he felt both an overwhelming affinity with the words, and a deep resentment for them. They both attracted and repelled him at the very same time. It was like standing at the edge of somewhere you had always wanted to be, but knowing the price of entry was more than you could pay.

For the briefest moment, he wanted so much for the song to be his, and at the same time, felt the deepest fear of the consequences. Like a moth before a flame.

He left the Church in a daze, unsure of what he was feeling. There was clearly something vitally important there, and while he struggled desperately not to lose the traces of what had gripped him, he fought to retain the sense of logic and proportion that would protect him.

He gathered himself up to shake hands with the vicar, and to secure the temporary loan of the hymn book he was still holding, forefinger firmly wedging it open on hymn 456.

While Laura took Nicholas in for coffee, Richard excused himself, and went to sit quietly on a bench at the far corner of the churchyard.

- In the top left-hand quadrant the chart displays the key performance measures for the area (department, process, section...), the target to be achieved, and the current level of performance.

- In the top right-hand quadrant, it graphs the performance measures and trend against forecast performance and target for the year to date, and thereby illustrates any issues in the pattern of performance over time.

- In the bottom left-hand quadrant, it provides a summary of the analysis that has been undertaken into any performance issues - whether overall performance or adverse trends.

- And in the bottom right-hand quadrant, it summarises the actions that have been planned to address the issues and bring the performance back into control.

The quadrant chart demonstrates clearly in a format that is straightforward, logical and easy to assimilate, what is being managed and what is not - it reports the basics baldly and provides little scope for hiding issues in a mass of rhetoric. And a quadrant chart is quick and easy to produce.

The various quadrants are explained in more detail below.

Quadrant 1: Performance

The top left-hand quadrant should list out the key measures of department performance, together with the agreed targets and current performance. These should be drawn directly from the process QFD (if one has been created).

The measures of performance should cover all that is important in the process or area to which it pertains, because the

Gazing out across the serried ranks of gravestones, he composed and centred himself, re-opened the hymn book, and re-read the words. Something vitally relevant had gripped him and he was determined to identify it.

He could see that the words echoed with what he had been struggling with over the last few weeks, the whole concept of adding value. But that was not it.

There was something more, something in the words that both compelled and frightened him.

It was the sense of sacrifice. The sense of not just wanting to add value, but of being willing to give things up to make it happen.

It was not cold, but something made Richard shiver, and he knew that he was on the edge of a decision. And the question, quite simply, was this: was he only willing to add value on his own terms, or was he willing to do whatever was necessary? It was this question that had struck him. He wanted to do both, and he wanted to do neither. He wanted to be real, but he felt he could only afford the sham.

"Sometimes," he thought ruefully, "insight can be far too bloody expensive! Ignorance can be a far more comfortable place to be!"

He knew that, at some point, he would need to make this decision, but at least now he knew what it was, he could put it to one side for a more appropriate venue. He stood up and walked toward the building where the sign invitingly advertised coffee and biscuits.

As he weaved his way through the gravestones, he puzzled on the enigma that was 'God', and for the first time considered, albeit only fleetingly, whether his unwillingness to believe in God was due to an excess of believing in himself and his own potential. "Sacrifice is a strange concept," he thought, "it opens up a whole new can of worms!"

The concept of sacrifice played on Richard's mind, off and on, all through the following week. He reflected on his earlier thoughts; of the need to make himself dispensable, and the parallels between that and sacrifice. He thought about the concepts of coaching, and the need to draw the best out of the other person, thereby foregoing your own opportunity to shine.

quadrant chart should be the one means of reporting all that is being managed in the area, and it should not need to be supplemented by any other form of report.

Practically this is likely to require three to seven[1] measures, if they have been well thought out. These measures should be practical and able to be recorded at least quarterly and preferably monthly, in order to ensure a level of responsive control over the outcomes. The targets are intended to drive improvement, and should be focused on areas that provide the greatest business or customer benefits.

Quadrant 2: Trend

The top right-hand quadrant of the report should provide graphical evidence of performance over time. Each measure listed in quadrant 1 should be clearly associated with a graph showing trend, forecast and target performance over the year.

These graphs provide a clear indication of how consistent and stable the management of each measure has been. They demonstrate clearly the level of control and improvement that has been achieved.

Each graph should include a forecast line, which clearly reflects the expected impact of any planned programmes to meet target performance by year-end. This time-based aspiration (sometimes called a flag plan) both reflects the level of thought and planning that has been invested in meeting the target, and provides confidence that current performance is to plan, even when it does not yet meet the final goal.

Measure	F'cast	Actual
1 Percent products ranked #1	60	53
2 Innovations copied by top 5 competitors	3	3
3 % standards set in favour of Cylex	15	28
4 Component and assembly variety ('000 items)	14.8	14.7
5 Cost of goods sold (COGS)	69	69
6 Production errors post pilot	5	18
7 Value of supplier licenses (£m)	21	21

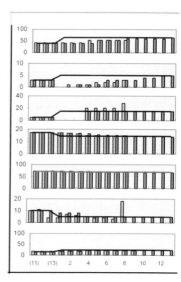

---

1   It is difficult to obtain a balanced comprehensive picture with less than three measures, and the thinking can lose focus with more than seven.

Sacrifice was a whole new way of thinking, was he really up to it? Did he want to be up to it?

He thought about the sacrifice of handing over Cylek UK to one of his team, once the management system was in place. It would be okay if there was a new better role for him to take on, but what would he do if there wasn't?

Would he hold things back, rather than move them forward?

Work on implementing the QFD seemed to be progressing well since the last management meeting. The level of activity gave him a good feeling. Most of his team had managed to clear their diaries, and had identified local performance improvements which would begin to deliver before the next meeting.

Even Daniel seemed to be playing ball. Richard did not really understand it, and suspected a rat.

Daniel had cleared his diary of two days a week to work on Customer measures, and that was clearly a step forward. However, Richard did have cause to wish Daniel had been a trifle more circumspect about how he arranged his time. He had already received two calls from irate customers with whom Daniel had cancelled previously arranged meetings, with no explanation.

Daniel's behaviour made him uneasy, but he was not sure what to do about it.

Lucy's *'Introduction to Problem-solving'* had now been attended by everyone from the management team, and by a fair proportion of their subordinates. And over half the processes now had at least one problem-solving project under way.

And while Richard had offered his own time, and additional contract resource, he was surprised at how little of it had been taken up. Only Abs, Susan, Peter, and Andrew had taken on contractors to spread the workload, and Richard's only involvement had been to comment on the various schemes and ideas proposed.

By the next management meeting, two of the projects had really begun to bear fruit. Inventory, though it was only down by 0.4%, was planned to reduce by 16% over the next three months. And order overdues had

Each graph in quadrant 2 should use a consistent 'house-style' so what they are saying can be easily and unambiguously interpreted.

Quadrant 3: Analysis

The lower right-hand quadrant provides an opportunity for the process team to demonstrate the objectivity with which they are addressing any unexpected shortfall in performance. Analysis entries should be brief and only focused on areas where the performance is below forecast or of adverse trend. In all other cases we trust that the team is in control.[1]

Analysis should indicate very clearly the systematic issue that has brought about the problem, and provide objective evidence for this. While it may be easier to associate a specific event with the problem, doing so provides little scope for preventing further occurrences or for ensuring performance over the longer term, and should therefore be avoided.[2]

Analysis should have been derived from the use (formally or informally) of a defined and agreed problem-solving[3] approach, and through this, analysis should clearly identify the proportion of the deficit that arises from the defined issues.

Quadrant 4: Action

The lower right-hand quadrant lists out the actions that are to be taken as a result of the analysis. All analyses should be associated with clear actions to resolve the issues and prevent future recurrence.

	Analysis
1	Delayed launch of MR6 has failed to sucure supremacy in high-spec OEMs market
2	
3	Surprise standard set intermodem interfaces standard at V984 compatible
4	Adverse trend caused by retention of KF range while MR6 issues sorted out
5	Delayed launch of MR6 will delay realisation of CoGS gains by two months
6	83% MR6 failures traced back to poor component tolerancing
7	

Def Above target, Trend up   Above target, Trend down

The greatest of faults, I should say, is to be conscious of none.

Thomas Carlyle
Scottish essayist and historian

---

1   If you cannot trust your team, you have a coaching issue, not a reporting issue.

2   A tool for helping the team to think this through can be found on page 302 and on the associated web-site (see Appendix 7).

3   An appropriate methodology can be found in Chapter 22.

reduced from 34% to 13%. Clearly still too large, but plans were in place to reduce it to less than 5% by the end of the next quarter.

Most of the measures presented showed some improvement, although Richard was convinced that much of it was merely due to the increased focus the measures gave the process teams. At this stage, it really could not be anything else.

Only one quadrant chart was missing. Daniel was off at an important sales conference, and his stand-in had been assured that Richard had a copy of the quadrant chart, and would present on it. Yes, the stand-in, was sure it existed somewhere, because he had seen Daniel working on it. No, he could not remember any of the data.

Richard was reluctant to push too hard. He did not want one of Daniel's people to think he was conducting a witch-hunt on his boss. Though clearly annoyed by this one dark cloud on his horizon of blue sky, Richard dropped the subject.

After the meeting had finished, and Richard had congratulated his team and promised them a party to celebrate, Richard and Lucy retired to Richard's office to compile the top-level Cylek UK quadrant chart, and to wing it on its way to Frank Delaney.

They looked with satisfaction at the finished article projected high on Richard's wall, and at the various graphs, each showing a little, or not so little, upward kick in their tails.

"You could not have got anything better if you'd fixed the data," said Lucy, grinning from ear to ear.

"Oh, I don't know," said Richard, a small frown on his forehead. "I'm really sorry that we haven't got the customer satisfaction measure. I'm sure that would have leapt up with the improvement in delivery performance, and with Deborah involving them in New Product clinics. And that's without the work that Daniel has been doing. I really could have done with that data. You know how hot Cyrus is on Customer Satisfaction!"

"Well, Daniel's in on Monday," suggested Lucy. "Why don't you wait till then and send Frank the complete thing?"

All the listed actions should have clearly defined owners, who have accepted responsibility for completing the action, and timescales for delivery. In practice, actions without delivery dates are uncontrolled, and drift. Dates need to be set that are consistent with the needs to meet target performance by year-end.

The planned actions should also be reflected in the forecast performance line of the 'Trend' quadrant. This will help to ensure that the thinking and planning has been diligent, and will help to stop the issue becoming over-managed in subsequent months.

Quadrant charts,[1] when designed and enforced appropriately, leave no place to hide poor management. Unlike a multi-page written report, they provide little opportunity for camouflage, rationalisation, distraction, or sleight of hand. They simply reflect the facts. But they are very simple and easy to complete, and far less bureaucratic than many other reporting systems.[2]

Action plan	Who?	By?
Cure production issues on MR6 (see measure 6)	MFA	21/07/2000
No action required		
Clear obsolete components to spares stock when MR6 released	TFF	10/08/2000
End of year target will be met. No further action required		
Review testing and quality routines for newly specified components and suppliers	SAB	23/05/2000

---

1   An example of an Excel™ based Quadrant Chart is available on the associated web-site (see Appendix 7).

2   This is true if the team are following a systematic approach. If they are not, quadrant charts are a real pig to fill in.

"I've thought about it, but I promised it to Frank tonight. I don't want to let him down. It would look unprofessional. I will leave sending Cyrus his copy until we've got Daniel's data though."

Richard attached the quadrant chart to a brief e-mail, and said: "So, who wants the honour of pressing the send button?"

Lucy simply reached across and clicked the mouse. "Go on. Knock their socks off!" she said.

Summary

Effective deployment of clear goals requires that the management systems and frameworks that support this are designed to reflect their importance, and to ensure that their pursuit remains meaningful to all involved.

In practice this can be achieved by:

- keeping meetings clean and focused, and ensuring that they do not become complex or confused by trying to do too much in them

- ensuring issues are addressed systematically and objectively through a defined and agreed approach to problem-solving

- establishing effective and simple means of communication between groups pursuing interdependent goals

- providing a means of reporting which focuses on the essentials, and ensures they are presented accurately and clearly.

How can you improve your own organisation's pursuit of its goals through the ideas presented in this section?

....

....

....

....

....

....

....

....

....

....

Relevant materials available on the web-site to support discussion and application of the ideas in this section

Presentation materials in MS PowerPoint™ format:

> Problem-solving training materials.

Basic tools in Adobe Acrobat™ format:

> Problem-solving guide

> Problem-solving tools

> Problem-solving exercise.

Workshop exercises in MS PowerPoint™ format:

> Developing the 'roof' of the QFD

> Managing the management meeting.

Basic tools in MS Excel™ format:

> Template for automatic quadrant chart.

Basic tools in MS Word™ format:

> Session plan for management meetings.

Copies of key diagrams in MS PowerPoint™ format.

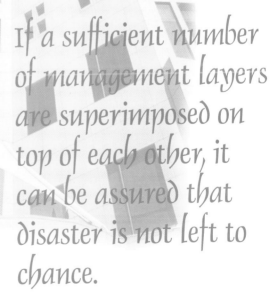

Section F

Coordinating QFD in large organisations

If a sufficient number of management layers are superimposed on top of each other, it can be assured that disaster is not left to chance.

Norman R Augustine

COORDINATING QFD IN LARGE ORGANISATIONS

The preceding chapters have described in general terms how QFD can be established within an organisation.

In this final section of the book we now turn to look at how this can be interpreted for larger and more complex organisations consisting of multiple layers of management.

Colin wiped away some moisture that had strayed away from his watering eyes, as he gazed again at the solid brass ship's-wheel.

"Well one thin's for sure," he said, "if we capsize, the keel is gonna have one 'ell of a struggle t' pull us back upright again!"

The laughter was replaced with applause, as the entire Cylek Gloucester workforce appeared to salute Colin's twenty-three years with them.

Colin turned round to face them, his eyes staring slightly over their heads as he mastered his emotions and thought of something to say.

"Well y'all know me!" he said, "I'm a man of few words." He paused to savour the quizzical looks, and then continued, "but I get a lot of use out of 'em!

"And today's the first day in a quarter cent'ry that any of you'll listen t' any of 'em, I 'spect. I 'ave t'admit I've bin looking forward ta this day for a long time. Twenty-three years workin' with great people, but through difficult times.

"We've 'ad problems, cut-backs an' redundancies over our 'eads for as long as I can remember. An' now, cruellest of fates, jus' when I'm leavin', you get the place lively an' 'ummin' an' fun."

People laughed where they were supposed to. Everybody liked Colin and they were really happy for him.

"I'm really gonna miss you lot, and I'm surprised ta say I'm gonna miss this place too. But keep up the good work, don't let it slip back to how it was. An' I'll welcome y'out for a sail if only ta remind ya what rough waters feel like!"

Pulling it all together

Over the preceding 24 chapters of this book, we have looked at the full range of approaches to implement and fully exploit QFD within an organisation:

- establishing clearly what is to be achieved by the implementation of QFD

- pulling the management group into a team focused on the achievement of common objectives by common means

- deploying responsibility for delivering the objectives to process teams, and soliciting their best ideas and endeavours

- ensuring that process teams use an objective approach to delivering their objectives

- developing an appropriate system of meeting and reporting to ensure progress is made

- adjusting the role of the leader to ensure that people are given space and support to grow in their new responsibilities.

In working through these ideas, we have endeavoured to reflect how generally applicable they are, and to emphasise their suitability to virtually any management situation.

As a result, we hope that, whatever your organisation or management environment, you have developed a coherent and comprehensive picture of how you can apply systematic management approaches to improve the quality of your work and the performance of your business.

However, the model we have been working with has been a simple one, applied to only one or two levels of the organisation. Therefore, we need now to consider how the model needs to be implemented in more complex organisa-

Examples of where QFD can be used effectively:

Complete organisations

Individual departments or sections

Special projects

Programmes or events

Alliances or joint ventures

Partnerships

Individual roles

Specific processes or services

Industries/markets

Pressure groups

Clubs and societies.

Chapter 25

The expected telephone call from Frank Delaney eventually materialised late on Monday afternoon. But it was not the warm pride and congratulations that Richard had been waiting for. Frank was distant, matter-of-fact, and his topic was like a bolt from the blue.

"Richard, we need to talk!" Something in his tone made Richard reply with a cautious "Ye-e-e-s?"

"The old man is doing his pieces over here, Richard, you know how obsessed he is by customer satisfaction. The least you could have done is given me some advance warning. What were you thinking of?"

Richard's mind whirled. What was Frank going on about?

Before he got the chance to ask, Frank continued: "Anyway, he says he wants to see you personally. You're booked on the red-eye, tonight, 9.15 from Heathrow. You'll get into here at 8.40 tomorrow morning, after a six-hour stop over in Chicago. You have only got yourself to blame for this one, Richard. Why didn't you at least ask me? I could have done something! Merged the data with the rest of Europe, or something, while you sorted things out."

"Whoa! Stop!" shouted Richard. "What are you on about? What data?"

"Your customer satisfaction data, Richard." Each syllable had been sounded emphatically and separately, as if impressing a point on a dense child.

"Sorry?" replied Richard. He had never furnished any such data. None existed as yet, Daniel had only just got around to establishing the system to get it.

"Richard, I admire your integrity and openness, but giving the Old Man cold data of this nature - that is just so naïve, so stupid!" The last word was almost spat out.

Light began to dawn on Richard, and he went cold. He could not believe what he was thinking had happened. He had to get off the telephone. "Frank, I will call you right back!" he said, and he severed the connection.

tions where it may need to coordinate performance management efforts over many levels.

Each level of an organisation can benefit from QFD, quadrant charts and systematic management disciplines. But the key question to answer in this chapter is: 'How do the QFDs, quadrant charts and meetings at one level of the organisation integrate with the same at a different level of the organisation?' Because it is only by providing an answer to this question that there can be any confidence in QFD representing a sustainable management tool for a large and complex enterprise.

In this chapter we will therefore explore:

- the hierarchy of organisations
- deploying QFD downwards
- reporting quadrant charts upwards
- using the right meeting at the right level of the organisation
- special cases of conglomerates etc.
- where to start with QFD.

The hierarchy of organisations

Your organisation may be an entire multinational conglomerate, or it may be a small part of one, or it may be an independent concern of any size. Whatever your organisation, QFD will help you to make it sustainably more effective and more efficient. But depending on the size of your operation, and how many organisational levels it has, the implementation of QFD may be very simple, or it may be a hierarchical sequence of QFDs, which operate in harmony to achieve your goals.

Consider for a moment the diagram over the page - it reflects a huge conglomerate of large businesses. However, by selecting only certain levels, it may also repre-

His legs felt like lead as he walked the few paces to Daniel's office. He looked coldly at the man behind the desk and trusted himself with only three terse words.

"Customer satisfaction data?"

Was that the faintest trace of a smirk? Daniel stood behind his desk, glanced at the floor to compose himself, and delivered some lines he had clearly been rehearsing: "Oh, I am surprised you took so long to respond to my memo. I did warn you of the effects of your new system some time ago, and now our chickens have come home to roost."

The picture became instantly clear to Richard. There had never been a memo, at least not to him. Richard moved towards the desk. "Do you have a copy of the memo?" he asked.

Daniel looked a little more tense. "Oh I am sure I can lay my hands on it somewhere," he said, and then, as though he could not resist it, he added: "Why? Have you mislaid your copy? I will have Anna bring you another copy round."

But Richard was thinking further ahead, and before Daniel could stop him, he had stepped round the desk and stood in front of Daniel's computer terminal. "It's okay, I will print another off, don't bother yourself."

Daniel had clearly not expected this breach of protocol, and short of physically ejecting Richard, he was stumped for options.

"Where will it be?" asked Richard.

"Well, I'm sure I don't know? Anna looks after that. I'm sure she will be back shortly."

"No matter," said Richard, and he deftly fired up the 'find' utility. He was frantically hoping Daniel had not already deleted it, but of course that was unlikely because he would need it later. However, he would bet it would not be on the server where such memos should go. He pointed the 'find' programme at Daniel's local hard disk, and put in his own name as the thing to search for. He then set it running and refocused his attention on Daniel.

Though Daniel was keen to pick a fight with anyone verbally, he was not good at physical confrontation. He appeared to flinch, to cower.

sent your organisation. For instance by selecting levels 3, 4 and 8 we can represent a small independent business, or by selecting levels 4, 5 and 8 we can represent a reasonable-sized process within a larger organisation.

Essentially, whatever your organisation, you may be able to reflect it as one, or a number of business units (3), which have a logical (possibly hierarchical) structure of processes (4-7) which coordinate activities (8). These business units may themselves be part of a coordinating structure (1-2) or could be entirely independent.

The principles explained in this book work best in harnessing the activities (8) - through however many levels of process are needed (4-7) to the objectives of the business unit (3).

1. Global corporation
2. Operating division
3. Business unit
4. Function / process
5. Sub-process
6. Sub-sub-process
7. ...
8. Activity

The initial sections of this chapter will explain that in more detail. How this then builds up into the corporate model will be explained in the section on special cases.

Deploying QFD downwards

At any level from the business unit as a whole, down to the smallest process subdivision (3 to 7 on the diagram), there should be sufficient focus in your objectives, and clarity about your operation, to enable you (and your team if you have one) to develop a QFD.

If you are a small and simple organisation, this may be all you need to develop clear objectives for each of your key staff, which they will then pursue enthusiastically.

If, however, your organisation is more complex, and your key staff in turn manage process teams of their own, they would be well advised to develop their own QFD to understand how their sub-processes can be used to best leverage their process objectives. And sub-process

Richard kept Daniel fixed with his silent glare, hoping that it would stop Daniel regaining control of the situation and his computer. It did, not for long, but long enough. Richard looked back at the search screen to find a list of 30 files, which contained his name. He had not expected this, but in hindsight, it was probably obvious.

Daniel flustered: "Hold on, they are my private files! You can't do that!"

Richard glared at him. "Haven't you heard of the Data Protection Act? My name is in each of these files, so I have a right to see them," he bluffed. He hoped Daniel did not know any better. He clearly did not!

Richard opened the most recent file. Bingo! There it was, the missing memo. His name in the 'To' field, but he knew it was only sent to the 'cc' recipients. He glanced down and sure enough, there was 'Dr. Cyrus Lerejecks'.

He smiled at Daniel, and Daniel smiled weakly back. Richard went to print the memo, and then on a hunch he selected all the files with his name on them and sent them all to the printer. Daniel went ashen, and moved to grab the keyboard, protesting: "Hey you can't do that." But Richard had had enough, and pushed him roughly back in his chair.

Daniel's face told him everything. There would be enough here to be rid of Daniel for good, if only Richard could survive tomorrow. He stood over the keyboard long enough for the computer to finish its work, and then grabbed the pile of printouts on his way out. But as he reached the door, another thought struck him, and he turned on his heel and walked back to Daniel's desk. Daniel looked like he was waiting for a tirade of abuse, but Richard just picked up the telephone and dialled the reception desk. It was a risk, he knew, but not as big a risk as leaving Daniel loose in the office, and he was sure he would find enough to justify his actions amidst the papers he was holding in his hands.

"Marilyn, could you send Security up to Mr Matthews' office? Urgently!"

Daniel looked perplexed and quizzical. But Richard just stood there silently until the security man arrived, and as he entered the office he simply said: "Daniel Matthews, I am suspending you forthwith on suspicion of gross misconduct."

Turning to the security guard, he said: "You are a witness to this, please note the time, and escort Mr Matthews from the premises. Remove all

teams may in turn benefit from their own QFD if they are still a sizeable entity.

QFDs may be cascaded down in this way (see the diagram on the right), until there is no further insight to be gained from doing so; until there is no further benefit from reconsidering the means to achieve the deployed objectives in order to better design or focus them. In some organisations it is, however, conceivable that this may bring you right down to specific staff, where individuals may want to develop their own personal QFD in order to better understand the potential in undertaking their role differently.

Where there is such a cascade of QFDs, each level should be reconciled as explained in Chapter 12, and the objectives stated in the (sub-)process QFD should clearly reflect the relationships in the relevant column of the QFD at the next level up.

Reporting quadrant charts upwards

Any individual, or team, with clear and quantified objectives that they are responsible for delivering, should be able to communicate their progress against these succinctly and regularly. This is especially true where their role is defined in terms of a business (sub-)process, with clear performance targets.

The quadrant chart[1] provides simple and clear evidence of how the team (individual) is fairing against their agreed objectives, and how they are dealing with performance issues.

Where a team is responsible for the collective performance of a group of (sub-)processes, for instance in a process or management team, they should expect

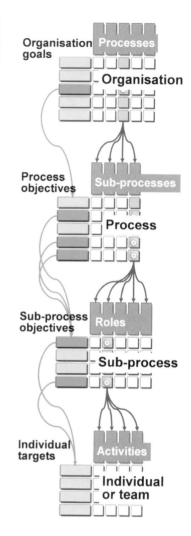

1   See Chapter 24.

security passes, and do not let him out of your sight until he is outside the building."

Without looking at either of their faces, Richard walked out of the office, and turned the corner. And as he did so, the adrenaline that had taken him through the last ten minutes, appeared to flood out of his body, and his knees almost gave way.

He was not sure of the protocol for gross misconduct or suspension, or even if he had used the right words. But he had bought himself some time, and that was what he needed most.

Back in his office, he called for Lucy. He would need her help with Cyrus if he was to survive the next 36 hours. She was in a meeting, but she would be free at 4.30pm. Fifteen minutes. That would give him time to pull what he needed from his printouts of Daniel's files.

Ignoring the offending memo, he flicked through the other sheets of paper, but they were mostly innocuous. Just draft reports and memos that he had previously received. He looked through the pages again, more carefully this time. But no, there was nothing.

He began to fret. What had he done? He was convinced he had Daniel by the look on his face, but now it appeared that Daniel had him. He had been too hasty! He had fired before Daniel was really in range, and now he was dead in the water. Had Daniel won after all?

He slumped, head in hands, on his desk. But wait a minute. Something had riled Daniel, and Richard was convinced it was not an act. He had clearly thought something was there, that was not. Could Richard have dropped it? He did not think so, and a quick check confirmed it. What then? Perhaps something Daniel had deleted, and then forgotten that he had done so.

It seemed unlikely, but Richard was running out of options. He telephoned John Trowell "John, it's Richard. Is there any way to get deleted computer files back?"

John replied that it was possible, if they were still in the recycle bin. "If they are you just select them, and 'Restore' them," he said.

Richard rushed back to Daniel's office. Anna was not yet back, for which he was grateful - he did not have the time, or the stomach, for explana-

to be furnished with quadrant charts for each of their (sub-)processes. In conjunction with their own measures of performance, these quadrant charts should provide the team with enough insight to make appropriate decisions, and to develop their own quadrant chart, which in turn should be reported to the next level up (see the diagram on the right).

Ideally, each level should only receive quadrant charts from the level immediately below, and should trust the people they have appointed as responsible for that (sub-)process to manage and report on their own affairs. In this respect, receiving quadrant charts from two levels below would create confusion over who exactly was managing the situation, and left unresolved could introduce significant over-management.

Using the right meeting at the right level

The logic of the process QFD would imply that all process performance could be traced back to the performance of the sub-processes. As such, the analysis already undertaken and the actions reported in a 'lower level' quadrant chart, can simply be copied into the quadrant chart for the next level up (see the diagram on the right). Performance review meetings[1] would then be an unnecessary overhead.

Unfortunately, because of unforeseen gaps in the logic of the QFD, and because of errors in the information provided, problems in the performance of higher level measures may not be fully described by performance issues that are being addressed in the (sub-)processes. And so meetings are necessary in order to identify these issues, and to ensure they are addressed.

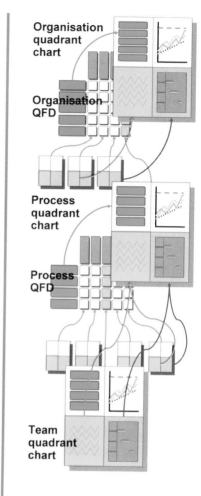

Organisation quadrant chart

Organisation QFD

Process quadrant chart

Process QFD

Team quadrant chart

Only a mediocre person is always at his best.

Laurence J. Peter
University of Southern California

---

1   See Chapter 21.

tions. He opened Daniel's recycle bin on the computer screen. There were literally thousands of files. Momentary panic was replaced by optimism that at least Daniel never seemed to delete anything properly. He selected all the files and 'Restored' them. It was quicker than he feared.

Then he just repeated the search for his name, and held his breath. Yes! Five more files came up. He quickly selected them and printed them, grabbed the printouts, and headed back to his office before Anna returned.

Back in his office he recomposed himself and looked at the first new printout. He could not believe his eyes. It was a transcript of the whole sorry speech that Daniel had given to Laura. Of course! Daniel was meticulous. He would have prepared himself carefully for that visit. He would have been word perfect.

Richard read the script for the first time. He could see Laura's face in his mind's eye as she heard each maliciously contrived lying detail. He could identify in his heart with the rending pain that Daniel must have caused her. And he could not stop the tears coming.

"Richard? Are you okay?" It was Lucy. Richard quickly turned away and mumbled something. When he turned back, he was composed again.

"Sorry about that. Have a seat. I need to discuss something with you."

Lucy was a bit hesitant. She had seen the tears. She had no idea where this was going. But she sat down anyway. Richard slid her the memo on Customer Satisfaction that Daniel had produced. She proceeded to read, and her eyes opened in surprise. She read quicker, seeking to gather in the information as fast as she could, her head jerking slightly as she worked to absorb it all. At the end, she looked up in surprise.

"This is bull!" she said. "Total crap! It is a biased selection; a subset of our customers and responses known to be poor, and then drawn out to represent a valid sample. He cannot write this!"

Without saying anything, Richard slid across the transcript of Daniel's speech to Laura. Lucy took it, and read it dumbfounded. She looked up at Richard, and simply shook her head.

"Daniel delivered that, word for word, to Laura four weeks ago. I am sorry, we should have told you. It caused both of us a lot of pain, but we worked though it, and we agreed not to get you involved."

The role of the meetings is fourfold:

- to understand current performance against forecast for all areas of the team's responsibility
- to understand where shortfalls in performance have already been identified, and are being addressed at a lower level of the organisation
- to define responsibility and set deadlines for addressing shortfalls that are not already being addressed (ideally these will be delegated back down to the relevant level)
- to address any observed issues arising in the quality of the management process, e.g. completion of actions or quality of data and reporting.

The structure and interrelationship of such meetings is reflected in the diagram on the right. The deliverable from each meeting should be a quadrant chart for the next level up.

At the lowest level of the business, these management meetings are likely to be fairly informal affairs. With no lower level quadrant charts to review, the meeting is likely to focus on reviewing the performance measures, and undertaking analysis directly.

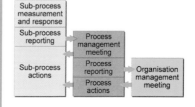

At the business unit level, the meetings may be heavily formalised, and if the quality of management is sufficient, it is likely that practically all issues will be being addressed at lower levels of the organisation. As such, the meeting may be extremely brief.

At the intermediate process level it is likely that the meeting will be a hybrid between the two:

- initially reviewing the overall measures of performance
- then reviewing the quadrant charts from the lower level, where they explain and address shortfalls

"But I was involved," she said. "It's here. I had a right to know!"

"Yes. I am sorry," Richard said simply.

"So why now?" she asked. "Why show it to me now?"

Richard told her the story, as much as he understood it. "And now, I am seeing the Old Man tomorrow, and I need your help." Lucy grunted for him to continue. "Basically I need some corrected data quickly. And I need someone he trusts to deliver it to him."

"Richard! You really don't know what you are asking!" she replied. "The systems aren't fully implemented at the moment, and even when they are, it will take us five days, at least, to get the finished data out of them!"

Richard shook his head. "It is as simple as this, Lucy. If you don't do it, I'm looking for work. We've taken this too far to give up now. And anyway, Daniel got his data without the systems, and I am betting you are better than him."

Lucy shot him a sideways glance, sensed she had been hooked, and smiled. "Can't stay here all day," she said, "I've got data to catch." And with a final: "Good luck with the Boss," she was gone.

Richard sat alone in the large dark marbled ante-room. He had been locked in the same position for the last fifteen minutes, almost lounging in it: his elbows on the square black leather arms; his entwined fingers apparently supporting his nose; his left foot slowly but distinctly tapping to some unheard beat; his dark, smartly-tailored suit jacket rising up over his hunched shoulders; a sullen and slightly bored look on his face.

But if he looked inactive, that belied his mental turmoil. His mind was running, and re-running, all the scenarios for his impending trial. In his briefcase was the sheet of data that Lucy faxed him at the reception desk. He only hoped he would get the chance to use it.

He was surprisingly sanguine about the whole thing. At the end of the next hour, he would either have a job, or he would not. That was what it all boiled down to. He could blame Daniel for his current predicament, but at the end of the day he should have handled the situation with Daniel far more directly, and that was the bottom line. He realised now that it was really only cowardice over the implications that had stopped him.

- then reviewing unexplained shortfalls and seeking to understand them enough to define clear responsibilities and timescales for addressing them.

Special cases of conglomerates etcetera

The pattern of QFDs, meetings and reporting reflected above, applies well to all levels of business unit and below. But it does not add so much value to management entities that reflect groups of businesses.

Does this mean that QFD has little to offer a conglomerate?

Actually, QFD has a tremendous amount to offer conglomerates, and not only in terms of improving the performance of its constituent business units. But to see the real value of QFD to conglomerates we may have to reconsider the role of the 'head office'.

At one level a conglomerate is simply an accounting feature. The performance of the conglomerate is simply the sum of the performance of its individual business units, and as such the head office may be seen as simply an accounting overhead. But that does not fully reflect their potential, and many reading this will probably be able to cite other valid contributions of a conglomerate, including those listed on the right. The QFD for divisions and conglomerates should therefore reflect these contributions, and should provide a focus for the head office to improve and refine their performance and their leverage in these areas. Financial performance has a habit of adding up (or subtracting) naturally, and does not require a QFD to do this.

If this seems a step too far, you might reflect on Chapter 19, and the idea of a personal QFD.

What is the role of the head office?

An overall strategic focus

A brand image.

Influence with investors and business partners.

Coordination of activity.

An effective culture and emphasis.

Efficient systems and practices.

Corporate services and expertise etc.

Cyrus would either disqualify him for that, or he would give him a second chance.

Cyrus's office door opened, and he heard the click of high-heeled shoes on the marble. Cyrus's secretary, immaculate in a red suit, slipped behind her desk and said: "Dr. Lerejecks will see you now. Would you like to go through?" She indicated the open door.

Richard breathed in deeply, launched himself out of his chair, gripped the handle of his briefcase on his way up, and walked towards the office door.

Cyrus sat behind a massive dark-oak desk, which was bare, except for a brass lamp like Richard's own, and three separate documents. Richard recognised all three: his quadrant chart, Daniel's memo, and Lucy's data. Not a bad start point.

Cyrus indicated that Richard should take the chair opposite him. Richard felt Cyrus's gaze steadily on him as he did so.

As soon as Richard was seated, Cyrus asked: "What is going on, Richard?" The voice was calm, matter of fact, without any trace of exasperation. Another good sign?

Richard opted for scenario C.

"I'm sorry Cyrus, I'm afraid that you have been troubled by a personality situation that I have allowed to get out of hand." He looked at Cyrus to see how he was taking this tack. So far so good.

"We have been implementing our plans as agreed with you on your visit to Gloucester, and as you can see we have begun to deliver the expected benefits. Unfortunately, during this time, one of my staff has been consistently fighting a rearguard action, even to the extent of supplying you a set of carefully manipulated data. But I'm in the process of dealing with the matter."

Cyrus stared back silently, and Richard felt a great compulsion to fill the gap. But he had said what he had planned to say. He really needed some input from Cyrus before he decided what tack to take next.

"Stiff British upper lip, eh?" said Cyrus after a while. "So why don't we cut through this bullshit, and you tell me what's really happening?"

A head office that simply adds up numbers is an expensive overhead. A head office that adds value has scope for using QFD to improve the efficiency and effectiveness of how it does so.

QFD has also been used very effectively to design and manage business partnerships. The structure and process has a dramatic impact on clarifying the shared goals, and in evaluating and defining the means of pursuing them.

Where to start with QFD

The place to start using QFD is the place where you currently are. If you are a junior manager in a larger organisation, it makes sense to pilot the ideas in your own area before you attempt to persuade your bosses that they ought to apply it more widely. It is not particularly compelling to have somebody advocate a process that they have not adopted themselves. As the saying goes: 'Never trust a thin Chef'.

If you are very senior in the organisation, and perhaps run a division, or the whole organisation, you would be well advised to apply QFD to the role of your head office before expecting your operating companies to do the same. You will be far better placed to coach, challenge and encourage their applications if you have personal experience of using the tool yourself.

If on the other hand you run an operating company, then you are at the ideal place to rapidly generate major business gains through QFD, and you can begin to involve your top team directly in the ways described in this book.

In working through the QFD model with your immediate reports, they learn how to apply QFD and its associated thinking to their own areas of responsibility, and so the approach can be cascaded down through the organisation.

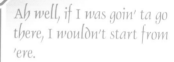

Ah well, if I was goin' ta go there, I wouldn't start from 'ere.

Anonymous country yokel

Richard stared blankly back, his mind racing for what stance to take, but before he could come up with any thoughts, Cyrus continued. "Let me lay my cards on the table, and you take a stab at playing them for me. I've got a well-respected Sales Manager claiming that you are killing the UK business. I've got a well-respected Consultant claiming you aren't. The consultant claims the Sales Manager is lying. The Sales Manager is claiming that you are sleeping with the Consultant. You claim that you're handling it, and the Sales Manager claims that you have illegally dismissed him out of vindictiveness. How do you suggest I play this hand?"

Richard stared doom in the mouth! He had not got a scenario that started like this. Ah well, the only way from here was up! Wasn't it?

"Seems to me that the first choice I would have to make, is about who to believe," said Richard in a flat tone, and simply stared back at Cyrus.

Cyrus smiled with his mouth, but it did not touch his eyes. "I'll do that in my own sweet time. Now, what I want from you is a detailed blow-by-blow account. I've cleared my diary, and I'm all ears. Just start at the beginning!"

Richard winced, and Cyrus saw it. He softened slightly. "Listen son, nobody does everything perfectly. I know this won't reveal you in a blaze of glory. I've got three sheets of paper that prove that. But just tell it as it is, and we'll see what we can do with the pieces."

Richard paused for a moment to compose himself and then launched into the whole sorry story of Daniel. All he left out were his own misplaced feelings for Lucy, he felt they were private to him, Laura and Lucy. Cyrus was a good listener, he remained in rapt attention right up to the end.

After he had finished, Cyrus continued to gaze at him, and Richard felt increasingly uncomfortable, but he did not flinch. He got that increasingly intrusive feeling that Cyrus could see into his soul.

After fully five minutes, Cyrus broke the silence.

"Okay, I believe you!" he said abruptly. "But you've got a huge mess to clear up back there, so you had better get on with it. I'll expect to see it all resolved by next month, and I'll expect to see further progress on these measures as well," he said, tapping the quadrant chart.

One implementation of QFD that takes a bit more thought, however, is the situation where an organisation has a collection of almost identical operating units, for instance regional retail outlets, offices, or manufacturing sites. In this situation, harnessing creativity needs to be tempered with consistency and not having to reinvent the wheel in every location. In these situations it is wise either to:

1. centralise process development, and charge the operating units with the application of those processes, or to

2. facilitate easy communication and adoption of QFDs and process solutions between sites.

Most successful implementations are likely to be a balance between these, where the organisation decides on which processes it needs to maintain tight control (and uses option 1) and where it wants to free off local thinking and ownership (and uses option 2).

In these cases, understanding the role of head office, through doing a QFD there first, can provide tremendous insight and can help create an efficient framework for the operating units.

If, however, you currently run one of those operating units, using QFD can highlight those areas where you can use the flexibility that you do have, to better advantage. And where you don't have that flexibility, QFD can help you to influence those who do.

This book provides all you need to start to profitably explore the hidden potential within your own organisation. If you start to use it for your current responsibilities, whatever they are, it cannot fail to add value to your thinking. So start where you are.

The meeting was clearly at an end, so Richard got up to leave. As he reached the door, Cyrus shouted after him: "And this time get some advice. That's what all this central edifice is here for. I don't pay a Legal Department to sit on their asses all day! Daniel is a tough cookie. You'll need to manage his departure carefully!"

Richard looked back and nodded sheepishly. And then walked out, still the MD of Cylek UK.

Summary

QFD can be implemented wherever you are within an organisation, but it needs to be led by you before you attempt to influence others of the need for it.

In this chapter we have looked at:

■ how you can apply QFD whether you are the MD of an organisation, one small cog within it, or the Chief Executive of a major conglomerate.

We have now explored all of the practical essentials to implementing QFD and using it to transform your management performance.

So what are you going to do next?

....

....

....

....

....

....

....

....

....

....

....

....

....

....

Epilogue

The people filing out through the sliding door were an odd mixture. Some were clearly on their own, they walked purposefully but with a distinct weariness, occasionally increasing their pace to pass slow moving well-laden trolleys. Others, also weary, were pushing those trolleys, and in some cases attempting to control small excited children.

Many of the people walking through the door eagerly scanned the faces of those standing the other side of the barrier, expecting to see a friend or a loved one.

But not so Lucy Derring. Her eyes quickly scanned the yellow signs over-head, located the one proclaiming Taxis, and without the faintest trace of fatigue she purposefully strode through the waiting hordes in the direction the sign had indicated.

Richard watched her sail right past him with amusement. He ducked under the barrier, and after a brief sprint fell into step behind her.

"Taxi, Ma'am," he said in a false gruff voice directly in her left ear.

Lucy looked round startled.

"Richard!" she exclaimed. And without the faintest trace of awkward-ness, she dropped her bag and embraced him in a huge hug. He felt it was perfectly safe to return it. The expression on her face, and her delight at seeing him, made the sacrifice of three hours sleep all worthwhile.

He picked up her case, and she linked his other arm. "So, this is a million miles from my last reception!" she said. "What gives?"

Richard grinned ruefully as he remembered the way he had been so rude to her at the start of her last visit, a little over nine months ago. "Oh I don't know," he said, "I didn't realise how expensive you were then."

She laughed, and said: "Shh! Not so loud! You'll give people the wrong impression."

Book continues normally...

He chuckled back, and then replied: "Seriously though. It really is good to see you again. Everybody has been looking forward to the next two weeks. Me included!"

She smiled at him.

"We've booked you into the Cavendish, but you're dining with Laura and me tonight, if that's okay with you."

"That's fine," said Lucy.

"And if you're a good girl," he said mockingly, "and of course, if you'd like to, Laura and I would like you to come with us this weekend to a mediaeval festival at Berkeley Castle."

She gripped his arm tightly and wheeled him round, her eyes wide with surprise and delight.

"Richard! Really? With knights and jousting?"

"And festive Christmas fayre!" Richard mocked gently. "We even get to stay in the castle overnight, and gorge ourselves on a mediaeval banquet. Sound okay to you?"

"Fantastic!" she said with relish. "Now don't tell me any more, or I won't be able to concentrate for the next five days. By the way, have you got a clear set of objectives for this exercise?"

Richard had asked Lucy over to undertake a Review and Audit of the past year's efforts. He wanted the team to understand clearly where they had approached things well, and also where there was still clear room for improvement. He also wanted to establish this as an annual cycle of learning for his team, so they could continue to improve each year. He outlined these intentions to Lucy as they walked out of the terminal.

When he had finished, she said: "So, tell me what's been happening in Gloucester while I've been away."

"Well, we have now exceeded all our targets, without exception, so in hindsight we were probably too conservative in setting them," he said.

"It didn't seem so at the time!" she interjected.

"No, you're right there," he agreed. He paused, and then said: "And I'll be moving on in the spring."

"Really?" she said, surprised, and just a touch disappointed. She was concerned that this might be one of Cyrus's little interventions. "Where are you going?" she asked.

"I'm not sure yet," he shrugged. Lucy's fear that this was a Cyrus intervention deepened. As she asked her next question, it was with the faintest trace of dread.

"Why? What's brought this about?"

"Well, it's time to hand the baton on to Deborah," he replied. "I've been coaching her for the last three months now, and very soon I'll be getting in her way. She's plenty ready to take the business forward, and we've agreed with Cyrus that she will be appointed MD around April time. In fact, it is her you'll be working with on this review, and not me."

"Wow!" said Lucy. "Good choice! But who will take over R&D? And what about you? What will you do?"

"As for R&D, or rather *'Developing products and processes'*," Richard said with mild reproof, "Jack De Witt has been running it for six months now. Ever since Deborah moved over to replace Daniel. And as for the sales area, I'm proud to report that Deborah has groomed successors as efficiently there as she did with Jack. To all intents and purposes, they are now running the two processes under Deborah with very little intervention from her."

"Yes, I remember Jack," said Lucy thoughtfully. "She did an excellent job with him as far as I can recall. But what about you? You can't just jack in a job without a new one to go to!"

"Oh, I don't know," he replied. "There's been some real changes in me since you've been away. I won't hold anybody back just to ensure I'm all right. And somehow, in my heart of hearts, I know I'm doing the right thing and that it will all turn out.

"Here's the car!" he said, and just in front of them the amber indicators on an S Type Jaguar flashed once as it unlocked itself.

They drove out of the airport in silence. Lucy took the opportunity to reflect on what she had heard. Finally she said: "I can see that all of what you said makes perfect sense. But it seems a little bit too ideal, almost like someone applied the textbook without seasoning it first with a modicum of good old self-protection and common sense. Forgive my bluntness."

Richard laughed. He found her bluntness refreshing. "Don't worry," he said, "others have said the same, but in more round about ways."

"So?" she challenged.

"By April, I will have ceased to add value to Cylek. By then, I won't really be able to do anything practical for it that I haven't taught it to do for itself. The machine is ready to fly the nest and so are its pilots. And I've been instrumental in making it happen. But I've made it happen, and all come together, because I've been focused on that goal. Because I have been single minded in making myself dispensable, I have taught it to be every-thing it can be for itself. And that is such a wonderful feeling. Do you know the song 'The Rose'?" he asked her. Lucy nodded.

"In it, there is a line," Richard continued: "It's the soul afraid of dying that never learns to live! I know for myself that I wouldn't have achieved all that I have achieved, if I was worried about me. My job has been the most fantastic experience over the last six months, and it's been that because I never once worried about keeping it. It seems that the more we want to hold on to something, the more we diminish it."

Lucy looked at him. She could see he was telling the truth. And it was not just his truth. She felt a new admiration for the man.

"So, April!" she asked. "Do you just become a street bum?"

"Oh, I doubt it!" he laughed. "I've already had three job offers, and I've got a story that anybody will listen to. Watch this space!"

"I wonder," posed Lucy, slightly mischievously, "Is it that you are so employable, that makes you so free to make the decisions you have?"

"Or is it that I'm so free to make the decisions I have, that makes me so employable? You decide!"

Lucy settled back into her seat, and peaceably watched the road pass by.

CONCLUSION

'Managing by Design' is a way of thinking. It is the challenge of never being 'under the circumstances'1. It is about developing a perspective that rises above any situation and enables you to make the very best of whatever opportunities there are. Throughout the process of writing this book we earnestly hope that we have contributed to your desire and ability to do that.

- In the introductory chapters, we outlined the challenge that global perspectives, faster communication and ever increasing rates of change represent to management, and how conventional management practice is ill-equipped to deal with these.

- Through Chapters 2 to 6, we looked deeper into the implications of traditional management. We explored its ineffectiveness in ensuring the persistent clarity of objectives needed to harness the full resources of the organisation in transforming performance. We challenged the 'professionalism' of traditional management approaches, and we looked at how a 'design' perspective – and in particular a design tool called QFD – overcomes these weaknesses.

- From Chapter 7 to Chapter 10, we saw how effective use of a design approach can: reconcile and clarify ambitious objectives; configure the resources of the organisation to best meet them; and inspire commitment and creativity in pursuing them. And we looked at the practical example of using QFD to establish a platform and a process for the management team to achieve this in practice.

- In Chapters 11 to 14, we recognised the importance of leadership in creating a supportive and nurturing environment to sustain the new management approach. We looked at how the leader was the critical element in reconciling: individual behaviours with their new responsibilities; local aspirations with the needs of the organisation; and corporate expectations with a new systematic perspective.

- And in Chapters 15 to 20, we addressed the personal implications this has for leaders, and the need for them to anchor themselves within a balanced and healthy perspective, so that they are well placed to take tough decisions regarding their own approach, and those of their colleagues.

- Through Chapter 21 to Chapter 24, we examined how the corollary practices in management, such as meetings, problem-solving, and reporting, could be best adapted to reinforce and make full use of the power of the 'Managing by Design' perspective.

---

1 Statements beginning "Under the circumstances..." are commonly a means for excusing mediocre performance. The alternative mindset is exemplified by a riposte attributed to Napoleon: "Circumstances? I make circumstances!"

- And finally, in Chapter 25, we looked at how the tools could be brought together to provide a complete solution for managing a large and complex enterprise.

The goal of this book has been to do everything that we can to enable you to understand and adopt healthy systematic perspectives to management.

- We have painted a vision through the novel.

- We have explored the reasoning through the textbook.

- We have provided practical steps for you to explore and experience the approaches for yourself through QFD.

- Finally, we have equipped you with a head start through the materials available on the web-site.

All of these things are necessary to assimilating fully the ideas of 'Managing by Design'. Only a fraction of the concept can be absorbed logically; far more is learned by living with the ideas and making them your own. And we hope that now you have completed the book you will go on to do exactly that.

But, before we leave you do so, it is important that we advise you of two real issues that you will face as you continue your journey.

The first is best illustrated by the closing story in Peter Senge's book, The Fifth Discipline, where he tells the story of Rusty Schweickart, an astronaut, looking back down on the Earth from space. From up there your perspective of the Earth and what is important changes dramatically, and it becomes almost impossible to embrace things again as you used to see them.

When managers engage with the ideas in this book, it totally changes their perspectives on responsibility. It opens up a whole new way of seeing things. Unfortunately, the new way of seeing things is so powerful that it ceases to be an option, and takes over your whole way of thinking; a bit like Pandora's box when you aren't able to get the lid back on. Amongst those who have already embraced the ideas in this book, a common phrase is: "I can't imagine how I used to manage, I can't see that what I was doing was really management at all!"

So the first point is: when you really start on the journey there is no valid way back!

The second issue is that the practical tools and methodologies propounded in this book are themselves a system. Are you not just as vulnerable to imprisoning your thought in this system as you were in the systems it replaced? Have you merely traded one set of cell walls for another? The real danger is that you might have done exactly that! It may be more difficult to fall asleep in your new prison, but over time, and with sufficient lethargy, you will find that it is still amazingly possible.

The tools proposed in these pages are a set of stepping-stones, a ladder to realise the idea of 'Managing by Design' practically. But they are not in themselves the idea, and if we are to learn anything from our history, we have to accept that the rungs of this ladder can all to easily become the bars of our cage.

The essence of what we have been pursuing is about taking a 'design' perspective to management; about lifting ourselves above the system and looking back down on it objectively, analytically and systematically. And this perspective is just as important to apply to our new system as it was to the old.

As you implement the tools and ideas we have outlined, you will be unlikely to do so perfectly the first time around. And even if you can, it is likely that they will suffer some corruption over time, or even be superseded by more efficient and effective mechanisms yet to be developed. We must always be mindful that we are ultimately the masters over the systems we create, and not vice versa; and that requires that we need to review even these systems objectively and analytically. We need to lift ourselves even over the systems we have used to lift ourselves.

The most common practical means for doing this is an annual cycle of review and audit. In this cycle the management team:

- reviews/audits the current state of progress and performance of the management system, usually through the means outlined in Chapter 5
- develops a workshop to raise and address any issues identified through the review, and to incorporate any new learning and ideas
- agrees further developments of the approach and sets about implementing them.

For convenience, the review and audit cycle is usually linked in with the planning cycle, and the workshop to reset the QFD for the following year. A more detailed explanation of review and audit can be found in Appendix 10.

Everything in this book has been drawn from the perspective of lifting yourself above the system to look back down and improve it. If over time all else fades this one principle must prove timeless. From this one principle all of the rest of the learning in this book can be recreated. And this is true whether we are talking about your business, your project, your role, or even your life itself.

From this perspective you are not restricted to any shallow horizon, even those of the specific approaches we outline in this book.

From this perspective, you really can fly!

SECTION G

Appendices	Page

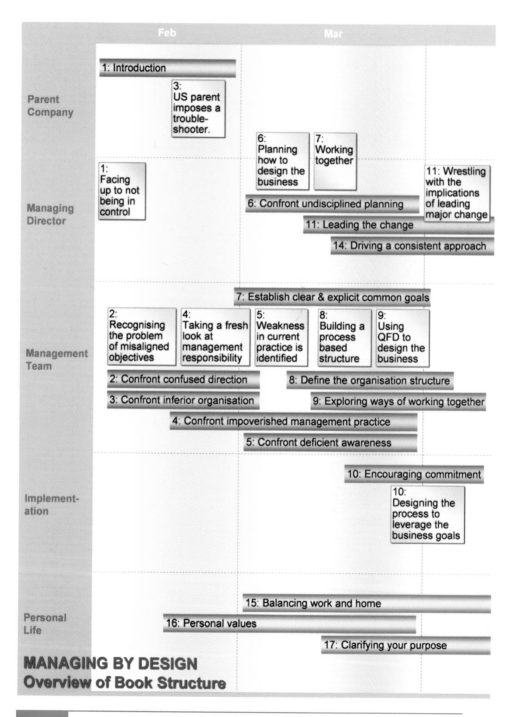

MANAGING BY DESIGN
Overview of Book Structure

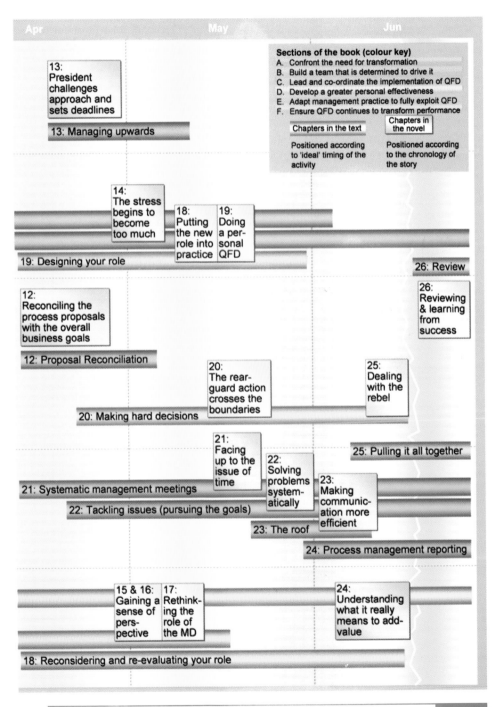

Apr   May   Jun

Sections of the book (colour key)
A. Confront the need for transformation
B. Build a team that is determined to drive it
C. Lead and co-ordinate the implementation of QFD
D. Develop a greater personal effectiveness
E. Adapt management practice to fully exploit QFD
F. Ensure QFD continues to transform performance

Chapters in the text
Chapters in the novel

Positioned according to 'ideal' timing of the activity
Positioned according to the chronology of the story

13: President challenges approach and sets deadlines
13: Managing upwards

14: The stress begins to become too much
18: Putting the new role into practice
19: Doing a personal QFD
19: Designing your role

26: Review
26: Reviewing & learning from success

12: Reconciling the process proposals with the overall business goals
12: Proposal Reconciliation

20: The rear-guard action crosses the boundaries
20: Making hard decisions

25: Dealing with the rebel

21: Facing up to the issue of time
22: Solving problems systematically
23: Making communication more efficient
25: Pulling it all together

21: Systematic management meetings
22: Tackling issues (pursuing the goals)
23: The roof
24: Process management reporting

15 & 16: Gaining a sense of perspective
17: Rethinking the role of the MD
24: Understanding what it really means to add-value

18: Reconsidering and re-evaluating your role

APPENDIX 2: BACKGROUND TO CYLEK UK
(EXTRACTED FROM 'A BRIEF HISTORY OF CYLEK UK'
WITH PERMISSION)

Cylek UK is a fictional company of around 800 people, situated near the entrance to the Westgate Industrial Estate to the north-west of the City of Gloucester in the West of England.

What now constitutes the UK arm of Cylek Corporation, originated as Balmore Brothers in 1952 to provide automatic switchgear to telephone exchanges. Business boomed during the mid-1950s, necessitating its relocation from the restored barn it operated from in Bishop's Cleeve to its current site on the outskirts of Gloucester City Centre.

Sadly the investment in the business move coincided with a change of government and a downturn in the telephony market, and Balmore's were acquired by BAEC to support major opportunities in Northern Europe, where BAEC already had a very strong marketing presence.

In the late 1980s a foresighted management team, recognising the potential of the newly burgeoning computer industry, persuaded the BAEC board to allow them to acquire the old Balmore business. Somewhat strapped for cash, BAEC agreed to the leveraged management buy-out, and Gloucester Computer Telecommunications (GCT) was formed as a result.

Having identified a niche market in linking computer installations through existing telephone infrastructures, business grew rapidly, and within two years the turnover of the business had doubled and profits had risen to an all-time high. At this point, GCT came to the attention of Cyrus Lerejeks; a well known North American entrepreneur in this field, who acquired GCT as a means for Cylek to expand into the European market.

During the 1990s, the organisation grew from 200 people to 800 as it took on more of Cylek's computer communications business in a rapidly increasing market.

Today, Cylek UK specialises in sophisticated high-quality modems for commercial and industrial markets throughout Europe. Roughly half of its staff works in a five-shift continental pattern on the highly automated flow-line manufacturing facility which occupies over 75% of the site. Multi-layer printed circuit boards are populated by computerised pick and place machines with surface-mount components. The boards are then wave soldered (for the non-surface-mount components) and assembled into rack mounted systems prior to being electrically soaked, surge-tested and inspected on sophisticated simulation equipment.

Cylek Organisation Chart (Pre-QFD)

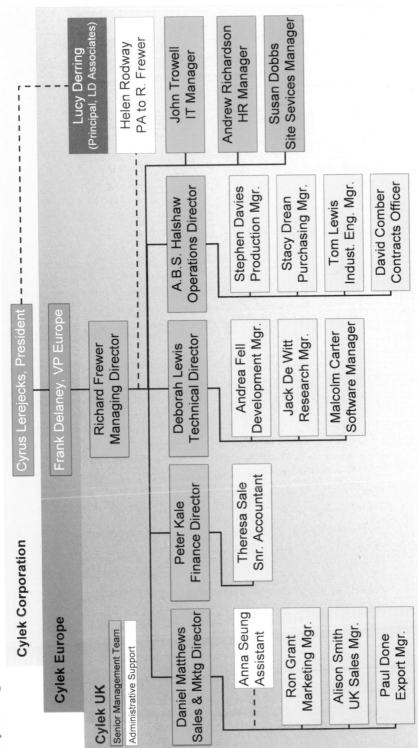

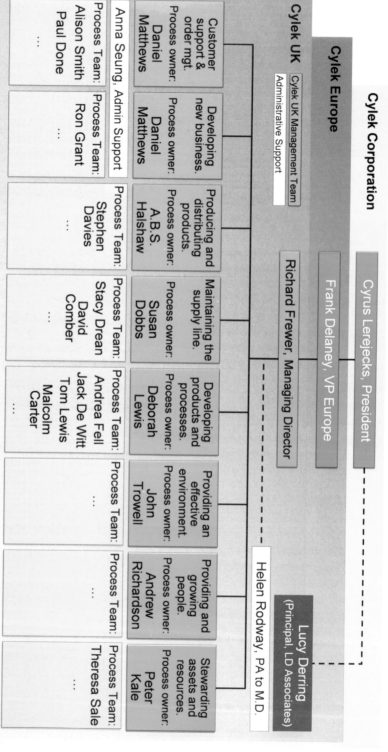

Cylek Organisation Chart (Post-QFD)

Cyrus Lerejecks, President

Frank Delaney, VP Europe

Richard Frewer, Managing Director

Lucy Derring
(Principal, LD Associates)

Helen Rodway, PA to M.D.

Cylek Corporation

Cylek Europe

Cylek UK

Cylek UK Management Team
Administrative Support

Anna Seung, Admin Support

Customer support & order mgt.	Developing new business.	Producing and distributing products.	Maintaining the supply line.	Developing products and processes.	Providing an effective environment.	Providing and growing people.	Stewarding assets and resources.
Process owner:	Process owner:	Process owner:	Process owner:	Process owner:	Process owner:	Process owner:	Process owner:
Daniel Matthews	Daniel Matthews	A.B.S. Halshaw	Susan Dobbs	Deborah Lewis	John Trowell	Andrew Richardson	Peter Kale
Process Team:	Process Team:	Process Team:	Process Team:	Process Team:	Process Team:	Process Team:	Process Team:
Alison Smith Paul Done ...	Ron Grant ...	Stephen Davies ...	Stacy Drean David Comber ...	Andrea Fell Jack De Witt Tom Lewis Malcolm Carter ...	...	...	Theresa Sale ...

APPENDIX 3: REAL EXAMPLES OF QFD APPLICATIONS

Cylek provides a useful device for helping people to understand QFD and systematic management at a very practical level. In many ways, it is an amalgamation and distillation of experience from a number of real business situations but, being fictitious, it offers the opportunity to be open and detailed in ways that would otherwise not be possible.

However, much of the feedback received in the early stages of writing this book suggested that there was still a need to provide a number of real examples; of real companies in real situations. That is the purpose of this appendix.

On the following pages you will find seven cameos drawn from different industries; addressing a range of different opportunities in a number of different ways. The examples provide insight into how QFD can be easily adapted to suit practically any situation, and present a 'warts-and-all' picture of these organisations' efforts to transform the management of their organisations. For this reason, the examples presented are anonymous, and where photographs of real data have been used to illustrate the tools, the precise detail of the text is intentionally illegible.

The table on the next page provides an overview of the seven cameos. The blue text in each column indicates where the information is further amplified in the main text of the cameo, which can be found at the page indicated in the second row of the table.

Situation			
Title	Driving performance	Harnessing innovation	Aligning business focus
Company	A (Page 434)	B (Page 439)	C (Page 445)
Business	Manufacturing	Research & development	Service management
Industry	Process Equipment	High Tech. Healthcare	Engineering
Context	Business Unit	Company	Operating Division
Size	<100	100-400	400-1000
History	Long established	Recently reorganised	New reporting structure
Key theme	Addressing major delivery issues	Challenging and inspiring highly intelligent sceptics	Pulling together entrepreneurial businesses
Approach			
Exploring the context and defining the objectives	Initially through adoption of higher level objectives. Subsequently through collating the implications of customer feedback through affinity diagram.	Objectives were developed through a full why-how chart analysis	Through 'SWOT' analysis of business position. Strengths & opportunities refined, prioritised, and built into objectives through affinity diagram.
Identifying measures	Syndicate work	Syndicate work arising from competition question exercise	Syndicate work, further refined off-line by separate teams
Setting targets	Discussion	Imposition of a 50% improvement mandate	Clothesline method
Determining the operating structure	Adaptation & clarification of the existing structure, through detail mapping	Development and optimisation of a logical process model, which overlaid existing structure	Identified interdependent processes running through independent Business Units
Deploying responsibility	Initial QFD workshop followed by cascade workshop involving the whole organisation	Quality function deployment. Responsibility deployed to part-time teams	Objectives linked to common processes through sticky-note based QFD
Mapping out communication	QFD roof developed by discussion in plenary	QFD roof developed by discussion in plenary	Common processes work closely together
Reconciling proposals	Process measures and targets agreed by discussion	Matrix 'B' to reconcile process & organisation objectives	Proposal flipcharts evaluated by means of reverse clothesline
Planning implementation	Clear implementation plan regularly reviewed. Cultural spectrum was used to plan culture	Clear implementation process mapped out. Cultural review of management values	Developed on a case by case basis with internal consulting team. Sticky-note plans developed.
Managing progress	Intensive use of quadrant charts, and prominent display of progress. Systematic management meetings and annual review workshops.	Balanced scorecard Systematic meetings Review and Audit workshop to set new targets identify key learning points	Progress monitored through modified version of 'balanced scorecard'. Progress reviewed through schedule of systematic meetings
Ensuring systematic improvement	Processes mapped and managed using systematic management approach	Processes mapped and managed using systematic management approach	Common processes mapped and developed by inter-business-unit teams.
Miscellaneous	Management team were fundamentally involved in the QFD workshop design	Approach developed by client staff by considering how scientific disciplines apply to management.	

Building full commitment	Making alliances work	Managing project mgt.	Leveraging partnerships
D (Page 450)	E (Page 455)	F (Page 461)	G (Page 466)
Supply Chain	IT	Projects	Sales & Marketing
Electronics	Retail	Healthcare	Computers & Telecomms
Business Unit	Project	Process	Function
400-1000	100-400	<100	100-400
In transition	New project	Newly established	Continuously developing
Ensuring radical change delivers results	Defining and managing joint venture performance	Improving the processes of project management	Getting the best from alliances & partnerships
Drawn from strategy document and further refined by single column QFD.	Objectives set through interviews with key players in both parent organisations.	Structured customer interviews using prede-fined feature cards and a positioning grid. Proposed objectives refined by consensus.	Interviews with key players; competitive analysis; corporate mar-keting strategy; sales targets. Joint objective reconciliation grid.
Syndicate work informed through detailed explo-ration of objectives	Syndicate work based on competition question	Syndicate work based on competition question	Syndicate work based on competition question
Clothesline method	Clothesline method	Clothesline method	Shared goals through clothesline method
Industry-standard process model refined by boundary discussions	Process model adopted from QFD work of parent organisation (for reasons of efficiency)	Process model adopted from generic model for project management and subsequently refined	Partnership processes identified between the organisations, and refined using sticky-notes
QFD; Rich pictures; Cascade QFD workshop led by process man-agers	QFD by combined team. Process responsibility deployed to mixed teams	QFD; preceded by sticky note modelling of key issues between objec-tives and processes	QFD; Preceded by sticky-note QFD, developed from process sticky-notes
QFD roof discussions between process teams	QFD roof discussions between process owners	QFD roof discussions between process owners	
Syndicates reviewing process proposals against each objective	Process proposals evalu-ated against criteria and prioritised	Syndicates reviewed process proposals against each objective	
Clear implementation process based on cultur-al spectrum	Implementation plan developed in syndicate using draft examples of plan activities.	Implementation reviewed by survey. Progress driven by clear targets on the cultural spectrum.	Linked to existing systems in both partner organisations
Progress managed through quadrant charts and systematic meet-ings. Local displays of workshop conclusions regularly updated	Progress managed through highly structured systematic meetings and quadrant charts	Progress managed through quadrant charts and systematic meetings. Spring clean workshop to make necessary adjust-ments to the QFD	Regular review meetings between the partner organisations to drive progress and address any performance issues
Processes mapped and managed using system-atic management approach	Systematic approach to improvement agreed by consensus using 6P model	Processes mapped and managed using systemat-ic management approach	
Emphasis placed on individual responsibility for managing systemati-cally	Implementation support-ed by internal consultants trained in QFD and sys-tematic management		Workshop design adjust-ed to meet the specific needs and maturity of each partnership

Driving Business Performance

Profile

Organisation 'A' is a manufacturer of process control equipment based in mainland Europe. Part of a major multinational; their role is to assemble the finished product prior to its installation at customer sites for all projects undertaken in EMEA (Europe, Middle East and Africa).

Issues

In the process industry deadlines are vitally important. Process plant often runs twenty four hours a day, seven days a week for fifty weeks of the year. In the other two weeks all major installation and maintenance work takes place. It is tightly scheduled to ensure that the process restarts on time; any delays are cripplingly expensive and penalty clauses are correspondingly high. It was therefore of major concern that the delivery performance of this particular organisation was less than 40%. Additionally, the finished goods and work-in-progress inventories which the organisation used to buffer their performance issues were coming under increasing scrutiny from a corporate initiative to reduce stock levels.

Objective

The organisation saw QFD as a means to systematically address the problem of performance while meeting the inventory expectations placed upon them. They believed that the structure of QFD would help them to identify and rethink their critical processes, and also support their arguments on how certain corporate behaviours exacerbated the situation.

Approach

Despite being a particularly lean and flat organisation, the management team took a very comprehensive approach to implementing systematic approaches to management.

Initially they adopted a very prescriptive, low-investment approach by using the framework and thinking of a sister company, which had been using QFD for some time. The result had a number of limitations in terms of insight and ownership, but it was sufficiently powerful to build the commitment of the management team to investing their time in a more fundamental approach.

In the second cycle (a few months later) the management team took a very direct role in the planning and implementation of the approach, to the extent of becoming fundamentally involved in the design and running of the workshops. The MD, a particularly foresighted and people-oriented individual, saw the 'process' of implementing a new management approach as an excellent development experience for his management team.

The organisation drew their objectives from their own experience of running the business, and from the wealth of corporate and customer feedback that they were already experiencing as a result of their delivery and inventory performance. The same feedback also gave them clear guidance on relevant measures and targets for the coming year.

The process model was drawn largely from their existing organisational structure. A subgroup of the management team developed a logical process diagram for the organisation based largely on the existing organisational structure. From this model, minor adjustments to the scope of each process were made by listing out the key activities and responsibilities on sticky-notes, sticking them on a wall under the title of their existing process group, and then moving them between processes to reflect appropriate changes. In this way, much of the existing structural and reporting arrangements were preserved, but the management team had ownership of the conclusion.

The relationships on the QFD were worked through using voting cards and consensus reaching. Through this process the team identified the need to take firmer local control for two processes which until then had been left with head-office to undertake on their behalf. The QFD is shown on the right. Ownership for each of the processes and for the various top-level measures was clearly identified on the QFD grid (see the darker blue areas at the top and to the right of the diagram)

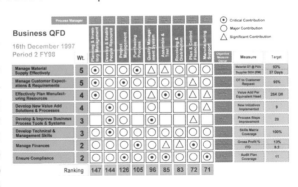

The management team decided that the cascade of the QFD into the objectives of the different processes should involve the whole organisation. They also decided that the cascade should reflect their commitment, as a management team, to this approach. Accordingly they set about designing and facilitating these workshops themselves. Their commitment in this regard should not be underestimated. The cascade was two off-site events of two days each. The management team shared the responsibility for these between them, and invested an average of six days each in: designing the overall structure; developing the relevant materials; rehearsing their presentations; and facilitating the event. Though they received external help, this was focused on ensuring that their planning time was spent productively and not on doing the planning and materials for them. However, this investment had a dramatic impact on the thinking and attitudes of the entire organisation, and was a key factor in their ultimate success. The diagram on the right shows the QFD they developed to design the cascade events.

The first cascade event involved the organisation in understanding the conclusions that had been reached up to this point: the overall objectives; the process structure; the grid of the QFD etcetera, and then in getting them to work out, in their process groups, how they could contribute to taking this forward. In outline, the event was structured as follows:

- Introduction of the background, which included: the issues the organisation is facing, its objectives in moving forward; and how the workshop fitted into that

- Overview of how the QFD and quadrant charts work in general, and what the various parts of the organisation's QFD and quadrant chart mean specifically

- In-process work to: establish the relationships and the dependencies between each process; map out each process and how it fulfils its responsibilities; identify priority areas for improvement; and establish clear performance objectives for each process.

The workshop was organised in a cabaret style with each process team organised around its own separate table but within sight and sound of all other process team tables. This enabled them to work on their own conclusions whilst taking inputs and liaising with other processes. To guide the activity a number of proforma sheets were used, an example of which is shown on the right.

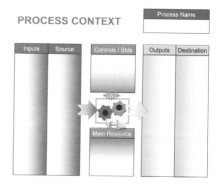

Following the workshop, the process teams worked to refine their conclusions, implement their operational measures, and identify performance targets which would fulfil their responsibilities to their customer processes and to the organisation as a whole.

The second event was held five weeks after the first, and was an opportunity for the process teams to share the conclusions they had developed between-times, and evaluate them collectively against the expectations set by the objectives and targets for the organisation as a whole. Once each process's conclusions had been approved, the workshop focused on the management and cultural implications of the changes. Through this, common routines for reporting and problem-solving were agreed, and a common plan developed for implementing the conclusions within the process management structure.

The implementation plan was essentially a step-by-step guide to establish a systematic approach to management within each process, and covered such things as communication, measurement, meeting structures, reporting, problem-solving etcetera. Progress against the plan was monitored methodically, see diagram on the right, and used to identify and address any issues in the implementation.

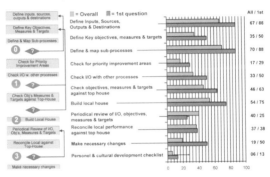

The pivotal tool for driving progress on performance, however, was the quadrant chart, a single-page reporting device which uses the objective clarity and ownership generated by the QFD as the fulcrum for ensuring any and all performance issues are systematically identified and addressed. The management team set in place a powerful discipline for using these single-page reports to focus attention on progress deficiencies, and ensure that appropriate improvement actions were rapidly set in place. The picture on the right shows one wall of the Managing Director's office, with the display boards of the QFD and the process quadrant charts.

All management reports were submitted in the form of a quadrant chart, and the analysis of these formed the main part of the monthly management meeting. During the meeting, all reported performance deficiencies were expected to have an associated root-cause analysis and corrective action plan. The quality of these varied considerably in the early months but the continuing emphasis on such systematic discipline, and the resulting questions and discussions, served to develop a culture in which all performance deficiencies were seen as important and their resolution systemic.

As a result of such discipline they were able to radically improve their delivery performance to better than 95%, at the same time as reducing their inventory to benchmark levels. The graph on the right is an actual excerpt of one of the organisation's quadrant charts. It is a graph of inventory turn-over performance (the inverse of inventory) and shows clearly the target increase driven by the corporate initiative (blue line) and the dramatic response achieved (pale-blue bars), virtually halving the cost of inventory.

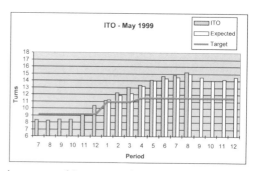

The impact on performance was such that the organisation went from being the corporate pariah to being the benchmark organisation for inventory and delivery performance. But the management team recognised that, while their results had been all that they had wished for, the manner in which it had been achieved still left some room for improvement. Much of the improvement had been created due to the sheer focus on the issues brought about by the clarity of QFD and the methodical discipline of the quadrant charts. But the organisation still felt it had some way to go in terms of refining performance by systematically redesigning the processes to meet the creative opportunities presented in the QFD.

In order to progress this issue, prior to setting even more challenging targets for the following year they undertook a 'Review and Audit': an internal and external survey of their approach against the six key aspects of systematic management. As a result of this they were able to maintain their performance despite a series of technical design problems (originating in a separate organisation) and a major shift in their product range.

Harnessing Innovation

Profile

Organisation 'B' is the corporate research and development facility of a Healthcare company focusing on high-technology products. It employs 200 people in the development of new technology and novel product concepts for a number of different markets. Their focus is on radical longer-term technical solutions, which they develop in close cooperation with the operating divisions, who then have responsibility for developing the final product and for marketing and manufacturing it profitably.

Issues

The development of radical new technologies is inherently risky. Success can bring a massive payback of many times the original investment, but many of the programmes never reach this point – technical and commercial uncertainties undermine their practicality well before they are launched as products. In addition, programmes can be several years long and each piece of work is unique in many different ways. Because of these factors, the management of performance is a particularly difficult issue (and often a source of contention) and as a consequence it is difficult to address the many sources of inefficiency that are often inherent in such operations.

Objective

While each research programme is unique, there are a number of metaprocesses (processes which determine how the work may be best undertaken) that are reasonably consistent and can be developed to reflect best practice (see diagram on the right). Unfortunately in many scientific communities the focus of interest is almost entirely on the technical challenges – the currency of conversation tends to be discoveries and achievements with little mind being paid to the efficiency of the approach.

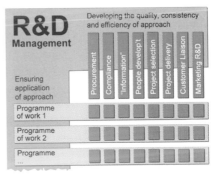

Organisation 'B' wanted to use QFD to explore exactly how these metaprocesses could leverage their performance of their objectives, and then to gain better control of the organisation through them. Contrary to the fear that process-emphasis can limit creativity, they felt QFD could enable them to develop the metaprocesses to stimulate an increase in creativity and innovation as part of a drive to improve performance and efficiency.

Coincidentally, at about the same time the parent organisation had grown concerned about value for money, and there was increasing pressure for 'B' to justify its performance in this regard.

Approach

A number of the management team were particularly confident in their own thinking and approach, and were deeply mistrustful, and even cynical, of management theories and business consultancy in general. However, it was vital that these people were won over if the conclusions were to be successfully cascaded down into the organisation.

Accordingly, their own scientific disciplines and expertise was used to draw out an approach to managing the business that they could feel comfortable with. In the event, the conclusion was little different from the originally intended approach, but the management team could now understand and appreciate it on their own terms.

The objectives of the research organisation had grown unclear as the parent organisation had grown and developed around it, and as a result there were almost as many different perspectives on the role of the organisation, and the relative priorities of any objectives therein, as there were members of the management team. To address this, the management team wrote out what they individually saw as the objectives, grouped them together where appropriate, and then used them to develop a Why-How chart. The resulting discussions did much to clarify a number of misconceptions, and to reconcile the different perspectives into one common, and commonly understood, set of objectives (shown by the blue band in the Why-How chart diagram on the right).

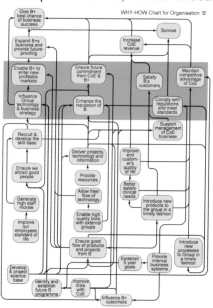

Measures were developed for the objectives using the output from the 'competition question'. This proved quite contentious in practice; scientific communities often pride themselves on the clarity and unambiguous nature of their conclusions, and they are very sensitive to ensuring they are able to defend their conclusions from criticism (which is traditionally a key form of quality control in scientific institutions). However, the nature of most practical business measurement is that it is at best a good indicator of future outcomes; the more one attempts to make it universally incontrovertible, the more impractical, burdensome and bureaucratic it becomes. In the end practicality won out, but only after several weeks of frustration and wasted energy.

To avoid target-setting inducing the same degree of academic debate as the measures had, which it was clearly threatening to do, the Managing Director cut across the discussions with a mandate of a 50% improvement target on all measures. While this would NOT normally be a recommended strategy, it was exactly the right thing to do at this time and in this particular situation, and after an initial backlash, far more energy was channelled into making progress far quicker than if the targets had been left open to debate.

The approach taken to identifying the processes was indicative of, and sympathetic to, the culture of the organisation. All of the main activities within the organisation were written on separate sticky-notes and three sets of the notes were developed, one complete set for each syndicate group who would work on the process model. The syndicate groups were then asked to use the sticky-notes to group activities into sets of 'processes' which they felt reflected a productive and insightful way of viewing and managing the business. The syndicate groups put the sticky-notes together in different ways to create what they saw as sensible affinities and relationships between the activities.

Each of the three models was presented, and the whole group reviewed each model in terms of the strengths and weaknesses of its potential for managing performance. These were listed as two columns on a flipchart beside each model. The group then decided, on the basis of this, which model would provide the best start point for incorporating the good ideas round the room (not necessarily the best model in its own right). Once this had been agreed, the group worked through the flipcharted weaknesses of the model to refine it with the perceived strengths of the other models. The end result was a process model which had clear potential to help the group manage organisational performance, and which was owned by the whole management team.

The grid of the QFD was developed in a conventional manner, using definitions of 'critical', 'major', 'significant'

Organisation B

Legend:
⊙ Critical Contribution
◎ Major Contribution
△ Significant

	Wt.	Procurement of materials & services	Gaining and maint-aining compliance	"Information"	People development	Project selection	Project delivery	Developing the B+ customer interface	Projecting B externally	Representing Group internals w externals	Est. & maint. Group policy/stds/strategy	Provide professional services
Influence Group tech./bus.strategy	4			○	○	⊙	○	○	⊙	△	○	○
Enable B+ to enter new profitable markets	4	△	○	○	○	⊙	⊙	⊙	△	○	△	○
Satisfy B's customers (CoE)	5	△	△	○	○	⊙	◎	⊙	△	○	△	⊙
Maintain competitive advantage of CoE	5	△	△	⊙	⊙	◎	⊙	○	○	○	△	⊙
Enhance reputation of B externally	3	△	△	○	⊙	○	○	△	⊙	△		△
Ensure future commitment from CoE/B+	3		△	○	○	⊙	⊙	⊙	△	△	△	⊙
Comply w. regulations & meet standards	1	○	⊙	○	○	△	○	△	△		△	△
Est. best practice stds. for B+ Group	4									△	⊙	○

and 'not-significant' for the contribution each process made to the delivery of each objective (marked respectively with a bulls-eye, a circle, a triangle and a blank). Sadly, these definitions proved too ambiguous, and while they succeeded in generating good debate they were insufficiently rigorously defined to get good differentiation in the scoring. This became obvious when they came to discuss the impact of 'Project Delivery' on 'Satisfying Customers' when they had already defined other far less important relationships as 'critical'. Going back to reconsider the earlier relationships was not an option; they had already spent three hours on the grid and the psychological impact of starting-over would have wrecked the whole thing. Instead, the team were allowed to 'play-their-joker' (an idea drawn from a TV game show called 'Jeux Sans Frontiers') and double the points of that specific relationship (and as it transpired one other relationship later in the grid). The end result was a working QFD diagram, continued productive discussions, and a surprisingly happy management team; perhaps because they felt more in control of the process that was being applied to them.

Process teams were appointed to take responsibility of managing the processes. Their first task was to develop objectives and performance targets for their processes that reflected the needs of the QFD and the potential of their process to address it (as defined by the grid relationships and the associated discussions). They were then to relate these back to the QFD objectives using what they called a 'Matrix B' and to agree their conclusions with the management team.

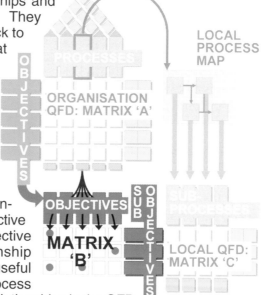

'Matrix B' was a QFD type grid which listed the organisation's objectives along the top, and the process objectives down the right-hand side, and mapped out the contribution of each process objective to each organisational objective using the QFD relationship symbols. This proved a useful device in getting each process team to reflect back on their relationships in the QFD and to ensure that they had developed objectives to fulfil those relationships.

Each process then went on to develop its own process QFD, which they called 'Matrix C', and from there to identify how the process needed to

be developed in order to ensure that the top-level performance objectives were met. Progress and performance were managed on a regular basis in the monthly management meeting. The overall structure of the implementation process is shown on the left.

Despite the challenging nature of the top-level performance targets, at the end of the year they were at least 80% met in 80% of the objectives. However, cultural differences between the management approach and the scientific perspective continued to dog progress, and as part of the proposed annual review it was agreed to address this issue directly.

The Review and Audit was scheduled for a point some eighteen months after the work had started, and consisted of customer and employee surveys, both by questionnaire and by interview. The results were fed-back to a sub-group of the management team and clearly illustrated two main interrelated problems. The first was that there was within the organisation a core of talented but deeply cynical people who consistently undermined and disrupted the process. Termed the 'dirty dozen', their common features were a degree of arrogance about their own abilities and insights, and an evasion of any system which might 'call them to account'. The second, and closely related, issue was that it was clear that management had not created a clear understanding of their own values within the organisation, and as a result the 'dirty dozen' were getting much more air-time with a far clearer agenda.

The Review and Audit Workshop was structured to spend one day on re-setting the objectives for the following year, and one day on addressing the two cultural issues. The issue of management values was tackled by sticking up flipcharts around the room; on each flipchart was a summary from the interviews of what each manager's subordinates felt their manager valued in their behaviour and approach. None of the flipcharts was titled, and each reflected a mixture of different things, very little of which was to do with systematically driving up performance through the processes and the QFD. To lighten up the event managers were awarded one point for each of their sixteen colleagues' flipcharts that they could identify, and ten points for their own, with a prize for the winner. Every manager identified their own and well over half of their colleagues. The workshop then moved onto what they wanted to appear on their flipcharts, and what they needed to do to have that happen; tackling 'dirty dozen' behaviours was an integral part of working that through.

The tool used to think through the management values and behaviours was the force-field analysis, shown in the diagram below. With this tool the managers first of all explored the drivers of behaviour in the organisation, and then reflected how they needed to bias the positive forces to change the equilibrium that existed.

After the workshop, the culture began to change, and gradually the 'dirty dozen' began either to change with it, or to leave the organisation altogether.

The success of QFD in improving R&D performance has since begun to lead to its adoption in the operating divisions, and also in parts of head office.

MANAGEMENT BEHAVIOURS THAT DRIVE OUR CULTURE

Hmm... well shall I behave in the way they want?

For(+)   (-) Against

Aligning Business Focus

Profile

Organisation 'C' has emerged from efforts to centralise all of the non-core activities (such as accounting, facilities, purchasing, IT, intellectual property, pensions, tax, legal etc.) within a large and diverse multinational engineering company. The organisation acts as a contractor to supply and manage all of these services, thereby freeing the operating divisions to concentrate on their core business, and also introducing economies of scale to keep the cost of the service to a minimum. Initially the organisation focused on providing a purely internal service, but more recently it has been contracting-out its services to other third-party companies outside of the group.

Issues

Until recently, organisation 'C' has been a collection of individual businesses working independently to sell their services within the parent organisation, and outside. Many of the heads of these individual business units were appointed for their entrepreneurial flair as well as their technical expertise.

With the drive to solicit more work externally, and to secure a greater percentage of the business within the parent group, it has become clear that there is now a greater need for the separate service businesses to work together. Where the market seeks to buy two or more services from the portfolio it expects a consistency between the offerings and approaches provided by the organisation, and in a competitive market there is also a need to ensure that a lead for one service is also recognised as an opportunity for others. Also, some organisations outsource their services en-masse and there is clearly a need to coordinate a coherent, even seamless, response to such opportunities.

Objective

Clearly QFD provides an excellent means to pull the organisation behind a coherent set of objectives. However, the organisation is culturally still very much a collection of independent (and sometimes fiercely independent) businesses and it was necessary to develop an approach that provided many of the insights and opportunities of QFD but avoided its intense dependency on consensus.

The goal therefore was to gain agreement on a common vision and to develop/define some basic common processes to support its achievement. At the same time it must allow the commitment of the business unit heads to evolve at their own pace.

Approach

Last year, organisation 'C' appointed a new Managing Director who is particularly skilled in QFD, and in systematic and facilitative approaches to management. In preparation for the work on QFD he established a small core team to develop four Common Processes to support each of the service businesses: business development; finance; HR and IT (shown in the diagram on the right). These provide a practical means by which approaches can be harmonised in a supportive and non-intrusive manner.

On the basis of a number of interviews with the heads of the various service businesses, and also with the owners of the Common Processes, two two-day workshops were developed. In the first workshop, the service business heads worked together to develop a common vision for the organisation, to translate that into clear measures and targets, and to understand the implications for the Common Processes. In the second workshop the service business heads reconciled their own performance targets to the overall vision and objectives.

Many of the business heads believed that the business was so diverse that a common vision was likely to be either impossible or expressed in trivial platitudes. However, by starting with a collective SWOT analysis of the business, they were able to identify a number of clear common goals for the organisation to be successful, and were able to translate these into agreed measures and targets for the business as a whole. The approach was as follows.

- The workshop was divided up into three syndicates; addressing services to 3rd party, headquarters, and the operating divisions respectively. Each syndicate developed sticky-notes (each group used a different colour) looking at the strengths, weaknesses, opportunities and threats facing the business in their area of concern, and stuck these in each of the four SWOT quadrants on a large grid.

- Following feedback from each syndicate, the group as a whole explored which strengths should be developed, or which opportunities should be pursued to address the key areas of weaknesses and threats. New sticky-notes were added to the SWOT grid as required.

(The SWOT diagram at this point is shown on the right).

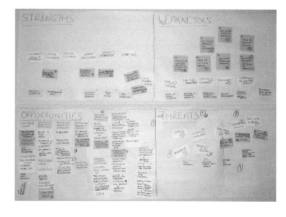

- The group then took the sticky-notes that were included under 'strengths' and 'opportunities' and grouped them using an affinity diagram. The groups were prioritised using sticky dots, and the most important ones were fashioned into appropriate elements of a vision by separate syndicate groups.

- The elements of the vision were then further refined by developing appropriate measures (using the 'competition question') and performance targets (using the clothesline)

By means of this stepwise approach, the organisation developed an agreed vision that for the first time brought the disparate service businesses under a set of common and shared objectives. The importance of this achievement should not be underestimated, since it was pivotal to the service business heads' engagement with the rest of the process.

Having agreed the objectives, the group moved on to develop a sticky-note QFD. It was felt that even with a rudimentary common vision, there was not sufficient buy-in to a 'collective model' to sustain the engagement and commitment necessary to develop a normal QFD grid. The sticky-note QFD however, enabled the group to see the potential of the four Common Processes to supporting them in their delivery of the objectives, and it did this while maintaining a sense of energy and engagement in the group.

The sticky-note QFD was a large matrix of the four Common Processes (columns) and the five objectives (rows) with each cell being a sheet of flipchart paper (as seen on the right). People wrote green sticky-notes to reflect the opportunity of a positive contribution by the process to the objective, and pink sticky-notes to reflect potential risks and negative contributions. These they stuck in the relevant cells. Individuals were free to place sticky-notes where they felt most appropriate, but in order to maintain some level of discipline, different groups looked at each of the columns to explore the potential of each process, and different groups looked at each of the rows to evaluate the extent to which each objective would be supported.

Following the first workshop the Common Process teams took away the columns of the QFD, and all the associated sticky-notes, and held workshops to develop appropriate performance measures and targets for their process. At the same time the service business heads looked at their, more direct, contribution to achieving the organisation's objectives (the organisation's performance would necessarily be the sum of the service business's performance). Each group were also required to develop a forward plan for how they were intending to deliver the performance improvements. A device that worked very well in this regard was to create a table of the objectives to be achieved, against the months of the year, and then to create sticky-notes of the activities needed to deliver the objec-

tives and to schedule them on the plan by placing them under the relevant month (see photograph on the right). This approach enabled all the team members to take part in agreeing the plan, and also allowed for tasks to be rescheduled in order to balance individual workloads.

At the second workshop, all of the service businesses and the four Common Processes had translated their intended contributions into clear measures and targets in line with the organisational measures and targets. These had been presented in a common format and stuck up on flipchart sheets on the wall of the room in which the workshop was being held.

Reconciliation of the service business and process proposals to the organisation's objectives was achieved by means of a three step process.

- Everybody reviewed the service business proposals (flipcharts); visiting each one of them in turn and providing direct feedback by writing on and sticking up pink sticky-notes (see photograph on the right). These were subsequently reviewed by the service business heads, and used to adjust their proposals.

- Having understood more clearly what was being required of them, the business service heads split into four groups and were conducted around the Common Process proposals, providing feedback as appropriate. These were subsequently reviewed by the process owners.

- Finally, the impact of the proposals on the organisation's objectives was evaluated and reconciled using a 'reverse clothesline'. People stood along the clothes line at the point where they believed the sum of the Common Process and service business proposals would take them, and debated their positions. Where consensus was below the original target, the group was asked what changes needed to be made to specific Common Process and service business proposals for them to move to the target. These changes were either made and 'accepted', or the organisational target was reconsidered as appropriate.

These workshops have done much to establish the organisation as a collective commercial force both within the parent organisation, and within the contracted-services market. Progress has been managed through regular meetings and disciplined performance reporting.

The organisation was already very familiar with the balanced scorecard format of performance reporting and so it was felt inappropriate to introduce quadrant charts because of the potential resentment and confusion this might engender. Instead, we built on the balanced scorecard format to ensure that each manager's response to performance issues would be systematic. This was achieved by requiring a monthly forecast against target, and by introducing supplementary sheets which summarised analysis and actions against any measures where the performance was below forecast.

The forecast against each measure was developed by assessing the impact for each planned improvement on the measure, and scheduling these performance increases according to the planned programme; in effect creating a 'flag plan' where problems in either performance or progress register as deficiencies against forecast.

'Service Business Unit' Balanced Scorecard		Actual / Forecast / Target
Customer		**People**
Cost reduction passed on to our customers	A: % / F: % / T: %	% Staff feeling aligned to our objectives and vision — A: % / F: % / T: %
% Score on customer satisfaction survey	A: % / F: % / T: %	% Score on employee satisfaction survey — A: % / F: % / T: %
% penetration of total accessible market	A: % / F: % / T: %	
Process		**Finance**
Percentage of invoice queries as a proportion of invoices raised	A: % / F: % / T: %	Value of new external revenue — A: M / F: M / T: M
Reduction in overhead costs	A: % / F: % / T: %	Profit - £M — A: / F: / T:
		Assets - £M — A: / F: / T:

Building Full Commitment

Profile

Organisation 'D' is part of a well-known electronics multinational with a reputation for innovative high-quality products. Over recent years more and more electronics manufacture has been sourced from the far-east where labour costs are significantly cheaper; as a result, electronics manufacturing has become a commodity with very low profit margins. Organisation 'D' was recently created in response to these economic pressures; it is a Global supply chain with world-wide responsibility for realising the company's innovative designs through a global network of dedicated suppliers, and for delivering high-quality product to its customers on very short lead-times.

Issues

The parent organisation's reputation and $1/3Bn business rested on Organisation 'D's ability to identify, develop and influence independent businesses to sustain exacting quality requirements and very short cycle-times at ever decreasing costs. The creation of Organisation 'D' represented a massive transformation for the business and its ways of working, with high rewards for success, but terminal consequences for failure. The organisation therefore used its best people for the task, and head-hunted a number of experts from external companies. The challenge then became one of forming them into an effective team with the means to harness their individual talents to ensure a successful result.

Objective

The MD of the new supply chain organisation recognised the power of QFD to harness a diverse group of people and talents in delivering an ambitious set of goals. Given the new and unproven nature of the organisation, he believed that QFD provided the best means for people to work through how the organisation needed to operate and to identify individual responsibilities therein. The objective for the work was to use QFD to:

- clarify the dimensions of success in terms of clear objectives and performance targets
- identify the key supply-chain processes, and define their responsibility for delivering the objectives
- explore the interdependence between the processes and establish how they needed to work together
- clarify how the processes would fulfil their responsibilities, and build commitment to that.

Approach

The overall responsibilities of organisation 'D' were reasonably clear, and had been defined through a strategy document commissioned by the parent organisation. However, there was still scope to translate them into a set of clear objectives, measures and targets for the organisation, and by means of this to build commitment and ownership for them within the team members.

This was achieved in two ways. Firstly, a draft list of objectives was presented – this had been drawn from a series of structured interviews with the team and with key players in the supply chain. And secondly, the role of Organisation 'D' was explored as a single column QFD against the objectives of the parent organisation, so that new opportunities to leverage value could be identified.

This initial draft was then further developed by means of flipcharts titled with each of the objectives and split into columns headed Scope, Sub-objectives, Success criteria and Benefits. In these  columns people stuck up sticky-notes that described what would be really important to them in a final set of objectives. To start with, this was done in silence, but was then reconciled into an agreed shared conclusion through discussion.

These objectives were then weighted; measures were developed in syndicates; and targets were set by means of the clothesline. A proposed embellishment to the clothesline was to include benchmark data on cards and include them along the length of the line, but unfortunately there was insufficient time to prepare for this.

Conventional processes for supply chain organisations are fairly well defined, and provided a very good starting point for appointing people to roles, and for getting them to think through the boundaries of their process reponsibilities and what was needed to make it happen. At the time of the workshop, each member of the management team had a reasonably clear idea of where things would work and where there would be issues.

In the workshop itself, adjustments were made by asking each manager to list the key current activities and responsibilities of their process on sticky-notes and place them in a column on the wall under their process title. The team were then invited to identify any overlaps or gaps, and to introduce new sticky-notes or move them around accordingly. Final reconciliation of each process was achieved by discussion – initially in plenary and then by having each manager meet with every other to clarify the boundaries between their processes and the qualities of any inputs or outputs that crossed those boundaries.

The grid of the QFD was developed in the conventional way, through voting cards and consensus reaching. But following this, each manager was asked to develop a 'rich picture' for their process. This involved them reflecting back on the opportunities in their column of the QFD, and on the interdependencies between processes, and translating these into a set of images of what excellence would mean for their process. It was a way of consolidating the learning from the discussions into a vision for their work; a way of reinforcing the left-brain logic with the more emotions-based right-brain visualising. The end result was very effective in stirring up energy and determination; and for developing even more enthusiasm for taking things forward.

Having established the top-level model of the organisation, and thereby the top-level supply-chain process, the next step was to cascade it down into the rest of the organisation. It was agreed to do this by means of one big event: a cascade workshop where the separate process teams (each focusing on a separate sub-process of the overall supply chain) could work both on their own, and with other processes, as they required. In

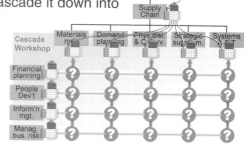

this way it was possible to develop ownership within each process team, but also to gain the support and commitment of the teams around it.

To run such a cascade successfully requires that each process manager knows exactly what he or she is trying to achieve with their team through the workshop, and takes full responsibility for using the structure and opportunities of the workshop to achieve it. Accordingly, it was made very clear that each manager was responsible for developing their own performance targets and QFD with their team in whatever way they chose, but that the cascade workshop would provide a useful vehicle for getting most of their work done – if they were suitably prepared to make full use of it. The diagram on the right was used to reflect the cascade workshop as simply one mechanism among many that the process owner would need to employ, if they were to develop full ownership for the agreed performance levels and approach within their people.

The workshop was developed with a subgroup of the management team, and was entirely led by them. Most of them were already very experienced in QFD and systematic approaches, and they wanted their full ownership of the event to signal that this was their way of managing, and not some separate consultancy approach driven by an outsider. The result of their ownership and commitment to the workshop was awesome in its effect on the commitment of their people and the quality of the work that their people produced.

The bullet points below give a detailed overview of the workshop itself.

- An introduction: to the workshop and to QFD; to the opportunities facing the organisation as a whole; and to the role of their particular process in meeting those opportunities.

- Within the process teams, each team member then had an opportunity to contribute their own ideas on how the process could fulfil its potential and to build further understanding and ownership through this.

- The tables were then rearranged to facilitate a 'roof type' discussion where each process team met with each other process team to discuss how they needed to work together and what their interdependencies were.

- Each process team then worked individually to develop a high-level process map of their process, reflecting the responsibilities of the top-level QFD and the key interdependencies with other processes. Where it transpired that key inputs and outputs had been forgotten, members of each process team could discuss and agree these with other processes 'on the hoof'.

- Each process team then defined a set of clear objectives for their process (using sticky-notes from earlier sessions supplemented by further ideas from the process mapping) and developed appropriate measures (using the competition question) and performance targets (using a clothesline) for each of these.

- The process team then developed a sheet for each of the organisation's objectives (one sheet for each cell in their column of the QFD). On this the team listed the specific measures and targets that related to their process, and which they believed would impact on the attainment of the top-level objective. These sheets were collected centrally and divided into piles for each objective – each pile containing a contribution from each process.

- The workshop then re-organised into six syndicates, each looking at one objective for the organisation and the proposed process contributions to achieving it. Each syndicate discussed whether the process contributions collectively ensured the top-level objective. If not, they discussed what more was needed, and where appropriate they made counter proposals on the relevant process contribution sheets. The results of each syndicate were fed back to the main group, and the process owners were asked if they approved the amendments to their process objectives and targets. Because the teams that made these recommendations included a representative from each process team, this proved to be fairly straightforward and, following a small amount of in-team discussion, each proposal was accepted without a problem.

- Having defined their objectives and had them approved, the processes then worked through a 'roof' discussion to agree what communication they needed between them. And then they individually developed implementation plans for their processes.

- The workshop finished with each process team developing their own composite rich picture for their process, and gathering all their outputs and conclusions into a display. Everybody was then given the opportunity to wander round the displays, and discuss the conclusions with a process team member; each display was manned on a rota basis.

The basic room arrangement for the cascade workshop is shown in the diagram on the right.

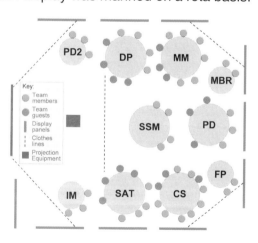

Following the workshop, each process team has made tremendous progress on implementing their conclusions, and the organisation is well on its way to achieving its vision of best-in-class response times with minimal stock and zero defects.

Making Alliances Work

Profile

Organisation 'E' was a 'virtual organisation'; a joint venture between a well-known computer company and a major UK retailer to develop and implement an innovative, efficient and customer friendly Point-of-Sale (POS) system – commonly referred to as a check-out. The organisation consisted of about 150 staff in total, based in two different locations: about 50 staff were employed by the retailer's IT department, and were based at head office, and the remaining 100 staff were employed by, and based at, the computer company.

Issues

Although the computer company had been appointed following a rigorous selection process, and it was already working with the retailer, the recent history between the two organisations was far from harmonious, and was imbued with a lot of mistrust and a tendency to blame the other party whenever things went wrong. Sadly, this drove both organisations to express their requirements in greater and greater detail; a strategy which was poorly suited to the inherent complexity and the rapid evolution of the technology.

Objective

Key people in both organisations recognised that if the venture was to be a success then the working relationships would need to change radically. The proposed project was critical to the retailer's short-term and long-term competitive strategies, and it was vital that the systems fulfilled their specification and were rolled out to schedule. Equally, the complex and evolving nature of: the competitive environment; the requirements; and the technical possibilities, meant that resolving trust issues through tight specifications would severely limit, and probably compromise, the end result.

- Capacity
- Flexibility
- Data gathering & analysis
- Ease of use
- Empowerment
- Data retrieval
- Data provision & trending
- Issues & follow-up
- Patterns
- Variable pricing
- Multi-buys & offers
- Loyalty card
- Task skills
- Guidance and help
- Job satisfaction
- Modularity & mobility
- Design & aesthetics
- Self scan etc.
- Speed of transaction
- Types of transaction
- Familiarity & tailoring
- POS Format
- Purchasing options
- Linkage to other systems

- Technology Awareness
- Systems Analysis
- System Development
- Infrastructure Expertise
- Coding Practice & Library
- Change Management
- Best Practice Awareness
- Competitor Awareness

Teamwork?

- Business Analysis
- Change Management
- Customer Understanding
- Retail Expertise
- POS Knowledge
- Marketing Awareness
- Relationship Management
- Trading Expertise
- Best Practice Awareness
- Offer Presentation Skills
- Competitor Awareness

The retailer had been using QFD in a number of other areas of its business, and recognised the potential of the tool to create and focus a higher level of teamwork and trust between the two organisations. Accordingly, it was agreed to use QFD to develop a 'virtual organisation'; an interrelated structure within two separate organisations, with common goals and agreed ways of delivering them.

Approach

Historically, the mistrust and resulting inefficiency existed at all levels between the two organisations. While the QFD was intended to directly address these issues within the team, most of the particularly disruptive interference originated at more senior levels within both organisations, outside the normal practical remit of the QFD process. However, it was felt that if the objectives of the QFD succeeded in explicitly reconciling the different needs of these two groups, then this would do much to manage and alleviate any heavyweight political influences on the team and its working processes.

Accordingly, it was felt prudent to interview all the key players on both sides, and to use the results of these interviews as input into the objective setting process. The interviews utilised a number of devices to solicit the aspirations of each of these directors, to bring some of their hidden agendas to the surface, and to clarify what was needed to sustain their confidence over the duration of the project. The results were analysed, grouped, and pulled into a clear set of objectives which were revalidated in a presentation back to the senior people in both organisations.

The objectives were then shared with the management team of the project, who were given an opportunity to further develop them through the competition question, by defining measures and setting performance targets.

The process model used by the team was adopted directly from the one used by the IT department. The reasons for this were practical. Firstly, it was a well thought out model of IT processes that had been proven in practice. Secondly, the rest of the IT department was organised along these process lines and was already using QFD to improve their performance in these areas. And thirdly, it meant that any process improvements arising from the department's QFD work could more easily be adopted by the team for the virtual organisation. The above arguments were put before the management team of the virtual organisation, and on this basis it was agreed to adopt the existing process model.

Having agreed the objectives and the process model, the QFD grid was developed in the conventional way using voting cards and consensus reaching. This was a particularly key piece of work for the combined team, because each grew to understand more about the

processes and approaches adopted in the other organisation. This understanding could then be used to develop new possibilities and to gain greater insights into why the other organisation behaved as it did. The end result was rich, not only in terms of the creative ways that the virtual organisation could pursue its objectives, but also in reflecting a deeper shared understanding of each other, and a renewed developing trust that was based on that understanding.

Having explored the potential of the processes to deliver the objectives, a suitable manager was appointed to head up each process (roughly an equal number from each organisation) and a team pulled from members of both organisations was appointed to help develop and operate the process. This further developed understanding and trust.

The first task for the process teams was to develop proposals for the contribution each process would make to achieving the top-level objectives. Rather than use a standard form for the proposals, the team worked together in a syndicate to develop a set of criteria which they would use to evaluate the quality of their proposals (and other people's). The syndicate was short (only about half an hour) but it gave the advantage that the managers fully understood what was required of a good proposal and why, and were committed to the conclusions. In the event, all the proposals were of a particularly high quality, and the winning proposal (as voted by the team as being the one that best fitted the agreed criteria) won a bottle of champagne for its author.

The biggest concern for the group was balancing the work of systematically managing and driving the performance of their processes, with the challenge of delivering project outputs to an onerous schedule. This was far from being a trivial issue, and it was concluded that process improvement was vital, but it had to be focused in a limited number of crucial areas if it were to avoid overloading the team.

By discussion, three of the four highest scoring processes were selected to be worked on and improved. The highest scoring process was not one of these, but was already the subject of extensive improvement within the retail IT group, and was of a nature that the team felt sure they would benefit from what was going on centrally.

The key challenge for the group was whether they could deliver sufficient improvement to meet their overall performance targets by only focusing on the priority processes. To evaluate this, the group split into syndicates to review each of the objectives and see how they were supported by the process proposals. Each syndicate group first reviewed the proposals of the priority processes to determine whether they alone could deliver the required performance. If they could not, they next determined whether an amendment to those process proposals could close the gap sufficiently. If it could not, they next worked through what they might need from any other proposal to ensure that the target would be met.

Their conclusions were marked on the QFD diagram as shown on the right. Pale blue grid squares illustrate where aspects of the original proposals have been accepted as-is. White squares reflect where the proposals were not needed to fulfil the objectives. And darker blue squares reflect where there

was a need for a greater contribution from the process proposal to meet the objective.

The grid illustrates that many of the objectives could be delivered mostly (or in two cases entirely) through the priority processes, with very little change in the proposals. However, there would be some need for improvement from the other processes, though not on the scale originally envisaged. With a few further adjustments it was agreed that the additional requirements could be fulfilled through special projects linked to the priority process work. This freed the non-priority process teams to focus on their normal work and support the priority processes where required.

The roof of Organisation 'E's QFD provided particularly valuable discussion. Because the team was situated on two sites, communication between the different processes was often difficult, with resulting inefficiency and mistrust. The roof discussion helped flag up these issues and to set in place communication mechanisms to address them.

Having agreed the priority processes and what they needed to deliver, the management team developed a plan for how the improvement was to be delivered systematically. The challenge here was to ensure that the process managers had enough say in what they were going to do that they were committed to delivering, while at the same time ensuring that their final plan was robust and systematic enough to ensure success. To achieve this, a number of planning cards were developed (an example of which is shown on the right) and the process managers were grouped in

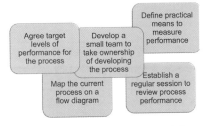

syndicates and asked to develop their forward plan. They were told they could use the planning cards, leave out any that they did not want, or add new ones if necessary. The end result was that they used most of the cards, thereby ensuring that their plans didn't miss out on key steps.

A second syndicate exercise gave the team a chance to think through what a systematic approach meant for them personally. Using the model of the 6Ps, the team agreed the practical elements that they would employ to ensure systematic progress in their process performance. From this agreement a highly structured monthly meeting was developed to review progress and overall performance.

The first part of the meeting (approximately half an hour) was concerned with ensuring an overview of performance; for the virtual organisation as a whole, for the individual processes, and for the management in completing actions from previous workshops. It is important to note that this last point was simply a measure of performance (illustrated on the right), it was not an opportunity to update people on actions that should have been communicated in preparation for the meeting.

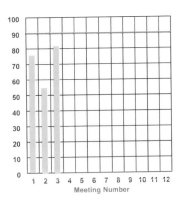

The second part of the meeting was focused on addressing the priority issues identified in the first part (including, on occasion, non-performance in completing actions on time), and ensuring they were actioned. It also provided an opportunity to reconsider any targets in the context of any external change.

The third part of the meeting was concerned with developing the management team's understanding of the key topics. It had long been recognised that the management team were largely reactive to new thinking, and not in a position to grasp new ideas as they came along and evaluate their possibilities for the group. To address this, the group developed a schedule of 'hot-topics'. These were allocated to members of the management team to 'research' with regard to their potential for the organisation. This third part of the meeting was for those members to feed back their findings on a rota basis, and where appropriate to present proposals to the rest of the team.

Two other points of note regarding Organisation 'E': Firstly, to further develop teamwork, they instituted a series of monthly teambuilding events, each looking at relationship building on a more personal and individual level – this provided a means for people to address the  more emotional and unstructured aspects of their relationships, and on occasion to blow off steam in a safe environment. Secondly, they made good use of internal consultants to support their work – these were a group of six people who had received extensive training to support their line managers (predominantly in other areas within the retail organisation) in the adoption of QFD and systematic management approaches.

Sadly, despite major shifts in both relationships and performance, the work on QFD did not bear fruit in this instance. A major political shift at the top of the company created a number of changes in the board, and with the new appointments came the intention to outsource all IT work. New brooms sweep clean, and the outsource company had its own agenda and its own way of doing things – accordingly it did not invest too much time in seeking to understand the existing approaches, even where they were working well, and the 'joint venture' was killed stone dead. In hindsight this is quite understandable – during high-pressure change it may be better to focus on a winning formula that you are familiar with, rather than distract key resources with things that might only serve to confuse the picture.

Managing Project Management

Profile

Organisation 'F' is the Project Management group for a global health-care business, where the timing and quality of products are crucial to commercial success. At the time of embarking on QFD, Organisation 'F' had been recently formed out of a reorganisation of the company's innovation processes, and was seen as the lynch pin of the company's future success. Employing approximately eighteen staff, most of whom were experienced in project management, albeit within the old line-management-based structure; its role was to manage all multidisciplinary product development projects through the newly adopted stage gate review process.

Issues

The reorganisation had been a response to historically poor performance in project delivery, and was seen as the way to ensure that future new-product performance supported the company's ambitious competitive strategy. Project Management, were now seen as responsible for improving deadline performance, but (in common with many project management teams) with no line authority over the resources required to achieve it.

Objective

Clearly, if the Project Management group were to be successful in their new task they would need to use every lever of influence they possessed to achieve their objectives. Their manager, who was already conversant with the QFD approach, saw QFD as the means to identify those levers, and to develop commitment in the team to apply them systematically in delivering project performance.

Approach

Influence is a personal thing. One person may not be influenced in the same way as the person next to them, and one person may be stronger in one form of influence while his or her colleague may be stronger in another. And yet the success of this Project Management group would ultimately depend on 'influence' and their ability to use it in forms most appropriate to the situation.

Therefore, before embarking on QFD, it was important to gain a coherent picture of how the Project Management group's influence stood currently, and also an understanding of what influence would be likely to work best in future (by understanding people's expectations and aspirations of the Project Management group). To achieve this, a series of interviews was conducted with key people within and outside the project-management process. The main section of the interviews used a set of cards marked with features of effective project management, an example of which is shown on the right. The interviewee placed each of these cards on a grid reflecting how they saw the relative importance of that feature (vertical axis) and how they saw its current performance (horizontal axis). They then talked about their reasoning and provided examples to support their conclusions.

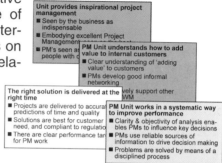

On completion of the interviews there was a clear understanding of what was important to the customers of Project Management, and where they saw the need for improvement. This provided an excellent basis for establishing the importance of doing something like QFD in the mind of the project managers, and also for determining the actual objectives for the left-hand side of the QFD. As might be expected, the choice of 'features' for the interview cards largely determined the final objectives for the QFD – but in practice, the 'features' were carefully thought through beforehand, and both the interviewees and the project managers were given opportunities to challenge them, to refine them and to take ownership for them.

In the event, the process used to build ownership within the Project Management group proved somewhat counterproductive. The project managers were asked to mark up on flipcharts what they liked and disliked about each objective and how it was worded, and then to prioritise the dislikes, and propose changes which would be discussed and approved or rejected by consensus. Many items were felt by the group to be important to resolve, but in the end only one word was changed on one objective. To be fair, at the end of the exercise the group had a far better understanding and ownership of the words, but from their perspective it seemed a major waste of time. People tend to need to see that they are being productive and in hindsight we hadn't realised how good our draft set of objectives was – were we now to repeat the exercise, we would probably use an intentionally flawed set of objectives as the start-point.

Unlike many organisations, the Project Management group is largely homogenous – one person's responsibilities and approach is much like another's. In this way, whatever the processes of project-management are, it would be inappropriate for people to specialise in any one of them – all project managers are likely to use all processes at various times. However, if such processes need to be improved, it does make sense

462

to divide the improvement effort up amongst the group, even though everybody will then benefit from the more efficient and effective approaches.

To this end, a model of the processes of project management was devised by the head of Project Management and tested with her project managers, who accepted the draft model and set to work on better defining what each process included. At the QFD workshop, they brought their outputs in the form of sets of sticky-notes, and set about refining the model collectively by resolving any duplications or gaps between the processes, and by agreeing the process boundaries.

Before building the QFD itself, the project managers built a large flipchart grid of the processes against the objectives, and used the interview feedback to identify key issues that needed to be addressed. These issues they wrote out on sticky-notes and placed them in the grid at the most relevant intersection of process and objective. This exercise gave a practical demonstration of what they were trying to achieve through the QFD process, and provided a good basis for stimulating the discussions necessary to create the grid of the QFD.

Processes	A	B	C	D	E	F	G	H
◉ Critical Contribution								
○ Major Contribution								
△ Significant								

Objectives	Wt.	Project Execution	Project Planning	Project Monitoring & Review	Project Team Development	Maintain and Gather Knowledge on Project Management	Project Risk Management	Customer needs and networking	Project Management PR
Continually leverage performance via teamwork	4	△	△	○	○	○	△	○	△
Identify and develop line reports and team members for the future	2	△	○	△	◉	○	△	○	△
Deliver right solutions at the right time at the right cost	5	◉	◉	◉	○	△	◉	◉	○
Understand how to add value to Project Management Stakeholders	4	△	△	○	○	○	△	◉	△
Work in a systematic way to improve performance	3	◉	○	○	○	△	△	△	
Provide Inspirational Project Management	2	○	△	○	○	○	△	○	○
Establish & develop relationships & deliverables with our suppliers	4	○	◉	○	○	○	○	○	△
Ranking		100	106	98	84	56	72	120	35

Following the development of the grid, responsibility for managing the processes was allotted to different project managers, and their responsibilities for developing them made clear. This responsibility was grasped enthusiastically; everybody could now see the potential for these processes to ensure the success of the group, and as a result they felt more in control of their destiny and were keen to address some of the issues they now recognised.

Understandably, they were very good at planning out their responsibilities into a clear milestone plan. But further to this, their manager is unusually talented at balancing a supportive, inspiring and empowering approach with the hard messages that are sometimes needed to make progress. She has the courage to be both sympathetic and direct at the same time and as a result her team's progress has been exemplary.

The grid of sticky-notes of the key issues from the interviews was transferred to their office, and has become an effective basis for monitoring and encouraging their progress. When an issue has been addressed by a planned process improvement it is taken off the grid, and when the group become aware of new issues, these are added back on to the grid.

As a result of their work, all projects are currently on target, and recent feedback reflects that the group has built up the respect and admiration of the company, to the extent that people are beginning to sit in awe of their achievements – an excellent position for a group whose success is largely determined by their ability to influence others.

As work progressed on the QFD, the project managers gained new insights that have changed their perceptions on a number of relationships and values within their QFD. This was an inevitable consequence of the work they had been doing to systematically improve their processes, but in most cases the insights merely added to their opportunities and any reconciliation with the QFD diagram itself could wait until the next planning round. It is important to maintain sufficient stability within the QFD that projects initiated to improve performance are not undermined by uncertainty about what they are trying to do. However, some insights reflect an original perception that was so flawed that to leave it unaddressed would be very likely to lead to confusion and wasted effort. Such issues can be addressed by means of a Spring Clean workshop.

In preparation for the Spring Clean workshop, the Project Manager's were surveyed to identify which elements of the QFD diagram needed changing in order to ensure efficient progress. Only items flagged up before the workshop were addressed so as to avoid opening the floodgates within the workshop and end up changing everything. The proposed changes concerned one measure, three cells, and the combination of three existing processes into one new one.

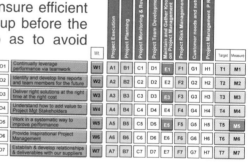

The Spring Clean workshop also provided an opportunity to begin work on the culture of the Project Management group. Although progress to this point had been good, the head of the Project Management group was concerned that more could be done to establish ownership within the group for systematically driving up performance. This was addressed in two ways.

Firstly, the group undertook a survey of how they had progressed against their original implementation plan. The results are shown in the diagram on the right. The group reflected on this picture by considering what had led to the result, in terms of what factors had supported progress with their implementation to date, and what factors had been a barrier to

PROGRESS ON PROCESS DEVELOPMENT

% Complete

	0 20 40 60 80 100
Process mapped and clearly defined, with boundaries and deliverables agreed	
Clear measures for the performance of the process established and routinely graphed/trended	
Performance targets set consistent with the needs of the customers and the top-level QFD	
Performance gaps identified, and root causes (reasons) objectively analysed	
Agreed milestone plan of improvement with resources justified and approved	
Performance impacts of the plan forecast, and used to assess effectiveness of progress	
Regular performance and progress reviews to identify and address new issues	
Clear improvements delivered and progress largely to plan	

progress. These factors were considered in more depth, and then prioritised and assigned as actions for the group to work on, both collectively and individually.

Secondly, the group used the cultural spectrum to evaluate their current position, and also the level that they felt they needed to be to ensure that their rate of progress was sustained over the year (see below). They then considered what actions they each needed to take personally in how they conducted their work to close the gap that they had identified.

Knowledge and desire to ensure "delight"	A clearly designed value set is evident	Developm't designed into work patterns	All process deliberately designed to "perform"	All activity consciously analysed & modelled	Systematic improvem't of overall "fitness"
Systematic focus on customer satisfaction	C'hensive standards rigorously prosecuted	"System of growth thru' challenge & coaching	"Key/critical processes have been "designed"	"Rigorous prediction & trending invoke PSD	"Fitness" is understood & steadily improved
Clear desire to satisfy customers	Standards exist and are actively pursued	Clear effort to involve, support and encourage	Processes have been mapped & developed	Measured deviations are clearly analysed	Clear strategy for improving perform'ce
Customer awareness is evident	A direction is evident but goals are unclear	Effortlargely a result of observed deficiencies	Some clear document'g and control of process	Perform'ce objectively monitored & recorded	Improv'ts take place on an ad-hoc basis
Largely task rather than role focus	Value set, if any, largely depends on individuals	No serious attempt to address developm't	Concept of processes is not evident	No objective perform'ce monitors	There is no clear planned improvem't

Both exercises worked well, and the team are working hard to build on their earlier success and ensure their effectiveness in delivering the projects on time.

The Spring Clean workshop finished with some champagne to celebrate the successes that had been achieved to date.

Leveraging Partnerships

Profile

Organisation 'G' is the Partner Services Group of a large, well-known software house. Their role is to increase the volume of software licences by inspiring, equipping and supporting a number of key partners in implementing their software as part of their partner's systems solution to the end-customer. Also by building relationships between the organisations which ensure that competitive achievements in this area continue to be built upon.

Issues

Partnership is a crucial element of the software house's competitive strategy, particularly as the company seeks to become a major force in new markets. But for a number of reasons it is not viable to be monogamous in these relationships, and as a result they can tend  to be opportunistic and ad-hoc in practice. As a result, partnership strategies rarely recognise all of the opportunities for growing business together and can often be weak at putting into place the mechanisms which will maximise the benefits to both parties.

Objective

The new manager of the Partner Services Group saw that there was a major opportunity here. His past experience of using QFD, and his extensive work on partnerships, made him well aware that it was possible to massively increase sales and thereby licences through a more effective joint planning process. The key was to develop enough commitment and trust in each partnership to enable ambitious strategies to be identified and fulfilled. He saw QFD as a means of doing exactly that, and of developing the outcome into an effective partnership plan.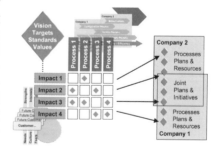

Approach

The QFD approach was initially applied, separately, to each of five partners. Each application had a number of common elements, but each differed slightly to take account of the specific needs of the relationship, the characters involved, and the learning from earlier applications.

In each case, there was a joint planning workshop, which was preceded by interviews with the key players in each organisation, and was followed up with regular progress meetings against clear plans and measures of performance. But in each case the nature of the workshop was adjusted to accommodate the needs of the key players, and the level of maturity of the current relationship.

The following overview of the first (pilot) partnership planning workshop may give some insight into how the process worked in practice. It was arranged at a hotel somewhere between both organisations' offices, and ran over two days.

- After an initial introduction and overview of what the workshop was trying to achieve, the participants were invited to introduce themselves to each other (many had not met before) by means of 'rich pictures'. This simple tool involves people drawing pictures on a flipchart to represent themselves, their interests, their work and their vision for the partnership. It works well because the degree of embarrassment it introduces tends to draw out humour and the beginnings of a bond between people. Also the pictures cause people to open up a bit more than they otherwise would, and tend to be more interesting and memorable than a written or solely verbal introduction.

- The results of the interviews were presented back to the group as a context for what they might be trying to achieve/address. Following this, the members of the two organisations were invited to draw their conclusions from the interviews into a clear set of objectives for what their organisation wanted to achieve through the partnership. These were written out onto sticky-notes (one objective per note) and were placed on a grid like the one on the right. Organisation 'G' stuck their objectives along the X axis according to their relative importance to them, and their partner stuck theirs along the Y

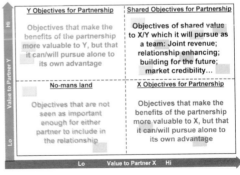

axis using the same convention. From that point on, either partner could move any sticky-note, but organisation 'G' could only move notes horizontally (according to the value they placed on the objective that was written on them) and their partner organisation could only move notes vertically. When the movement had settled down (in some cases following a bit of discussion) the objectives in the top right-hand quadrant were seen as the shared objectives for the partnership and the basis for the objectives on the QFD.

- The objectives were grouped (using an affinity diagram), weighted in terms of their importance (using voting cards and consensus reaching), further refined through identifying suitable measures (using mixed syndicates), and associated with performance targets (agreed through the clothesline approach). The collective interactive nature of the approaches used did much to ensure a clear understanding of the different perspectives and a shared commitment to the conclusions. It was clearly noticeable how each group continually gained new insights into the partnership and its history to date. The clothesline method is particularly useful in this regard. Seeking arguments and perspectives to persuade partners toward your targets and ways of thinking can help to develop a closer and more transparent relationship. Similarly, better understanding of the practical barriers can also develop and this provides the possibility of finding more creative solutions, or for ensuring a greater degree of support within the partnership.

- The process model was originally proposed to the group, but was then further refined by the group using sticky-notes to define and adjust the content and responsibilities of each process. This was then further refined by reviewing the interview feedback for specific issues, and then allocating them to be the responsibility of appropriate processes (once again using sticky-notes). This helped both organisations grasp a more systemic perspective on the operation of their partnership and its potential for delivering the competitive wins they both wanted.

- Prior to developing the QFD using voting cards and consensus, the group reorganised the sticky-notes under each process to place them in rows against the objectives that they best supported – thereby forming a sort of sticky-note QFD. This helped all the participants gain a better understanding of what they were trying to do via the QFD, and to organise their thoughts and ideas for the grid discussions. As a result the QFD discussions progressed smoothly, and once again there was a large amount of understanding and insight into the approaches adopted in each organisation, and also creative ideas for how things might be progressed in the future.

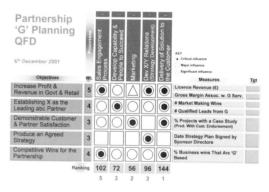

- Finally, joint owners were appointed to each process, one from each partner, and each pairing was asked to develop a joint vision for their process in terms of a rich picture. The mechanism for taking processes forward was agreed and monthly follow-up meetings scheduled

The result of the workshop was a set of ambitious targets – in some cases doubling the performance of the partnership to date – with a partnership team that was confident and committed to achieving them. At the end of the year the partnership had out-performed all its important targets by a significant margin and had driven up end-customer satisfaction from 86% to 94%; more than halving the gap to perfection.

Following the success with the pilot workshop, the approach was adopted with other key partnerships. The main variations in these are listed below.

- In later workshops, a simple SWOT analysis replaced the feedback of interview conclusions. Four sheets of flipchart paper were placed in the standard 2x2 SWOT grid and the representatives from the two partner organisations each separately developed sticky-notes that reflected their organisation's perception of the partnership's strengths, weaknesses, opportunities and threats. Each organisation used different colour sticky-notes but they were all mixed up on the same grid as a composite view. During the feedback from this session, knowledge of the interviews was used by the facilitator to gently ensure that all the issues and opportunities were flagged up.

- In one workshop, where three mutually interdependent organisations formed the partnership, it was not possible to use the 'values' grid to agree shared objectives because of the limitation of two axes. Instead a Venn diagram was used (see right). The partners placed their sticky-note objectives in their own

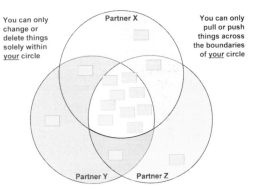

circle where it did not overlap any other circle. From then on other partners could adopt objectives by pulling them across their own boundary into their circle, but were not allowed to push them across anybody else's boundary. This meant that any sticky-notes that arrived in the centre of the diagram must have been adopted by all three partners. (It takes some conceptualising but it is actually very simple in practice if people just follow the rules, and it worked well in reconciling objectives in the workshop).

- In a couple of cases, the partnership was simply not ready for a full-blown QFD. Key people were unwilling to invest the time that it would require, and this would have been likely to undermine the whole process. In these cases we used a sticky-note QFD which did much to help the partnership to think through how it was going to deliver its objectives – while they did not get full exposure to the creativity and insight that grid discussions can stimulate, they certainly got as much as they were likely to want to use in the next twelve months of the partnership. It soon became clear that the full-blown QFD is an excellent tool where the partners already have a deep commitment to each other that they want to build on, but a sticky-note QFD is more than sufficient to explore opportunities and set them on a good footing where the relationship is a bit more tentative.

A key part of the success of these partnership QFDs has been the regular methodical review of progress against what has been planned. These are typically scheduled on a monthly or bi-monthly basis and last approximately one to two hours. The clear measures, targets and relationships defined in the QFD are used as an objective means to assess progress by the partnership as a whole. Deviation from the forecast levels of performance are recognised early, and addressed quickly in order to ensure the long-term success of the plan. The examples on the right illustrate two of the simple spreadsheet models that are used to keep track of progress and actions.

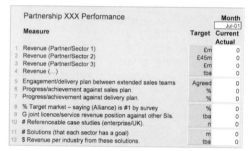

Partnership XXX Performance		Month
		Jul-01
Measure	Target	Current Actual
1 Revenue (Partner/Sector 1)	£m	0
2 Revenue (Partner/Sector 2)	£45m	0
3 Revenue (Partner/Sector 3)	£m	0
4 Revenue (...)	tba	0
5 Engagement/delivery plan between extended sales teams	Agreed	0
6 Progress/achievement against sales plan.	%	0
7 Progress/achievement against delivery plan.	%	0
8 % Target market – saying (Alliance) is #1 by survey	%	0
9 G joint licence/service revenue position against other SIs.	tba	0
10 # Referenceable case studies (enterprise/UK).	n	0
11 # Solutions (that each sector has a goal)	m	0
12 $ Revenue per industry from these solutions.	tba	0

APPENDIX 4: DISCUSSION STARTERS

Books are very useful devices for conveying ideas and information, but they are very limited in their ability to share real experiences, to develop a consensus of understanding and to build a collective commitment to do something practical. In practice this is much better achieved through discussion. Sadly, it is often the case that much of the really important discussion and reconciliation takes place in response to decisions and action, rather than the other way round. It often seems that only current problems and real risk can validate this sort of investment in shared learning.

The purpose of this appendix is to provide a mechanism whereby, within forward thinking teams, such investment in learning and reconciliation can take place. It is intended to be used by any group of managers who are working through the book together. Taking the form of a series of discussion starters, it provides thought-provoking questions designed to draw out the experience of the group and reach consensus on what they believe for themselves (rather than what the book suggests they should believe).

By using the questions appropriately, the leader should be able to identify where there is any shortfall in understanding, use the perspectives and arguments of others in the group to address this, and understand where there is the greatest collective energy and enthusiasm for moving forward. If in saying this, you think that we may have got leadership confused with education, we have! Transforming management performance is first and foremost a work of education in its deepest sense, and we believe that such education should be undertaken using best teaching methods, hence the inclusion of this appendix.

In using these questions we would offer the leader the following advice.

- Persuade the group to read through the book at the same pace, section by section, with a discussion scheduled at the end of each section.

- Confirm the 'educational' nature of the discussion session and address any negative reactions up front, rather than allow them to develop and fester underneath the discussion. But ensure also that the group has a correct perspective on 'education' – that it is something they can do for themselves, and that it is empowering rather than remedial.

- Select a few questions, out of those listed for the section, which seem most relevant to the learning needs of your group, and where the 'correct' answers may also be drawn out of the group. In other words set the learning at the right level, not too easy but not too far in advance of where the group currently is.

- Start by asking what questions the group has on their reading, and only introduce your questions as and when discussion dries up. Use your knowledge of the questions and the group to guide discussion into productive areas.

- Recognise that very little in this life is 'absolutely true' and that your people (and especially your resident cynic) will be able to identify many situations where the 'learning' does not apply. Accept the limitations, and draw the group on to thinking about where it does apply. The extent to which we would rather find fault in others than improve ourselves never ceases to amaze, but sadly it is the least productive of responses.

- Keep the discussions well facilitated, ensuring that they remain productive, that everyone is involved, and that they result in clear conclusions that have practical value for your organisation. And be aware that some issues are better followed up with individuals outside meetings.

Section A

1
What feelings and emotions do we associate with Richard, as he sits alone in his office at the opening of the book?

How common are those feelings within our own organisation, and when are they most likely to occur?

What tends to be the cause of such feelings?

2
How would we describe the consistency and clarity of Cylek's objectives as outlined in Chapter 2?

How did Richard attempt to illustrate inconsistencies in his management's perceptions of the objectives? How successful was he?

How serious does Richard believe the apparent inconsistencies in the efficient running of the business are? Are we inclined to accept his perspective? Why? Does our own organisation have similar inconsistencies?

What implications could this have for our efficiency and effectiveness? Do we have any evidence to support this?

How do we feel about Richard's observation that Cylek is not a democracy? Why do we feel that way?

In what areas should our own organisation seek to be more democratic? And in what areas should it seek to reduce an expectation of democracy?

What new areas of thinking did the Why-How chart method open up for Cylek? What is it about the method that brings this creativity about?

In what ways might a commonly agreed Why-How chart be useful for our organisation?

3
How do we feel about Richard's perspective that business design can benefit from insights and approaches drawn from product design?

What are the key factors that determine when a product design becomes 'obsolete'? Do similar factors apply to the design of organisations?

When was our organisation last 'designed' in the full sense of the word? How might those factors have changed since our last 'redesign'?

How did uncertainty affect Richard's team's determination to follow Richard's plans?

To what extent do we feel that uncertainty was an excuse to take the easier option of avoiding extra work? Do we tend to do that?

How much do Richard's prejudices about Lucy resonate with us? To what extent might they serve any purpose for him?

In what way does Cyrus' sponsorship of the situation affect Richard's decision making? What implications does that have for our sponsorship of change?

How would we describe Lucy's approach to Richard? What benefits does it offer her, and are there any real disadvantages?

4

How would we describe Lucy's approach to her meeting with the management team? What do we imagine the impact on the team to be? What advantages will this give her?

How relevant will the 'competition criteria' developed by the Cylek team be in evaluating their own performance? Do we have a clear handle on the criteria that are relevant to us?

Do we agree that growth in performance of the 'criteria' is a measure of the quality of management? What does the rate of growth of our performance say about our quality as management?

Would it be fair for Cylek to rationalise their comparative weakness in performance as due to outside factors, such as limited investment, exchange rates, etc.?

How would such rationalising limit their determination and opportunities to be the best? How might it affect their creativity and enthusiasm?

Conversely, how would a determination to win, with whatever hand they are dealt, affect their creativity and enthusiasm? And even if they don't win, how might this attitude affect performance?

What do we feel about Lucy's argument on the returns available from freeing up management to transform performance? How much investment in management could this justify?

5

What were the pros and cons of Richard having a pre-meeting on the results of Lucy's survey? What would we have done in Richard's position? To what end?

What is our view on the statement 'Total Quality Management is more about the quality of management than it is about the management of quality'? Do companies still make the same mistakes? Do we?

To what extent do the six principles, outlined by Lucy, reflect what we would see as best-practice management?

Taking each principle in turn, what are the consequences of not doing it well? How well does our management practice reflect these six principles? What proportion of our time do we spend on this?

During Daniel's attack, what advantages did Lucy's pause bring her, both immediately and as a consequence of that? What should she have done if no one had stepped in?

To what extent did we find Lucy's conclusions consistent with the picture of Cylek that has been developing in our own minds? Why might that be the case?

6

Why did Lucy want to draw out where Richard's energies and interests lay, rather than propose her own ideas? What would have been the risks of doing otherwise? What evidence, in the book or otherwise, is there to support her perspective on this?

To what extent do we seek to draw out other people's plans and passions before introducing our own? Why? What is the impact of this (including practical examples) within our own organisation?

What are Richard's feelings about Management by Objectives (MBO)? What does he see as the disadvantages of the approach? What methods do we know about for deploying objectives down through an organisation? What do we know of their advantages and disadvantages in practice?

In practical terms, what would our implementation of QFD need to achieve if it was to address the shortcomings in our current method of deploying objectives? How might QFD be able to do this?

Lucy feels that QFD has the potential to address the issues raised in her survey – which of Cylek's issues do we feel would begin to be addressed through effective use of QFD? In what way?

How does Lucy address Richard's reservations at the end of the chapter? What insights might we draw about the balance between vulnerability and influence? Is there a paradox here?

Section B

7

Why is Lucy being totally open about the information she is sending to Cyrus? What would be the consequences if she had some criticisms to make in it? Why might she still see this as an advantage?

To what extent has Lucy been over-structured in developing a four-page session plan for the QFD meeting? How much effort should it take to design a meeting that is efficient and effective?

How efficient and effective are our meetings? What proportion of our management business takes place through meetings?

To what extent is it conceivable that, with excellent design, preparation and participation, our meetings could be made more efficient or more effective? How much would this be worth?

Do we have any experience of meeting approaches or techniques (maybe in special events or workshops) that achieved their objectives quickly and effectively? Why did they work?

Why don't we think more creatively and objectively about the design of our own meetings? To what extent is preparation time an issue? To what extent is wasted time in meetings an issue?

8 What does Lucy present as the main arguments for thinking about the organisation in process, rather than departmental, terms? How do we feel about these?

To what extent is our own organisation structured around processes? What would be the opportunities and the risks of periodically rethinking our core processes and restructuring around them?

Why might Richard be so concerned about a confusion of accountabilities? How do we feel about Lucy's observation that it will make accountabilities clearer?

To what extent are accountabilities blurred by the boundaries in our own organisation? How do we deal with this in practice?

Why does Richard so easily see the risks in redesigning the processes? To what extent do we let our fear of things going wrong deter us from a course of action, rather than encourage us to put in more checks and balances? How does Lucy handle Richard's concerns?

How do we feel about Lucy's observation about cost and value? Why might this means of judging value have some validity? To what extent might it make us a hostage to perpetual external support?

Why does Richard feel vulnerable to Daniel's actions? What would our strategy be for dealing with this sort of situation?

9 What did Cylek's management team gain from the discussions on the grid of their QFD? Why might they have remained oblivious to these things for so long?

Is it common for a company not to recognise all the different and creative ways in which its operations can contribute to its objectives? What are the consequences? Are there opportunities here for us?

Why did the discussion at Cylek become so entrenched on particular cells? Are there similar issues that we have between ourselves? How important is it that we work to resolve these things?

Why might the 'old surface need to be physically broken before the organisation would reveal new secrets and opportunities'? Why is this hard work and potentially painful? What aspects of our business might represent our 'old surface'?

How valuable were the 'disciplines', which Lucy introduced to the meeting, in ensuring that progress remained efficient and productive? How do we feel about using them in our own meetings?

Why would such methods normally be sneered at? Is our proclaimed 'maturity' over such methods really manifest in how we behave at meetings?

To what extent do we share Richard's optimism in the impact it is having on his people? Can we imagine such discussions having the same effect on us? Why? How important is it to capture such discussions and conclusions for future reference?

10 Why does Lucy try to get the process team to think radically about their contribution to Cylek and its objectives? What might the implications be, if our teams thought radically about what they could contribute to meeting our objectives?

What are the advantages of getting the process team to think what would win the 'contract', rather than have Cylek's management team work out performance objectives for the process?

How might a team that had proposed a 'contract', and had it accepted, behave or think differently from a typical internal department? How could this be reinforced? How might it change things here?

Why does Tom have problems thinking beyond specifics? How might the Cylek culture encourage or reward people thinking about events rather than performance? Does our culture do this?

How much value did Andrea get out of the interviews with her customers? Does it appear that way from the outset? Why do we get the impression that the process team thinks it can fulfil its role without meeting its customer's requirements?

How do we feel about Deborah's approach to time allocation? What are the practical implications of loading all resources to 100%? Why is there so much pressure to do what is bad for us?

What are the advantages to the process of developing a process map? Does the difficulty of producing such a map bear any relationship to its value? Could we benefit from more process mapping?

Why does Deborah concede taking on the paperwork objective? Does her reason make sense? To what extent are we tempted to select measures that look good rather than drive change?

Section C

11 What are the main factors in why Lucy is finding progress so difficult? Why does she believe that Richard is a factor in this? To what extent is she correct?

What do we think might be the factors in why Richard has been so poor in ensuring forward progress in his managers? To what extent do we tend to fall foul of the same things ourselves?

How do we feel about the level of understanding Susan has developed for her process? Has she done more than is necessary? What benefits might such benchmarking and background provide us?

What do we feel are the implications of John's approach to the meeting, in terms of its efficiency and effectiveness? How do we, individually and collectively, avoid such pitfalls?

Overall, what is our perception of Richard's management of the meeting? To what extent should effective meeting management take place before the meeting?

Who's attitudes and behaviours pose the biggest threat to Richard's effective leadership of the group? In what way? To what extent is the same true for ourselves?

12 Why does Andrew think that the QFD will ensure the top-level objectives? To what extent is he guilty of seeing QFD as more than it actually is? Are there any principles that we should follow in maintaining an appropriate perspective on the 'tools' we use?

Why doesn't QFD automatically ensure the objectives will be met? How do we feel about Lucy's way of checking that the proposals add up? To what extent does it feel subjective and unstructured? How do we fulfil this responsibility currently?

What might the impact of the reconciliation process be on the ownership and commitment of the groups who developed the process proposals – both positive and negative? How might it be kept positive?

13 In what ways can Lucy's leadership of the meeting be seen as more effective than Richard's? What do we believe are the key things that contribute to this?

How would we describe the relationship between Richard and Cyrus? What does this achieve from Cyrus's perspective? To what extent is Cyrus's stance well suited to the geographic and organisational distances in the relationship? Does Cyrus's approach have any disadvantages?

How does Richard attempt to break through Cyrus's mindset? Is he right to do this? To what extent might challenging existing paradigms be an important element of managing upwards?

How could Richard have been better prepared for shifting Cyrus's paradigm? What advantages might this preparation have brought him in the meeting?

Do we believe that it is conceivable that Cylex could improve its performance by 50% in two to three years? What do we feel about Lucy's perspective that "if you could not design [any] business to perform 50% better, you were clearly not seriously trying"?

What did Richard gain by implicitly contrasting Cyrus's grubby fax with the rigour of his planning process? To what extent was it a good strategy in managing Cyrus?

Why did Cyrus ask about the problems? Why do we think that Richard chose to answer the question openly and honestly? Was he right?

Is Lucy right about the cultural differences between Cyrus and Richard? How could recognising these from the outset have helped Richard?

14 What took Deborah's team 600 man hours? What do we think they achieved with that time? Do we feel that was a worthwhile investment?

To what extent is it important that the other processes do the same things as Deborah's team has done? Will Richard achieve his longer term performance aims without it? Could it be realistically achieved in less time?

How do we imagine that Cylek's senior managers spend their time? How does this affect our perception of their priorities and their competence?

What do we think about Richard's perspective on the economics of this work? Would similar economics be true of our own organisation?

How might we describe Richard's state of mind as he approached the meeting? What were the consequences of this?

15 How would we describe Richard's attitude to his family up to this chapter? To what extent might this be explained by what you know of Richard and the decisions he has made?

What inferences might we draw about Richard's character? To what extent are the choices that he has been making likely to encourage his healthy growth and development as a person?

How might the personal development we gain through a full engagement with our 'home' life be different from that we gain through a full engagement with work?

How do we make decisions when there isn't a financial 'bottom line' to reflect 'right' and 'wrong'? What can we learn from wrestling with things that cannot be resolved through our logical models?

Why did Laura apologise to Richard, when she clearly felt that he was largely in the wrong? What was the impact of this?

How could Richard's growth become stultified if he doesn't keep a better balance in his life? How can we become shallow if we don't keep a balance in ours?

16 To what extent has Richard been trading his soul for the World? What exactly might he have been giving up, and to what end? Why do people find it so easy to do that?

Why might Richard have been so sensitive to the words of the reading? What unresolved tensions and uncertainties in his thinking might generate such a level of 'paranoia'?

To what extent do we accord with the preacher's views on how the singular pursuit of success can distort our ability to enjoy it? What examples have we seen of this?

Who is Richard – his position; his achievements; his relationships; his values? And how does who he is, affect what he does, and the decisions he makes?

Who are we – our position; our achievements; our relationships; our values? And how does who we are, affect what we do, and the decisions we make?

To what extent might Richard's search for tangible success, and his cynicism about 'spiritual' things, be bound up in his desire to have complete and unquestioned control over his own life?

Why might facing up to the idea that Richard was not who he really wanted to be, make him calm and resolute rather than increase his mounting panic? Has this ever happened to us?

17 Why is it so important to Richard that there should be some common purpose to the two halves of his life? What benefit would there be for him in finding something that reconciled work and home?

To what extent do we think that Richard is being 'too hard on himself'? What is wrong with doing things to be admired? Why do we think Richard is so upset by his conclusions?

To what extent do we not explore our own motives too deeply because we might find something that, once it has become clear and explicit, throws our comfortable life choices and self-image into question?

Why might Richard never have questioned his picture of success? To what extent is our picture of success cast on a point in the future, or based on appreciating the moment? Is our picture of success dependent on the material, or is it founded in the spiritual? What are the implications of this?

Why does Richard feel embarrassed at the words he writes on the top of his Why-How chart? To what extent is sophistication stacked against 'goodness'? Why might this be so? And what sort of language does our own organisational culture reward?

What is our purpose? What are our individual purposes?

18 What is Richard trying to achieve in his meetings with Susan, Deborah, Andrew and Peter? Why is he trying to do this?

To what extent do we agree with Richard's motives? To what extent do we try to achieve the same thing here? How good are we at it?

How would we describe Richard's approach to developing his role? What other things could he do to ensure that he is successful in what he is attempting? What are the risks in Richard's approach?

How successfully could the approach Richard has taken be applied by us in our own organisation? What would we need to do differently, to ensure our success?

How might we measure the extent to which we are successfully developing our role?

19 To what extent is Richard right to use QFD on his own role? How appropriate is the tool to this individual type of application?

What logic does Richard use to reason that Cylek's results are not his job? How do we feel about his conclusions? Why does Richard see these conclusions as 'almost heretical'?

What then does Richard see as his job? Is he right in believing that if he does that job well, results will naturally follow?

To what extent might Richard have to get involved in the 'first camp' because he doesn't currently do the 'second camp' well enough? How true might that be of our own organisation?

What are the key lessons for Richard out of his QFD? Why are the conclusions such a surprise to him? Why do the implications frighten him?

What is our perspective on Richard's conclusions? Would we expect to see the same pattern emerging in our own personal QFDs?

What should Richard do next?

20 How would we describe the relationship between Richard and Daniel? What is actually happening in their meeting at the beginning of Chapter 20?

What do we think Daniel is trying to achieve by his attitude to Richard? And what is Richard trying to achieve out of this meeting?

What have been the upsides and downsides of Richard's approach to Daniel? What other options did he have? What do we believe he could have done to resolve things more effectively?

Do we have any Daniels (to any degree) within our own organisation? How effective is our approach to them? Do we need to do anything different as we move forward?

After the events at the end of Chapter 20, what would be the likely consequences of Richard simply firing Daniel on the spot? (This may depend on the employment laws that pertain in your country!)

Section E

21 Why does Lucy propose to split the management meeting into two sections? To what extent can we appreciate her arguments? Can we think of any additional arguments for, or against, her proposal?

How key will Lucy's facilitation be, in making the meeting work? What will be the key things that she needs to manage?

How much does our experience of meetings accord with Richard's? How good is our prioritisation of where we spend the time? Do we have a clear and appropriate process for working through issues?

How big a factor is the structure, frequency and quality of meetings, on how we spend our 168 hours per week? To what extent would improving the design, membership and effectiveness of meetings help us to spend time where it is most needed?

How does Deborah's view of management differ from Daniel's? Where does our view of management fit against these? What proportion of the time and thought we invest in meetings is actually focused on our 'management' responsibilities?

Is Daniel right; is this form of management purely a dreary clerical exercise? Or is Lucy right; is this the platform from which new and exciting challenges will emerge?

Does Lucy's vision carry any implications for how we design and run our meetings?

22 How accurate is Peter's assessment of the situation? To what extent would Peter's three reservations be likely to apply in our organisation?

How appropriate is Richard's response to Peter's reservations? How relevant would they be to what might emerge in our own organisation?

What are the main steps that Lucy takes the group through, in tackling the issue of time? How effective are these steps in ensuring the problem is fully explored?

How did Lucy develop a common definition of the problem? What questions did she use to gain a clear definition? In what way did having this common definition help move things forward?

What process did Lucy use to identify the main causes of the problem? How effective was this? Why didn't she narrow down the list of causes to a root cause in this instance?

Why does Lucy encourage the group to list out all options and avoid debate? How could Lucy have improved the way the options were selected?

How methodically do we address issues? What would be the advantages of tending more toward Lucy's approach?

23 To what extent is it valuable for the process owners to understand the potential conflict or synergy that their objectives may have with other processes' objectives?

How well do we understand the conflict or synergy that exists between our own processes/departments? How might a better understanding on the part of the process or department managers help us?

How might a better system of planned communication between processes/departments help the efficiency of our full management meeting?

24 Do we know what Richard means by 'standing on the edge of somewhere he had always wanted to be, and knowing the price of entry was more than he could pay'?

What are the links between 'sacrifice' and 'adding-value' that Richard is wrestling with? To what extent does adding-value need to contain an element of sacrifice, however small? To what extent might we be held back from adding-value in a major way because of the sacrifices that it requires?

To what extent does the process of developing effective measures of performance require some level of sacrifice? What sort of sacrifices might be required? What would make those sacrifices easier to bear?

Pulling it all together

What are the opportunities and threats posed by taking a more systematic approach to how we manage our business? What aspects of our management would benefit from being more systematic?

How can we use the resources available to us to implement a more systematic approach to our business? To what end; how would we describe success in this?

APPENDIX 5: EVALUATING STRATEGIES WITH QFD

The Grid of the QFD provides an excellent structure for teams to explore how their processes contribute to achieving their objectives. This was outlined in Chapter 6, and further amplified in Chapter 9.

Because of the structure and disciplines involved, the grid also has the potential to fulfil a wider role in evaluating strategies and prioritising processes. In this appendix we look at how the QFD can be developed to support the management team in:

- reviewing strengths and weaknesses in the strategy
- prioritising the processes
- evaluating the importance of the objectives (more sophisticated weighting)
- incorporating benchmark data

Reviewing strengths and weaknesses in the strategy

The diagrammatic nature of the QFD makes it relatively easy to identify where your strategies have not been fully thought through and linked up. Such gaps in thinking are normally indicated by rows or columns containing very few major (and no critical) relationships.

Where such a condition occurs in a row, it is a clear sign that your current strategies for your processes may not support the attainment of the objective. Weakly supported objectives may indicate one of three things.

- Certain processes may need to be developed in different ways to ensure that the objective is met. New strategies for extending the role and performance of a process, make it possible to create new relationships in support of the objective.

- A process crucial to the attainment of the objective may have been totally missing from the thinking to this point. This occurs most frequently when the organisation relies on a service from outside, and has not fully considered its responsibilities for 'managing' this service.

- The objective is surplus to what is really needed. It sometimes happens that the organisation has to reconsider what its role really is, in terms of its objectives, when it finds that it simply does not have, or want, the processes required to support them. Recognising what we are not going to do is as important as planning what we will.

In the case of a column with few strong relationships, there is a clear implication that your current objectives do not warrant any significant investment in that process. This may be for a number of reasons.

- Certain key objectives that do require the process are missing from the thinking and need to be included. This happens were certain aspects of role and routine are taken for granted.

- The potential for the process to leverage the achievement of other objectives has not been fully recognised or explored. Both this point and the point above are often reflected in a nagging doubt over any suggestion of abandoning the process; sometimes all our logic may indicate that a process is superfluous and yet instinct tells us that it is important. If this is the case, using your feelings to drive your creative and analytical faculties can be very useful.

- The process really has outlived its strategic usefulness and should perhaps be cut right back and/or subsumed into one or more other processes.

Prioritising the processes

The relative strategic importance of each process in achieving your objectives can be evaluated very quickly within the QFD. This was outlined briefly in Chapter 6 but is explained in more depth below.

Each cell of the QFD represents the potential contribution of a single process to the attainment of a specific objective.

The importance of the 'cell' to achieving that objective lies in the strength of that relationship. Its value to the organisation lies in the strength of that relationship *and* the importance of the objective, e.g. a cell which provides a weak contribution to an important objective may be as valuable as one which provides a strong contribution to a much less important objective.

By giving each different relationship a numerical value, which reflects the strength of the potential contribution, and multiplying it by the weighting assigned to the objective, we have a means to determine the relative value of each cell (relationship) to the overall aims of the organisation.

Key to QFD symbols

⬤ **Critical:** the process is fundamental to progressing the objective

◯ **Major:** the process is key to achieving the target performance

△ **Significant:** the process will significantly contribute to the result

Each process has a number of such relationships. By adding up the relative value of each cell under a process, we have the means of estimating the overall value of the process to the aims of the organisation. The relative value of each process provides a guide to prioritising how the improvement effort should be invested in those processes. QFD, thereby, provides a useful mechanism for prioritising the strategic importance of each process.

From experience, it has been determined that attributing values of: nine, for a critical relationship; three, for a major relationship; and one, for a significant relationship, provides an effective means of differentiating the relative importance of the processes. The relative importance of each cell can then be calculated by multiplying the weighting of the objective (1-5) by the value of the relationship (0, 1, 3 or 9), and these can then be added up within the columns to assign values for the strategic importance of each process (as shown by the diagram on the right).

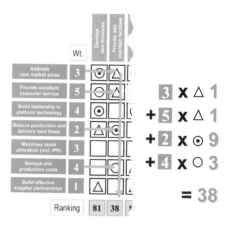

$$3 \times \triangle 1$$
$$+ 5 \times \triangle 1$$
$$+ 2 \times \odot 9$$
$$+ 4 \times \bigcirc 3$$
$$= 38$$

More sophisticated weighting

In the examples we have used of organisational QFDs, the weighting of the objectives has been a single column with a simple 1 to 5 scale (as shown above). In product QFDs the weighting scale has evolved into a number of columns reflecting different aspects of importance, such as: customer perception; market leverage; and performance gap, which are then multiplied together to form a compound weighting.

This compound weighting provides an opportunity to combine a number of factors in considering priority processes. Suitable columns for an organisation QFD might be: impact on this year's business results; long-term potential; influence on market dominance; performance deficit. These columns can be weighted differently in order to reflect the relative importance, so for instance market influence could be rated from 1 to 3 while long-term potential may only be rated from 1 to 1.5, thus ensuring that the compound figure reflects an appropriate balance.

The example below shows how this can work:

Weighting due to impact on:	Year-end results	Market influence	Future potential	Overall weight
Objective Scale	1 – 5	1 – 2	1 – 1.5	1 – 15
Address new market areas	3	1.5	1.2	5.4
Excellent customer service	5	2.0	1.1	11.0
Maximise asset utilisation	3	1.0	1.2	3.6
Reduce production costs	4	1.2	1.0	4.8
Build supplier partnerships	4	1.2	1.2	5.8

In each case '1' is a neutral value, because it has no effect when the numbers are multiplied together – thus it forms the bottom of each scale. The top of each scale should therefore be 1 + x, where 'x' is the relative importance of the weighting to what the organisation is trying to achieve.

Compound weighting may also be a solution if debate on simple weighting becomes confused because those involved in the discussion are struggling to take account of too many different factors. By looking at the separate impacts the objective has on different areas of what the organisation needs to achieve, the discussions can be made a lot clearer, and the overall weighting simply falls out mathematically at the end.

Incorporating benchmarking data

The QFD model lends itself extremely well to capturing and presenting benchmark data. Using a simple 5-point scale, the current performance of the organisation, vis-à-vis its main competitors, can be graphed against the objectives that the organisation has chosen (see the vertical graph at the far right of the diagram). The comparisons can be generated either as an index of objective measurement data, or on the basis of customer perspectives on your organisation and its competitors.

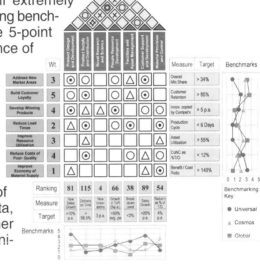

The same can be achieved for comparative measures of process performance. The resulting picture can then be used to decide strategies, to drive target setting, and to check the organisation's logic. This last point can be best illustrated using the diagram above. If we assume that our organisation is 'Universal', we seem to be of the opinion that we are outperforming our competitors on the last (seventh) objective (see right hand graph). When we look in the body of the QFD we see that the predominantly contributing process (seventh column) is significantly underperforming the competition. This would indicate a disparity which requires further understanding. In this way the QFD can use benchmarking data to highlight where our information or logic needs further investigation.

It is a truly unfortunate aspect of management, that the ideas that support it come in and out of fashion. Over recent years, I have seen a number of such cycles, the main planks of which have been: Total Quality Management; Business Process Re-engineering; The Balanced Scorecard; Just-in-Time; Single Minute Exchange of Dies; Moments of Truth; Benchmarking; Concurrent Engineering; Knowledge Management; Emotional Intelligence; The Learning Organisation; …

What has been sad, is that they have been fashions. Each one of these approaches contains new, and largely timeless, insights into good management practice that still hold true today. Yet, all too often, they have been initially adopted with such fervour that one might think that they were the only way to manage, and then subsequently neglected as though they had lost their usefulness. Neither of these responses seems appropriate to what are, essentially, good elements of a holistic and systematic approach to the profession.

But perhaps that is part of the problem – perhaps management is not yet a real profession. It is difficult for managers who don't have a professional grasp of the process of management, to place these tools into context, and to adopt and adapt them into their appropriate places within a mature management approach. Within an impoverished management process, the benefits promised by these new tools and concepts can seem overwhelming, but without the complementary disciplines in place the results are often disappointing. And so one management idea is replaced by the next rather than complemented by it.

Sadly, my own profession has been a factor in this – partly inadvertently, but also with a fair degree of opportunism. In order to get new business themselves, many consultancies promoted the latest thinking, but in order to promote it they often polarised the arguments to make them simple. As a result, a lot of the necessary richness in the ideas listed at the top of the page were forgotten. Further to this, in order to sell their work, consultancies tended to understate the real implications for management responsibility, and to compensate for this by putting in more of their own people's time. The end result was a fully functioning system, but with a management that was sadly ill-equipped to drive it and adapt it to their changing needs. As a result, the fashions tended to have a steeper entry and exit, but it didn't really matter because the next fashion was already pulling in. In a previous consulting organisation, I regularly had people telling me that Total Quality was old-hat and that I should focus on Business Process Re-engineering. It did no good to tell them that, done properly, they were virtually the same thing with different emphases.

I do not want QFD to fall victim as another management fashion. I neither want the hype that draws new converts unthinkingly to apply it, without first considering the full implications and its dependency on other good practice. Nor do I want it to be abandoned, when poor implementations are blamed on its 'fundamental impracticality', rather than its poor implementation or the lack of understanding of those attempting to adapt it.

QFD needs other good management practice to deliver benefits (see Chapter 14) and it also benefits from the best management practice to make those benefits even better. Whatever new ideas come along, they will need good planning and design – and good planning and design will always need other good practice to fulfil its dreams.

The purpose of this appendix is to look at aspects of current management thinking, and to show how QFD can work effectively with them, and through that to stimulate the reader to think through how QFD can guide and harness other management concepts and thinking as they develop over time.

QFD and Agility

The biggest barrier to agility is not the lack of resources to apply to a new project or opportunity – it is not knowing the implications of those resources, or that opportunity, on existing plans and commitments.

To the novice, the existence of a clearly thought through structure like QFD would imply a lack of flexibility to adapt to new opportunities. The converse is true. At one level, for an organisation that wants to be agile from the outset, QFD provides a means to think through how best to structure and manage the organisation such that its goals of 'agility' are best supported. At an entirely different level, for the organisation facing a new and unexpected opportunity, QFD provides a way to quickly think through the consequences of change, and to communicate adjustments succinctly and accurately with the minimum of unwanted side effects.

The supposedly 'agile' organisation that lacks good design, is either massively inefficient in the first place, or is probably destined for a fall.

QFD and the Balanced Scorecard

QFD benefits tremendously from any good measurement system. My own preference has been the Quadrant Chart (see Chapter 24) because of its focus on analysis and action, and because of the ease with which measures can be linked to the objectives on the QFD.

However, because of their existing competence with the Balanced Scorecard, some organisations have used these to drive their QFD, and an example of this can be found on page 449.

The key advantage of the Balanced Scorecard is that it ensures that measures are identified in all areas that are a factor in the ultimate health of an organisation, and it does so by proposing four empirically correct measurement areas. QFD, by virtue of the process by which the objectives are developed, also ensures that measures are identified in all the crucial areas, but it does so in a way that is specific to your organisation. Of course, there is no harm at all in using the Balanced Scorecard as a checklist to ensure that whatever measures you do ultimately identify, cover the four areas of: Finance, Customer, People and Innovation/Process.

QFD and Customer Focus Programmes

QFD also goes by the name: 'The voice of the customer'. In product design the left-hand side of the QFD (the objectives) is explicitly drawn from customer interviews using customer phrases, and the purpose of the QFD diagram is to translate this 'voice of the customer' into a clear performance specification for the product.

In Organisation QFD, the 'customers' reflect a far wider range of stakeholders, and it is important to keep these expectations of the organisation in balance with its long-term vision. But the left-hand side of the QFD provides an excellent opportunity not only to emphasise customers, but also to ensure that this emphasis is translated down into an appropriate response from all the top-level (and lower-level) processes.

Customer focus can also be reflected in the weighting given to the objectives. In the examples we have used of organisational QFDs, the weighting of the objectives has been a single column with a simple 1 to 5 scale. In Product QFDs the weighting scale has evolved into a number of columns reflecting different aspects of importance, such as: customer perception; market leverage; and performance gap, which are then multiplied together to form a compound weighting. For a slightly more detailed explanation, please see page 484.

QFD and Knowledge Management

Knowledge Management is described as 'The leveraging of collective wisdom to increase responsiveness and innovation' (Knowledge Management Yearbook 1999-2000). It covers all aspects of assimilating, accessing, combining and using knowledge; whether human, technical or organisational; whether conscious or intrinsic. For some organisations, knowledge management has been translated into the knowledge repository systems and the cultures that encourage their use, but the original concept is far wider than that.

QFD provides an excellent vehicle for both using and driving knowledge management. The construction of the QFD diagram itself forces the assimilation, sharing and combination of the knowledge of the organisation. And the deployment of objectives into processes, drives their systematic refinement, thereby harnessing the knowledge and creativity of the people into the very fabric of the organisation, its processes and systems. Finally QFD, and its documentation, provide guidance for specific information/people systems to ensure that their design is focused on the organisations objectives, and that their performance is objectively managed.

QFD is Knowledge Management in a very real and living sense. It drives learning, and it drives the relationships that make use of that learning.

QFD and the Learning Organisation

The above section clearly outlines QFD's role in the 'learning by assimilation' aspects of the learning organisation, but there is also another vitally important aspect to the learning organisation, and that is to ensure that 'learning by accommodation' takes place. To illustrate the differences between these two types of learning: assimilation is where new information can be accepted into an existing mental model without distorting it; accommodation is where the learner has to accept that his or her mental models are wrong and need to change. In short, learning by assimilation is not threatening, while learning by accommodation can be a very humbling experience.

In fact, learning by accommodation can be quite painful, and we therefore tend to continue to work with flawed mental models well past the point when we should have accepted that they need to change. And the more we invest in shoring up our mental models and denying that we have a problem, the harder it ultimately tends to be to face up to the fact that we are wrong and need to change.

QFD, when used in conjunction with a good measurement reporting system like quadrant charts, helps this process by forcing the learner to recognise the need for change early. The clarity of the targets and the reality of the measures flag up issues in a way that forces early realisation of the issue, and encourages change at a point well before 'backing-down' really becomes an issue.

QFD and Total Quality Management (TQM)

QFD is ideally suited to support TQM. My own initial adoption of QFD was to address shortcomings in the TQM work I was undertaking. All too often, I saw massive investments in TQM fail because, although people within the organisation had become well versed in TQ techniques, their senior management failed to recognise the implications of this for their own role.

QFD was a means to get senior management to move their thinking up a level, and to make space for people to grow beneath them. Working through QFD provided an opportunity for management to take a more objective look at the design of their business; and it provided a clear structure and goals in which those people who were equipped with TQ skills could really make use of them.

QFD and Business Process Re-engineering (BPR)

Business Process Re-engineering (BPR) is a set of tools and principles for removing inefficiency from key business processes, and for focusing them on their objectives. In an early incarnation, the proposed approach was somewhat dramatic, but subsequently the approach was developed to make better use of what already existed in the organisation. A common dimension of most BPR implementations is IT systems.

QFD provides a clear context for BPR. Once the key business processes have been identified (Chapter 8), the grid of the QFD, and the cascade approach, ensure that the objectives of each process are made clear, and that the results are managed against what was first agreed. Within the QFD, stretching goals can be set, and the grid discussions provide guidance on where real benefits can be gained from BPR, and where an incremental approach may be more appropriate.

QFD thus provides a framework in which the work on BPR can be integrated and harmonised with the rest of the business.

QFD and Competencies

One of my earliest applications of QFD was on the subject of Competencies. A well-known news organisation was undergoing a major restructuring that placed a whole new set of demands on their people. We used QFD to help them articulate what those demands might be, and then to map out the key competencies that the different roles would need in order to fulfil those demands. QFD was excellent at helping them to think through and design appropriate competency sets.

Within that particular organisation, the QFD on competencies was done as an isolated exercise. However, where organisational QFDs exist, it is significantly easier to accurately identify the expectations of any role, and thereby to develop appropriate competency QFDs. Furthermore, the roof of the QFD provides an opportunity to think through how teamwork can be used to combine and deploy the competencies effectively and efficiently.

QFD and Emotional Intelligence (EQ)

Emotional Intelligence (often shortened to EQ to reflect a parallel perspective to IQ – Intelligence Quotient) is the ability to monitor and discern emotions, both our own and other people's, and to use that understanding to guide appropriate and effective responses.

In and of itself, QFD has very little to offer EQ directly. However, indirectly, QFD provides an environment in which EQ can be drawn on, developed and nurtured. From the outset, the discussions around developing the QFD provide an excellent opportunity for people to use, monitor, develop and provide feedback on EQ skills.

Further to this, the resulting clarity of objectives and issues, removes a lot of the noise and confusion from interpersonal interactions, and so EQ issues are easier to identify and address.

Finally, the dependency on teambuilding and empowerment within the QFD-driven organisation will help to discern poor management in all regards, including EQ, so that appropriate support can be put in place.

QFD and Complexity

Complexity is the boundary between logic and chaos. Logic is the arena where events can be analysed and predicted with a reasonable degree of accuracy, and so models of operation can be developed and used to guide thought and action. Chaos is the arena where events are discontinuous and defy rational explanation.

Complexity then is the grey area between them, where patterns are beginning to be discernable, but models are not yet capable of accurately predicting outcomes. In complexity, small entities exhibit non-random behaviour as they come together in a state of interdependence.

This 'self-organising' aspect of complexity is what particularly interests business thinkers. It is an area, beyond the reach of our current thinking, where new insights can be gained and new theories formed, and complexity is the means to navigate through it. It is the means to achieve success where conventional planning would be too cumbersome, and prey to the uncertainties involved.

But it is very important to note that complexity is the means to convert what we do not understand into what we do understand, and not vice versa.

QFD provides the means to differentiate between those parts of the business that are to be managed logically, and those parts where complexity is to be explored. It provides the mechanism to objectively evaluate success, and the framework to gradually incorporate the resulting models as they develop. It provides the structure to maintain what we do understand, while we experiment with what we don't.

QFD and Benchmarking

The QFD model lends itself to providing a very clear focus to benchmarking activities and data. The clarity of processes and objectives provides excellent guidance on where benchmarking may be most profitably pursued, and the basic diagram can be enhanced to reflect benchmark data. For a slightly more detailed explanation, please see Appendix 5.

QFD and Non-Linearity

The relationship between QFD and Non-Linearity was covered at the end of Chapter 22.

QFD is simply a tool for thinking through what you are trying to do and how you are trying to do it. As such it has much to offer management and little to condemn it as a management fashion. It is my fervent hope that the examples above have illustrated that the limitations of QFD are far more likely to be found in its blind and narrow application, than intrinsically in the nature of tool itself.

APPENDIX 7: TOOLS AVAILABLE THROUGH THE WEBSITE WWW.TESSERACTS.COM

Over the past decade, we have gained a lot of experience in the practical application of QFD and systematic approaches, in a wide variety of organisations.

As a result of this, a lot of the materials that you might need to support your own implementation of the ideas contained in this book have already been created. To save you time and effort, these have been made available through the website:

www.tesseracts.com

which also provides further expansion of many of the ideas outlined in this book. The materials are available free of charge to all owners of this book, to support their work on implementing QFD within their own organisations, providing they are willing to abide by the terms and conditions outlined in Appendix 8.

The materials are outlined in lists at the end of each section, and these lists are reproduced below.

The material is provided 'as-is' in good faith. All of the materials provide a good platform for anybody who has read and understood this book, and who has a good working knowledge of Microsoft Office™, to adapt and develop to suit their particular situation. Tesseract Management Systems is not organised to provide technical support on these materials (it is not on their QFD!).

In addition, the author has made most of the diagrams and some sections of the text of this book available to support training and communication activities. These too are available through the above website.

In support of Section A

Presentation and workshop materials

- Why-How charting and how it works
- The concept of business design
- The 'top-box' role of management, and its responsibilities
- Surveying current management practice
- Introduction to QFD
- Competition question
- Group of scientists question

Survey materials

- Customer interview & questionnaire forms
- Employee interview & questionnaire forms

In support of Section B

Presentation and workshop materials

- The concept of business processes
- Process ownership and its responsibilities
- Process visioning
- Performance Measurement

- Process Mapping
- Developing effective measures & targets
- Defining processes for the organisation

Templates and tools
- Session Plan
- Process Proposal
- QFD model

In support of Section C

Presentation and workshop materials
- Developing Process Proposals
- Template for 'Managing Upwards'
- Process Management
- Process Proposal reconciliation

Guidelines
- Time Management

Templates and tools
- Self Assessment vs. Systematic Approach
- Session Plan for Process Management Meetings
- Quadrant Chart Template

In support of Section D

Presentation and workshop materials
- Developing Vision
- Developing a personal QFD

Templates and tools
- TOP-BOX planning form
- 'Drawing out the Systematic' checksheet
- Personal evaluation form
- Personal QFD Template

In support of Section E

Guidelines
- Problem-solving Training Materials
- Problem-solving Guide
- Problem-solving Tools
- Problem-solving Exercise

Presentation and workshop materials
- Developing the 'Roof' of the QFD
- Managing the management meeting

Templates and tools
- Template for automatic Quadrant Chart
- Session plan for Management meetings

In support of Section F

Presentation and workshop materials
- Review and Audit slides
- Spring Cleaning Slides

Miscellaneous
- Diagrams contained in this book
- Excerpts of the Text
- Excerpts of the Novel
- Excerpts of the Appendices

APPENDIX 8: USE OF COPYRIGHT MATERIALS

Code of practice for using 'Tesseract Management Systems' copyright materials

The web-based materials, outlined in Appendix 7, contain much of the contents of this book, and are the property and copyright of Tesseract Management Systems Limited, and of the Author.

Tesseract Management Systems have given permission for these materials to be used in support of the work described in 'Managing by Design', providing the user complies in full with the 'Conditions of Use Agreement' described on the associated website.

The following is an outline of the main points of that agreement:

...within your own organisation

The rightful owner of a copy of the book 'Managing by Design' may view, copy, modify, present, or circulate the materials provided on the website, for use within their own organisation, as part of a non-commercial arrangement, providing:

- All copies of the material contain the Tesseract Management Systems copyright message.

- Any use of the materials clearly acknowledges their original source

- The person copying, using or presenting the materials has read the book in its entirety

- The materials are used solely in support of the work and ideas described in the book

- The user assumes full responsibility and risk of loss resulting from the use of these materials, and will indemnify Tesseract Management Systems Limited against any risk of legal action arising therefrom.

...to support a third party organisation

The rightful owner of a copy of the book 'Managing by Design' may view, copy, modify, present, or circulate the materials provided on the website in supporting a third party (client) organisation on a commercial basis, providing:

- All the conditions listed above, regarding use within an organisation, are met, and...

- The 'client' is provided with a copy of the book 'Managing by Design'

- All materials supplied to the client are of professional quality

- The user is an experienced consultant with well developed analysis, planning and facilitation skills, and a good understanding of the client's business

- The materials are used as part of a contracted programme of work to ensure the 'client' becomes self sufficient in some or all aspects of the work described in the book

- The user's experience (or lack of it) in applying the materials in similar situations, is made explicitly clear to the client in the contract document

- Any supplementary materials developed by the user, and used in support of the 'client' in this work, are made freely available to the 'client' for their use in continuing this work themselves

- The 'user' does not claim any official relationship with, or approval from, Tesseract Management Systems, nor is such implied

- Ten percent of the commercial revenue arising from the use of these materials is paid to charity via the Peinao Trust, Account B10130103, Charities Aid Foundation, Kings Hill, West Malling, Kent, ME19 4TA, England – all such proceeds will be used to benefit suffering people throughout the world through officially recognised charities (see below)

- The 'user' assumes full responsibility and risk of loss resulting from the use of these materials. In no event will Tesseract Management Systems Limited be liable to any party for any direct, indirect, incidental, special, exemplary, consequential, or other damages

In the event of any disparity between this brief overview, and the detail of the agreement on the www.tessracts.com website, the wording of the agreement on the website applies.

About the Peinao Trust (Peinao is the Greek word for hunger)

The Peinao Trust seeks to financially support and encourage other charities in their work to alleviate the causes and effects of physical, emotional or spiritual hardship throughout the world. The trust recognises that physical and emotional hardships often arise, or are sustained, as a result of spiritual deficiencies elsewhere (such as greed, hate or selfishness) and therefore places special emphasis on those charities which seek to equip and inspire their beneficiaries to go on to help others, or who attempt to address the systemic causes of hardship. 100% of all monies received by the Peinao Trust are passed on to charities that meet the above criteria, and which can demonstrate that the money they receive from Peinao is used directly and productively to benefit those in need.

The financial affairs of the Peinao Trust, and a complete list of its beneficiaries, will be posted annually on the www.tesseracts.com website on March 31st each year.

Appendix 9: A Brief Guide to Consensus Reaching

Consensus can be described as unanimous individual agreement to implement and fully support a decision, even when some or all of the participants may have preferred a different conclusion.

In reaching a decision, it would be great if everybody agreed whole-heartedly with the conclusion, and were fully committed to making it happen.

Sadly, such a situation rarely arises, and for good reason. Often there is a lot of uncertainty in the process of reaching a conclusion: key pieces of data are missing or incomplete; implications and future conditions cannot be forecast accurately; people distort subjective data with their own perceptions; and side-effects are often unforeseen. And yet a decision still has to be made – sometimes the only really wrong decision is to delay the decision until all the facts are available.

As a result of all the uncertainty, it is quite common for people to disagree with the conclusion because they hold a different perspective, either on the likely outcome of the missing data, or because they have a different perspective on the probable implications and their importance. The danger is that this can lead them to be unsupportive of the conclusion, and to feel vindicated when they are proved right when the decision fails (sometimes more due to lack of support than to flawed guesswork on the data).

Lack of support for a decision is often a bigger problem in practice than inaccuracy. Where the decision is fully supported, it is very clear when the facts are at variance to the assumptions. But where the decision is poorly supported, it is not always clear whether the problems are due to flawed assumptions, or a lack of support – and so politics arise, and feedback isn't trusted, and poor decisions are pushed way past the point when they should have been abandoned. And good decisions miss out on vital corrections that could save them.

But how do you get full support when the data aren't available? The answer is 'by process'. People are usually willing to support a collective decision, even when on balance they feel it is likely to be wrong, if it has been arrived at by what they see as a good and fair process. Consensus reaching is such a process.

The principles that underpin consensus reaching are simple.

- All pertinent information needs to be understood by all decision makers.
- Everybody needs to feel that they have had a fair and complete hearing.
- When all the information is known and understood by everybody, the majority viewpoint is most likely to be the right one.

The process is simply a matter of arriving at this point.

The way that this is achieved is relatively simple too.

- The process (and reasons) for consensus reaching are outlined, and the group agrees to abide by the process.
- A clear and unambiguous proposal is made to the group.
- The protagonist lays out clearly and concisely the reasons for their proposal, being careful to stick to objective information as far as possible.
- A straw poll is taken for who are in agreement with the proposal and who are against it, so that any facilitator can see where to bring in other perspectives.
- If everybody is in agreement, then the proposal is carried.
- If one or more people are against the proposal, they are invited to provide their reasons, once again in clear, concise, objective terms.
- Other new pieces of information are placed before the group as people present them, and each time the facilitator should check that everybody is hearing and understanding what is being said.
- Repeated or restated information is discouraged because of its potential to discourage listening and generate argument. People are trusted that they listened to things the first time they were said.
- Emotive language and arguments that tie people's conclusions to their character (such as 'only an idiot would agree to this') are discouraged.
- When no new arguments are forthcoming, the group is asked to confirm that they have made and heard all the arguments, and that nobody will be making their decision on anything that has not been said round the table.
- People are asked if they are willing to abide by, and fully support, the majority decision. If they are not, such issues must be addressed before any vote is taken.
- A vote is taken, and the majority view is taken as the decision.

Consensus tends to work very well because it is fair, but it often needs good facilitation or chairmanship to work properly. People abide by the majority decision because they know that a decision is necessary, and they know that this is the fairest way of delivering it. It takes a fairly arrogant person to believe they are right when they are in a minority amongst their peers, and when their peers are in possession of all the facts. Sometimes the group does contain an expert, but we tend to find that in these cases the group is swayed by the expert unless there is good reason not to be.

An example of consensus reaching can be found in Chapter 9 of the novel.

APPENDIX 10: A BRIEF GUIDE TO REVIEW AND AUDIT

"The seeds of every company's demise are contained in its business plan"

Fred Adler, CEO, Adler & Co. Inc Magazine, February 1987

Once you have established QFD effectively within your organisation, it will efficiently and relentlessly drive the pursuit of the goals that you have set. But while it is doing so, the world moves on and the goal posts shift. And your thinking moves on; you see things differently, and often more clearly.

Your QFD may, in a few short months, represent a future you no longer fully believe in. If you do not remain alert to this possibility, you may find that you have invested a vast amount of effort in a large white elephant (with black spots).

Some people use this reasoning as an excuse to avoid planning in the first place. But people who never engage their brains, are even more ineffective than those who engage their brains to start with and then switch them off. The important thing is to keep thinking all the way through; to establish QFD, and then to periodically review it against your developing understanding, and against your ever changing environment.

In this chapter we will look at two types of review:

- annual review, to provide the opportunity for a total rethink
- spring cleaning, to fix specific issues

Annual review

The annual review provides an opportunity to review your QFD, and further develop it so that it continues to drive your organisation to its full potential.

- To reassess the logic in your Why-How chart, and to agree new objectives and targets.
- To reconsider the processes of your organisation, and develop a model that provides more insight and leverage.
- To identify new design opportunities within those processes, and to set process objectives that ensure they will be fulfilled.
- To re-harness your organisation to another year of transformational performance.

It is not essential that you totally redevelop your QFD every year, but you should at least face up to the question as to whether it would help your organisation it you did so.

Reconsidering your original Why-How chart, provides the opportunity for you and your team to reflect on how much your situation has changed, and whether you can simply establish new performance targets for the coming year, or whether you would benefit from a total reconsideration of the nature of your role and your objectives.

And by reflecting on your process model, your team can consider how much potential improvement is available by continuing to see the business in this way, or whether changes to the model will provide even more potential for resolving inefficiency and driving up performance.

The result of exploring these issues will help you to determine whether you need to develop a whole new QFD grid, or whether you just need to introduce new ideas and understanding into the old one.

Whatever you decide to do in the top-level QFD, reconsidering the process columns will provide each part of the organisation a chance to think through how radically they wish to redefine their own role.

This annual review cycle provides an opportunity, not only to reset the direction and thrust of the organisation, but also to learn from how well change has been managed.

By preceding the annual review with an audit of how well the implementation of QFD and systematic approaches has taken place, the available lessons can be collated into improvements in management as well as improvements in the organisation; a sort of top-box over the top-box. In this way management can regularly improve not only what they do, but also how they do it.

The audit can be effected by using some of the tools described in Chapter 5.

Spring cleaning

Subsequent to each reworking of the QFD, your people will gain new understanding of the business as they work to implement its conclusions. Some of these insights will cast doubt on some of the premises contained within the QFD. In most cases this may only be a small proportion of the QFD, but failing to correct the resulting inaccuracy may prove a major hurdle to progress.

On the other hand, constantly altering the QFD every time new insight is gained, can create uncertainty and confusion, and can mean that longer-term improvement projects lose direction and impetus.

The challenge then is to maintain the QFD with sufficient accuracy such that it remains a valid driver of the business, and yet maintain sufficient stability in its conclusions that teams can practically work on achieving it.

Spring cleaning provides a means to do exactly that. One day, scheduled some three months after the completion of the QFD, in which those parts of the QFD that have been proposed as major barriers to progress are reconsidered and adjusted by the team. In a spring cleaning session, the objective of stability is clearly spelled out, and only individual items of the QFD, proposed in advance and with clearly defined arguments circulated before the meeting, are open to being changed.

In practice this means that only those aspects of the QFD that have to change are changed, and often this is only one or two measures, the odd definition, and about 5% of the cells.

An example of spring cleaning can be found on page 464.

APPENDIX 11: BIBLIOGRAPHY

The application of QFD to organisations is still fairly new, and is sadly not at all widespread. In Japan and America it is sometimes applied as part of Hoshin planning: a process of cascading strategic intent into improvement actions – Yoji Akao was the architect of both Hoshin Planning and QFD in Japan, and Glenn Mazur has been a driving force in getting both approaches adopted in the USA. Very little has been written regarding its application to the holistic design and management of organisations, but some relevant papers do exist and I am grateful to Tony Lowe in the UK for his research of the subject, and for bringing most of the following to my attention.

- QFD for Small Business – Mazur – Proceedings of the 6th Symposium on QFD, Novi, Michigan, 1994
- Strategic Policy Management for Small and Medium Enterprises – Mazur – International Symposium on QFD, Sydney, 1998
- Organisations Can Apply QFD as Strategic Planning Tool – Maddux, Amos & Wyskida – Industrial Engineering, September 1991
- Using QFD in Business Planning at a Small Appraisal Firm – Susan & William Ferrell – The Appraisal Journal, July 1994
- QFD in Strategic Planning – Lyman, Buesinger & Keating – Quality Digest, May 1994
- Policy Management through QFD – Sullivan – Quality Progress, June 1988
- Using QFD to Align Business Strategies and Business Processes with Customer Needs – Barnard – Transactions from 4th Symposium on QFD, 1992
- UK User's Guide to QFD – Lowe & Ridgway – Engineering Management Journal, June 2000
- The Road Map to Repeatable Success – Bicknell & Bicknell – CRC Press, 1995

For those wishing to explore the subject of QFD further, the definitive texts on the tool itself are probably as follows.

- QFD and CWQC in Japan – Masao, Kogure & Akao – Quality Progress, October 1983
- Listening to the Voice of the Customer – King – National Productivity Review, 1987
- The House of Quality – Hauser & Clausing – Harvard Business Review, May-June 1988

- Quality Function Deployment: How to Make QFD Work for You – Cohen – Addison-Wesley Publishing, 1985

In the context of this book, QFD has been a pivotal tool in transforming the performance of a number of organisations and management teams. But it is just a tool (albeit an extremely powerful one), and I have endeavoured to present it in the context of the management thinking and disciplines that are vital to harnessing the creative power and focus that it can unleash.

In creating an effective management context to QFD, I would specifically like recommend the following books which have been influential in my own thinking, either in stimulating a new line of thought or in confirming my existing prejudices (both of which can be useful at times).

- The Fifth Discipline, The Art and Practice of a Learning Organisation – Senge – Century Business, 1990
- The Learning Company – Pedler, Burgoyne & Boydell – McGraw-Hill, 1991
- The Manager's Book of Quotations – Eigen & Siegel – Amacom, 1989
- The Seven Habits of Highly Effective People – Covey – Simon and Schuster, 1989
- The NIV Study Bible – International Bible Society – Hodder & Stoughton, 1987
- The Dilbert Principle – Adams – Boxtree, 1996

And in support of specific areas of a systematic approach to management, you might like to reflect on the following texts and papers (ordered according to the six principles outlined in this book).

Purpose

- The PIMS Principles – Buzzell & Gale – Free Press, 1987
- Managing the Delight Factor – Lynch – IFS International Limited, 1993
- Corporate Imagination and Expeditionary Marketing – Hamel & Prahalad – Harvard Business Review, July 1991
- Marketing Intangible Products and Product Intangibles – Levitt – Harvard Business Review, May 1981

Philosophy

- Gods of Management – Handy – Pan, 1985
- The Living Company – de Geus – Nicholas Brealey Publishing, 1997
- Strategy as Stretch and Leverage – Hamel & Prahalad – Harvard Business Review, March 1993

People

- The Tao of Coaching – Landsberg – Harper Collins Business, 1997
- The One Minute Manager Meets the Monkey – Blanchard, Oncken & Burrows – Harper Collins Business, 1994
- The One Minute Manager Builds High Performing Teams – Blanchard, Carew & Parisi-Carew – Harper Collins, 1992
- Talk Language – Pease – Positive Paperbacks, 1989

Process

- Competing Against Time – Stalk & Hout – Free Press, 1990
- Business Process Analysis – Darnton & Darnton – International Thomson Business Press, 1997
- The Profit Zone – Slywotzky & Morrison – Wiley, 1998

Predict

- Benchmarking, The Search for Industry Best Practices – Camp – ASQC Quality Press, 1989
- Six Thinking Hats – de Bono – Pelican, 1985
- Techniques of Structured Problem Solving, Second Edition – Van Gundy – Van Nostrand Reinhold, 1988
- The Memory Jogger Plus – Brassard – Goal/QPC, 1996
- A Quality Harvest – Lowell Jay Arthur – Quality Progress, April 1993
- The Balanced Scorecard - Measures that Drive Performance – Kaplan & Norton – Harvard Business Review, January 1992

Perfect

- Po: Beyond Yes and No – de Bono – Pelican, 1972
- Business Beyond the Box – O'Keefe – Nicholas Brealey Publishing, 1999
- Teaching Smart People How to Learn – Argyris – Harvard Business Review, May 1991
- Evolution and Revolution as Organisations Grow – Greiner – Harvard Business Review, May 1998
- Building a Learning Organisation – Garbin – Harvard Business Review, July 1993

APPENDIX 12: WHAT IS THE MOTIVATION FOR THIS BOOK?

The Author of this book is unashamedly a Christian. Should that worry you? Should that affect the credibility you extend to what is written in these pages?

I believe the answer to both of these questions is 'no', and the purpose of this section of the appendices is to offer you some additional assurance that this is the case, and to provide some insight into why this book has been written, and why so much material has been made freely available in support of it.

My perspective is that the main reason it might worry you, is that questions concerning the judgement and emotional maturity of someone who espouses what might seem from the modern perspective to be a antiquated superstition. Some years ago that was very much my own perspective, together with a few more less charitable judgements I am sorry to admit to.

Since then, it will probably be obvious to the reader that I have changed my mind, and this book is part of the outworking of that, for reasons that will become clear later on.

Despite my life choices, I would dearly like to retain your respect for two main reasons: the first is that I am affected by what people think of me; and the second, and more important reason, is that the value you get out of this book will in large part be determined by the confidence you place in what it says.

Why would a sane and rational person believe in profane and irrational things?

It is true that many people come to Christianity during periods of emotional and psychological weakness, and often in a state of some desperation, but that does not mean that faith itself is only for the weak and desperate, it just means that faith provides answers which supports people through times of weakness and desperation. It does not mean that is all there is to it, and it does not mean that those are the only people you will find within it.

My own journey has been somewhat different. And as I look back over it, I see that there were three crucial questions that I had to work through, both academically and psychologically. These were:

- Does our grasp of science, technology and logic describe everything in the world, or are there things that are still beyond our understanding, and maybe even beyond our awareness?

- If there are things beyond our awareness, could they really be a factor in the creation of our universe, and thereby in forming me and who I am? And if that is so, what should be my response to that?

- Amongst such a plethora of possible answers to the above question, how can I even begin to identify the right answer?

The fact that I personally was unable to answer unequivocally the first two questions, led me to wrestle with the third. And in addition, there is a fourth question which I continue to wrestle with today:

- If I am right in my conclusions to the above three questions, why is there so much around me that appears to point to them being wrong?

Perhaps the above questions are enough to convince you that I have not stumbled into Christianity blindly, but for those of you who would like to understand a little more, I have included my own conclusions on those questions on the web-site associated with this book. But before you read them, I would like to make the following point clear: they are only my own personal conclusions, and should not be taken in any way as *the answer*.

Why has this book been written, and supporting material been made freely available?

I do believe that the above questions are good for anybody to engage with, but if they do, it is important that they identify their own answers for themselves.

I believe that people grow when they honestly and earnestly wrestle with questions bigger than themselves, and as they grow, they add value to the world – not necessarily in the form of answers, but in the form of empathy, understanding, forgiveness, support and encouragement; the very things that combat greed, resentment, intolerance, hate and all the things that make our world a worse place. As we wrestle with the big questions, we learn to build relationships rather than to destroy them; we equip ourselves to embrace and repair them, rather than to escape by rejecting them.

But all too often, we hide from the big questions. We are frightened by the implications of their conclusions and we feel ill-equipped to address them, so we push them to the back of our minds and we busy ourselves with smaller details which distract us from the big questions. And as a result, we don't learn techniques to tackle the big questions, and we don't build up experience in them, and so the situation continues.

Sometimes of course, we have big questions thrust upon us, such as: 'What is friendship?' or 'What is parenthood?' or 'What do I become when the person who loves me is no longer there?' and through working our way appropriately through these questions, we grow. But sometimes, faced with such questions and being so unfamiliar with them, we still hide from them when they are thrust upon us – and at this point we can be in danger of retreating further inside ourselves, further away from growth and relationships and the things that fulfil us as human beings.

It should be clear to anybody reading this that I believe that people benefit from actively engaging with questions like: 'Why?'

I believe, and have demonstrated, that organisations benefit from engaging with such questions too, and in some small way, this book is intended to support and build on this process within your organisation, but in doing so, my fervent hope is that it will achieve four things.

- Firstly, it will give those who work with it, practice in wrestling with such questions, and build their confidence in doing so.

- Secondly, through the practical benefits that result, it will demonstrate the value of asking such questions and build a commitment to doing so.

- Thirdly, that the result of using these approaches will remove some of the clutter of the small detail questions that distract us from the big questions.

- Fourthly, that having gained confidence in the relatively safe environment of work, people will begin to extend such challenges to their personal and spiritual lives.

If this book at least does something toward achieving that, then I will have achieved riches beyond that which money can buy. I will have built a new relationship, and that new relationship will do something to add value to the world.

I am sorry it sounds trite and naïve, but as Richard discovered in the book – sometimes the Devil owns all the sophistication.

Yours, with God's love,

Michael

APPENDIX 13: ACKNOWLEDGEMENTS

The development and application of QFD to business situations has been a privilege and a source of great satisfaction for me over the past decade, and the opportunity to write this book has proven to be the icing on the cake. I feel particularly blessed by my experiences, and eternally grateful to those who have helped to create them, and have helped to navigate me through them. And this is my opportunity to acknowledge some of those contributions publicly.

Amongst so many that have influenced my thinking, I would particularly like to thank Peter Diplock and Michael Slade for first bringing the tool of QFD to my attention; Jürgen Maier for working with me to develop the first application of QFD to business; David Winder for the vision and opportunity to develop a complete management system based on QFD; Dilip and Bharat Popat for their encouragement and support in applying QFD as a solution to complex business situations; Len Pendle, Dave Rawlings, Mark Richardson and Jonathon Chappel for helping me to develop the concepts that anchor QFD into a systemic approach; and Dietmar Harteveld for demonstrating the power of Quadrant Charts in support of QFD and for his particular words of encouragement at times when I needed them. I would also like to thank fellow travellers: Helen Cole; Kevin Downes; Johan Verhoeven; Amanda Studd; Phil Mitchell; Tracy Tomlin; Chris Stockdale; Diana O'Reardon; Angus Martin; Barry Veal; Tim McGuire; Paul Reid and Susan Baulch who have at various times shared the load of helping and encouraging others to apply many of the concepts contained in this book.

I hadn't realised, until after it was too late, how much work was involved in translating what has been written into what can be read. And so, for ploughing through earlier versions and for providing copious feedback, I thank again many of those listed above, and also Hywel Benjamin, Andrew Bolton, Win Brooke, Peter Cresswell, Malcolm Denham, Peter Desmond, James Griffin, Kelvin Heywood, Andrew Jackson, Roy Knight, Martin Lane, Dave Lawson, Gareth Lloyd-Jones, Chandra Lodhia, Chris Martin, Chris Merkin, David Newey, Graham Phillips, Martin and Sarah Price, Phil Ranson, Peter Strode, Andy Withers, and in particular Ann Marshal for her continuing, tireless, advice, encouragement and prayers.

And, on the home front, I would like to thank my wife Joanne, and my children Alison and Ian, for making many sacrifices to allow me to do the work I love.

Finally, I would like to thank God for the strange set of circumstances that led to this book, and for the sense of purpose, peace and tranquillity that enabled me to use those circumstances productively.

APPENDIX 14: GLOSSARY AND INDEX

Abstraction 30
The process of making an idea less specific by broadening its application to a wider set, e.g. from 'cars' to 'motor vehicles' or from 'paint' to 'surface coating'

Activity 108, 114, 120, 304, 310, 312, 314
A specific sequence of actions, normally undertaken by an individual or small team, which result in a change in the state, location, or potential of a particular thing (item, person, information…)

Adoption 72, 170, 190, 246, 366, 414
The process of making a particular set of actions or behaviours part of an individual's or organisation's normal routine

Affinity diagram 447, 468
A simple mechanism for quickly sorting ideas or other pieces of information into manageable groups

Agenda 94, 140, 144, 146, 344
A list of topics and associated timings which define the intended sequence and schedule of a meeting or other people-based event

Align 152, 252, 346
The process of ensuring that all the people, processes and policies are headed in the same direction toward the same goal, thereby minimising effort wasted in confusion and inefficiency

Alliance 398
A partnership between two or more organisations using different strengths in each of them to achieve a common goal or enhance their individual performance/potential

Ambition 72, 196, 198
A specific expectation or intent, set at some point in the future, to achieve more or perform better than is currently the case

Analysis 48, 62, 126, 178, 242, 334, 390
The process of breaking down a situation, event or entity to understand the main factors and underlying reasons that make it what it is, or prevent it from being what it is not

Analytical 60, 62, 64, 358
Having a nature of analysis

Animation 132
A feature within some presentation software (such as Microsoft PowerPoint) where events (such as items appearing, or slides changing) can be set to occur automatically after a defined period of time has elapsed

Annual review 74
A discipline whereby the manner and extent of an organisation's progress over the previous year is objectively surveyed and analysed to identify key learning points for the next year

Appointment 122, 146
The process of contracting with an individual to undertake a specified role with defined responsibilities, resources and terms of reference, for agreed rewards (salary, benefits, bonus…)

Aspiration 28, 102, 196, 388
A desired level of performance or achievement that is in excess of what is currently being attained

Audit 76
The process of evaluating existing practices against a defined standard in order to identify instances of deficiency or risk

Authority 120, 122, 138, 156, 176, 178, 262
The power to make decisions and incur their implications on behalf of an organisation

Balance 362, 366
The fourth step of PROBLEM: Collating a (set of) solution(s) to a problem into a cost effective plan of action which appropriately addresses both long and short term needs

Balanced scorecard 449, 490
A format for reporting key organisational performance measures, which reflects an appropriate balance of financial and non-financial factors

Balancing 42, 226, 250, 252-262, 282, 314, 326
The process of comparing (and sometimes combining) the impact and/or implications of different options in order to optimise the outcome

Behaviours 188, 238, 246, 288, 304, 324, 328
Consistently repeated actions and/or responses from an individual or group. These are likely to reflect a combination of factors including situation, environment, competence and attitude

Bottom-box 14
Management of an event or outcome by undertaking and/or directly influencing the actions that are currently delivering it

Bureaucratic 140, 152, 236, 392
Associated with excessive levels of reporting and control, the costs of which exceed the observable benefits resulting from them

Burning platform 24, 186
A means of establishing the need for change through making explicit the unacceptable implications of not changing; on occasion, by precipitating those implications

Business 26, 398
A commercial entity which combines the resources of its shareholders and suppliers with the efforts and competence of its staff to meet the needs of its customers

Business context 266, 356
The salient characteristics of a business's environment and the nature of its customers, its competitors, its suppliers, its employee base, its shareholders and its product or service

Business interfaces 62
The boundaries within and around a business where information, services and physical items move from being the responsibility of one group to being the responsibility of another

Business planning 78-88
The process of determining clear objectives for a business, and then developing the strategies and plans (operational, financial, and developmental) to ensure those objectives are achieved

Business process 82, 106, 108, 110, 112, 116, 118, 128
A sequence of activities which transform an input into an output. A repeatable means of delivering a service, an operation or a faculty of the business

Business unit 402, 408, 410
Part of an organisation which operates as a distinct business with its own staff, customers, suppliers and budgets

Car park 142
A simple means of managing important issues that arise, but that are outside the objectives of the meeting, so that they do not disturb the agenda of a meeting

Cascade 404
The process of deploying organisation-level objectives into practical lower-level objectives that are appropriate to guiding and focusing the efforts of teams within the organisation

Catch 22 294
A situation that is impossible to resolve because all perceived solutions are invalidated by the problem. Named after Joseph Heller's book which illustrated the concept

Challenge 164, 204, 284
An expressed need or expectation which requires a demanding improvement in performance for its fulfillment

Champion 270
An individual, usually in a senior position, who commits themselves to promoting and supporting a particular cause at every available opportunity

Closed loop control 70
A means of performance control where feedback is used to adjust the process variables until the desired output is achieved and sustained

Clothes line 100, 204
A method of setting and agreeing targets that uses numbers pegged along a piece of rope to stimulate discussion and facilitate consensus

Coaching 190, 200, 240, 246, 296, 326
A process of one-to-one development of an individual, in which skills and knowledge are transferred in response to emerging needs, that arise from undertaking a challenging task

Commitment 50, 54, 92, 114, 148-170, 198, 216
The determination to ensure that something is achieved, even at the cost of other desired objectives and opportunities if necessary

Committee 28, 94, 152
A group of individuals (or representatives of other groups) who work together to make decisions on common matters, which collectively benefit them and further their individual objectives

Communication 86, 120, 176, 232, 346, 374-380
The process of transferring information between individuals and/or groups and/or organisations. Communication can be in a variety of forms, including written, verbal and electronic

Competence 62, 240, 282, 306, 308
The ability of an individual or group to successfully undertake a specified task or role to a desired standard (quality, time, cost)

Competition 56, 58, 98, 158, 162
A situation where a number of companies compete for the business of potential customers by providing better, cheaper or more convenient solutions than the others

Competition question 56, 58, 98, 162
A simple exercise designed to help identify the most important areas of performance for your organisation

Competitor 58, 214
A business that seeks to attract your current and potential customers away from your products and services and on to theirs (see competition)

Concession 212, 218, 226
A relaxation of the standards, rules or expectations in response to known difficulties, or in order to provide the flexibility necessary to nurture an important project

Confidence 212, 228, 358, 388
The degree of expectation and trust that requirements will be fulfilled and the necessary outcomes delivered in an appropriate manner

Conflict 34, 50, 80, 174, 318-330, 376
A state of tension that arises when two or more incompatible objectives are pursued at the same time, often by different groups of people

Conglomerate 400, 410, 416
An organisation that contains a number of distinctly separate businesses each of which operate in different markets

Congruence 286
Alignment of objectives, will and behaviour, sometimes known as 'walking the talk'

Consensus 100, 102, 116, 144, 204
Unanimous individual agreement to implement and fully support a decision, even when some or all of the participants may have preferred a different conclusion

Consistency 414
The quality of regularly delivering a result with minimal variation in its key features (form, function, quality, timeliness, cost...) either good or bad

Contract 48, 130, 158-164, 208, 220, 328
A formal and often well-defined agreement to exchange one thing of value for another, e.g. money for goods, wages for time, one service for another

Contribution 132, 162
The degree of impact that the outcome of a process can have on the fulfilment of an objective. In the grid of the QFD this is usually estimated on a four-point scale: 'insignificant' to 'critical'

Cost of quality 76
An accounting procedure which evaluates all the wasted time, materials and opportunities in an organisation and reports them in financial terms, often as a % of turnover

Creativity 32, 100, 366
The ability to identify new ways to achieve an objective or eliminate a problem, either by thinking up new solutions, or by finding new applications for existing solutions

Criteria 32, 56, 58, 122, 198, 210, 220
Tests or conditions by which to evaluate an option's suitability (hurdle criteria – whether the condition is met) or relative value (benchmark criteria – how fully a condition is met)

Culture 224, 320-326, 336, 437, 441, 444, 464
A stable, and often self-reinforcing, pattern of behaviours, values and underlying assumptions which collectively reward certain attributes or actions and penalise others

Customer 48, 68, 124, 158, 168, 236-238
The intended recipient or beneficiary of an organisation, process or action. Customers can be external to the organisation or internal (such as another staff member, process or department)

Customer focus 236
A philosophy of ensuring that all action and thought is undertaken in the context of the overall purpose for doing it, through ensuring consideration of the customer's expectations for it

Customer satisfaction 68, 124, 126, 238
The extent to which your products, service and relationship (actual and perceived) are meeting the needs and expectations of your customers

Cynic 324
Someone who is determined only to see and publicise the downsides and risks of a venture and who openly mistrusts, trivialises or makes fun of any positive perspectives

Deficiency 92, 188
A shortfall from the expected or desired standard, for instance where the output performance falls below the target performance

Delegation 192, 294, 408
The process of transferring the authority and responsibility for undertaking a task from one person to another, usually from the manager to a subordinate

Delight 58, 72
An emotional response generated when expectations have been exceeded in such a way that there is a sudden and significant growth in empathy and trust in the relationship

Deploy 28, 90
To apportion responsibility and resources in a structured and logical manner consistent with achieving the overall objective

Design 32-58, 80, 166, 170, 304, 344
The process of determining appropriate configurations of resources (materials, components, facilities, system, information, effort...) to address and fulfil a clearly defined objective

Detail 30-38, 114, 234, 290, 344
The precision of the information that distinguishes one specific thing from other similar things, and the degree of categorisation this provides

Direction 26-40, 50, 238
A sustained, consistent and shared picture of the things that the organisation should be working toward and the ways that it should be developing and improving

Disciplinary process 324, 328
A formal legal means of confirming dissatisfaction with behaviour, of resetting expectations and, ultimately, of applying sanctions for continued poor performance

Discipline 44, 48, 58, 138, 164, 182, 242, 360
A defined methodology, and the expectation that specified activities and situations will be addressed by its systematic application

Discretionary surplus 270, 272
Wealth (tangible and intangible) generated by an organisation that is in excess of that needed to fulfil and sustain the relationships with its key stakeholders

Disenfranchise 180
To diminish or remove the power of any individual or group to influence decisions and direction of the organisation

Distraction 54, 392
Something that diverts attention away from the main objectives or issues

Dormant potential 214
Capability that would be of value to the organisation, but that is not being recognised, developed, and utilised by it

Effective 26-52, 250, 258, 270, 336, 368, 412
Successful at realising and delivering its objective

Efficient 52, 140, 200, 270, 340, 412
Provision of progress or performance with minimal waste (frugal consumption) of resources

Empowerment 330
Development of the ability of an individual or group to take full responsibility for a specific task or role, including the provision of the necessary skills, knowledge,

authority and resources

Environmental stewardship 224
A sense of responsibility for maintaining the quality of the environment through minimising or neutralising any negative impact of the organisation on it

Evaluate 362, 368
The sixth step of PROBLEM: Measuring the impact of the solution on the effects of the problem and comparing this against what is expected

Evaluation 74, 106, 198, 222, 234, 362
Comparison of methods and results against an expected standard

Experimentation 48, 62, 360
The process of adjusting variables in a controlled manner and monitoring the results in order to develop and test hypotheses, thereby increasing understanding and improving performance

Facilitation 36, 146
Assisting the effective and efficient learning and decision making of a group through the provision of a process (sometimes transparently) and through supporting their use of it

Facilities 42, 58, 62, 106, 108, 110, 266
Physical structures, environments, equipment and systems that help the members of the organisation to fulfil their roles and responsibilities

Fire-fighting 64, 178, 358
Focusing on the direct and immediate resolution of current problems and issues, without identifying and addressing the systemic causes of those problems

Fitness 72
The capacity of an organisation to develop the competence and the performance of its people, its teams and its processes

Flag plan 388
An 'improvement focused' derivation of the milestone plan, which forecasts the implications of each milestone on the

intended performance benefits and uses this to evaluate progress

Flipchart   114, 142, 188, 256, 282
A freestanding pad of A1 paper used for recording or presenting ideas and other information in meetings. Completed sheets can be stuck on the walls so that they remain visible to the group

Focus   94-100
A narrowing down of attention from an overview to a specific, intentionally limited, area, with the intention of making faster and/or more robust progress in that area

Forecast   350, 382-392, 408
A considered estimate of future performance or conditions, taking account of the current position, anticipated changes in important factors, and intended progress on plans

Forum   184, 334, 380
A place or event where information and ideas are shared and debated, for example a meeting, a notice board, or a virtual (computer based) community

Framework   68, 74, 82, 218, 278, 370, 374
A structure which provides a logical and operational context to the components which function and interrelate within it

Function   38, 62, 82, 88, 106
A piece of work or service, and sometimes the part of an organisation that fulfils that work or service

Global   46, 102
Relating to the whole world and all the markets and organisations therein

Goals   26-40, 46, 94-102, 270, 282, 298
Articulated accomplishments, status and associated privileges to which the organisation, team or individual aspires but has not yet attained

Goal-setting   26, 168, 236, 374, 382
The process of determining and agreeing goals

Grid   128-136, 310, 312, 374, 376
A matrix of columns and rows used for exploring and recording relationships between different sets of things; in the case of QFD it is between the set of processes and the set of objectives

Ground rules   132, 138, 142, 326
A short, simple set of rules agreed by the participants in a meeting, for the purpose of ensuring that the interactions within the meeting are healthy and productive

Harmony   88, 374, 400
A sense of fellowship that evolves when two groups pursue compatible objectives which inherently support each other or support a common goal

Harnessing   42, 88, 402, 414
The process of engaging and channelling effort, skills and creativity to effectively progress an objective, and of building commitment therein to the delivery of that objective

Head office   410, 412, 414
Part of an organisation that coordinates other parts of the organisation through directives and budgets, and sometimes through the provision of inspiration and support

Hierarchy   32, 34, 66, 400
A structure of control for managing large organisations, in which one individual directly manages a number of individuals, who each manage numbers of individuals, and so on

Holistic   88
Taking account of the whole system and the influence each part has on the others, and the overall impact that results

Hoshin planning   196
A derivation of 'Management by Objectives' which focuses on specific areas for improvement but encourages groups to contribute their own proposals

Identity 44, 250, 258
A description of an individual or group and what they stand for, and the influences (intentional and unintentional) that they have on the people and situations they connect with

Impact 60, 126, 204, 282, 300, 304, 376
The influence that one thing has on another, and particularly the extent to which changes in one thing brings about changes in another

Implementation 174-188, 246, 318-322, 360, 366, 412
A process of making adjustments to facilities, practices, policies, systems and competences in order to effect a planned change in operations

Incremental 100
A modest increase in progress or performance consistent with making improvements in existing practices, but without fundamentally changing the nature of those practices

Inefficient 52, 340
Provision of progress or performance through considerable waste (excessive consumption) of resources

Initiative 106, 212, 222, 224, 354
A specific project or programme of change, usually intended to address some major issue, or to introduce a new idea or method of working

Inspiration 144, 148-156, 288
An enlightened enthusiasm born from the combination of a cause you believe in and a confidence that you can contribute (often creatively) to it

Institutionalised 340
Having become an established and unquestioned part of the way the organisation works; part of the accepted fabric

Interaction 86
Where one thing affects another, and often where it is in turn affected vice versa, either directly or indirectly through other things

Interdependence 38, 128, 130, 158, 254
Where things are dependent on the success of other things for their own success, as would typically be the case in a system

Interpersonal commitment 92
A commitment between members of a group to support each other in pursuing their objectives. Often this may include emotional and spiritual support as well as physical and intellectual

Interpersonal skills 148
The skills of effective communication through methodical use of questions, summaries, checks, involvement, recognition, etcetera (both verbal and non verbal)

Interview 74
A structured meeting by which one person (the interviewer) gathers information and perceptions from another (the interviewee), usually face to face or by telephone

Involvement 52-54, 150, 168, 224, 294, 330, 352
The process of developing a sense of ownership through seeking the input and ideas from those who are likely to need to implement or support the conclusions

Job description 122, 124, 182, 220
A document outlining the requirements of a job such as key responsibilities and any terms of reference and reporting expectations

Landmine 328
An issue selected and escalated (forced) in order to polarise opinion and thereby discredit or even derail aspects of an intended change

Launch 362, 368
The fifth step of PROBLEM: Implementing the plan to solve the problem and project managing its progress to completion

Lazy goals 198
Goals or objectives that can be achieved easily with minimal effort or creativity

Leadership   174-192, 248, 264, 288, 298, 304
The quality of setting out clearly where you are heading, and inspiring and encouraging people to follow you and play their part in making it happen

Learning   134, 194, 232, 300, 302, 368
The process of assimilating new information, acquiring new skills, accommodating new models and adapting to new realities in order to successfully grasp and exploit new opportunities

Leverage   32, 48, 100, 198, 272, 402, 410
A concept reflecting using those things that can be controlled directly, such as processes, to act as levers to force into being those things that cannot, such as objectives

Linear   370, 372
Future performance that can be predicted and extrapolated from past performance because even though the variables change, the formula remains constant (see 'incremental')

Maintain   64, 166, 168, 228, 268, 414
The last step of PROBLEM: Integrating the confirmed solutions to a problem into the normal operating practices and routines of an organisation, thereby ensuring they are sustained

Making a difference   264
Seeking to ensure that your presence has some distinct beneficial impact on whatever you involve yourself in

Management meeting   184, 324, 336-354, 382, 408
A meeting of the managers of an organisation with the purpose of reviewing current performance in order to secure or improve future performance

Management process   138, 334, 352, 408
The process by which managers review the current situation, assimilate new learning, and apply that learning to ensure that future performance meets or exceeds what is needed

Management protocols   138
The conventions and codes of practice (often unwritten) that describe the management culture and establish the expected behaviours and ways of working together

Management reporting   382
The process by which management at one level of the organisation communicate their progress, their issues, and their response to managers at the next level up

Management team   92, 232
A group of managers who collectively take responsibility for ensuring the overall performance of the organisation or for a discrete element of it

Manager   56-64, 120-126, 188, 232, 240, 244, 306, 342
An individual who takes responsibility for systematically ensuring that future performance in his or her part of the organisation will sustain the goals and aspirations of the business

Managing for shareholder value   268
A mechanism by which the business is configured and managed solely to maximise the monetary value of its shares and share earnings

Matrix   80, 82, 84, 104
A rectangular array of elements set out in columns and rows (see also 'grid')

Measures   70, 96-100, 160, 168, 242, 308, 368, 386
Stable dimensions or scales along which performance or progress can be compared or evaluated consistently

Metaprocess   112
A process which acts on other processes, e.g. to create, evaluate, control or modify them

Methodical   178
Taking a structured, logical approach

Milestone   366
A point in time defined by the fulfilment of specific criteria, e.g. 'When the first functioning prototype is available'

Milestone plan 234, 463
A graphical representation of a forward schedule where the conclusion of key activities are evaluated by milestones

Mobilise 94, 214
The act of engaging and energising your resources to do useful work

Modelling 244
A process of approximating observed reality through combinations of mathematical formulae, and using these to predict the likely outcomes of different circumstances and decisions

Monkey 294, 298
A metaphor for a problem or issue

Motivation 270, 292
The incentive or desire to get involved in a situation and to use personal resources to see it to a satisfactory conclusion

Multidisciplinary 106
Incorporating a number of different disciplines or skill sets

Nine dots exercise 278
A simple exercise which illustrates how unrecognised paradigms can limit and constrain a person's thinking

Non-linear 370, 372
Improvements in performance that are sufficiently radical that they cannot be extrapolated from past performance, usually because the mechanisms of delivery have fundamentally changed

Objectives 26-40, 44, 48, 78, 82, 92-102, 160, 204, 238, 280, 306, 356, 404
Clearly defined achievements, often further clarified through measures and targets. Objectives are likely to be significant parts of (steps to) the attainment of a goal

Operating division 402
One or more companies that form part of a large organisation (usually a conglomerate), which are administered together because they focus on similar or associated market areas

Operational 62, 76, 224, 242, 328, 348
To do with the day-to-day functions of the business and its operating, delivery and housekeeping routines

Optimise 34
The process of achieving the best balance of benefits in two or more potentially conflicting result areas, usually by adjusting one or more variables (e.g. adjusting inventory levels to balance overhead costs with delivery accuracy)

Optimum 34, 42, 48, 80, 240
The ideal balance achievable through 'optimising' (see above)

Options 46, 48, 128, 298, 366, 370
The third step of PROBLEM: Identifying and evaluating a comprehensive range of solutions to resolve the root causes of a problem and/or to attenuate their effect

Over-management 406
Where an undue amount of management effort is being applied to a situation, often leading to wasted effort in bureaucracy and responding to conflicting or superfluous expectations

P45 342
A UK colloquialism for losing your job. The P45 is a legal form that every individual is given in the UK if and when they leave their employment

Paradigm 274, 276, 278
An unquestioned pattern of behaviour or thought which improves the efficiency of many thinking processes and actions, but which can limit the recognition of new opportunities and threats

Partnership 216, 270
An enterprise of two or more bodies (organisations or individuals) who work together to achieve a common objective for their common benefit

People 68-74, 240
The third of the 6Ps (aspects of good management practice): Developing people's abilities and attitudes in a planned and productive manner

Perfect 70-72, 244
The last of the 6Ps (aspects of good management practice): Planning to continuously improve through a strategy of actively learning from oneself and others

Performance 66, 78, 110, 120, 128, 204, 234, 242, 306, 350, 386, 404, 410
Ongoing and sustained achievement

Personal life 250, 254, 256, 258, 260, 266, 290, 332
Time not contracted to the organisation, and what an individual does with that time. Often described in terms of the relationships and interests pursued outside of the organisation

Personal values 262-274
The objectives, causes and codes of behaviour that are intrinsically important to an individual

Philosophy 70, 238
The second of the 6Ps (aspects of good management practice): Establishing clear targets for improvement of performance, and a value culture which ensures they are actively pursued

Pike syndrome 276
A behaviour that has outlived the original (and sole) reason for its adoption

Pioneer 212
A group or individual who is the first to attempt to adopt a new way of working, and therefore have no recourse to proven ideas, experience, resources or even support

Plan 52-54, 78, 140, 182, 346, 366, 392
A structured schedule of intent, outlining the necessary actions, sequence, responsibilities and timings to achieve one or more objectives by a specific date

Plenary 200
Attended by all the members of an event or assembly

Policy 218
A statement of how the organisation will address particular situations, and

thereby a set of rules and required practice for people undertaking work within or on behalf of the organisation

Potential 42, 78-88, 128, 156, 280, 310
The capacity of an organisation, individual or entity to develop to fulfil different (often more demanding) roles and responsibilities, and/or to better fulfil current ones

Potential problem analysis 164
A tool for exploring the risks inherent in a situation or forward plan, and for developing strategies to avoid, eliminate or reduce the likely negative consequences

Practice 24, 56, 66-76, 182, 294, 334, 360
Usual or customary ways of working

Predict 70, 242
The fifth of the 6Ps (aspects of good management practice): Measuring process performance objectively and using a disciplined approach to solving current or potential performance issues

Prevention 360, 368, 390
The practice of making systemic changes in order to remove the likelihood of error or the risk of problems arising

Principle 100, 158, 206, 232-244, 252, 354, 402
A guiding statement or rule consistent with achieving and/or sustaining a defined (and usually very important) result or benefit

Prioritise 78, 84, 102, 196, 202, 370, 382
The process of selecting and scheduling actions or options based on their relative urgency and importance to the organisation

PROBLEM 362
A seven step discipline for methodically resolving issues and improving performance: Profile; Root Cause; Options; Balance; Launch; Evaluate; Maintain

Problem-solving 242, 362, 366, 370, 382, 394
The process of identifying, understanding, correcting and permanently resolving performance deficiencies within the organisation

Problem tracking 76
The process of looking back along the path of a problem (usually a major incident) in order to identify the systemic issues that gave rise to it

Procedure 314
A document providing precise guidance on the preferred (and often prescribed) method for undertaking a process, or a part of a process (e.g. a specific activity or task)

Process 68, 70, 72, 240
The fourth of the 6Ps (aspects of good management practice): Developing the processes which effect performance, using methods which aid disciplined thinking and collective involvement

Process map 118, 126, 166, 240
The diagrammatic representation of a process showing the sequence of activities and how they feed into each other

Process model 108, 110, 112, 120, 160
A logical picture of how the operations of the organisation can be explained in terms of a limited number of distinct processes

Process owner 120-124, 150, 152, 234, 352, 378, 380
A manager who has taken responsibility for ensuring, in a systematic manner, that the performance of a process fulfils the organisational expectations of it

Process proposal 156-164, 194, 198, 200, 204, 212
A formal document that sets out: how the process supports the organisational objectives; its performance targets to fulfil that role; and the means by which it will achieve those targets

Process review 76
A tool, normally used as part of an annual audit, for reviewing the quality of process management and its implications

Process team 150-156, 184, 194-208, 232, 398
A team of people who, with the process owner, take responsibility for managing and improving the performance of a process

Process variables 62
The aspects of a process (inputs, controls, sequence, effort, timing etc.) that can be adjusted to improve or diminish process performance

Profile 224
The first step of PROBLEM: Objectively determining the dimensions of a problem in terms of its impact, its area of influence, and its salient features (timing, location, …)

Progress reporting 228
A formal means of regularly communicating how well an agreed plan is being fulfilled

Project 106, 146, 234, 336, 356-362
A one-off set of activities intended to achieve a specific aim or objective, usually the research, development or implementation of something

Proposal reconciliation 194-208
The activity of reviewing process proposals against the overall objectives of an organisation in order to confirm that they are consistent, or to make adjustments so that they are

Purpose 70, 236
The first of the 6Ps (aspects of good management practice): Ensuring a clear understanding of customer needs and issues, and inspiring a desire to find new ways to serve them better

QFD 80-88
Quality Function Deployment: A tool for methodically and creatively relating **what** you are trying to do, to **how** you are trying to do it

QFD cascade 148-170, 402
The process of using a QFD at one level of the organisation to guide and validate

the development of QFDs at the next level down

QFD column   104-126
A vertical set of cells in the QFD diagram that reflect the complete potential of a particular process to contribute to the organisation's objectives

QFD row   94-102
A horizontal set of cells in the QFD diagram that reflect how a particular objective can be supported and leveraged by all the processes of the organisation

Quadrant chart   384-392, 400, 404, 406, 408
A single page mechanism for reporting the essentials of process management: performance; trends against forecast and target; analysis of issues; and planned actions to address them

Quality   70, 124, 270, 360, 398
The extent to which a product or service fulfils the requirements (including function, reliability, timeliness etc.) that have been set for it

Quality assurance   106
The process of ensuring 'quality' in a product or service

Rebel   324-328
An individual, or group, who not only disagrees with an intended change or action, but who also seeks (often by both direct and indirect means) to undermine and derail it

Recognition   148, 224, 226, 238, 246, 292
Showing appreciation for something or somebody, usually not financially but in some form of communication, either publicly or privately

Reconcile   168, 178, 298
The action of making one thing compatible and consistent with another, usually by making adjustments to one or both

Resources   48, 66, 78, 120, 122, 202, 206
All of the things that are available to an organisation to help it to fulfil its role and achieve its goals, including materials, facilities, people, relationships, equipment etc.

Responsibility   120-126, 180, 234, 262, 300, 318, 392
A duty or commitment for ensuring a satisfactory result. Having the ability to respond (which, by convention, usually infers some sense of obligation to do so)

Review and audit   416
A process, usually annual, of objectively evaluating past progress (and the means of delivering it) in order to learn for the future

Reward system   40, 62, 240, 324, 328
The processes of providing incentives (financial and structural) to encourage and honour people who have actively pursued the desired objectives, efforts and behaviours

Rich picture   452, 454, 467, 469
A rough pictorial representation (usually on a flipchart) of something that would normally be communicated by words, such as a vision, background, personal details, etcetera

Role   56, 62, 92, 104, 120, 128, 138, 152, 192, 244, 290-316, 336
The responsibilities and activities expected of a particular position or assignment

Roof   374-380
The triangular grid that is located at the top of some QFD diagrams, which reflects the interactions and communication needs between processes

Root cause   126, 162, 362, 364, 366, 370
The second step of PROBLEM: Identifying and confirming the key factors and underlying causes that are the greatest contributors to the consequences of a problem

Salient   134, 144, 384
Important and relevant, likely to have some bearing on the situation

Scope 118
What a process includes within its boundaries (usually in terms of the activities that make it up)

Selling the plans 212
The process of developing a commitment within the board (or anybody else to whom the organisation reports) to support the proposed efforts

Session plan 140, 350
A meeting or event schedule that lists each of the main sessions together with: the session objectives; the process by which it will be delivered; timings; inputs and outputs

Shareholder 50, 274
An individual or institution which owns all or part of the organisation, normally via shares

Shortfall 66, 202, 206, 350, 354, 390
The amount by which a result falls short of the target or expected return

Silo 106
A metaphor for a part of an organisation which focuses on itself and does not link well with other parts of the organisation (particularly with regard to improvement)

Six Ps (6Ps) 236
Six empirically proven aspects of good management practice, each of which begin with the letter P: Purpose; Philosophy; People; Process; Predict; and Perfect

Smart 26
An acronym for remembering the key qualities of a clearly defined objective: Specific, Measurable, Agreed, Realistic and Timebound

Solution 44, 46, 48, 50, 244, 302, 358-372
A defined mechanism, way of working or other change that, when implemented, corrects or resolves the problem it was intended to address

Spartan 352
Strict and austere, stripped down to the basics

Spring clean 416
A process of tidying up the QFD to resolve any barriers to progress, but without disrupting progress and momentum in other areas

Stage gate 461
A milestone point in a research or development plan which serves as a point of project review; normally a point where a significant area of uncertainty has been resolved

Standard 182
An accepted or approved example against which others are judged or measured

Standard form 140
A document that requires its recipient to provide information in a particular way, and thereby a useful device for ensuring that the underlying reasoning has been comprehensive and rigorous

Stewardship 222, 262, 264
Responsibility for the care, protection, maintenance, and fulfilment of a thing. Stewardship can be applied to people, animals, events, resources, ideas and even the world as a whole

Sticky-note 94, 114, 280, 310
A small piece of paper which can be written on one side, and has a strip of non-permanent adhesive on the other. A good example is the Post-it™ note manufactured by 3M

Strategic 306, 344, 346, 370
Related to the goals and overall direction of something

Stretch targets 100
A proposed increase in performance, the attainment of which is likely to require a degree of innovation and risk

Structure 104-118, 24, 82, 374, 402
A model or perception of how things are organised and how they relate to one another

Subjective 58, 200
Based largely on opinion with very little data or comprehensive evidence to

support it

Sub-objectives 32
Clearly defined achievements that are part of a larger objective, and combine with each other to deliver it

Sub-process 150, 350, 358, 382, 402
A group of activities that link together to form a functional part of a larger process

Survey 68, 76, 366
The process of researching an objective picture of current perceptions and realities concerning a particular topic or situation

Symbiosis 266
A mutually beneficial and supportive relationship between things, where the products of one serve as nutrients to another and vice versa

Syndicates 114, 200
Sub-groups of a larger meeting, which have been split out to enable a higher degree of focus and involvement in the discussions and decision making

Synergy 376
A situation where the whole is greater than the sum of the parts, sometimes described as 'one plus one equals three'

Systematic 70-74, 176-184, 300, 336, 362, 382
Methodical, ordered and underpinned by a logical and comprehensive perspective

Systemic 60, 182, 228, 382
Relating to the entire system in context, and the relationships and influences therein

Target 98-102, 160, 204, 238, 308, 386, 404
A numerical value that represents the extent of desired (and intended) progress along a specific dimension or measure of performance

Task focus 72
Where all attention has been concentrated on an activity and its completion, to the exclusion of any ongoing consideration of the original intent. A focus on

'what' without 'why'

Taylor 42
F W Taylor, who introduced a method of management which used detailed analysis of tasks to determine the optimum means of undertaking them

Team 72, 92, 104, 150, 348, 374, 404
A group of people who are working together toward a shared common goal, and who are willing to suppress or forgo their individual personal agendas for its achievement

Team of scientists question 58
A simple exercise intended to encourage a group to explore scientific perspectives on management

Technical 236, 290
Relating to the technique of undertaking a task, particularly where the technique requires a degree of skill and intelligence

Time management 252
The means by which tasks are prioritised, scheduled and actioned in order to optimise both the organisational benefit and the quality of life of the task-holder

Tool 78, 138, 162, 166, 250, 294, 366
An implement, mechanism or device intended to facilitate or ease the execution of a task, and often requiring some skill in its effective use

Top-box 60, 64, 90, 192, 294, 296
Management of an event or outcome by designing and developing the processes which will ensure its effective and efficient delivery

Top-level objectives 200, 204
Objectives that concisely reflect the overall aims of the organisation as a whole, and against which all other objectives within the organisation should be validated

Tragedy of the commons 340
A phenomenon where individual opportunism within a balanced system leads to a worse situation for all parties

Transformation 24, 100, 172, 232, 276, 334
The process of radical, almost magical, improvement beyond that which can be imagined purely by extrapolation

Trending 388
The process of understanding rates of change by developing a line graph of performance measures (or other numerical data) over time

Types of meetings 346
A means of classifying meetings by their purpose, and thereby in terms of their most suitable structure and format

Unambiguous 74, 94, 96, 356, 382
The quality of a description or definition, that it is understood and interpreted in the same way by all who hear or read it

Value 182, 262-274, 278, 286, 318, 320, 326
A thing (often a behaviour) that is important to an individual or organisation, to the extent that its manifestation is both sought and rewarded

Value set 44, 188, 238, 240, 272, 274
A definition of the current or intended values of an organisation

Value-add 160, 264, 274, 278, 294, 412
The concept of providing benefits by identifying the key areas of value to the customer and ensuring that they increase in worth

Vision 30, 50, 144, 154, 186, 270-274, 298
A picture of the organisation in the future (what it achieves, and how it achieves it) that is intended to provide a direction and focus for determining goals and objectives

Voting cards 132
Cards used to indicate the strength of opinion of the various members of a group, so as to aid facilitation during consensus-reaching sessions

Wastage 50
Channelling or leakage of effort and resources into non-productive activities

or results, usually as a result of (or in order to correct) a mistake or inefficiency

Weighting 102, 136
A number assigned to reflect the level of importance attached to an objective and often used mathematically to select or prioritise options for its delivery

Why-How chart 34-40, 82, 98, 162, 280-286, 290
A mapping system used to reflect relationships between objectives

APPENDIX 15: FINAL COMMENTS ON QFD

In a blatant attempt at persuading the reader to now go away and begin to implement what he or she has read, I include the following quotes from those who have undertaken the journey before you.

This single idea transformed my whole view of what managing a team really meant. QFD has transformed how I and my team look at managing our business in a way that has engaged, motivated and ensured sustainable improvement - I am now unshakeable in my belief that this message must be shared with others

Mark Richardson, R&D Director, Smith & Nephew Wound Management

As a manager in an International organisation, I had been introduced to most of the concepts and ideas about management, but the issue has always been how best to link these concepts and ideas and put them into practice. Systematic management and QFD did it for me!

Dietmar Harteveld, World-wide Supply Chain Director, Emerson Process Management

GlobalNetXchange is a global electronic marketplace, created by 8 of the largest retailers in the world and operational within months. My team is culturally diverse, and the QFD has given us a common management framework for rapidly developing the organisation to be effective and manage the complexity of our global and technological task.

Bharat Popat, V.P. Product Management, GlobalNetXchange, SanFrancisco, CA.

Management by QFD gives complete transparency to the inner workings of an organisation; everyone can see why we are doing something and how our efforts contribute to the big picture.

Andrew Jackson, Programme Manager, Smith & Nephew Endoscopy

The two-day initial QFD session taught me more about my organisation than working there for the previous eight years! QFD provides the business overview and structure to manage the operation effectively

Jelle Struijk, Systems Support Engineer, Fisher Rosemount Systems Assembly Europe

I have experienced the QFD process and witnessed the transformation from demoralised, dysfunctional groups to effective, progressive organisations. I know of no other method which is as systematic and repeatable in achieving this as QFD.

Chris Merkin, IT Projects Manager, Micro-Motion Inc.

It's easy to create a new approach to management – the bookshelves are crammed with them. It takes real insight and powerful logic to create an enduring approach. Mike Clargo has achieved this by applying a tool borrowed from engineering. He has used QFD to reduce the complexity of management to simple principles which, when combined and applied, have the power to transform organisations - and to continue to develop them in response to the changing environment.

Kevin Downes, Technical Manager, Wound Management Business Unit, Smith & Nephew plc

QFD is an effective means to ensure that an organisation's objectives are supported by its various operating processes. Once the QFD is established, the matrix of processes against objectives makes it clear where the value adding or value destroying issues lie. It ensures the allocation of clear process ownership and it breaks down functional silo thinking and encourages an holistic approach.

Rama Venchard, Business Support Manager, Whitbread plc

We see QFD simply as the mechanism by which we can more effectively live our visions and values and bring what can often seem abstract to employees, into real focus in their daily lives. Applying discipline to management activity is not easy, as we tend to see it as a natural gift; only when methodology is applied do we appreciate what can really be achieved.

Gareth Lloyd-Jones, Managing Director, Smith & Nephew Group Research Centre

QFD is invaluable in creating understanding of what needs to be delivered, how we might go about it, and how we can measure achievement. Better still, it can be used at many levels, with the resultant QFDs clearly linked. Thus we can drive strategy from board level with one QFD, deliver programmes of change across a division with a second QFD and make improvements in operational departments with a third. All linked, all relevant to the level at which they are being applied. QFD effectively uses people.

Chris Stockdale, Business Change Consultant, Sainsbury plc

QFD is the only tool I have seen that allows a manager implement cultural, structural, and process changes in to an organisation whilst still being able to keep an overview. It allows me to monitor progress on all aspects of change and focus my attention appropriately, safe in the knowledge that I understand why I need to focus attention in that area, and sure that it will give me a sustainable change in the performance of my department. As a consequence of QFD, and the resulting clarity of the goals, aims and vision, the whole department is more focused, but also having more fun despite the difficulty of their task.

Clare Healy, Programme Manager, Wound Management Business Unit, Smith & Nephew plc

QFD is the best management framework I have ever come across. It gives you a model to manage your organisation from Board level right down to the individual teams, and it achieves the focus and collective commitment of the stakeholders to deliver benefits. QFD enables you to manage complex business environments, simply.

Dilip Popat, Service Manager, Partner Practice, Enterprise Services, Microsoft Limited

QFD, within one process, reconciles the apparently irreconcilable: simultaneously dealing with politics and planning; with opinions and organisation; with ideas and exploration. It provides a structure that enables structured social thinking to be applied from the outset, and that captures the conclusions like a camera can capture a million pieces of information in a fraction of a second. It is a high performing strategy/planning process, and as a means of managing complexity and controversy into confidence and commitment, nothing else can touch it!

Martin Price, Principal Consultant, PMProfessional

I used QFD to successfully recover from the chaos following the dual disaster of a $24M fraud and a widespread corrupt system implementation. QFD helped improve productivity in the Finance department by 33% in two years – it provides the raison d'etre and focus for every activity in the business. I have never known these QFD tools to fail. QFD opened the mind of an internally focused and autocratically inclined bean-counter to what real empowerment was and showed him what he had to do to get the combined efforts of the whole organisation, across all functions and workgroups, to be brought to bear on the goals of the organisation.

Phil Ranson, Finance Director, Control Techniques plc

My experience of organisations in need of surgery is that they don't usually lack people with enthusiasm, creativeness and drive. The key to creating their success is very often the creation of a common vision and a systematic approach to management, which channels all efforts in one direction to achieve this vision. QFD has helped me personally achieve this in several different organisations

Juergen Maier, Managing Director, Siemens Shared Services Ltd

Having been part of a Team that used QFD to turn a business around, it is now endemic to how I do my job. I simply would not want to operate without the clarity and structure the QFD process gives to the business.

Kevin Thompson, Material Manager, Emerson Process Management

QFD was originally conceived as an aid to product development. Using it to run a business is a truly novel concept, perhaps too novel for some people, but the clarity and simplicity of the view it gives is invaluable in moving management out of the process and into the monitoring and guiding position where it needs to be. The experience of working through the process had a huge impact on our management team, and the result has been a better-formed team with a common language.

Dave Rawlings, Director of Quality, Planning & Information, Smith & Nephew GRC

QFD has allowed us to truly understand, what we do, whether we should be doing it, and how we can do it better. It has given us a clear understanding of what we need to achieve, at all levels of the organisation, and helped us to work as a team to deliver it. It has improved my performance, that of teams I work with and the company as a whole. I know of no other management tool that would have achieved what QFD has done for us.

Len Pendle, HR Director, Smith & Nephew Group

When I was first introduced to Systematic Management, including QFD, I was an electronics Manufacturing manager buried in a period of extreme growth. Volumes of product grew six fold and staffing levels doubled over a period of three to four years. Quality was around 50 to 60%, on time delivery was around 70% and the organisation was in chaos. Using the tools described in this book, I was able get everything under control and to improve on time delivery to over 90% and quality levels to around 98%. I do not know of any other tool that would have allowed me to do this

Roy Knight, World-wide Demand Planning Director, Emerson Process Management